TOBACCO
ARMS
AND POLITICS

STUDIES IN 20TH & 21ST CENTURY EUROPEAN HISTORY

VOLUME 1

Edited by
Mogens Rüdiger and Mogens Pelt
University of Copenhagen

Mogens Pelt

TOBACCO
ARMS
AND POLITICS

Greece and Germany
from World Crisis to World War 1929-41

MUSEUM TUSCULANUM PRESS • UNIVERSITY OF COPENHAGEN
1998

Mogens Pelt: Tobacco, Arms and Politics
Studies in 20th and 21st Century European History, vol. 1

© Museum Tusculanum Press 1998
Translated from Danish by Rasmus Chr. Dietz
Linguistic consultant: Marion Fewel
Layout and composition by Ole Klitgaard
Cover design by Erik Pelt
Photos on front cover by Mogens Carrebye Fotografi, Billedhuset A/S
and Carsten Esbensen, Plan Design
Printed in Denmark by Narayana Press, Gylling

ISBN 87 7289 450 4
ISSN 1398 1862

Published with the support of
The Danish Research Council for the Humanities

Museum Tusculanum Press
University of Copenhagen
Njalsgade 92
DK-2300 Copenhagen S
Denmark

ACKNOWLEDGEMENT

I have received more help with this book than I can adequately acknowledge here. Nevertheless, I shall try, albeit running the risk of omitting deserving people who should be named.

The basic research for the book, carried out from 1990 to 1992, was supported by the Faculty of Humanistics of the University of Copenhagen. During that period I was a research fellow at the Institute of Contemporary History, University of Copenhagen, writing my Ph.D.

Knud Højgaards Fond was also very generous in supporting my various trips to undertake research abroad.

I owe much to the Danish Research Council for the Humanities: the council fully financed my research for more than tree years, from 1993 to 1996, while I was a senior research fellow at the Danish Institute at Athens; it also played a crucial role in turning my thesis into a book by financing both the linguistic revision and the publication. My thanks also go to Marion Fewell, who took care of the linguistic revision of my manuscript, and to Ole Klitgaard, who patiently supervised the publication process.

I am further grateful to the Danish Institute at Athens and to the Consul General Gösta Enboms Foundation for their part in supporting the work of turning my thesis into a book. My thanks also are also extended to Rasmus Dietz, who translated the manuscript from Danish into English.

I owe much, as well, to archivists and librarians at the following institutions: Public Record Office, Kew Gardens, Surrey, the Politisches Archiv des Auswärtigen Amtes, Bonn, Bundesarchiv, Koblenz, and Bundesarchiv Abteilung Potsdam as well as Bundesarchiv-Militärarchiv,

5

Freiburg, the Imperial War Museum, London, the Greek State Archives, Athens (Genika archia tou kratous), the Archives of the Greek Ministry of Foreign Affairs, Athens (Archia tou ipourghiou eksoterikon), the Historical Archive of the National Bank of Greece, Athens (Istoriko archio Ethnikis Trapezas) and the library at the Bank of Greece.

I would also like to thank my colleagues at the former Institute of Contemporary History, University of Copenhagen, and at the Danish Institute at Athens.

Special thanks go to Lecturer cand.mag. Carsten Due-Nielsen who was supervising my Ph.D. project; and last but not least, to professor fil. dr. Carl-Axel Gemzell: without his inspiration and sage support none of this would have come to pass.

I also owe much to Winnie Irene Dietz and dr.phil. Søren Dietz, director at the Danish Institute at Athens 1992-1997, for their love and friendship, support I could not have managed without. The same is true for my parents Anna and Erik Pelt, who not only supported me but also took care of Christian and Sebastian. Further tanks go to my father for all the time and skill he spent on suggestions regarding the graphic dimensions of my book.

The story and the opinions set out below, however, are the responsibility of the author alone. Needless to say, this also applies to any mistakes or inaccuracies that are found in the book.

CONTENTS

PART II:
RECOVERY, REARMAMENT AND TRADE IN ARMS 1934-1937

INTRODUCTION

On 4 August 1936 a dictatorship assumed political power in Greece. Five years later, in April 1941, Greece was occupied by Germany. Both events were conditioned by conflicts which the economic world crisis in 1929 had unleashed and which significantly marked both the internal development of Greece and Germany and the evolution of their foreign relations.

These conflicts were connected to tobacco production, to rearmament and to the trade in war materials, as well as to Germany's determined efforts to dominate central and south-eastern Europe and the repercussions this generated within the international system. Foreign trade constituted a large part of Greece's total national production, while at the same time Greece was connected to the world market in a monocultural way. Tobacco comprised almost half of Greece's total exports and of this Germany bought about 50 per cent. Greek-German trade was based on counter trade through a clearing agreement. As Greece did not import the same quantity of goods from Germany that Germany did from Greece, Greece in fact was financing a substantial part of her own exports to Germany at a time when the Greek economy was in sore need of capital and foreign exchange. However, the tobacco trade not only affected exports. Production was concentrated in northern Greece, an area which had only recently been incorporated into the country. Furthermore, 70 per cent of a total of 1.2 million refugees who came to Greece in the wake of the disastrous Greek campaign in Asia Minor were settled in northern Greece. This made them a crucial factor in the social, political and economic stability of Greece and resulted in northern Greece facing extensive social and political problems. This state of affairs caused a series of crises in the inter-war period, culminating in 1936.

After the establishment of the dictatorship, Greek credits on the clearing account were liquidated, mainly through imports of arms and military technology from Germany. Trade policy falls in the borderland between economy and politics and between internal and external policy. This is especially true in the case of the arms trade, as a result of the great political significance innate in transactions of this nature.

Research into trade policy has been inspired by the school which originated around Fritz Fischer and his pioneering works: *Germany's Aims in the First World War*, London 1967[1]2 and *War of Illusions*, London 1975.[2] Fischer's thesis posits that the origin of the First World War was a result of Germany's ambition to become a political and economic world power on a par with Britain. His theory provoked much discussion and aroused deep feelings, as, to a large extent, he held Germany responsible for the First World War and thus suggested (albeit very cautiously) similarities between this conflict and the Second World War. Instead of concentrating on the events of July and August 1914 and viewing the war as a result of a political situation that had got out of hand, as German historiography had done so far, thus implying that no-one was really to blame, Fischer used a wider chronological framework. He believed that the First World War was the culmination of tensions which increasing German economic and political power had been creating in the international system since the end of the last century, and he explained political events in structural terms.

Methodologically, Fischer transcended the narrow approach of diplomatic history. He included social factors, industry, business and finance as important parameters, on the same level as politicians and diplomats in the historical process. Fischer did indeed focus on foreign policy, but emphasized the importance of internal politics and, in particular, the interaction between external and internal factors.

It took years of historical work for his views to become accepted.[3] Attention has been concentratated on the so-called "problem of continuation", i.e. the identification of structures which connect the Third Reich to the Weimar Republic and imperial Germany and whether it makes sense to talk about continuation at all: today there is a broad consensus of opinion that it does.

Germany's expansion and plans for political domination of central and south-eastern Europe have been singled out as an important link connecting imperial and inter-war Germany. Domination of central and south-eastern Europe, including the Ottoman Empire, was an important political aim in imperial Germany, most conspicuously symbolised by the Berlin-

Baghdad railway which was to connect Germany and central Europe to the Balkans, as well as to Anatolian and Middle Eastern tracts of Ottoman land. This direction of expansion also remained a goal in German political and business circles throughout the inter-war years.

Fischer's work has inspired a whole generation of German historians, who have all tended to emphasize German commercial policy towards south-eastern Europe during the 1930s. Bernd-Jürgen Wendt, one of Fischer's students, has suggested that Germany gained political control in south-eastern Europe during the period by means of commercial dominance, even though the area was financially linked to the Western Powers. This took place despite Britain's launching of an active financial and commercial counteroffensive between 1938 and 1940 to prevent German hegemony in the area.

Wendt points out that Britain, in contrast to Germany, was never able to coordinate the interests of the state and business and for that reason failed to establish a joint effort in south-eastern Europe. This is explained by Britain's close commercial ties to the Empire, by Whitehall's traditional reluctance to connect the aims of trade with power politics and, finally, by the appeasement policy. In other words Wendt sees Britain's inefficient foreign policy in south-eastern Europe as a result of various internal and external structural weaknesses. When Britain finally decided to launch a counter- offensive, it was too late. This was mainly because at that time industry in south-eastern Europe, and in particular the armament industry, had become technically dependent on German know-how to an extent that made it impossible to break the connection with Germany. However, the situation was also due to Germany's dominant political position, which made it possible for her to force the governments of south-eastern Europe to compel the arms industry (including those companies which were controlled by British capital) to submit to German interests.[4] Thus the final success of Germany in the area is primarily explained by her relative structural superiority in comparison to that of other Great Power rivals.[5] In his investigation of Germany's trade policy towards south-eastern Europe, Wendt focuses on the relative strength and weakness of the Great Powers and he pays only slight attention to the actual interaction between Germany and the individual states in that area. In this way he gives the impression that Germany's political dominance and military occupation of south-eastern Europe in the early 1940s was a direct and simple consequence of the area's economic dependence on Germany. Thus he

13

depicts these countries as mere pawns in German policy, and not as individual subjects with their own objectives and strategies.

Alan S. Milward has criticized Wendt for this and exhorts historians to "... turn their attention to the successful exploitation of Germany's economic weakness before 1939 by the small economies of central and south-eastern Europe".[6] This approach makes it important to treat every single country separately and requires an investigation that considers the characteristics of each individual state and its relationship to Germany.[7]

Greece is situated between Europe and the Orient. Geographically and geopolitically she belongs to both south-eastern Europe and the Mediterranean. Moreover she has traditionally formed part of Britain's sphere of interest.

Relations between Greece and the Middle East were strong in the period between the wars because of the presence of large and influential Greek communities in the area and because of Greece's position as a commercial nation. These close links make Greece especially interesting in an interpretation of Germany's ambitions.

This book tells the story of the intricate relationship between Greece and Germany between the years of the Great Depression and Germany's occupation of Greece and it focuses in particular on the impact of Germany's trade policy on Greece and on the way in which that country responded to the new challenge. A central thesis advanced here is that Germany's trade policy towards Greece significantly affected not only economic but also the political developments in Greece and that the establishment of the dictatorship of General Ioanis Metaxas in 1936 must be seen in the context of Germany's penetration into south-eastern Europe in the 1930s. There have been numerous studies of Germany's policy towards south-eastern Europe as a whole, as well as accounts of her policy towards a number of individual countries in the area, such as Bulgaria, Romania, Turkey and Yugoslavia.[8] However, no thorough studies have been made of Greece using this point of departure.[9]

A second central thesis advanced in this book is that the basing of a substantial part of Greece's rearmament programme on German military equipment and know-how played a crucial role in the development that brought Metaxas to power. Furthermore, it posits that the Greek-German trade in war materials and military technology was of central importance to the development of Greek-German relations until Italy's attack on

14

Greece on 28 October 1940. A certain amount of space is devoted to the Greek armament industry and its extensive trade in war materials, as these important matters have not hitherto been subject to research. The Greek armament industry supported by German technology, went through a period of dramatic expansion and entered the international arms market as an important factor.

This relates to a third central thesis, namely that the Greek trade in war materials played a crucial role in Greek-German relations as well as in the economic and political development of Greece. The Greek arms trade produced a substantial revenue in hard currency of which a part went to Germany. Furthermore, Greece served as a platform for Germany in politically difficult arms deals, such as supplying weapons to the Republicans during the Spanish Civil War. Furthermore, the intensification of Greek-German relations affected Metaxas' position *vis-à-vis* the pro-British King, George II. Scholars of this period of Greek history have tended to emphasize that the King was in firm control of the country and that the dictator was dependent on the King;[10] their works, however, have primarily concentrated on Greek-British relations and have been based on British evidence. For this reason it is important to stress that evidence of German provenance shows that Germany regarded Metaxas as an important asset to German interests in Greece. Indeed until 1938, German observers within the armaments field were convinced that Germany had no stronghold in south-eastern Europe like the one she had in Greece, a fact which they primarily contributed to Metaxas, whom they regarded as a guarantee for this position.

Germany's conquest of Central Europe in 1938, by means of *Anschluss* and the Munich Agreement, and in 1939 by the march into Prague, combined with the prospects of a general war in Europe, resulted in increasing discomfort in Greece about her dependence on Germany. This state of affairs also caused concern in Britain. During 1938 and 1939, as a response to this, the British government attempted to establish a counter-offensive to reduce Greece's dependence on Germany. However, it soon became impossible to make private business align with the government in such efforts. After the outbreak of war in Europe, and especially until mid 1940, Greece conducted a policy of benevolent neutrality towards Britain while at the same time her economic dependence on Germany remained considerable. During the same period Greece continued to rely on Germany in matters of armaments. Germany believed it important to continue to supply Greece in this field, as this would enhance the political position of Metaxas whom Germany saw as the best guarantee against Greece being drawn into the war on the side of Britain.

As a result of Germany's sweeping campaigns in Scandinavia, Holland, Belgium and France during the first half of 1940, as well as, of Italy's entrance into the war, Metaxas approached Germany for protection against Italian aggression. Germany did intervene towards Italy but in the end did not manage to prevent Mussolini from attacking Greece. This point relates to a fourth central thesis in this book, namely that German-Italian relations were primarily marked by rivalry and antagonism in respect to Greece. Some historians have already noted this as a characteristic feature of the relations between Germany and Italy. The findings in this book will corroborate the point and show that Greece at times even served as a platform from which Germany could decoy Italian resources away from central and south-eastern Europe.

This book is divided into three parts. The division of material roughly follows the different phases of the trade cycle in the 1930s and represents what I consider to be the most suitable periodization needed to explain the intricate interaction between internal responses in Greece and Germany and external challenges and the way in which these affected the development of Greek-German relations.

In the first part of the book, which covers the Depression during 1929-1933, the dominant development is taken to be the impact of the world crisis and the responses in Greece and Germany to this.

Both countries had to reorganize their economies to cope with the crisis and with rising protectionism on the world market. This laid the foundation for a substantial increase in Greek-German trade which became a dominant issue in relations between the two countries for the rest of the decade. Furthermore, in 1933 important changes in government power took place: in Germany by the advent of the National Socialists and in Greece by the anti-Venizelists winning a majority in parliament.

In the second part of this book, which covers the period from 1934 to 1937, the dominant development is taken to be the economic recovery and especially the lauching of a comprehensive rearmament programme in both Germany and Greece. As to the former the initiation of the so-called *Neuer Plan* in 1934 resulted in a substantial rise in Germany's trade with south-eastern Europe including Greece and led to a significant enhance-

16

ment of Germany's position in that country. This, in turn, affected the overall development in both countries and brought about Greek dependence on imports of German arms and military know-how. In the realm of politics the new groups which had come to power in Germany and Greece managed to strengthen their positions. In Germany the National Socialists successfully strove to conquer the state, while Hitler became the country's dictator. In Greece the anti-Venizelists gained control over the armed forces in 1935 and succeeded in restoring the monarchy in the same year. In August 1936 the King made the radical anti-Venizelist Metaxas dictator of Greece.

In the third part of this book, which covers the period from the recession in 1938 until Germany's occupation of Greece in April 1941, the dominant development is taken to be Hitler's launching of an overtly aggressive policy intended to obtain his goals by means of war. In the period stretching from Germany's conquest of central Europe in 1938 by means of *Anschluss* and the Munich Agreement to the German occupation of Greece, Germany's dominance in south-eastern Europe rose by leaps and bounds and unleashed reactions, not only from Germany's Great Power rivals Britain and the Soviet Union, but primarily from Italy. In the realm of politics Hitler gained more and more control over Germany's foreign and military policy and managed to overturn the remaining exponents of traditional national conservative policies. In Greece Metaxas enhanced his personal power *vis-à-vis* the pro-British King.

Part I

Depression,
Reorganization
and Counterstrategies
1929-1933

GREECE

National Unification and Political Instability

The Depression of 1929-1933 was of decisive significance for Greece's internal and external development throughout the rest the 1930s. To understand this it is important to consider certain structures in the social, political and economic edifice of the country. These emanated from Greece's previous history and became, in their interaction with the consequences of the crisis, determinative for Greece's development in the 1930s and her relationship with Germany.

The establishment of the Greek nation state in the first half of the nineteenth century marked the end of more than 350 years of Ottoman hegemony. The Greeks in the Ottoman Empire belonged to the so-called Greek *millet (rum i-milleti)*, a culturally and religiously autonomous society headed by the Patriarch in Constantinople. It is important to stress that this was a confessional and not an ethnic identity, in that every Orthodox subject in the Ottoman Empire, whether he spoke Greek, Slavic, Arabic or Turkish, was defined as Greek.[11]

Along with nationalism, the creation of the Greek national state made the so-called Great Idea (*I megali Idea*) a popular ideology which provided an effective means of political mobilization. In its broadest sense the Great Idea implied the foundation of a new Byzantium. Of crucial importance was the dream that Constantinople, The City, (*I Polis*) as it was called according to this terminology, would return to Greek hands.[12]

During the same period the accelerated disintegration of the Ottoman Empire dealt a severe blow to the balance of power in the eastern Mediterranean and in the Balkans, and turned the whole area into an object of intense rivalry among the Great Powers: this became known as the Eastern Question.

21

This Eastern Question in turn exposed various Greek governments to pressure from both public and military quarters to redeem the Ottoman orthodox subjects; politicians thus became dependent on the power and success of the army as well as on diplomatic and military support from the Great Powers.

For almost a century the majority of Greece's economic and political power was sacrificed to the process of national integration. This prevented sufficient resources from being channelled into modernization. It also hampered the development of well-entrenched political institutions, and intensified Greece's dependence on the Great Powers.[13] Moreover, it aggravated the difference between those citizens within the new inde-pendent Greek nation state and the many Greeks outside its borders: those belonging to the diaspora. The latter, and particularly the inhabitants of urban centres like Constantinople, Smyrna and Alexandria, were more open to western modernization of the economy and of society.[14]

The Balkan Wars and the First World War doubled Greece's territory. When the Greek army landed in Smyrna, on the western coast of Asia Minor, in May 1919, the Great Idea seemed to have reached its fulfilment, only to vanish three years later in central Anatolia.

In August 1922 the Greek army was decisively defeated by the Turkish Nationalists; in September of the same year, Mustafa Kemal's troops marched into Smyrna. This caused a massive uprooting of the Ottoman Greeks, of whom Greece received more than a million refugees.

The initial territorial expansion followed the disintegration of Greek society in Anatolia meant that the majority of all Greeks for the first time in modern history lived within the borders of the Greek nation state, and, for this reason alone, 1922 marks a watershed.

The defeat in Asia Minor, as well as the traumatic exodus from Anatolia, also provided fertile soil for a continuation of the political conflicts that had disrupted Greek society and the diaspora before 1922.

Disagreement about Greece's participation in the First World War had divided Greeks into supporters of Eleftherios Venizelos, the Prime Minister, on one side, and King Constantine I on the other, respectively Venizelists and anti-Venizelists or Royalists. The King wanted Greece to remain neutral, while Venizelos called for participation on the side of the Entente. In 1916 Venizelos formed a provisional government in Salonika called The National Defence (*Ethniki Amina*), after the King had relieved him of his duties several times. In practical terms this meant that two

22

governments ruled the country: a royal government, with its foundation in the areas which constituted the bulk of Greek territory before the Balkan Wars 1912-1913, the so-called "Old Greece", and Venizelos' provisional government, with its base in the new areas, the so-called "New Greece". In Greek history this is known as The National Schism (*Ethnikos Dichasmos*). The Schism was further intensified when the Entente powers forced the king to abdicate in 1917. In this way Venizelos became Prime Minister of a unified Greece and it was under his leadership that Greece emerged victorious from the First World War.

In November 1920 Venizelos surprisingly lost the elections and Constantine was subsequently restored to the throne. It was during his leadership that the Greek army was defeated in 1922. The army and a huge part of the population held the king responsible for the defeat; in the same year, a military government forced Constantine into exile, where he died shortly afterwards, and executed six leading anti-Venizelist politicians and army officers, whom they held responsible for the disaster in Asia Minor. After an abortive Royalist *coup d'etat* in 1923, the Venizelists proclaimed a Republic in 1924.

In this way the disaster in Asia Minor and its immediate political sequel became incorporated into the National Schism, while at the same time Venizelists and anti-Venizelists were divided into opposed camps regarding the constitutional issue.

"Greek politics are in reality nothing but a struggle between two factions for control of the armed forces..." wrote the British Minister in Athens, characterizing Greek politics in his annual report of 1935.[15] Although this is a simplification, it is true that Greek politics were dominated primarily by a struggle between the two factions, the Venizelists and the anti-Venizelists.

However, democracy was also rooted in a socio-economic climate quite different from that of Western Europe. Traditonal pre-modern "patron-client relationships" played an important part in Greece's social organization.[16]

Clientilism[17] was also decisive in relations of loyalty within the Greek army and in the army's relations to politicians.

Indicative of this is the fact that it was the army that transferred power to Parliament in 1924. During the following year and a half, various Venizelist governments ruled the country, until Theodoros Pangalos, a Venizelist general, seized power in June 1925 by means of a *coup d'etat*. In August 1926, Pangalos was toppled by Georgios Kondilis, another

Venizelist general. In the following six years, until 1933, the arena of politics was left to parliamentarians.

On 5 March 1933, at the immediate conclusion of a parliamentary election, Nikolaos Plastiras, a Venizilist general and leader of the 1922 revolution, attempted a *coup d'etat* to prevent the victorious anti-Venizelists from gaining power. However, his move was abortive and on 10 March 1933 the anti-Venizelist Panages Tsaldaris formed a government. This produced a situation in which the anti-Venizelists were dominant in Parliament and the Venizelists were in control of the army: this contributed significantly to widening the breach between army and government. Furthermore, the situation led to a revival of the National Schism[18], an issue which coloured the development of Greek politics until the establishment of Metaxas as a dictator on 4 August 1936.

Integration of Refugees

After protracted negotiations Greece and Turkey signed a convention at Lausanne on 30 January 1923 concerning the compulsory exchange of populations. By this, Greece renounced her right to reinstall Greek refugees in Turkey. Moreover, the signatory parties agreed to a compulsory exchange of members of the Greek Orthodox church in Turkey and Muslims in Greece, with the exception of those members of the Greek Orthodox church who had had permanent residence in Constantinople prior to 1918, and similarly Muslims in Western Thrace to whom the same provision applied. These two groups became a bone of contention between the Turkish and Greek authorities in the years to come. This conflict was further intensified by a disagreement about compensation for the property abandoned by the refugees.[19]

The Lausanne agreement meant that Greece had to accept between 1.2 and 1.5 million[20] refugees from Turkey on a permanent basis, while only 365,000 Muslims left Greece.[21] This left Greece with a surplus population of almost a million, constituting some 20 per cent of her total population.

Two-thirds of the refugees were settled in "New Greece". Out of a total of 337,397 refugees who were settled in "Old Greece", Athens and Piraeus between them received 230,565.[22]

About half of the refugees were settled as farmers. The integration of these proceeded relatively smoothly. In June 1926, 551,939 persons, or some 80 per cent of those who were to be settled as farmers, were relocated on a permanent basis.[23] About 50 per cent of these were provided with abandoned Turkish or Bulgarian land, while the rest were offered land made available by expropriation and division of agricultural holdings[24] as well as by land reclamation.[25]

With about 90 per cent of the refugee holdings situated in Thrace and Macedonia[26] the agricultural interests of the refugees were closely linked to northern Greece. This made them far more sensitive than any other social group to agricultural changes taking place in Macedonia and Thrace.

The integration of refugees in the cities proceeded more slowly than in agricultural areas. About 60 per cent were placed in and around the large cities, Athens and Salonika, and contributed substantially to the growth of these two urban centres.[27]

It is difficult to assess the impact that the refugees made on Greece's development. However, a report from the League of Nations made in 1926 stated that the refugees contributed considerably to the development of industrial production in Greece. An investigation into Greek trades and professions carried out in 1961 notes that 25 per cent of all entrepreneurs were originally refugees, i.e. proportionately more refugees than Greeks.

In this context it is significant that modern cities like Constantinople and Smyrna, which functioned as trade and industrial centres in the decades before the exchange of populations, lost their positions to Greece after 1922. Thus in 1925, Maurice Davies, the governor of the Banque Nationale de Crédit de Paris, observed that an increasing number of foreign businessmen were directing their attention to Athens rather than to Constantinople.[28] The exodus of the Ottoman Greeks led to a recession in Turkey within trade, crafts, mining and agriculture, and, as a result, French, Italian and Dutch firms followed the Ottoman Greeks from Asia Minor to Piraeus. The Greek port became an important *entrepôt* between Europe and Asia. It is not an exaggeration to say that the disintegration of the Ottoman Empire and, in particular, the construction of the Turkish nation state, resulted in the structures commercially connecting Europe and the Orient being shifted from Anatolia to the Greek nation state.[29] In this way Greece gained a new and important role during the inter-war period as a platform for commerce with the Middle East.

The refugees constituted a distinct social group, quite different from the society of which they were now a part. As a result of this they established exclusive networks unattached to existing patron-client relations.[30] The refugees also organized themselves politically as a group. Most identified with the Venizelists and, in particular, with Venizelos himself.[31] This, however, should not obscure the fact that they had conflicting interests with regard to several issues, a point clearly mirrored before the Parliamentary election in 1926 when the question of economic compensation became an urgent issue, and influential refugees started to campaign independently. Four days before the election, Kondilis succeeded in initiating the payments, and thus prevented the constitution of separate refugee lists.[32] Kondilis was one of many so-called Refugee Fathers (*prosfigopateres*) characteristic of the inter-war period. These were politicians who championed the cause of the refugees in order to gain political influence. Kondilis became one of the most important refugee fathers in the inter-war period and is a good example of the close political relationship between Venizelists and refugees that characterized Greek politics.

The political bonds between the refugees and the Venizelists were strained when Greece and Turkey, under the leadership of Venizelos, agreed to the so-called Ankara Convention in 1930. This agreement settled the question of compensation to refugees once and for all. The refugee organizations, however, felt that the agreement neglected their claim for sufficient economic compensation, and prominent refugee fathers, like Kondilis, rejected the convention and joined the ranks of the anti-Venizelists, who had taken the opportunity to set up an alternative proposal to consider the interests of the refugees. The consequences were decisive in the 1932 and 1933 elections, when the Venizelists lost their parliamentary power.[33]

Agriculture

According to the census of 1928, 61 per cent of the Greek population was employed within agriculture, while 23 per cent worked within industry, mining or transport.[34] Greek agriculture was divided into a sector concerned with production for home consumption, or for a small local market, and a sector oriented towards exports, producing mainly tobacco and currants. As Greece did not grow enough cereals for her own needs she had to import grain and foodstuffs. From 1922 onwards, various governments emphasized the development of import substitution production.

The import substituting effects of wheat and cotton production became increasingly important. The degree of self-sufficiency in wheat grew from an average of 35.9 per cent between 1928 and 1932 to 67.5 per cent in

1937.[35] In 1928, 72 per cent of the Greek consumption of cotton was met by imports. This figure dropped to 41 per cent in 1934 and to 12.7 per cent in 1938.[36]

The expanding wheat and cotton production during the anti-Venizelist administrations, and in particular in the period following the establishment of the dictatorship of Metaxas,[37] must be seen as a continuation of an already existing policy of national self-sufficiency launched by Venizelos' government, during 1928-1932.

Export Production of Tobacco and Currant
The tobacco grown in the Balkans and in Anatolia is the Oriental type, which is used mainly for cigarettes. After the conquest of Thrace and Macedonia, Greece became the world's leading producer of Oriental tobacco, with a share of a little less than 50 per cent of the total sale. In addition to Greece, Bulgaria and Turkey were the major producers of Oriental tobacco.[38] More than two-thirds of the tobacco production was concentrated in the northern Greek provinces of Macedonia and Thrace.[39] This meant that Macedonia, Thrace and tobacco replaced the Peloponnese and currants as the pivotal point in Greece's export economy and shifted the centre of gravity in Greek trade from currants and Britain to tobacco and Germany.

In 1925, 33 per cent of tobacco production was in the hands of refugees,[40] while, in 1927, tobacco producers became the largest group within agriculture, supported by loans from the National Bank of Greece.[41] Although tobacco producers constituted only about 10 per cent of the total number of farmers in Greece, half of the revenue from taxation from agriculture came from this group.[42] The important impact of tobacco production is further underlined by the fact that about 25 per cent of the total revenue from taxation in Greece originated from this sector.[43]

Most of the tobacco was sold on the world market, an average of 67.7 per cent between 1933-1937, while 21.7 per cent was stored and only 8.5 per cent was sold on the domestic market.[44] This made tobacco prices extremely vulnerable to fluctuations on the world market. The Depression and the contraction of world trade caused the prices of primary products and raw materials to slide down a deflationary spiral. This in turn precipitated the Greek tobacco trade into an acute crisis as the price of tobacco collapsed, reaching its lowest point in 1933, when it constituted only 27 per cent of the 1929 level.[45]

The state tried to stabilize prices through subsidized purchases. In 1936 a more systematic achievement was attempted by means of various laws that restricted the cultivated area for tobacco growing and decided which plots could carry tobacco. Moreover, in 1938, the so-called "Tobacco Protection Committee" was established to coordinate efforts to stabilize and improve tobacco production.[46]

Similar arrangements, to ensure the stability of the market, had existed within currant production since 1895. However, contrary to the situation on the tobacco market, Greek currant production had relatively little foreign competition, thus making it easy to manipulate prices through subsidiary purchase by the state.[47]

Industry

The industrialization of Greece began in the latter half of the ninetheenth century. Typically production was run on family lines, with a small number of employees manufacturing consumer goods from local agricultural products. Thus firms with 1-5 employees constituted 91.7 per cent of the total in 1920.[48]

However, the so-called decade of war, i.e. the years between 1912 and the war against Turkey, 1919-1922, changed this situation radically. First of all, the introduction of import control in connection with the war stimulated industrial growth. Secondly, the Greek merchant fleet gained enormous profits during the war, which, combined with the multiplied value of emigrant remittances, raised additional capital in the post-war period.[49] Furthermore, in 1919 there was a considerable shortage of manpower, so that the influx of refugees from Asia Minor, and the cheap labour that resulted from this, was a welcome development in the industry. The latter factor, and the introduction of protective duties in 1926, constituted a substantial stimulus to industrial development. However, the structure of Greek industry was divided into a countless number of small, technologically and financially underdeveloped family businesses on the one hand, and a limited number of large modern corporations on the other; these huge industries were mainly based in and around the large cities of Athens, Piraeus and Salonika.[50]

28

The most important industries were the food industry, the textile industry and the chemical industry, which together made up 59 per cent in 1923 and 66 per cent in 1938 of the total industrial production.[51] The tobacco industry constituted only a small part of this, but, because of its position in relation to the Greek foreign economy and its labour intensiveness, played an important role in Greek industry.

The tobacco industry constituted a small and declining percentage of the total industrial production between 1923-1938. According to the census of 1928, 48,000 out of 430,000 workers were employed in the tobacco industry, or 11.2 per cent of those registered.[52] 46 per cent of employees in the tobacco industry were refugees, more than twice their proportion within the total population.[53]

The tobacco workers were the best unionized of any operatives in Greece. According to a report by the Greek Ministry of Labour dated 1928, 55,507 out of 167,507 workers, i.e. 33 per cent, were from the tobacco industry.[54] These figures diverge from those shown in the census; this may be due to the fact that work within the tobacco industry was seasonal and additionally many workers, although members of the tobacco workers' union, were registered under another occupation.

Most tobacco workers in the Macedononian tobacco centres Serres, Drama and Xanthi owned their own land, thus securing an income outside the season. Nevertheless, the income for most workers in Kavalla was seasonable. In order to avoid serious social problems the government undertook the maintenance of non-property-owning workers outside the season. This was financed through a special tax imposed on workers and employers during the season.[55]

The tobacco workers' union had strong connections with the Communist Party of Greece (*Kommuniski Komma tis Eladas*, KKE). This turned the tobacco growing areas in northern Greece, Thrace and Macedonia into strongholds of the Communist Party. At the parliamentary elections held in 1926 the Communists gained between 10 and 15 per cent of the votes in the important ports of disembarkation, Salonika and Kavalla. However, the success of Venizelos and his liberal party two years later dealt a hard blow to the Communists, who faced a considerable decline in 1928.[56]

An indication that the Venizelists took the challenge from the Communists seriously is the fact that in 1929 they issued the notorious so-called special law (*Idionimon*). This law was meant to stifle the Communist Party but was also used to suppress the tobacco workers' unions whether or not they had allegiances to the party. However, this repressive action, combined with the world crisis, weakened the Venizelists and at the elections in January 1936 the Communists reinforced their position in Greek politics with 5.6 per cent of all votes, comprising 15 to 20 per cent of the votes in the tobacco producing areas and about 25 per cent of the votes in the area around Kavalla.[57]

According to an American report, the tobacco workers were the only group among the Greek working class to agitate efficiently and campaign for their rights.[58] This action reached its climax in May 1936, when northern Greece and Salonika formed the backdrop for the most extensive labour dispute in modern Greek history. At the beginning of May, the tobacco workers throughout Greece went on strike in support of a wage claim. On 9 May this culminated in a bloody confrontation in Salonika between the police and the workers; 10 workers were killed and 150 were injured.[59]

Social stability and the integration of the refugees in northern Greece were thus heavily dependent on tobacco production.

In turn, the economy of Macedonia and Thrace in general and the economic welfare of the tobacco producers and the industry in particular, were highly sensitive to changes and fluctuations on the world market.

"The tobacco nerve" made the entire Greek economy, as well as her social and political structure, extremely vulnerable to both internal and external factors, and resulted in a heavy dependence on Germany.

GERMANY

The Depression and the Development of Germany's Trade Policy

The Treaty of Versailles severely circumscribed Germany's opportunity to pursue an independent foreign policy extending into the realm of international commerce: it was not until 10 January 1925 that Germany was allowed to conduct an independent trade policy.[60] The suspension of this ban and the fact that Germany provided the second largest market in the world made trade policy an important consideration for various German governments in terms of foreign affairs. This resulted in an intensification of the relations between state and business, as industry and agriculture now had a more powerful say in the conduct of trade and foreign policy.

In 1925-1926 the proposal to create a European customs union, the so-called Loucheur Plan, which was intended as a first step towards the establishment of a "United States of Europe", unleashed a dispute between various branches of German industry. The export industries, already co-operating with French industry, took a firm stand in favour of this plan. They argued that such a union would enhance their ability to compete on third markets, in particular overseas and in the French dominated parts of south-eastern Europe. Heavy industry, in contrast, rejected the plan, primarily for reasons of power politics. It emphasized the narrow and necessary connection between preserving the independence of a national heavy industry and the possibility of rebuilding Germany's military power.[61] This approach was shared by agriculture and by ministerial bureaucracy: both stressed that Germany's trade relations were to be based on bilateral economic relations instead of being regulated by a multilateral system, as implied in the Loucheur Plan.[62] Such strong German opposition to international economic co-operation affected German-French relations throughout the following decades. French-German co-operation represented a corner-stone in the foreign policy of Gustav Stresemann, Germany's Minister of Foreign Affairs between 1923 and 1929. The importance of this maxim, however, was significantly reduced by his successors and disappeared as a goal in Germany's foreign policy during the Depression.[63]

The impact of the crisis varied substantially according to the various branches of the industry affected. While the total recession in the German economy was significant, the production of industrially manufactured goods experienced only a small decline. In this connection it is notable that the German export industry was capable of expanding its relative share of the international market, primarily at the expense of American but also of British industry. In Germany this made export an important crisis management strategy, with the slogan: "export Germany out of the crisis".

TABLE 1

The four countries with the largest share in the global export of manufactured goods.[64]

	Germany	Britain	France	USA
1927	16.5%	22.7%	11.4%	16.4%
1928	17.3%	21.8%	10.5%	17.2%
1929	18.6%	20.6%	9.8%	18.3%
1930	19.8%	19.4%	10.2%	15.4%
1931	22.5%	17.1%	10.5%	13.3%
1932	21.6%	19.4%	10.6%	11.1%
1933	20.2%	20.8%	10.8%	10.3%

Table 1 shows that the relative share of Germany's export industry increased in the first years of the Depression. It fell in 1932 but remained higher than before the world crisis.

The Depression made it a matter of urgent importance for Germany to find new directions and means of economic expansion. This made central and south-eastern Europe subject to new initiatives in Germany's trade policy. A German-Austrian tariff union was planned as a prelude to a later political *Anschluss* and as an alternative to the so-called Europe Plan, a modification of the Loucheur Plan, submitted by Briand, the French Minister of Foreign Affairs, in 1930. Such German schemes had to be dropped in March 1931 because of resistance from Italy and France.[65] This did not curtail Germany's ambitions to establish bilateral connections with south-eastern Europe. On 27 June 1931 and 18 July 1931 Germany concluded trade agreements with Romania and Hungary respectively. These were bilateral and preferential agreements that departed considerably from the most-favoured-nation principle and from multilateral trade, seen as the foundation of international trade by the French and, not least, by the Americans. According to these agreements, Germany would lower the tariffs on a series of agricultural products, while Romania and Hungary would reduce the duty on imported industrial goods.[66] However, complaints from the United States and opposition from German agriculture prevented the agreements from being realized.[67]

The plans outlined above can be interpreted as an initial attempt to establish a bilateral trade agreement system in south-eastern Europe to be dominated by Germany.[68] Furthermore, they should also be seen in the light of German fears of an agricultural coalition between the Danube countries and her resistance to the Tardieu Plan in 1932.[69]

During the world crisis another important change took place: the electrotechnical and chemical industries began to actively support plans for a central and south-eastern Europe dominated by the German economy. Carl Duisberg from IG Farben regarded a German-Austrian customs union as a step towards an economic opening of south-eastern Europe, which he described as a natural extension of the German home market.[70] Furthermore, by 1931, IG Farben and Siemens had become active in the *Mitteleuropäischer Wirtschaftstag* (the Central European Economic Congress). This was an important step in many respects: *Mitteleuropäischer Wirtschaftstag* provided German industry and the German state with an influental platform for planning and debate.[71]

It is important to stress that export-oriented industries preferred plans for a central European customs union to bilateral preferential agreements. This can be explained by the fact that, in terms of international law, a customs union worked in accordance with the most-favoured-nation principle and would therefore cause little damage to German export interests on other markets.[72] Like the engineering industry, the export-orientated industries saw co-operation with France as important as a result of their own positions on the overseas markets. IG Farben considered a closed European economic bloc "from Bordeaux to Odessa" as a preliminary condition in maintaining the position held by European industry on the world market.[73] This, as will be demonstrated below, was reflected in a series of cartel agreements between German and French industry. As a result, German industry gained substantial control of Czechoslovak industry through cartel agreements; due to the central role of the Czechoslovak industry in south-eastern Europe, this in turn resulted in increasing German control of the markets in this area.[74] Furthermore, German industry used the old imperial capital Vienna as a base for expansion towards south-eastern Europe. Thus, Siemens established an Austrian department in Vienna on the grounds that the existence of "old connections [between Austria and south-eastern Europe] makes it superfluous [for us] to establish new ones".[75]

In 1932 Germany started to conduct her commercial exchange through countertrade: the so-called clearing trade. This made it possible to exchange goods without the transfer of currency, in that payments for imports from Germany were placed on an account in Berlin and could only be liquidated by purchases in Germany.

Cartels and Know-How

Verena and Harm Schröter have demonstrated that Germany tried to overcome the economic crisis by means of export expansion. The clearing trade, cartels and know-how proved to be efficient tools in this respect. In November 1925 several leading German chemical companies amalgamated and founded IG Farben. IG Farben became the largest chemical enterprise in the world and gained a dominant position on the international market for production of synthetic dyes.[76] The same trends characterized developments within the German steel industry. In 1926 Vereinigte Stahlwerke was established, becoming the largest steel corporation in Europe and rendering the German steel industry a dominant position in the cartel, Internationale Rohstahlgemeinschaft, founded the same year.[77] The concentration of German industry also made it possible for it to "speak with one voice", a fact which was acknowledged and appreciated by the German government.[78]

Furthermore, on a global level, German firms led the way in production that was heavily dependent on research and development, and on advanced technology. This was especially true of branches like the chemical (IG Farben) and electrotechnical (AEG and Siemens) industries and of mechanical engineering.[79] Such technological and scientific advantages made it possible to control and dominate rivals by means of know-how, patents and licences.[80] The chemical industry, in particular, used such means to force its way into new markets, especially in areas where industrialization had just begun.

As noted above, these industries were intensely export-oriented, meaning that growth and stability were dependent on global economic and political conditions, as well as on their own international competitive edge. In the latter field their highly developed technological and scientific knowledge gave them a strong hand in negotiations with rival firms and placed them in a position to dominate a number of international cartel agreements. Verena Schröter points out that cartel agreements constituted an essential element in the strong position of German export-oriented industry in the years of the Depression.[81] Indicative of this is the fact that German firms were signatories of 60 to 70 per cent of all cartel agreements, making Germany the best represented nation.[82] In relation to this, it is significant that, in the period 1929-1937, between 30 and 50 per cent of total world trade was regulated by cartel agreements.[83] As a result German industry, and in particular the chemical and electrotechnical industries, gained a very strong position in international trade. This in turn made issues such as the direction of expansion as well as the goals of such activities of ever more topical interest in the conduct of Germany's foreign and trade policy.

Grossraumwirtschaft

Between 1929-1933 global demand was reduced and world trade declined. The total import in 75 countries fell from 2.9 billion gold dollars in 1929 to 1.1 billion gold dollars in 1932, and represented a mere 38 per cent compared to 1929.[84] This provoked several contradictory reactions: international competition intensified while the concentration of the industry increased and protectionism on the world market flourished. Moreover, the leading industrial nations raised tariff barriers around their home markets. The Smoot-Hawley Tariff Act of 1930 made access to the US market difficult. By the Ottawa Agreement of September 1932, Britain set up protective barriers around the markets of the UK and her colonies and dominions. France also turned towards her own Empire[85] and, in 1938, 70 per cent of the world trade was carried out within bilateral trade systems.[86]

German economy and trade were also severely hit by the Depression. Thus, the total value of Germany's exports fell from 13.5 billion RM to 4.9 billion RM in the period 1929-1933.[87] Germany did not have overseas possessions like France and Britain and neither did she have a domestic market of the same size as the United States: she was therefore obliged to conquer new markets and to use export as a strategy to overcome the crisis. This made the concept of *Grossraumwirtschaft* (literally: Big-Space Economy) a central and popular maxim in the planning of Germany's trade policy. This was to be understood as a regional economic autarchy under German leadership and control, in which south-eastern Europe produced primary products geared to Germany's needs, while Germany was to be its industrial centre.

Resistance from agricultural protectionists, led by Alfred Hugenberg, Minister of Economic Affairs, prevented this policy from being realized for a while, but, at the turn of the year 1932-1933, Franz von Papen joined forces with heavy industry, with the army and with Adolf Hitler. As a result of this coalition it became possible to define a trade policy based on the exchange of German industrial goods for agricultural products. In the summer of 1933 Hugenberg resigned as a result of pressure from Hitler, Hjalmar Schacht, President of the German Reichbank, *Mitteleuropäischer Wirtschaftstag*, Bernard von Bülow, State Secretary, and Constantin Neurath, Minister of Foreign Affairs. Subsequently, Kurt Schmitt, who enjoyed good relations with industry, was appointed to the post.[88] This contributed significantly to the weakening of opposition from agriculture. In connection with the World Economic Conference in London 1933, Hitler suggested that the industrial nations agree to reduce the export of capital goods in order to slow down the industrialization process in agricultural countries.[89] Furthermore, in 1933 the German government strengthened its influence on the disposal of scanty currency reserves and raw materials by delegating the control of exports and imports to several so-called *Aussenhandelsstellen* (Foreign Trade Offices). These came under the jurisdiction of *Auswärtiges Amt* and the Treasury Department, channelled through a *Reichsstelle für Aussenhandel* (Reichs Office for Foreign Trade).[90]

It is important to bear in mind that *Grossraumwirtschaft* was more than just an export strategy put forward as a response to the economic crisis. The idea originated before the First World War and was connected to economic doctrines in the army which aimed at autarchy. According to this point of view it was essential to move Germany's trade from overseas countries to the European continent in order to make her immune from a blockade such as the one that had had such crippling consequences during the First World War. According to the ideology of National Socialism, *Grossraumwirthschaft* in its broadest sense was defined as the entire 'space' between Gibraltar and the Urals and from North Cape to Cyprus and in which the community of race was seen as the uniting factor.[91] *Grossraum-wirtschaft* has been aptly characterized as a compromise between strategic and economic demands.[92] As noted above, racial considerations also played a part in the concept. This means that *Grossraumwirtschaft* had certain affinities with the idea of *Lebensraum* (Living Space), that is the colonization of the Slavic areas east of Germany by the German people. It is important to bear in mind that the concept of *Grossraumwirtschaft* was not an unambiguous term. It has been stressed that the definition was dependent on who defined it, which in reality linked the exact meaning of the term closely to the on-going power struggle within the German hierarchy.[93] However, there exists a broad consensus of opinion that an important precondition for the establishment of *Grossraumwirtschaft* was that Germany should be surrounded by a circle of politically friendly trading partners, a so-called *cordon économique*. Thus an early priority in Germany's policy towards south-eastern Europe was to strengthen relations with old friends and to acquire new ones.[94]

When the National Socialists seized power, issues relating to the strengthening of the German armed forces were given an increasingly prominent position in the policies of the regime. On 3 February 1933 Hitler stressed to the commanders of the army and navy that the build-up of armed forces was an important precondition for political strength. Hitler asked the following question: "...How is political power to be used when first acquired? At present it is impossible to say. Perhaps to conquer new areas for exports. Perhaps – and even better – by the conquest of new Living Space in the East and the reckless Germanification of it..."[95]

The statement reveals a conflict in the long-term aims of German policy: namely the economic plans for trade expansion on the one side and the idea of *Lebensraum* on the other.

Before the First World War, south-eastern Europe, that is to say the areas of the Habsburg Empire, former Ottoman land in the Balkans and the Ottoman Empire stretching to the Middle East as far as the tracks of the Berlin-Baghdad railway, constituted a goal in German economic and political expansion. As a result of continuity within the ministerial bureaucracy, as well as in the armed forces and business, such efforts towards expansion in this direction soon regained importance in Germany's foreign and trade policy in the inter-war period. The so-called

Central Europeans, represented in the Economic Department of *Auswärtiges Amt* by Karl Ritter, Emil Karl Josef Wiehl and Ernst Eisenlohr, primarily regarded Vienna, the capital of the former Dual Monarchy, as an important base for German penetration into the Balkans and Turkey.[96] A first step in this direction was to bring about an 'economic and legal' *rapprochement* between Germany and Austria, a second to have the French-dominated security system, the Little Entente between Czechoslovakia, Yugoslavia and Romania, dissolved in order to weaken the position of France in that area. A final step was to turn Vienna into a platform for German economic and political hegemony over south-eastern Europe and Turkey.[97]

A memorandum called *Raumpolitik-Kulturpolitik* (Space Policy-Culture Policy) dated 1934 notes that Germany's 'natural space' included East and South Europe, the Near East and Egypt. In this connection the Balkans were depicted as a bridgehead to Asia Minor, Turkey and the Middle East. The memorandum was written at Joseph Goebbels' request in order to examine methods of improving and intensifying relations between Germany and the Middle East.[98]

GREECE AND GERMANY

Greek-German Relations until the 1920s

Political and economic connections between Greece and Germany in modern times are closely linked with German policy towards the Orient at the end of the nineteenth century. The strengthening and maintenance of the Ottoman Empire was of vital importance to German interests in the region, and Greece's needs were only secondary in this respect.[99] German investments played a conspicuous part in the modernization of the Ottoman economy and of Ottoman society.[100] A good example of this is the fact that the Ottoman army was reorganized and modernized using German support.[101] Politically, the German-Ottoman *rapprochement* reached its climax in the German-Ottoman alliance during the First World War.[102]

The so-called Berlin-Baghdad Railroad became a symbol of German involvement in the Near East and caused French and British fears of German *Drang nach Osten*, i.e. German advances towards British areas of interest around the Persian Gulf, in Iran, in Mesopotamia and especially in India.[103]

Pro-Greek initiatives in German policy were on several occasions motivated by the economic significance of the Ottoman Greeks, whose goodwill was considered to be of great importance to Germany's commercial interests in the Ottoman Empire.[104] Similarily, Germany's financial commitment in Greece was dictated by her interest in the Orient. The only important direct German investment in Greece was represented by the Banque d'Orient, founded on the basis of parity between the National Bank of Greece[105] and National Bank für Deutschland. Operations were soon discontinued when it became blatantly obvious that the German bank was primarily interested in the Ottoman Empire, while the National Bank of Greece regarded Greece as the most important field of interst.[106]

In the realm of politics, the closest ties between Greece and Germany were found in a small circle around Crown Prince Constantine, later King, and his so-called 'Little Court'. Constantine, who was a great admirer of the German monarchy, had visited the German military academy and also studied politics in Germany. A number of Constantine's close supporters were sent to Germany; among these the best-known was Metaxas.[107] During the decade before the First World War, Constantine and the 'Little Court' also attempted to reorganize and modernize the Greek army using German support, but had only a limited degree of success.[108]

Greek-German Trade in the Years of Crisis 1929-1933

As noted previously, export-oriented German industry increased its relative share of global exports during the crisis. Table 2 shows that Germany's relative share of the Greek import grew between 1929-1933. Moreover, the nominal value of German exports to Greece remained quite stable during the first three years of the crisis, although from 1932 it began to fall.

TABLE 2

Greece's trade with Germany 1922-1933.
In billions of Drachmers, as percentage of total trade, and trade balance:

| | EXPORT | | | IMPORT | | | TRADE | |
	Dr.	%	Index	Dr.	%	Index	Current	Total
1922		21.1%			6.0%			
1926	1.19	21.9%	73	0.76	7.6%	88	0.44	
1927	1.29	21.4%	79	0.94	7.5%	87	0.35	
1928	1.63	25.8%	100	1.07	8.7%	100	0.56	
1929	1.61	23.1%	99	1.25	9.4%	109	0.37	
1930	1.39	23.3%	85	1.10	10.4%	121	0.30	
1931	0.59	14.0%	36	1.07	12.2%	141	-0.485	-0.485
1932	0.69	14.5%	42	0.76	9.7%	112	-0.072	-0.557
1933	0.92	17.9%	56	0.86	10.3%	118	0.054	-0.503

During the same period Greece's exports to Germany declined in both relative and nominal terms, and between 1928-1931 they were more than halved. In 1933 the average price per ton of exported tobacco reached an absolute minimum by constituting only 27 per cent of the level in 1929.[109]

This brought the tobacco industry to a point of acute crisis. The Greek state purchased the surplus production of tobacco at prices considerably higher than those on the world market, so as to mitigate the social and economic consequences. This was undertaken by the so-called "Central Committee for the Purchase and Administration of Tobacco". This committee was established by the state on 20 October 1931 with financial support from the National Bank of Greece. In 1932 the committee had 7.5 million *okkar* of unsold tobacco, thus posing a substantial economic risk to the state as well as to the National Bank of Greece.[110] The situation on the tobacco market grew worse during the first half of 1932, when Greek-German trade almost came to a standstill. This state of affairs arose because the Greek government had decreed a prohibition against the export of currency. This blocked the way for a settlement of Germany's assets in Greece. Table 2 demonstrates the way in which Germany's outstanding account in Greece had increased since 1931. However, protracted negotiations between the leading German tobacco company Reemtsma of Hamburg and the Greek government paved the way for the establishment of a general clearing agreement between the Bank of Greece and the German Reichsbank, as Reemstma declared itself ready to accept a certain quantity of Greek tobacco against a reduction of the German assets in Greece. The clearing agreement was signed in August 1932.[111]

To give a clearer and more precise view of the development of Greek-German trade and its impact on Greece, the following sections will investigate Greece's international political and financial position.

Greece's International Political and Economic Position
The disintegration of the Austro-Hungarian Dual Monarchy and the Ottoman Empire in the wake of the First World War led to a disruption of south-eastern Europe and the Middle East, and resulted in the foundation of a number of new nation states whose borders often ran across the original economic, political and cultural structures.[112] This state of affairs, combined with the defeat of Germany and the Russian Revolution, also created new economic and political opportunities for the victorious Great Powers: Britain, France, Italy and the United States.

At the San Remo conference held in 1920, Mesopotamia, Palestine and Transjordan came under a British mandate resulting in the emergence of a British Empire, which included Egypt in the Middle East.

France strove primarily to gain a leading political and economic positon in central and south-eastern Europe. To this end she allied herself with the newly established anti-revisionist successor states, Czechoslovakia, Yugoslavia and Romania, and created the so-called Little Entente. The alliance was mainly directed against German expansion into central and south-eastern Europe as well as against resurgent revisionism on the part of Hungary and Bulgaria. Finally, it was directed against a restoration of the Habsburg Monarchy.[113] Furthermore, France was entrusted with Cilicia and Alexandretta in Asia Minor, while, at the San Remo conference, Syria and Lebanon were placed under her mandate.

During the war between Italy and the Ottoman Empire, in 1911-1912, Italy landed troops in Libya and occupied the Dodecanese with its Greek Orthodox population. At the London agreement, signed in 1915, Italy was given sovereignty over the area of Andalia on the south coast of Asia Minor. Moreover, in accordance with the St. Jean de Maurienne agreement, signed in 1917, Italy was promised the area around Smyrna. The Tirana treaty in 1926 marked the beginning of the construction of Italian hegemony in Albania. In 1928 Italy signed a treaty of friendship with Hungary and in 1930 with Austria, and thereby made it clear that she also had ambitions in central and south-eastern Europe. The United States did not have any territorial claims in the region but both the government and business regarded access to the oil reserves overseas as a national interest.[114]

Greece's ambitions for territorial expansion in Asia Minor involved her in the complicated arena of power politics. Claims on Smyrna clashed with Italian interests and the two countries plunged into conflict. However, as Greece had political support from Britain and the United States, Italy decided to withdraw.[115] After the return of Constantine and the launching of the grand offensive against the Turkish Nationalists' bastion, Ankara, Greece gradually came into conflict with the Great Powers. In February 1921, France and Italy reached an agreement with Mustafa Kemal and renounced their claims on Cilicia and Andalia.[116] In April the same year, the Great Powers, including Britain and the United States, declared their neutrality in the Greek-Turkish conflict; this resulted in a weapon embargo on Greece. At the same time, France and Italy delivered military equipment to the Turkish Nationalists.

At the Lausanne Agreement, signed in 1923, the Greek-Turkish borders were finally fixed. However, the issues of compensation and the right of the Patriarch to remain in Constantinople continued to disturb Greek-Turkish relations: the decisive breakthrough came in 1930, when Venizelos and

Kemal Atatürk signed a declaration of friendship and neutrality on 26 and 30 October. The agreement secured the Patriarch the right to remain in Constantinople and settled the question of compensation to the refugees once and for all.[117] The Greek-Turkish *detente* meant that Greece had her flank towards the east covered. This enabled her to release resources for other purposes and especially for internal development. The agreement was one of the most stable diplomatic treaties in the inter-war period and led to yet closer relations between the two countries.[118]

Tensions between Greece and Italy culminated after the Lausanne Agreement, when Italy bombed and occupied the Greek island of Corfu. This resulted in British interference and the Italians withdrew. In 1926 Greek-Italian relations improved and in 1928 Greece and Italy signed an agreement of friendship.

Greece's interest in south-eastern Europe was underlined by a military pact. A *rapprochement* between Yugoslavia and Bulgaria in 1933 aroused fears in Greece and Turkey that a Great Slavic state in the Balkans would be created. Based on a Romanian initiative, the victorious Balkan states of the First World War, Romania and Yugoslavia, signed non-aggression pacts with Turkey. In February 1934, Greece, Turkey, Yugoslavia and Romania signed a general non-aggression pact, the so-called Balkan Entente. The latter guaranteed the borders stipulated in the peace agreements drawn up after the First World War. As a result of demands from Greece and Turkey the signatory parties agreed to set aside the Balkan Entente in the event of aggression from a non-Balkan country. In this way, Turkey hoped to avoid provoking the Soviet Union, while Greece hoped to stay on good terms with Italy.[119]

Greece's Financial Position

The First World War and a general drive towards modernization throughout the world created a huge demand for capital which could not be met by local accumulation alone. This gave exports and the import of capital a key role in the economies of south-eastern Europe. In the 1920s, capital flowed into south-eastern Europe as transfers and export income. The financial position of the United States was strengthened after the First World War, whereas the economic position of Britain was slightly weakened. The financial position of France in contrast was shattered. Huge capital investments were lost in the wake of the Russian Revolution, and the total of

France's foreign investments was reduced by 50 per cent.[120] The foundation of the Soviet state also meant that one of the most important areas for international capital export prior to the First World War vanished. After 1918 an increasing proportion of the international capital export became directed towards south-eastern Europe, and the region became the third most important area for foreign investments, after the British Empire and Latin America.[121]

After the First World War, Britain, the United States and France remained the most important capital exporting countries in the world, while Germany, before the war one of the leading creditor nations to south-eastern Europe, lost her position.[122]

TABLE 3

Total global investments made by France, Britain and the United States in 1930. In Billion US$.[123]

Investments in:		World	Europe	Europe's share of total.
From:	Britain	18.3	1.5	8.0 %
	USA	15.7	4.3	30.0 %
	France	2.8	1.6	60.0 %

American and British capital flowed into the old centres of the Austro-Hungarian Empire, i.e. Vienna, Budapest and Czechoslovakia, which in the inter-war period provided economic access to south-eastern Europe. French investments were primarily directed towards the countries in the French treaty organization, the Little Entente.[124]

The pattern of state to state or portfolio loans, set up in the 1920s, remained the same until the outbreak of the Second World War, as south-eastern Europe was cut off from the international capital market in 1931. This meant that foreign trade and the internal development of south-eastern Europe in the 1930s became increasingly dependent on export earnings. Whereas capital movements of the above-mentioned nature can be measured, it has not been possible to reach a precise quantification of direct investments. However, Alice Teichova points out that direct investments in Czechoslovakia were concentrated in firms that were already financially strong, technically advanced and strategically situated for export.[125] Thus, the figures in table 4 below do not reflect a complete pattern of the total foreign investments in south-eastern Europe.

44

TABLE 4

Total foreign investments in south-eastern Europe.[126]

Distributed by the following sectors: Public Finances (I), Trade (II), Banking (III), Insurance (IV), Industry (V), Transport, Communication and Construction (VI), Miscellaneous (VII).

	I	II	III	IV	V	VI	VII
Yugoslavia	67.7	3.3	6.4	0.1	20.2	1.9	0.4
Romania	74.6	0.8	1.8	0.3	22.1	0.8	0.2
Bulgaria	82.6	2.0	2.8	0.1	12.2	0.1	0.3
Greece	70.7	7.7	7.1˙		3.5	7.3	3.5
Turkey	54.0	3.0	7.2	4.0	5.0	23.0	3.8

TABLE 5

Distribution of foreign investments as public loans in south-eastern Europe.[127]

Creditor / Debitor	France	Britain	Italy	USA	Sweden
Yugoslavia	32.0		38.0	20.1	9.8
Romania	12.9	55.8	5.8	5.8	11.5
Greece		67.0		17.7*	

* including French capital

The Position of Foreign Capital in the Greek economy

Tables 4 and 5 show that capital exports to Greece were primarily directed towards public finances, as in all other south-eastern European countries. In Greece, contrary to the rest of south-eastern Europe, only a fraction was directed towards industry.

TABLE 6[128]

Distribution of foreign investments other than state loans.

Creditor / Debitor	France	Britain	Belg.	Italy	Germ.	Czech.	Switz.	USA	Aus*
Yugoslavia	20.5	19.8	4.4	4.9	6.6	13.3	10.3	5.2	1.6
Romania	16.4	20.6	10.8	7.4	2.0	5.6	1.6	5.8	4.5
Bulgaria	11.2	1.4	28.5	9.8	5.3	6.3	23.4	8.4	4.2
Greece	9.0	53.0	5.0	4.5	5.0		2.0	8.0	
Turkey	46.5	16.3	6.0	4.5	23.0		0.4	2.8	

* Austria-Hungary

TABLE 7

Distribution of the nominal value of foreign capital in south-eastern Europe, in US$, 1930.[129]

	Total	per capita
Romania	US$ 0.896 billion	US$ 49
Greece	US$ 0.515 billion	US$ 80
Yugoslavia	US$ 0.268 billion	US$ 22

The most important direct foreign capital investments in Greece were directed towards transportation, banking, mining, insurance and public utilities, while the most dynamic sectors in the 1930s, agriculture and industry, were largely neglected.[130]

Foreign investments played a relatively large role within insurance and mining. Nevertheless, capital in the insurance companies made up only two per cent of the total share capital in Greece.

In 1939 about 33 per cent of the total workforce in mining were employed in enterprises that received foreign capital. Almost half of these employees worked in the British dominated Anglo-Greek Magnesite Company or the French Lavrion Works. Because mining only constituted one per cent of Greece's national product, foreign, and in particular British, capital in these sectors played only a minor role in the Greek economy as a whole.

Within banking British capital played a significant role for only a few banks, of whom the Ionian Bank Ltd. and the Greek Mortgage Bank were the most important.

46

However, British capital occupied a prominant position within public utilities and transportation. The Athens-Piraeus Electricity Transport Company was the most important single holding of British capital, with a value of between £4.5 million and £5.5 million.[131] British capital also dominated the Piraeus-Athens-Peloponnese Railway (SPAP), with a share in 1939 of £0.7 million.[132]

However the 1930s proved a problematic decade for foreign vested interests in Greece. A harsh monetary policy made capital transfers out of the country difficult and at times impossible. Until 1937 the return on shares was typically between 0 and 3 per cent. Thus during the 1930s total direct foreign investments in Greece declined and dropped from £26.4 million in 1933 to £20 million in 1939.[133]

Greece's Financial Assets

Unlike other south-eastern European states, Greece had substantial international financial assets. These consisted of international Greek shipping, emigrants' remittances and capital investments overseas.

In 1938 the Greek merchant fleet was the ninth largest in the world, with 1.9 million G.R.T. Furthermore, with a total of 97 per cent of its tonnage engaged in the tramp trade, it dominated world-wide competition within this field. The Greek merchant fleet operated at competitive costs throughout the world and was known for its willingness to engage in high-risk trade during times of war. The Greek merchant fleet dominated the shipment of wheat from Argentina with a share of 40 per cent in 1937. Moreover, it carried about 13 per cent of the wheat imported into Britain. The Greek flag ranked as number four in British ports, thus strengthening relations between the two countries considerably.[134] This connection was further enhanced by the fact that Greek ship-owners transferred substantial amounts of their earnings to banks in Britain.[135]

Emigrants' remittances primarily came from the United States, a country which had received just over 90 per cent of the total emigration from Greece in the period leading up to the Second World War.[136]

Table 8 shows that emigrant remittances reached a peak in 1930. Thereafter, they fell, reaching a minimum in 1934 and constituting about 33 per cent of the 1930 level. From 1934 they began to rise again, until 1938, when recession in the United States dealt the world economy a heavy blow. It is important to note, however, that emigrant' remittances are generally estimated to have been higher than the figures suggest.[137]

TABLE 8

Emigrant remittances in billion Dr.(nominal rates)[138]

		US$ Mil.	£Mil.
1928	2.4	31	
1929	2.9	37.6	
1930	3.1	40.2	
1931	2.4	31	
1932	1.5	11.2	
1933	1.7	11.7	
1934	1.0	9.2	
1935	1.1	10.1	
1936	1.8	16.6	
1937	2.3	20.6	
1938	1.9	17.1	
1939	2.1		3.9
1940	2.0		3.6

Capital investments were mostly directed towards the Levant, and in particular Egypt, where Greek interests were represented in export firms, industry and the financial system. Thus two large Greek banks, the National Bank of Greece and the Athens Bank (*Trapeza Athinon*) both had branches in Egypt.[139]

When the Greek population was driven out of Asia Minor in 1922, the Greeks in Egypt constituted the remains of the diaspora in the former Ottoman Empire. Including those Greek Orthodox Egyptian citizens who spoke Greek and were descendants of Greek emigrants, the total Greek population in Egypt numbered about 200,000 in 1920.[140] Alexandria was the principal stronghold of the Greek-Egyptians, followed by Cairo and the cities along the canal: Port Said, Ismailiya and Suez. However, the existence of Greeks in the provincial towns in Upper Egypt, the Sudan and the Ethiopean plateau demonstrates the way in which the Greeks had formed a network stretching from Alexandria via Khartoum to Addis Ababa.[141]

The Greek community represented an important factor in the Egyptian economy and its affluence was a significant asset for Greece. In 1937 Greek commercial houses handled 21 per cent of the total cotton exports from Egypt.[142] Economically the colony was integrated into Egyptian society[143] and only loosely tied to Greece financially. Nevertheless, the members of the colony considered themselves Greeks and reacted to developments in the Greek nation state. This gave the Greek community in Egypt an important economic potential for Greece. Thus, during the 1930s, capital from the colony took over the majority of shares in the Athens and Piraeus Water Company.[144] In connection with the modernization of the Greek army, wealthy Greeks living in Egypt funded the purchase of four fighter aircraft for the Greek Air Force.[145] However, the Greeks in Egypt also made Greece dependent on developments in the Middle East, and thus tied her closer to the Western Powers and, in particular, to Britain.

The Impact of the Depression on Greek Foreign Trade

The world-wide Depression caused a decline in Greece's export earnings, a reduction in the revenue from invisibles and a suspension of the flow of foreign capital into her economy.

In 1929 Greek foreign trade amounted to 55.8 per cent of the total national income. Due to an export structure that was mainly based on agricultural products and minerals[146], the price collapse on the international agricultural and raw material market hit Greek revenues in foreign trade severely.

In 1933 total export earnings reached a minimum, a mere 60 per cent of the average in the period 1922-1930.[147] However, as a substantial part of Greece's imports, more than 50 per cent, were constituted by agricultural products and raw materials, the terms of trade in 1934 had only declined by 7.8 per cent compared to the average of 1922-1930.[148]

The decline in invisibles, namely the revenues from shipping, the tourist trade and emigrant remittances, as well as the reduction in the yields from overseas investments and the suspension of the flow of foreign capital, brought Greece to an acute liquidiry crisis.

In 1932 the Greek government decided to default on the service of her foreign debt. In the second half of 1932 an agreement was made with the Council of Foreign Bondholders that aimed at a 30 per cent service of the debt. This resulted in the expenditure for amortization of the foreign debt falling from 23 per cent of the total budget in 1932 to 9 per cent in 1933/34; by the end of 1930s, it constituted about 8 per cent. In this way the Greek Treasury saved 8.5 billion Dr., corresponding to the total government expenditure in 1933/34. Furthermore, the moratorium made it possible throughout the remainder of the decade for the government to keep expenditure for all purposes other than the debt service at the same level as before the crisis.[149]

However, the default on the debt did not solve the capital and exchange crisis, which still posed a serious threat to the Greek economy. For this reason, a series of laws passed on 15 May 1932 made imports subject to quantitative restrictions and introduced a stringent exchange control. As a result, an increasing part of the trade became subject to clearing agreements.[150]

Greece recovered relatively quickly from the immediate effects of the crisis. In 1933 the nominal value of the national product exceeded the 1928 level. Similarly, in 1933 the wholesale price index passed the 1929 level.[151] Part of the explanation for this must be due to the fact that the Greek drachma was devalued in 1932 and that accounts were worked out at current prices. Finally, it is important to note that the terms of trade deteriorated significantly less than in most other raw material exporting countries.

The Depression affected different sectors within the Greek economy unequally. The revenue from industry fell by 1.4 per cent between 1928 and 1931, when it reached its minimum, whereas the revenue deriving from agriculture declined by 34 per cent in the same period.[152] Within agriculture the depression was worst in export production, and first and foremost within the tobacco sector, where prices fell by nearly 70 per cent.[153]

While the Greek economy quickly recovered from the immediate effects of the crisis, secondary repercussions, namely the results of political and economic changes in response to the crisis, marked the country's development throughout the 1930s.

The decline in invisibles and the lapse of credit facilities gave an increasingly central role in Greece's foreign economy to export. In this way, Greece's dependence on her export markets rose.

The Development of Greek Export
In 1930, 71.5 per cent of Greek export and 52.9 per cent of Greek import was distributed among the five Great Powers: Germany, Britain, the United States, Italy and France. While in 1938 the total share of Germany, Britain and the United States remained roughly the same, respectively 72 per cent and 54.1 per cent, the share of Italy and France declined signifi-

cantly: France's share of the import fell from 7.2 per cent to 1.5 per cent, while her share of the export fell from 6.1 per cent to 2.9 per cent. Italy's share of the import fell from 6.1 per cent to 3.4 per cent, and her share of the export fell from 14.1 per cent to 5.2 per cent.[154] The United States's share of the import fell by nearly 50 per cent, while the Greek export to the United States rose.

TABLE 9

Distribution of Greek export (X) and import (M).[155]
1930=100 (index)

	Germany				Britain				USA			
	percentage		index		percentage		index		percentage		index	
	X	M	X	M	X	M	X	M	X	M	X	M
1927	21.4	7.5	91	72	11.4	13.5	90	103	21.8	16.0	149	102
1928	25.8	8.7	109	84	13.8	14.5	110	111	19.9	15.6	136	102
1929	23.2	9.4	99	90	11.7	12.7	93	97	16.1	15.7	110	100
1930	23.6	10.4	100	100	12.6	13.1	100	100	14.6	15.7	100	100
1931	14.0	12.2	60	117	15.5	13.2	119	101	10.2	13.8	70	88
1932	14.5	9.7	61	93	23.7	13.7	188	105	10.2	13.8	70	88
1933	17.7	10.3	76	99	18.9	14.4	150	110	12.5	5.8	86	37
1934	22.5	14.7	95	141	17.4	16.7	138	127	14.7	6.3	101	40
1935	29.8	18.7	126	179	12.6	15.5	100	118	16.9	6.3	115	40
1936	36.4	22.4	154	215	12.2	16.1	97	123	14.3	7.1	98	45
1937	31.0	27.2	131	262	9.7	11.0	77	84	16.5	4.3	113	27
1938	38.5	28.8	163	276	8.3	13.0	66	99	17.7	7.3	117	46
1939	27.6	30.0	116	288	13.9	12.0	110	91	21.6	7.0	148	45
1940	37.8	23.5	160	226*	7.4	11.1	59	85	25.0	11.4	171	73
1940	27.1	13.9	115	133*								

* See notes 156-157

Germany's position declined during the crisis years, but was strengthened as a trading partner from the middle of the 1930s. Britain retained her position after a period of expansion during the crisis.

Tobacco made up nearly half of the total revenues from Greek exports.[158] Germany and the United States were the most important buyers of tobacco, whereas tobacco only constituted a fraction of British purchases in Greece. These were dominated by currants, which made up some 70 per cent of Greek exports to Britain. Furthermore, Britain took about 80 per cent of the total Greek exports of currants.[159]

TABLE 10

Destination of Greek export of tobacco beween 1928-1939 (per cent).

	Germany	USA	Italy
1928	44.59	17.04	18.04
1933	42.00	17.63	5.32
1934	41.03	21.09	2.81
1935	44.05	19.87	2.80
1936	56.65	16.40	0.02
1937	44.22	22.23	3.51
1938	52.81	14.21	2.88
1939	48.67	21.78	0.00

TABLE 11

Tobacco and currant as a proportion of the Greek exports between 1929-1938 (per cent)[160]
1930=100

	1929	1930	1931	1932	1933	1934	1935	1936	1937	1938
Tobacco:										
Share	56.6	56.5	53.5	38.3	32.1	37.0	50.3	46.1	45.9	45.5
Index	100	100	94	68	57	65	89	82	81	81
Currants:										
Share	15.1	16.3	22.2	27.3	25.0	26.0	17.3	17.7	14.9	12.4
Index	93	100	136	167	153	159	106	109	91	76

The American and British export markets were of particular interest to Greece because trade was settled in hard currency. Greek-British and Greek-American trade were based on most-favoured-nation agreements from, respectively, 16 July 1926 and 9 October 1925.[161] Greece had a deficit in her trade with Britain between 1927 and 1940, but a surplus in her trade with the United States from 1933. However, this was only sufficient to compensate for the deficit in the trade with Britain in the years 1937, 1939 and 1940,[162] so that Greek-British trade during most of the period had a draining effect on Greek currency reserves.

Germany's dominant role as an export market was further boosted when Greece was no longer able to obtain loans abroad and also as a result of the decline in invisibles. In 1931 invisibles made up 87.5 per cent of the exports but were almost halved, to 44.4 per cent, in 1938.[163] As most of these invisibles originated in Dollar or Sterling areas, the decline further tipped the balance in Greek foreign incomes from Dollar and Sterling areas in favour of Germany.

At the same time, however, it is important to stress that invisibles constituted an asset which the other south-eastern European countries did not possess.

While, until 1938, Greek foreign revenues became increasingly dependent on exports to Germany, the development of the total foreign sector shows a tendency to decline in relation to the growth in the overall Greek economy.

TABLE 12

The development in the value of foreign trade as a share of the total Greek economy and the relation between export and import.
1930=100[164]

	The share of foreign trade in the total Greek economy.		Export as a percentage of import.	
	%	Index	%	Index
1927	51.7	109	...	...
1928	48.0	101	...	...
1929	55.8	117	52.3	92
1930	47.6	100	56.9	100
1931	39.9	84	48.0	84
1932	34.0	71	60.5	106
1933	31.9	67	61.2	108
1934	31.3	66	62.3	109
1935	36.3	76	66.5	117
1936	36.5	77	61.7	108
1937	43.0	90	62.8	110
1938	40.0	84	68.8	121
1939	...	...	74.3	131
1940	...	...	74.9	132

This development must be seen as a result of the Depression, which forced the Greek government to rely on the country's own resources to a greater extent than it had previously done. A more efficient utilization of these resources could compensate for a decline in the income from the external sector and limit the dependence on this, and such tendencies therefore became increasingly marked in the planning and organization of the Greek economy during the 1930s.

Clearing, Cartelization and Know-How

As already demonstrated, the three most important tools in Germany's crisis management strategy were: know-how, cartel agreements and clearing. No surveys exist to show the role of international cartels or know-how in the Greek economy. Nevertheless, the results of research within this field indicate that the influence of neither Czechoslovak nor Austrian industry and finance reached as far as Greece, except that Österreichische-Siemens-Schuckert Werke held a share of 75 per cent in Siemens Hellenic Electrotechnical Co. Ltd. Athens. (Siemens griechische electrotechnische AG).[165]

A cartel agreement, valid from 1929 to 31 December 1968, between IG Farben, the interest organization of the French dye industry, Centrale des Matiéres Colorantes (CMC) and the Swiss IG Farben, the so-called European Dye Cartel (Dreierkartel), gave the markets in Scandinavia and south-eastern Europe to IG Farben and Swiss IG Farben.[166] The Greek market was encompassed by this agreement.[167] On 26 February 1932 Imperial Chemical Industries joined the cartel, which was now renamed the Vierkartel. The production quotas were allocated as follows: IG Farben 65.5 per cent, Swiss IG Farben 17.4 per cent, Imperial Chemical Industries 8.5 per cent and CMC 8.5 per cent. The Vierkartel controlled 75 per cent of the global production of dyestuff, and 90 per cent of the total exports within this trade, thus enabling it to impose its own price policy on non-participant competitors.[168] In 1938 the German IG Farben accounted for 75 per cent of the dyestuff imported into Greece, while the Swiss cartel partner accounted for 11 per cent,[169] indicating that the cartel provided at least 86 per cent of all Greek dyestuff import. Furthermore, the firm which represented IG Farben in Greece, Athanil, concluded an agreement of friendship with its only competitor in the area, Societé des Matiéres Colorantes du Pirée S. A. Oeconimides & Co, in order to control prices and stabilize the market.[170] This agreement strengthened IG Farben's position

54

in Greece considerably and must be seen as extremely important in view of the intimate relationship between dyestuff and textile production and the fact the Greek textile industry during the inter-war period expanded to become the largest industry in the country, contributing significantly to substitute imports within this field.

However, during the second half of the 1930s, the German chemical giant lost some of its control over the dyestuff market in Greece, as a number of rival firms manufacturing this were founded. In this respect it is important to note that this challenge did not originate from foreign competition but from local production, the existence of which relied on a protectionist policy. Research has demonstrated that German industry was incapable of preventing the emergence of local competitors as a result of state protectionism.[171]

IG Farben also dominated the production of artificial silk. The sole Greek firm within this trade, ETMA, based its production of viscose on an IG Farben patent.[172]

On 25 February 1930, IG Farben, Imperial Chemical Industries and Norsk Hydro established the so-called DEN Group (Deutschland, England und Norwegen). This was a production and sales cartel within saltpetre, a basic component of fertilizers and explosives.

According to this agreement, IG Farben would control 80.5 per cent of the production, while the remaining 19.5 per cent was allocated to Imperial Chemical Industries. Moreover, IG Farben were given the sole and exclusive rights of sales in the European market, while Imperial Chemical Industries were allocated the countries in the British Empire as their exclusive market. The rest of the world was open for competition.[173]

While the establishment of local chemical production contributed to a reduction of Greece's dependence on manufactured chemical goods, the expanding Greek chemical industry became increasingly dependent on imports of basic and heavy chemicals from Germany.

The electrotechnical market was divided into high- and low-voltage accessories. The high-voltage market in Greece was dominated by British industry, represented by the Athens-Piraeus Electricity Company and Electric Transport Company. This firm, also called 'Power', was owned by Prudential Assurances and Whitehall Securities Corporation: it supplied Athens with electricity and ran her trolley buses and trams.[174]

During the dictatorship of Pangalos, 'Power' established a 60 year monopoly on production, transformation, supply and distribution of electrical power to the capital, including an area within a 20 kilometre range of the city centre. Moreover, the firm gained a monopoly on the establishment and development of buses and trams in this area, plus the service of the electric railway between Athens and the northern suburb of Kifisia.[175]

In a cartel agreement with Philips and General Electric, the German low-voltage company, Osram (a branch of Siemens & Halske and AEG), gained central and south-eastern Europe as its exclusive market. Greece was not specifically included in the agreement but Osram owned the incandescent lamp factory Sté Hellenique des lampes à l'incandescence, one of two electrotechnical enterprises in Greece.[176] In 1937, 56 per cent of the total consumption of electric bulbs was met by local production (in which German industry held a prominent position), while the rest was imported from Germany, Austria and Hungary.[177] As Österreichische Siemens-Schuckert Werke dominated the production of bulbs in Austria and controlled two production units in Hungary, the bulk of Greek imports within this field came *de facto* from the German industry as well.[178]

In 1930 Siemens & Halske gained a concession to extend the Greek telephone network and later acquired a majority share in the Greek Telephone Company. During the 1930s Siemens increased its sale of telephone equipment to Greece tenfold.[179] In 1939 Germany provided 65.5 per cent of all telephonic and telegraphic instruments imported by Greece.[180]

Furthermore, Siemens founded the above-mentioned Siemens griechische elektrotechnisches AG, so that ultimately electrotechnical production in Greece came under total German control.

In comparison with the general pattern of cartelization in Europe, it is important to note that German industry held a significant, albeit less dominant, position in Greece and that British industry dominated the electrotechnical high-voltage sector.[181]

However, in conclusion, it is also clear that during the crisis internationally powerful German electrotechnical and chemical companies strengthened their existing positions or gained new ones on the Greek market. Furthermore, throughout the remainder of the 1930s, German industry succeeded in creating a monopoly within the electrotechnical low-voltage sector, by means of international cartel agreements, concessions and the establishment or takeover of production facilities.

Part II

Recovery, Rearmament
and Trade in Arms
1934-1937

GREECE

The Resurgent National Schism, Political Crisis and the Establishment of the Metaxas Dictatorship

The assumption of power by the anti-Venizelists in March 1933 soon caused the National Schism to resurface, and resulted in a bitterly intensified polarization within the political world and the armed forces. Following Plastiras's abortive *coup d'etat* on the night of the election, 5 March 1933, Venizelos survived an attempt on his life in June 1933 under dramatic circumstances. Because the Chief of the Security Police, recently appointed by Tsaldaris, turned out to be the mastermind behind the plot and because the subsequent legal investigation was sabotaged, relations between the two factions were further poisoned.[182]

The anti-Venizelists' powerbase was constituted by recently acquired governmental power, whereas the Venizelists retained control over Senate and Army. In order to counteract this state of affairs, the anti-Venizelists launched plans to reform the power structure in the Army and to change the electoral system to reduce the impact of the refugee vote. Furthermore, plans were worked out to curtail the power of the Senate.[183] On 20 January 1934, Kondilis, the Minister of War, passed a bill to reduce Venizelist power in the Army, but was forced to withdraw the proposal when the opposition threatened to call for approval by the Senate.[184] This set the scene for a series of manoeuvrings of an extra-parliamentary nature by both the Venizelists and by the anti-Venizelists. In May 1934, Kondilis informed Metaxas that he was planning a *coup* for 15 August 1934 in order to overcome Venizelist resistance to the reform of the Army. At the end of the day, however, Kondilis, did not carry out the *coup*.[185] At the same time, Venizelist officers were preparing to bid for power. The prospect of an anti-Venizelist majority in the Senate resulting from a forthcoming election in April 1935 caused the conspirators to make their move on 1 March 1935 under the leadership of Plastiras.[186] In this way, Greece was precipitated into her worst national crisis since the *débâcle* in Asia Minor. For more than a week the country was on the brink of disintegration similar to the old cleavage between anti-Venizelist 'Old Greece' and Venizelist 'New Greece'.

However, it soon transpired that the conspirators had failed to muster sufficient backing from the Army and the population as a whole. Within 24 hours, loyalist troops re-established total control of Athens. On 8 March Kondilis mustered an army 45,000 strong to fight the rebels in northern Greece; within two hours he managed to neutralize all resistance and on 10 March Thrace and Macedonia were recovered. Finally, on the night between 11 and 12 March, Venizelos fled the country.

In the aftermath, Kondilis, assisted by Metaxas, promptly launched a massive and thorough purge of Venizelist officers.[187] This, combined with the abolition of the Senate and the large-scale dimissal of Venizelists from the administration, resulted in overwhelming anti-Venizelist dominance in the state apparatus and in the armed forces. Furthermore, the Venizelists lost all their influence in parliament, as they decided to boycott the election in June 1935.[188]

This significantly enhanced the power and prestige of Kondilis among the anti-Venizelists. On 10 July 1935, Kondilis further strengthened his own position, as well as that of other radical anti-Venizelists, when he made parliament pass a resolution providing for a plebiscite on the constitutional issue to be held before 15 October. Parliament then went into recess until 10 October.[189]

On the day that parliament was due to convene, 10 October, Kondilis and the three chiefs of the Armed Forces overthrew Tsaldaris and took control of the country by the use of dictatorial powers. The Junta abolished the Republic and proclaimed the restoration of the Monarchy

On 3 November a rigged plebiscite ratified the restoration of the Monarchy, with 97.87 per cent of the votes in favour. From the day of his arrival in Greece on 25 November, King George II, who had been living in Britain for almost 12 years, made it clear that he was determined to reconcile the factions within the political world. On 30 November the uncompromising anti-Venizelist Kondilis resigned as a protest against the attitude of the King. George II pardoned the Venizelist participants in the March *Coup* and appointed a caretaker government which was to stay in power until a political cabinet could be formed after the election to be held on 26 January 1936.[190] Kondilis's resignation has been seen as a result of his disagreement with the King over the latter's wish to placate the Venizelists and grant an amnesty to those involved in the March uprising. It has also been suggested that the King would not agree to act as Kondilis's puppet.[191] Both explanations are reasonable. It must be stressed, however, that the King was as adamant as Kondilis in his rejection of the reinstatement of the Venizelist officers; apparently their disagreement did not estrange them irreparably, as shortly after they found sufficient grounds to plan joint action should the Venizelist officers demand reinstatement. According to the German Counsellor of Legation, the King held Kondilis in reserve should his conciliation attempt with the Venizelists fail. Furthermore, Kondilis had told the German Counsellor of Legation quite frankly that he was ready to prevent, if necessary even by a revolution, any attempt to reinstate the Venizelist officers, "if some government should prove ready to re-admit the 'March traitors' into the Army."[192]

The elections on 26 January 1936 ended in a political deadlock, as neither bloc could form a majority government without the support of the Communist Party.[193] The deadlock soon turned into a prolonged political crisis. On 5 March 1936, as a reaction to rumours that the Venizelists and the Communists were negotiating, the Minister of War, Alexandros Papagos, informed the King that the army would not accept a government formed by Communists and Venizelists. However, the King refused to tolerate such interference by the armed forces. He immediately dismissed Papagos and assigned the Ministry of War to Metaxas, who also became Deputy Prime Minister.[194] On 13 April 1936, Konstandinos Demerdzis, the leader of the caretaker government, died, and a few hours later the King appointed Metaxas Prime Minister. According to the German Counsellor of Legation, the King did this in order to have a strong man at hand ready to act firmly should parliamentary chaos threaten Greece.[195] This is quite plausible. On 30 April 1936, Metaxas suspended parliament for a period of five months.[196] On 22 July 1936, the leaders of both the anti-Venizelists and the Venizelists informed the King that they were ready to form a government when parliament met again in October. The agreement was based upon the reinstatement of the purged Venizelists officers. This, however, would spell trouble for the anti-Venizelist army and could pose a serious threat to the power bases of the King and, not least, Metaxas. On the following day, 23 July, Metaxas told three of his close associates that the King had given him *carte blanche* to establish a dictatorship within 10 to 15 days.

On 4 August 1936 Metaxas decided to act. His official justification for establishing the dictatorship was to forestall a Communist inspired revolution. According to Metaxas this was planned to coincide with a 24-hour general strike declared for 5 August.[197] By cracking down on the Communists, Metaxas maintained in an interview with the daily newspaper, *Vradini*, he had prevented the kind of bloodshed that characterized the strikes in May. Furthermore, he declared that in the long run he intended to win over followers from the Communist Party to his side.[198]

According to contemporary diplomatic observers, however, the prospect of a Communist revolution was quite improbable.[199] These observations are supported by historians, who tend to explain the establishment of the dictatorship in terms of the protracted political crisis and the successive deaths of several leading political figures, such as Venizelos, Kondilis and Tsaldaris, within a short span of time.[200] As will be demonstrated below, the impact of German policy also played a significant role in this development as well as in the decisions that resulted in the establishment of the Metaxas regime.

The Metaxas Dictatorship

Metaxas suspended democratic rights and introduced strict censorship.[201] The Security Police reorganized and launched an efficient and brutal persecution of opponents to the regime, specially Communists. To this end, the so-called Special Security Department was established. It functioned as Metaxas's personal guard and was assigned duties concerning security and crowd control in Athens. Furthermore, the department became responsible for the torture and execution of dissidents.[202]

The regime strove to promote an image of itself as antiplutocratic, as an alternative to trade unions, political parties and professional and industrial bodies. The First of May became a national holiday, rebaptized and celebrated by the regime as the 'National Day of Celebration of Work'. Labour legislation was decreed which sanctioned compulsory arbitration and planned to increase the minimum wage and enhance social welfare. The regime paid great attention to the actual enforcement of the labour legislation and the Ministry of Labour did not refrain from fining employers if working hours in offices or factories were exceeded.[203]

The regime was adamant on this point to the extent that in 1938 it chose a major confrontation over just such an issue with the British dominated firm, 'Power'. When the company declined to conclude a collective agreement, as stipulated by Greek law, its managing director was arrested and the firm was ordered to pay a considerable fine.[204]

According to official figures, 616,000 workers and 141,000 public servants were covered by the labour legislation carried through in 1939.[205]

Wages increased by a nominal rate of 50 per cent from 1935 to 1940, yet real growth was little more than five per cent due to an increase in consumer prices.[206]

Regarding unemployment insurance, 37 million Dr. was paid to tobacco workers in the period 1937-1939, according to figures published by the regime, while the assets of the social funds totalled 3 billion Dr.[207] However, Spiros Linardatos states that the figure was significantly lower, 850 million Dr., as the regime used social funds to finance rearmament.[208] Job creation was an issue of central importance for the regime. According to the German Legation, the Greek government succeeded in bringing down unemployment from 128,000 to 26,000 during its first year in power, and in 1939, according to the same source unemployment was down to 15,000.[209] The key factors, according to the German Legation, were the state promoted stimulus of industrial growth and the efficient implementation and surveillance of labour legislation; the latter had set the working day for industrial workers at eight hours and for office workers at seven hours.[210]

The above figures, however, should not be taken at face value: the regime wished to promote itself as 'pro-labour' and as an alternative to Communism and free trade unions. However, it is a fact that the period under Metaxas was one of sustained industrial growth. This is particulary true in terms of the armament industry, as the regime launched a massive rearmament programme based on national self-sufficiency and on an extension of the military infrastructure.[211]

The policy of the Metaxas regime can best be described as one of national efficiency, modernization, and integration, implemented through the extensive use of brutality and at the expense of parliamentarian principles and democratic rights. In the realm of economics, the Metaxas regime continued the trend of 'crisis management' set by previous Greek governments as a response to the impact of the Depression, with the important exception of the focus which Metaxas placed on rearmament. In the implementation of its 'crisis management' policy, the Metaxas regime differed from previous governments by ruling without interference from the two main groups in Greek political life. In its attempts to establish a corporate organization of the labour market and by its vision to organize the political apparatus and society according to the same principles, it also departed from policies followed by previous governments.

The following chapters will investigate Metaxas's rearmament programme as well as the realization of these politics within the armed forces and in the field of industrial rearmament.

Rearmament

The main historical sources relating to the rearmanent are Papagos's book, published in 1945, concerning the Greek Army in the inter-war period[212], a publication issued by the Greek General Staff on the same subject, published in 1969[213], Annual Reports from the British Minister and contemporary German documents.

Papagos was closely linked to the political faction which governed Greece during the most intensive period of the country's military build-up and preparation for war. Papagos was one of the leaders in Kondilis's *coup* agaist Tsaldaris in October 1935. He served as Minister of War for a short period and during the Metaxas dictatorship was Chief of the General Staff. Papagos gained fame and reputation as the organizer of the successful Greek campaign in Epiros and Albania against the invasion by Italy during the winter of 1940-41. In this way he acquired a comprehensive knowledge of the rearmament programme. Papagos's book was published after three and a half years of German/Italian/Bulgarian occupation, which left Greece a deeply divided country on the verge of civil war. The Resistance claimed that the King, who fled the country with his government in the wake of Germany's invasion of Greece in April 1941, had betrayed his people and therefore did not have the right to return unless approved by public vote. Papagos took the side of the government in exile and his book is, generally speaking, an apology for this administration. According to Papagos, Metaxas's merit was the strengthening of the armed forces.

Papagos concludes his book by claiming that the Greeks would be guilty of ingratitude if they failed to recognize this achievement. At the same time, Papagos takes the opportunity to emphasize that he, more than anyone else, had a clear vision as to the necessity of building up a strong defence and that Metaxas, especially in the first couple of years, was too restrictive in expenditure *vis-à-vis* the rearmament programme. There is little reason to believe that Papagos exaggerated the expenditures for the rearmament programme, as this would only diminish the merits of his own foresight; furthermore, in 1945, Papagos's own military and political ambitions were high.[214] However, it is conceivable that Papagos has toned down the prominent role of National Socialist Germany in the rearmament programme out of consideration for Greece's reputation in the postwar world, and in order not to fuel the Resistance's already sharp criticism of the establishment: that its power was based on foreign support and on collaborators as well as on traitors.

Another useful historical source is the publication issued by the Greek General Staff. This work is mainly based on Papagos's book, but also contains documents from the archives of the General Staff. Like Papagos's book, the foreword praises Metaxas for his rearmament programme, and concludes with an allusion to the successful Greek campaign against Italy, so that "thanks to this [the rearmament programme], the long-standing toil of the Greek officer corps and the high morale of the Greek people it was possible to decorate the Greek arms with a triumphal wreath". The work was published during the Military Dictatorship of the Colonels, 1967-1974, which depicted its *coup* as 'The Revolution of Twenty First of April' (the military *coup* was carried out on 21 April 1967), clearly alluding to the Greek revolution of 1821, which colloquially and in textbooks is normally referred to as 'The Revolution of Twenty One.' In order to corroborate this allusion further, the Colonels adopted the revolutionary symbol from 1821, the Phoenix, and portrayed the regime as embodying "the renaissance of healthy Greek virtues", namely those stemming from the Greek War of Independence and from the reign of Metaxas.

To the extent that it has been possible to compare the works of Papagos and the Greek General Staff with contemporary sources of British and German provenance and with documents from the Greek Air Force, discrepancies in information and figures (apart from Papagos's toning down of Germany's role) are not significant and none of the deviations seem to be systematic in either direction. Thus, both Papagos's book and the publication issued by the General Staff provide valuable insights into the Greek rearmament programme. Furthermore, the overall picture which these works give of the general state of affairs regarding the preparedness of the Greek army is supported by contemporary American and British diplomatic reports. According to these, it was, more than anything else, due to the reorganization and rearmament implemented during Metaxas's leadership that, for the first time in the inter-war period, Greece could be counted as a substantial military factor in the Balkans. Until then, as the American Ambassador Lincoln MacVeagh puts it, "the typical Greek officer has been the lowest form of reptile life, a creature who lived for promotion to be wormed out of influence in political antechambers and drawing rooms interested in nothing as little as its own troops..."[215]

The Abyssinian Crisis in October 1935 unleashed a state of panic in the Greek army, as it highlighted the fact that Greece was unprepared for modern warfare. This sparked off a series of initiatives to redress the state of affairs and to reorganize and modernize the Greek Armed Forces. In October 1935 the Greek General Staff established a so-called 'Special Office for Civil Mobilization' to study and organize industrial mobilization. Emphasis was placed on safeguarding the supply of shells, gas masks, boots, medicine, etc.[216] In November 1935 an investigation was initiated into the need for anti-aircraft defence[217], and in January 1936 it was decided to coordinate the control of the three services in a so-called Supreme Council for the National Defence.[218]

The rearmament was divided into two phases. The first phase was intended, on the basis of a supply of equipment already at hand, to prepare the armed forces to meet an attack from Bulgaria. The second phase was intended to make mobilization possible to meet an attack from any of the Balkan countries. During this phase old military equipment was to be replaced, to achieve homogeneity and modernization. Furthermore, great emphasis was placed on self-sufficiency.[219]

A memorandum dated 12 May 1936 put forward by the so-called 6th Office of the General Staff, which was in charge of economic mobilization, stressed that experience from the First World War and the Italian attack on Abyssinia had proved that the industrial capacity of a country consti-tuted the basis for her military strength. As a consequence of this, the most important missions of the General Staff were to be accomplished in the factories and in the chemical laboratories. For this reason the memoran-dum strongly recommended that Greek industry be organized, as far as possible, with an eye to the national defence and to self sufficiency. To achieve this, it was further recommended that the General Staff establish a special organization to, as the memorandum put it, "discipline and manage the industry". It was stressed that such ends would be furthered if the organization could act "a little dictatorially". The organization and development of the war industry had to be linked to an overall industrial policy. Subsequently the memorandum enumerated certain firms within the production of metal, chemicals, rubber, textiles and concrete, which were in a state to commence armament related production almost

66

immediately.[220] In other words, industrial rearmament implied a policy which encompassed Greek industry as a whole.

Furthermore, the memorandum stated that production of arms and munitions required specific initiatives which had not previously been connected to a general industrial policy. Such production was to be organized by the state or through specialization by already existing private enterprises. The financial basis was to be established through long-term credits and regular orders.[221] This latter feature is significant, as the Greek armament industry actually entered the international market as an important supplier of war material during the second half of the decade.[222]

On 9 December 1936, the 6th Office of the General Staff was instructed to supervise and guide the development of the productive forces in Greece in order to meet her economic demands in case of war.[223]

This emphasis on self-sufficiency may appear to be a continuation of policies pursued by various governments since the Depression. However, the emphasis on rearmament also constitutes a break, because such production shifted the priority of the government from the civil to the military sphere.

The following pages will explore the extent to which Greece succeeded in realising these ambitions, and, in order to do this, will concentrate on defence expenditure.

Defence Expenditure

Total expenditures (ordinary and extraordinary) on defence increased considerably under Metaxas's regime and remained on a higher level than any other government's since the end of the war against Turkey.

In the period 1930-1936 total expenditures on defence constituted 2.0 billion Dr. on average per year, compared to an average figure of 4.4 billion Dr. per year during Metaxas. In the period 1930-1936 expenditures on defence made up 19.33 per cent of the total state expenditures, compared to 32.0 per cent in 1936-1939, an increase of 65.6 per cent.[224] Papagos makes a distinction between ordinary and extraordinary expenditures. While ordinary appropriations were mainly spent on maintainance, salaries and rearmament, extraordinary expenditures were exclusively for rearmament.

In the period from the *débâcle* in Asia Minor in 1922 to the Abyssinian Crisis in 1935 a total of three billion Dr. was approved as extraordinary appropriation for rearmament. Of this total, two billion Dr. was spent prior to the world crisis in 1929 and the remainder in the period until 1935.[225]

By the end of 1935 6.1 billion Dr. was approved as extraordinary appropriation for rearmament. Of these 3 billion was for the Army, 1.8 billion for the Navy and 1.25 billion for the Air Force.[226] However, the financial conditions in 1935 prohibited immediate allocation and it was not until 1936 that the state managed to raise the funds necessary for the implementation of the plan.[227] In this connection, it is important to note, as demonstrated below, that financial considerations played an important role in the placing of Greek orders abroad.

The Army

TABLE 13

The distribution of extraordinary appropriations for the Army in 1936-1941 in billions Dr. and as a percentage.[228]

	Dr.	%
Artillery	2.6	38.0
Logistics	1.5	22.0
Fortification	1.48	21.7
Barracks	0.6	8.8
(Various)	0.62	9.1
Sum	6.8	99.6

About 30 per cent of the extraordinary appropriations was spent on military installations, which could be constructed largely on the basis of Greek products. Papagos mentions that Greece was self-sufficient in concrete, electric light bulbs, metal wire, mechanical waterpumps and, from 1939, metal for bridge building.[229]

The actual total expenditures of 2.6 billion Dr. on artillery equipment constituted 38.8 per cent of total extraordinary expenditure for the Army between 1936-1941.

TABLE 14

Expenditure on artillery equipment in 1936-1941 in million Dr.[230]

	price upon order		paid for	
	Dr.	%	Dr.	%
1) Anti-aircraft guns	1.019	32.9	961	36.9
2) Ordinary ammunition	784	25.3	611	23.5
3) Vehicles	325	10.5	221	8.5
4) Hand and auto. weapons	240	7.7	208	8.0
5) Mine equipment	207	6.7	177	6.8
6) Chemical warfare	183	5.9	158	6.1
7) Artillery (in general)	98	3.2	64	2.5
8) Cavalry (equipment)	91	2.9	91	3.5
9) Tank/anti-tank weapons	85	2.7	42	1.6
10) (Various)	68	2.2	68	2.6
Total	3.100		2.601	

The expenditures on artillery equipment can be placed in the following approximate categories:

1) new acquisitions;
2) purchase of accessories and spare parts for old equipment;
3) improvements or changes made to old equipment.
Categories one and two were dependent on delivery from abroad, whereas improvements and changes to old equipment were made in Greece.

Anti-aircraft and anti-tank defence was almost non existent at the time when the rearmament programme was launched. The following equipment was acquired in the period 1936-1941:[231]

24	88 mm Anti-aircraft guns
54	37 mm do.
108	20 mm do.
24	37 mm Anti-tank guns

Including accessories and ammunition the acquisitions amounted to 961 million Dr.[232]

Papagos does not mention the source from which the equipment was purchased, but, as noted below, it was bought in Germany. According to the German export cartel, *Ausfuhrgemeinschaft für Kriegsgerät* (Export Organization for War Material), in the period 1 January 1936 to 30 June 1938, Greece contracted for 33 88 mm guns, 128 37 mm guns and 97 20 mm guns.[233] The discrepancy in the number of 88 mm and 37 mm guns recorded by Papagos and the German export cartel may be due to the fact that some weapons were never delivered. Another possibility is that Greece resold the guns. As will be demonstrated later Greece did resell war material to Spain. The discrepancy in the number of 20 mm guns is likely to be due to the fact that the calculations from the German export cartel end on 30 June 1938, and therefore do not cover the whole period.

98 per cent of a total of 221 million Dr. spent on vehicles was used for new acquisitions. About 136 million Dr., or 61 per cent of this total, was spent on equipment from Germany: 177 Daimler trucks, 50 Opel trucks and other material. It is notable that the Daimler trucks were for transport of the 88 mm and 37 mm anti-aircraft guns, indicating that the guns and trucks constituted a part of a package.

55 million Dr. was spent in France on: 48 Samoua trucks, 50 Renault trucks, including accessories.[234]

137 million Dr., or 86 per cent of the expenditure on chemical warfare, was used for gas masks. Papagos mentions that the order was originally for 500,000 gas masks, but he does not say where the orders came from.[235] However, the annual reports from the British Legation in Athens mention that the gas masks were ordered in Germany; the number according to this source was 400,000.[236] The report published by the Greek General Staff claims that 105,000 gas masks were purchased in Germany and 101,000 in France.[237]

Total expenditure on new weapons for the infantry, plus accessories and improvements, was 207.6 million Dr.[238] New acquisitions amounted to 118.1 million Dr., or 56.9 per cent, accessories to 48.8 million Dr., or 23.6 per cent, and improvement and preparation of existing equipment to 34 million Dr., or 16.4 per cent.[239]

The majority of existing weapons in the infantry were French, British, Italian or Belgian: Lebel rifles, Hotchkiss automatic weapons,[240] Maxim automatic weapons,[241] Mannlicher rifles and Mauser rifles.[242] New acquisitions were made within these brands. Thus 50,000 7.92 mm Mauser rifles were purchased in Belgium for 115 million Dr.[243]

70

Additionally the Army's supply of automatic weapons, consisting of 6,000 light and 1,752 heavy Hotchkiss machine-guns, was replenished with 600 new 7.92 mm Hotchkiss guns at the cost of 32 million Dr.[244]

Apart from a purchase of 300 German Schwartlose machine-guns, the Army continued to rely on French Hotchkiss weapons.

The British annual reports mention that the Greek Army was seeking to standardize the calibres of the machine-guns and the rifles, and that the Greek Powder and Cartridge Factory conferred with French and Belgian companies to this effect.[245] This work was carried out locally and amounted to 34.7 million Dr;[246] the delivery of tools needed for such work was charged separately.[247]

Thus, considerations regarding the standardization of old and new equipment seemed to be of paramount importance: for this reason new acquisitions of weapons and accessories were primarily directed towards countries which produced equipment that the Greek Army already had in its possession, namely towards France, Belgium and Britain.

The only new artillery acquisition was the replacement of a destroyed 155 mm cannon.[248] 64 million Dr., or 69 per cent of the total, was spent on supplementary equipment for modernization of existing material, while the remaining 30 per cent was used for renovation, repairs and improvements, that is to say tasks that could be carried out in Greece.

Like the infantry armament, but unlike anti-aircraft and anti-tank armaments, the artillery was trying to adjust purchases to existing material. This had mainly been bought during the 1920s from Schneider or Daglis (France) or from Skoda (dependent on France) and only in a very few instances from Krupp (Germany).

Of the 611 million Dr. spent on ordinary ammunition, the artillery and the infantry were supplied with new ammunition for 292 million Dr., or 47.8 per cent, and 265 million Dr., or 43.4 per cent, respectively.[249]

According to German calculations, 80 million Dr.'s worth of cartridges for light weapons were bought in Germany in the period between 1 January 1936 and 30 June 1938.[250]

Papagos mentions that the Greek Army made a 0.6 billion Dr. order for ammunition from the Greek Powder and Cartridge Company,[251] so it is reasonable to assume that the major part of the ammunition was supplied from there.

The supplies for anti-aircraft and anti-tank defence came from Germany. If the latter is included with the purchase of vehicles, equipment for chemical warfare, automatic weapons, artillery ammunition and light weapons, total expenditures on equipment bought in Germany between 1936-1941 amounted to about 1.7 billion Dr or 42.6 million RM, the equivalent of 65 per cent of the total Greek expenditure on military equipment. In addition there was expenditure on logistics, etc.

The acquisitions from France amounted to 151 million Dr. (if we suppose that all the supplies for artillery equipment were bought in France) or about 6 per cent of total expenditures on material.

Problems regarding quality and supply seem to have constituted a major obstacle for the development of a Greek rearmament based on French material. Thus, Papagos mentions that various new acquisitions from the French armament industry had been planned, but that only very few were actually realised. To cite an example: when Greece ordered 40 cannon in calibres of 75 mm, 85 mm and 105 mm, France could not deliver a single weapon.[252]

Moreover, the Greek General Staff rejected a French offer consisting of six 155 mm cannon and a batch of mines because France was only able to offer equipment dating from 1914. The fact that France was dealing with obsolete equipment is most clearly illustrated in the case of tanks: France was only able to offer antiquated Renault tanks dating from 1918. The Greek General Staff decided to turn down the French offer when it appeared that these were only capable of a top speed of between 2 and 6 Km/h, a velocity that was completely inappropriate to the mobility required in modern warfare.[253]

For these reasons the French armament industry turned out to be less than suitable for the modernization and rearmament of the Greek Army.

In this context it is also important to note that one of the crucial points in the rearmament programme was to develop Greece's self-sufficiency, so it is reasonable to expect that the needs of the Greek Army would gradually be based on material produced in Greece.

The Air Force

At the end of 1929 the flying squads of the Army and the Navy, as well as those associated with civilian aviation, became subject to control by a government department. Thus, by 1930, the Greek Air Force had 132 aeroplanes at its disposal, out of which 77 were fighter aircraft. In the fiscal

72

year 1930-1931, 46 new fighter aircraft and 16 training aircraft were purchased.[254] Together these aeroplanes, mainly of French and British origin, constituted the backbone of the Greek Air Force until 1937.[255]

The rearmament programme also launched a fundamental modernization of the Air Force, which, according to the plan, was to be completed in 1942.[256] The Air Force estimated that the cost of this rearmament would be 2.3 billion Dr., but initially only half of the amount, about 1.25 billion Dr., was granted.[257]

Although 240.7 million Dr. was raised through a nationwide campaign, the programme was far from completion. A note to Metaxas from the Secretary of the Air Force, dated August 1938, made it clear that an additional 480 million Dr. was needed in order to accomplish even half of the modernization programme scheduled. A completion of the programme would cost 1.2 billion Dr. more, meaning that total expenditures would amount to 3.2 billion Dr., that is considerably more than estimated when the programme was launched in 1935. The 480 million Dr. was approved, but it has not been possible to establish whether the 1.2 billion Dr. was made available.

In the following pages, the acquisitions made during 1935 to 1939 will be examined in more detail. The modernization of fighter aircraft had the highest priority and the aim was to muster 26 squadrons by 1942.[258] In connection with the attempted *coup* by the Venizelists in March 1935, Yugoslavia delivered five Czechoslovak Avia aeroplanes as well as engines, spare parts and ammunition.

In the days following the Italian attack on Abyssinia in October 1935, the Greek authorities asked the British and German governments in vain for an immediate delivery of 50 fighters of the most modern type. In September 1936 the Greek authorities ordered 36 PZL fighters from Poland instead: this was both technically and economically preferable for the Greeks, because 90 per cent of the costs could be settled in tobacco.[259] Total expenditures on aeroplanes and spare engines (Gnome Rôhne) amounted to 170.2 million Dr.[260] Moreover, the Greek Air Force was further strengthened by two Czechoslovak Avia 534s and two British Gloucester Gladiators, all four being gifts from Greeks living in Egypt.[261] By the end of 1938 orders were made for 12 British Supermarine Spitfires.[262] However, according to the account published by the Greek General Staff, the aeroplanes were never delivered.[263]

The decision regarding which bombers to buy caused a protracted tug-of-war. Certain circles within the Greek Ministry of Aviation were in favour of Dornier Do 17 planes; nevertheless, these plans were abandoned due to the high costs of the German aircraft.[264] In 1937, the Greek authorities planned to order 36 Bristol Blenheims from Britain but at the end of the year the decision was altered to 24 French Potez aeroplanes. Although the British Blenheims were judged to have superior fighting qualities, the price and credit conditions relating to the French aeroplanes were the decisive factors. The Potez aeroplanes were 40 per cent less expensive and payments could be stretched over four years.[265] The price including spare engines was 206 million Dr.

The account published by the Greek General Staff notes that eleven Bristol Blenheims and eleven Fairy aeroplanes were bought.[266]

In February 1937 twelve German Dornier 22 aeroplanes were ordered for anti-submarine activity at a cost of 27.9 million Dr. German aircraft were preferred to their British counterparts mainly because the time of delivery and the financial conditions were more favourable. Three Junkers Ju 52s for civil aviation were purchased from Germany and 42 Avro training aircraft and 131 Armstrong Siddeley Lynx engines were ordered from Britain at a price of 152.5 million Dr. Furthermore, 30 Avro Tutor aeroplanes were ordered from the Aircraft Factory at Phaliron, which was manufacturing Avro aeroplanes under licence.[267]

On 22 April 1938 the Greek Ministry of Aviation agreed with the German aircraft factory, Henschel, to the delivery of 16 Henschel Hs 126 aeroplanes.[268] At the beginning of 1940 the Greek Ministry of Aviation made an agreement with the German Air Ministry for the delivery of 32 Henschel Hs 126 aeroplanes and twelve Fieseler-Storchs.[269] The account published by the Greek General Staff states that 16 Henschel aeroplanes were delivered before the German occupation of Greece, while no reference is made to the Fieseler-Storchs.[270]

Total costs for the armament of the Air Force amounted to 338.2 million Dr. Expenditures on machine guns totalled 98.2 million Dr. Of this, 56 million Dr. was spent in Belgium, 32 million Dr. in Czechoslovakia and 10.2 million Dr. in Britain. The principal item consisted of bombs costing 240 million Dr., or 71 per cent of all expenditures on armament: this order went to the Powder and Cartridge Company. Finally, 132 million Dr. was spent on the construction and improvement of airports.[271]

The Aircraft Factory at Phaliron was originally attached to the Navy and was organized for repair and maintenance of aircraft and engines as well as

74

for licenced production. The factory was founded with British help,[272] and an agreement made in December 1924 handed over the management of the factory to the British-owned Blackburn Aircraft Factory at Phaliron.[273] At the turn of the year 1937/38 the factory became part of the Greek Air Force.[274]

The Greek Ministry of Aviation saw the factory as an important element in the initiative to make Greece self-sufficient, in order to achieve which it was considered necessary to renovate old machinery and tools and to enlarge the plant. Appropriate equipment was purchased in Germany for a total of 118.7 million Dr.: tools (21 million Dr.), radio equipment (48.4 million Dr.), meteorological instruments (5.5 million Dr.), electrical fittings (22.3 million Dr.) and photo-technical apparatus (11.5 million Dr.)[275]

By the end of the 1930s it was decided to expand licenced production to encompass a wider range of training aircraft.[276] Additionally, the manufacture of the Polish PZL 37 bomber was planned. This, however, was never realized, due to the outbreak of war in 1939.[277]

In April 1939 Greece bought the right to manufacture the German Henschel Hs 126 aeroplane.[278] In the first years of the war, the factory was adjusted to the production of this aircraft,[279] and, at the beginning of 1940, the Greek authorities ordered material for the production of an additional 40 aeroplanes of this type as well as material for Fieseler-Storchs.[280]

Like the Army, the Air Force endeavoured to reach an advanced stage of self-sufficiency. This was particularly evident from the outline of objectives relating to the Aircraft Factory at Phaliron. However, it must be stressed that the Aircraft Factory was limited to production on the basis of licence agreements and foreign know-how.

As in the case of the Powder and Cartridge Factory (for a thorough examination of this, see below) the technical updating of the Aircraft Factory was based on German equipment, but, even when the Greek state took over the factory in 1938, the technical staff remained British.

Whether the increasing technological dependence on Germany and the licence agreements with Polish and German companies crowded out the British, or would have done so, is impossible to know. However, the above-mentioned agreements indicate that the Greek government regarded the facilities of the Aircraft Factory as capable of more than just the production of British training aeroplanes. It is reasonable to expect that the Germans, by providing machinery and licences, were in a position to increase their influence over the factory and thus over the Greek Air Force. With the outbreak of war and the disruption of the above-mentioned plans, however, this must remain a speculation.

In one area of production, the Greek plans for the self-sufficiency were implemented extensively: the Powder and Cartridge Company succeeded in reaching a level at which it could deliver all the bombs required by the Air Force (see below). Thus, as was the case in its relation to the Army, the Powder and Cartridge Company held a central position in the rearmament of the Greek Air Force, and was therefore of paramount importance to the rearmament programme as a whole. This, and the fact that the factory was dependent on German production facilities, know-how and semi-manufactured articles (see below), means that the Greek Air Force was considerably more dependent on Germany than the above examination indicates. It therefore also makes sense in the case of the rearmament of the Greek Air Force to talk about a combination of Greek produced material based on German technology.

The Navy

The main task of the Navy was coastal defence and the maintenance of a free passage to the Black Sea. In constrast to the situation before the First World War, when it was important to maintain a strong fleet against the Ottoman Empire, the rearmament programme of 1935 aimed primarily at meeting dangers related to war on land. In the rearmament programme this rendered the Navy a less prominent role than the other services.

According to British assessments, the Greek Navy was inadequate until April 1936, and its efficiency almost sank to zero in the wake of the failed March *coup* of 1935. This was ascribed to extensive purges within the naval officer corps, which was, generally speaking, Venizelist.[281]

The Navy's rearmament programme was directed towards coastal defence, because the fleet was to a large extent unable to defend itself against air strikes. By the end of 1938 the Navy had modernized most of its defence along the important sea routes between the trading and industrial centres Piraeus, Volos and Salonika. In addition, plans to place heavy batteries at Cape Sunion and Hydra were implementated in order to protect shipping entering and leaving Piraeus from aggression from the seaward side. Whether this work was completed before the German occupation is uncertain.

76

Total expenditures on acquisitions amounted to 22 million Dr.; the place of origin of the arms is not known. However, a German mission went to Greece to give advice about the construction of the coastal defence.[282]

The fleet was enlarged by two destroyers built in Britain. The order was originally meant to be placed in Germany and in this connection a Greek naval commission was sent to Germany at the time when Kondilis was Minister of War. Nevertheless, the purchases in Germany were ultimately restricted to cannon and financed by the clearing account.

Like the Army and the Air Force, the Navy put great emphasis on self-sufficiency. The most important step in this direction was the construction of a shipyard at Skaramanga, to be completed by the end of 1939. The Skaramanga Shipyard was planned to provide necessary maintenance, repair and construction facilities. The running of the yard was put out to tender, while the technical back-up was based on tools, machinery and cranes from Germany.[283]

In expectation of the shipyard being finished shortly, the Greek Navy delayed orders abroad for two destroyers and withdrew an order for two 600 ton submarines.[284] The initial order was for four 500 ton submarines, and on this occasion the large German armaments firm Rheinmetall-Borsig was commissioned to find suitable German contractors.[285]

Unlike the two other services, the Navy did not deal with the French. It was British, and, by the second half of the 1930s, German influence which was dominant.

To summarize, it was evident that Greece did not reach the level of self-sufficiency within the armed forces to which she had aspired at the beginning of the rearmament programme.

French weapons still played an important – albeit considerably reduced – role in the Army and the Air Force. Nevertheless, apart from French bombers, the dependence on French equipment was based on old weapons, and it was quite clear that problems relating to quality and unreliable delivery dates made French equipment unattractive in relation to the rearmament programme. British influence was most significant within the Air Force and the Navy, yet credit problems seem to have reduced the possibility of basing the rearmament programme on British supplies: this was especially evident in the case of British bombers.

Regarding military matters, the most conspicuous change in Greece's relations to foreign countries was that Germany gained an increasingly important role *vis-à-vis* the Greek armed forces. Thus, Germany became the main supplier of cannon and ammunition to the Greek Army and, moreover, German aeroplanes, technology and know-how played a substantial role in the modernization of the Air Force and the Navy.

Metaxas's rearmament represented, in both size and quality, a new departure for Greek politics. The programme not only included the armed forces but also the organization of Greek production apparatus, which in turn led to the development of a military-industrial complex.

The Powder and Cartridge Company

In the second half of the 1930s the Greek Powder and Cartridge Company (Elliniki Eteria Piritopiiou ke Kalikopiiou) developed into Greece's largest and most modern industrial enterprise.[286] It was a private company, managed and controlled by Prodromos Bodosakis-Athanasiadis (known as Bodosakis).

According to an American report from the 1940s, based on sources from the inner circle of the decision-making body in Greek economic politics and on information from prominent business-men, including Bodosakis himself, by 1939/40 the Powder and Cartridge Company consisted of five industrial plants employing a total of 12,000 people and operating twenty-four hours a day.[287]

The following plants were included in the Powder and Cartridge Company:

1) A factory in Imitos producing cartridges in all calibres for hand-held guns and heavy machine-guns used by the infantry.[288] In addition, this factory was capable of producing artillery shells in calibres used by the artillery, ie. 75 mm – 155 mm, mortars, bombs weighing from 30 to 500 pounds, hand-grenades and anti-tank mines.

Moreover, the factory had a foundry and a modern engine works and was thus self-sufficient in tools. The technical facilities had been installed by Rheinmetall-Borsig, and, according to the above-mentioned American report, this factory was the largest in the Near East.[289] Furthermore, the factory had its own packaging facilities and a joiners' workshop producing boxes. Finally, the Imitos factory was self-sufficient in electricity, so appears to have been fully equipped for a war situation.

2) A factory at Dafni for the production of powder and explosives. These products were at the disposal of the cartridge factory in Imitos, thus making Greece independent of supplies from abroad.

3) A factory in Elevsis producing anti-aircraft grenades in all calibres (except 80 mm) used by the Greek Air Force.[290] The powder used at this factory was manufactured in the Dafni factory.

4) A gas mask factory in Athens.

5) A shipyard in Piraeus which included a foundry for machinery castings and a workshop for the production of marine boilers.

A comparison between the output of the company in 1936 and in 1939 reveals a considerable expansion of its productive strength, as table 15 shows.

TABLE 15

Production of the Powder and Cartridge Company

1) Daily Production of the Cartridge Factory:

A) Cartridges for light weapons		B) Grenades for 75 mm artillery:	
1936:[291]	0.16 million	1936:	300
1939/40[292]	1.2 million	1939/40:	2,000

2) Annual production of powder at the Powder Factory:

1936:	0.6 t.
1939/40	15.5 t.

In comparison it is notable that Italy's production of cartridges in 1940 was 1.2 billion p.a., or 3.2 million per day.[293] Moreover, the factory had a daily production of 60,000 cartridges for heavy machine guns, 4,600 grenades with calibres of more than 75 mm (including mortars), and, as already noted, bombs, mines and hand grenades.[294]

Papagos quotes lower figures for production by the cartridge factory (0.8-1 million cartridges for light weapons, 3,000-4,500 grenades for heavy artillery). On the other hand he states that the production of powder was 40-50 t. in March 1941 and that the Powder and Cartridge Factory had a daily production of 2,500-3,000 shell cases of the Rheinmetall-Borsig type and 1,000 of the Brandt type. According to Papagos, at the outbreak of the Second World War, the production of the Powder and Cartridge Company was too small to meet the demands of the artillery, but sufficient for the use of the infantry.[295]

Nevertheless, in spite of the above-mentioned discrepancies it is safe to conclude that the Powder and Cartridge Company had reached an output and technological stage at which it was capable of fulfilling a central role in the policy of the Metaxas regime, namely self-sufficiency within ammunition.

According to assessments by British military staff, the quality of the factory's products was high.[296] The Germans reached the same conclusion, and, in the wake of Germany's occupation of Greece, it was decided to dismantle the factory's assembly of machinery and move it to Germany, so that "the high quality facilities" (hochwertige Einrichtung) of the Powder and Cartridge Company did not fall into the wrong hands.[297] There were also voices in the German government advocating the retention of the factory intact in Greece, as it was important for the German armament industry, in its function "as the future armoury of the Great European space" (der zukünftigen Waffenschmiede im grosseuropäischen Raum), to preserve companies of a modern standard, like the Powder and Cartridge Company, outside the German Reich.[298]

The enterprise also expanded vertically. Thus, Bodosakis gained control of ETMA, the only company in Greece producing artificial silk. Moreover, in 1937 Bodosakis bought the Greek Wool Factory (Elliniki Eriourigia) and the National Rubber Factory. The former was acquired with an eye to the production of uniforms, blankets, etc.,[299] while the latter would provide rubber for the Greek Gas Mask Factory (Anonimos Elliniki Eteria Kataskevis Antiasfiksiogonon Prosopidon, EKAP).[300]

In the same period the Powder and Cartridge Company took over Ateliers & Chantiers Helleniques Bassiliades S.A. (until 1939 the only shipyard in Greece able to produce steel ships, machines and marine boilers)[301] and the Greek Wine and Liquor Company.[302] The latter was the second largest company in Greece and its production included carbon disulphide, in which commodity it was aiming to make Greece self-sufficient.[303] In August 1937 the firm started the production of acid sulphite, while a new factory was established for the production of methanol and formaldehyde; the production was planned to begin in the summer of 1939. Moreover, Bodosakis controlled a sister company to the Wine and Liquor Company in Cyprus. This company had an important export market in the Middle East, where Egypt, in particular, was of interest because her payments were settled in hard currency.[304] In addition, Greece's leading and most modern chemical enterprise, the Chemical Products and Fertilizer Company Ltd. (Anonimos Eteria Chimikon Proiondon ke Lipasmaton), which employed between 3,000-4,000 people, supplied the Powder and Cartridge Company with various basic chemicals for the production of powder and explosives. Some of its production was even adjusted to that of the Powder and Cartridge Company, as in the case of nitric acid, where the latter was the only customer.[305] According to a report from IG Farben, the Chemical Products and Fertilizer Company Ltd. was the most important chemical enterprise, not only in Greece but in the whole of south-eastern Europe and the eastern Mediterranean.[306]

By the end of the 1930s the Powder and Cartridge Company constituted the most important source of investments for the National Bank of Greece, the largest financial institution in the country. In 1939 the Bank's investments in the Powder and Cartridge Company amounted to 1.2 billion Dr., or 23.45 per cent of its total investments in industry.[307]

Thus, Bodosakis became the most powerful man in Greek industry and to a large extent a crucial factor in the way in that the industry developed. In addition to the Powder and Cartridge Company, several other civil industries under his management were directed towards armament production. Furthermore, large-scale investments by the National Bank of Greece in the Powder and Cartridge Company meant that funds that would otherwise have been invested in the civil sector were directed towards the armament sector. This trend was further strengthened by the fact that the interests of the Bank were tightly bound up with the economic well-being of this particular company.

These factors resulted in an industrial development in which the military-industrial sector became increasingly important; it also meant that industrialization during the Metaxas regime was based heavily on the war industry and production related to armament.

In this connection it is notable that there are signs that the government became worried by the dominant position of Bodosakis's industries within armament production and thus with their leading role within industrial mobilization as a whole. Papagos mentions that the Army tried to limit its dependence on the Powder and Cartridge Company. In June and August 1939 the Army placed an order worth 100 million Dr. with the firm Ath. Kosta. However, this firm did not have the capacity to meet these demands, so the Ministry of War had to ask Ath. Kosta to request assistance from the Powder and Cartridge Company, which, in October 1940, finally took over the Ath. Kostas factories.[308]

GERMANY

The *Neuer Plan*

In order to reach a fuller understanding of Greek-German relations, it is important to explore certain details of the development of German internal power structures and to analyse these quite closely. Germany's currency reserves fell dramatically in 1930 in the wake of the Depression. Concurrently, supplies of raw materials caused similar worries and stocks of cotton, rubber and fuel were running out.[309]

In September 1934 the so-called *Neuer Plan* (New Plan) was launched in an attempt to ameliorate this threat. The slogan was *Aussenhandelsverlagerung*, reorganization of the foreign trade. The aim was, as Hjalmar Schacht, Director of the Reichsbank and responsible for the New Plan, put it, to ensure that Germany "purchased solely from her own customers" and "only if they could pay". To this effect allocation of currency became subject to control by a central government office, while additionally imports became subject to control by the so-called *Überwachungsstellen* (Control Offices). Concurrently, efforts were made to promote exports, both through selective support schemes and by demanding countertrade from Germany's trading partners. Due to the latter measure and the scarcity of currency resulted in an increasing part of Germany's commercial exchange being settled through clearing accounts.[310] This led to a growth in the commercial exchange with northern Europe, south-eastern Europe, Latin America and the Middle East.[311] Simultaneously, exports to the British Empire and the United States fell considerably. In this way, Germany's trade became increasingly based on commercial exchange with less developed states producing raw materials, while trade with the industrialized countries took a less prominent role.

The expanding German purchase of agricultural products and raw materials from south-eastern Europe between 1934-1936 led to a rapid accumulation of credits on the clearing accounts in favour of these countries. The fact that the south-eastern European countries bore the risk of these outstanding amounts, and thus *de facto* financed their own exports to Germany, gave Germany an efficient lever in forcing these states to increase their import of German industrial goods.[312]

Thus, the important goals of the *Grossraumwirtschaft* were met. Germany had established herself as the core country in a network of commercial exchange in which her industrial products were sold against agricultural products and raw materials from a less developed periphery. It is reasonable to regard this intensified and extremely determined German commercial drive, especially towards south-eastern Europe, as a result of the *Neuer Plan*.[313] Nevertheless, the nature and the *raison d'être* of the *Neuer Plan*, as well as the effects it had, have been subject to some dispute among historians. Milward, who primarily bases his argument on statistical material, depicts the *Neuer Plan* as a response to the crisis in Germany, an *ad hoc* solution to deteriorating economic conditions. In this way he emphasizes the emergency aspects of the *Neuer Plan* at the expense of its long-term aims.[314] William S. Grenzebach, who bases his approach on a vast quantity of diplomatic material, in turn underlines the point that the plan aimed at a long-term structural revolution in the political economy of Europe.[315] In this way, and in contrast to Milward, he stresses the far reaching perspectives of the *Neuer Plan*. Grenzebach's approach is shared by Wendt and Hans-Erich Volkmann, who both regard the Plan as an important landmark in Germany's efforts to establish *Grossraumwirtschaft*.[316]

Milward has been justifiably criticized for his narrow statistical approach and his neglect of diplomatic history. This results in his failing to see the long-term aims behind Germany's trade policy and in his missing the point that this was intimately connected with Hitler's foreign and military policy. Germany's aggressive foreign policy and her war of plunder must be seen as a means to realize Hitler's goal of acquiring *Lebensraum* by force and can only be understood as an innate consequence and natural extension of her economic policy. In this context, trade policy played a crucial role in Germany's relations with central- and south-eastern Europe. However, Milward is right in emphasizing the *ad hoc* nature of the genesis of various political devices, which were created by different and often rival power bases in Germany's (at times almost anarchic) governmental structure in order to pursue the long-term goals of Hitler's foreign policy. In the following pages some devices of importance for Greek-

84

German relations and for the role of Hermann Göring, who played a crucial part in Germany's policy towards Greece, will be examined further.

Rearmament and the Four Year Plan

In 1935 Germany's preparation for war advanced significantly. The government launched a massive rearmament programme and reintroduced universal compulsory military service.[317] Moreover, in June 1935 Germany concluded a naval agreement with Britain allowing the German battle fleet to attain a size corresponding to 35 per cent of the British one. All these initiatives marked a radical departure from the constraints imposed on Germany by the Treaty of Versailles. The significance of these initiatives for the internal economic development of Germany was that they moved investments from export-oriented sectors of the industry to armament production,[318] and in this way also exacerbated the shortage of currency. In 1936, the rearmament programme was seriously threatened by a shortage of hard currency and raw materials, triggering a conflict between the interest groups of the export-oriented industry and the armament sector. Hitler intervened on behalf of rearmament, which he wished to augment, and, in September 1936, he launched the so-called Four Year Plan.[319]

In a confidential memorandum dated August 1936, addressed only to Göring, Werner von Blomberg (the Minister of War) and (later) Albert Speer, Hitler stressed that the German war economy must be reinforced quickly and unscrupulously. All complaints from particular interest groups were to be ignored. The one and only concern was the nation, that is to say, the ensuring of German self-sufficiency and preparedness for war within a four year period.

Hitler placed specific emphasis on the production of synthetic armament-strategic raw materials and on a more intense utilization and exploitation of low-grade German metal deposits, regardless of micro economic calculations of profits. Hitler summed up his position well when he expressed the opinion that Germany was better off producing expensive German tyres than buying "theoretically" cheap tyres abroad, the importation of which was prevented in any case by a shortage of hard currency.[320]

"Export-steigerung durch Einschaltung in die Industralisierung der Welt"

The Four Year Plan has often been referred to as the IG Farben Plan, because various important appointments on its board of directors and working committees were held by employees of IG Farben. Moreover, the emphasis on the production of synthetic products gave IG Farben, in its position as the world's leading chemical firm, a crucial role in the success of the Plan. Since 1934 IG Farben had been supporting *Mitteleuropäische Wirtschaftstag* with technical and scientific assistance in its attempts to expand the production of soya beans in Bulgaria and Yugoslavia and thus meet German import demands.[321] In this way IG Farben was, from an early stage, engaged in projects with a close affinity to the philosophy of *Grossraumwirtschaft*.

In the first half of 1937, Max Ilgner, President of IG Farben, prepared a report, *"Die Exportförderung im Rahmen der Vierjahresplan"* (Export Promotion within the Framework of the Four Year Plan). The report was based on ideas he had previously discussed with Schacht and Göring. The essence of these was that export-promoting measures were an absolute necessity if the Four Year Plan was to succeed and that German industry must participate in the global process of industrialization. Ilgner launched this concept under the slogan *"Export-steigerung durch Einschaltung in die Industrialisierung der Welt"* (Export Expansion through Participation in the Industrialization of the World).

According to Ilgner, the best opportunities for German industry were offered by the markets in Eastern Europe and the Near East, followed by those in Latin America, East Asia and Africa. The highly developed markets in Western Europe and North America were ranked as the least promising. Thus, Ilgner regarded the possibilities for *"Export-steigerung durch Einschaltung in die Industrialisierung der Welt"* as most fruitful in underdeveloped areas where modern economic and technological development was in its initial phase. It is important to note that Ilgner characterized the relationship between Germany and these so-called 'new' markets in terms which in the postwar period would have been labelled neocolonialism: "...one might address the case as a new and modern epoch of the colonial issue – or perhaps even better as the colonial issue in an age of trends towards nationalization and industrialization..."[322] Within this framework of new conditions, the easiest way for an industrial country to maximize its long-term political and economic influence, according to Ilgner, was to participate in the development of the [periphery]: "...in a long term perspective, that highly developed country which has actively participated as an ally [of the host country] in the exploitation of the existing opportunities will stand the best chance of anchoring its political and economic influence [there]..."[323]

Ilgner's concept can be seen as an extension of, or as a supplement to, the ideas of *Grossraumwirtschaft*. It constituted an extension in the sense that Ilgner stressed complementary economic relations between Germany and the periphery as being beneficial to German interests. However, contrary to the concept of *Grossraumwirtschaft*, Ilgner emphasized the industrialization of the periphery as an important stimulus to German export. This must be seen primarily against the background of the fact that the chemical industry was one of the so-called new industries. The export opportunities of these new industries would to a large extent benefit from some level of industrialization in those countries which mainly produced raw materials. This was because a number of finished and semifinished products necessary for the industrial development in such countries were not or could not be produced locally. A further explanation is suggested by Wendt. He notes that *"Export-steigerung durch Einschaltung in die Industrialisierung der Welt"* also offered a way to move production from Germany to other countries. This would relieve the strain on the German labour market and on the capacity of the armament industry, which, by this time was strained to breaking point.[324] In any case, as will be demonstrated later, the political and economic relations between Greece and Germany within important sectors of the Greek economy developed along lines which were compatible with this concept. In addition, the forced pace of rearmament placed a severe strain on the German economy which called for urgent solutions: these will be discussed below.

Raw Materials and Currency

The forced pace of the rearmament and the ensuing weakening of the competitive power of the export industry, made exportation of arms an attractive means to finance the armament industry as well as to procure currency and raw material.

Article 170 of the Treaty of Versailles prohibited all German import and export of war equipment.[325] However, on 4 May 1928 the German Ministers of War and Finance reached a secret agreement which constituted an infringement of Article 170: the German authorities involved connived at arms trade with other countries, as long as this was conducted via Stettin and under cover.[326] At this time several German armament firms were already conducting an international arms trade through shadow firms established abroad.[327]

By the early 1930s the German armament industry was heavily engaged in business with China, where the civil war had sparked off a boom in war materials. In June 1933 the armament company Rhein-Metall (later Rhein-metall-Borsig) applied for permission to deliver war material to China worth some 10 million RM. This request caused some inter-governmental disagreement, as the German Foreign Ministry opposed the idea for political reasons, while the *Reichswehrministerium* (Ministry of War) was in favour of such transactions.[328]

After protracted negotiations the Ministry of War had its way. At the beginning of 1934 the *Reichswehrfürung* launched a series of deliveries of arms to China. This business was conducted through two parastate commercial organizations, Handelsgesellschaft für industrielle Produkte mbH. (HAPRO) and Stahl- und Maschinengesellschaft mbH. (STAMAG).[329] Transactions like these were called compensation business, simply meaning that the total price, or a part of the total price, was – in contrast to the clearing trade – settled in hard currency or in raw materials considered important for the German armament industry.

In November 1934 a number of German ministries agreed to introduce a state subsidy on exports of war equipment, as the urgent shortage of hard currency left little choice but to encourage an expansion of the trade in war materials. However, such trade was still to be conducted in secrecy.[330]

As a result of the escalating Abyssinian-Italian conflict in Africa in 1935, Abyssinia received, in the second half of the year, a secret delivery from Germany of 10,000 Mauser rifles, 10 million cartridges, machine guns, hand-grenades, 36 Oerlikon cannon and 30 37 mm Rheinmetall-Borsig anti-aircraft guns plus ammunition.[331]

At about the same time, on 24 June 1935, Werner von Blomberg called for a repeal of the ban on arms exports. He depicted trade in arms in a civil and military economic context as the only way to finance the German armament industry: "...The promotion and facilitation of German exports of war material and the trade in arms and ammunition with other countries is highly desirable for economic and defence reasons. The manufacture of arms for exports is, in the long run, the most important, indeed the only, way of keeping our armaments firms productive and financially independent..."[332]

88

A few days later, on 27 June 1935, *Auswärtiges Amt* stressed, in response to Blomberg, the political implications innate in exports of arms. The Minister of Foreign Affairs, Constantin Neurath, pointed out that the combination of legal arms export from Germany and extensive sales to China and Abyssinia could have a negative impact on Germany's relationships with Italy and Japan.[333] On 9 July 1935 Hitler clarified his position, stating that he considered the ban on arms export as no longer in force, but adding that time was not yet ripe to make this official.[334] On 16 August 1935 the umbrella organization of German industry, *Reichsgruppe Industrie*, and the Ministry of Economy agreed to establish a cartel for exports of war material, the above-mentioned *Ausfuhrgemeinschaft für Kriegsgerät* (AGK). This was done in order to promote the export of war equipment and to divide larger orders between the German armament companies in order to avoid underbidding. The contracting firms included leading armament companies like Rheinmetall-Borsig, Mauser, Krupp, Zeiss and Siemens,[335] whose participation meant that the cartel gained the virtual monopoly of Germany's trade in arms. Furthermore, *Ausfuhrgemeinschaft für Kriegsgerät* also gained the status of a semi-state institution because of its close co-operation with the Ministry of Economy, the Ministry of War and the Ministry of Foreign Affairs. In October 1935 the decision was made to inform trading and banking institutions of the existence of *Ausfuhrgemeinschaft für Kriegsgerät*; shortly afterwards the export cartel was in business.[336]

On 6 November 1935, immediately after Italy's attack on Abyssinia, the German government openly legalized armaments trade through the so-called *Gesetz über Aus- und Einfuhr von Kriegsgerät* (Law governing Exports and Imports of War Material). Simultaneously, Germany declared her neutrality in the conflict in Africa and decreed a ban on exports of arms to the belligerent powers. In this way, the German government hoped that her attitude, combined with grave concerns in Britain and France about Italy's war in Africa, would mitigate and circumscribe possible negative responses from the Western Powers to the unilateral German abolition of article 170 of the Treaty of Versailles.[337]

The outbreak of civil war in Spain created a new market for German arms. Sales of German war equipment were handled by two parastate organizations, Compania Hispano-Marroqui de Transportes (HISMA) and Rohstoff- und Waren Kompensation-Handelsgesellschaft mbH.(ROWAK). Both companies were organized on the model of *Reichswehrsfürung*'s so-called China Organization and HISMA and ROWAK gave Germany a dominant position on the Spanish market during the Civil War.[338]

The armaments trade with China produced considerable amounts of hard currency, and in 1936 and 1937 this connection became Germany's most important source of hard currency. In 1937, when it reached its peak, it amounted to 42.6 million RM. This is an impressive figure if we consider that in 1937 total German gold and exchange reserves ran at 70 million RM.[339] Prompted by encouraging results in the procurement of hard currency and raw material, resulting from both the trade with China, and, in the second half of 1936, with Spain, it was decided that the compensation business should also be tested in trade with south-eastern Europe. A further aim of this business was to make a breakthrough into the area in terms of power policy and in this manner pave the way for the realization of a German dominated *Grossraumswirtschaft*.[340] In early 1937 *Ausfuhrgemeinschaft für Kriegsgerät* was anticipating sizeable armaments deals with the south-eastern European member states of the Little Entente, Yugoslavia and Romania.[341]

By the middle of 1937, however, it became increasingly obvious that the Czechoslovak Skoda works were successfully launching a counter offensive against German interests in south-eastern Europe. Furthermore, the British armaments company, Vickers, was supporting the Czechoslovak industry in its competition with the German armament companies. To this effect Vickers and Skoda directed their attention and interests towards the Austrian industry and made an attempt to disengage Österreichische Alpine Montangesellschaft from its influence on German heavy industry.[342] Furthermore, the Skoda works won orders to construct an iron plant in Yugoslavia, while British interests were expanding their investments in another major Czechoslovak company important to armament, the Vitkovice Iron and Ore Plant. Additionally the Czechoslovak armament industry received orders from the Romanian Army.[343]

In a statement of affairs dated 1937, *Ausfuhrgemeinschaft für Kriegsgerät* reached the conclusion that internal political resistance in Yugoslavia and Romania against German efforts to penetrate the armaments market, as well as an efficient offensive by the Skoda Works, meant that the French dominated Czechoslovak armaments plant had managed to win all orders for artillery equipment for the Yugoslav Army.[344] In addition to this, *Ausfuhrgemeinschaft für Kriegsgerät*'s trade with south-eastern Europe only yielded 4 million RM in hard currency in 1937.[345] Thus, exports of arms to south-eastern Europe did not succeed in increasing Germany's supply of hard currency and raw materials for armament production to any significant degree. It is also notable that the armaments trade did not bring Germany a breakthrough in terms of her power policy towards south-eastern Europe, something that Göring, in particular, had hoped for. Finally, it seems reasonable to conclude that the regional power structures, and not least those of the local armament industry and the army, which tied the region to the Western powers, constituted an insurmountable obstacle to such German efforts.

The following section will examine the rise of Göring within the German power hiearchy, because he, more than any other politician or military leader in Germany, emphasized at an early stage the economic and political importance of south-eastern Europe to Germany, and played a decisive role in the expansion of Greek-German relations.

Göring

The development of Germany's internal and external politics until 1937 contains a number of important elements of continuity in respect to the preceding period.[346]

To seize power, Hitler had to ally himself with national conservative forces. Göring became a symbol of such alliances and his political career reached its peak in this period.

An important feature of Göring's tactics in his way to power consisted in forging informal contacts locally and abroad. In this way he obtained two goals, namely to enhance his own political influence and to bypass established government institutions and ministries. This gave him a large degree of independece but also resulted in a series of severe clashes with such institutions. Furthermore, Hitler appointed Göring as head of important newly established offices and institutions, such as the Raw Material and Foreign Exchange Office and the Four Year Plan.

Göring played an important role in the arms trade with China and in so doing invoked strong resentment from Neurath and caused distrust in diplomatic circles.

By his appointment as Minister of the Air Office, on 5 May 1933, Göring managed to shift the control of war aviation from the two other military services to his own office. Against strong protests from the Ministry of War, and after months of protracted political strife, Göring finally wrenched the right to develop aeroplanes and arms for air warfare from the

Army and the Navy.[347] On 1 March 1935 Göring achieved another important policy goal, when the *Luftwaffe* was established as the third military service. This strengthened his position even further *vis-à-vis* the two other military services in a struggle for allocation of scarce raw materials and resources. This struggle, and the fact that aircraft technology required certain metals, like bauxite from south-eastern Europe, caused Göring to direct and sharpen his attention towards that area.[348]

On 4 April 1936, Hitler appointed Göring to head the so-called *Rohstoff-und Devisen Stab* (The Raw Material and Foreign Exchange Office), the specific task of which was the procurement of raw materials necessary for armaments and hard currency.[349]

Shortly after the outbreak of civil war in Spain, Hitler made Göring solely responsible for the management of German-Spanish relations. His influence on the conduct of Spanish affairs became so dominant that Spain was at times referred to as "Göring's economic fief".[350] Indeed it was primarily the economic aspects rather than the political dimensions of the Spanish Civil War that concerned Göring, to an extent that Franco's military success became a matter of only minor importance.[351] In order to maximize the economic turnover resulting from his engagement in Spain, Göring took the arms dealer Colonel Josef Veltjens under his protection. Without the knowlege of the rest of the German government, but with Göring's connivance, Veltjens supplied both sides in the Civil War with military equipment.[352] In this connection it is important to note that the Republicans were in control of the Spanish gold reserves. In addition, freight rates for cargo destined for Republican ports were three times higher than for delivery to Nationalist ones.[353]

This obviously made arms deliveries to the Republicans highly attractive in strictly economic terms, and was apparently also politically acceptable to Göring, as long as such business did not attract too much attention. Göring's involvement in these transactions stresses that, generally speaking, his behaviour was guided by pragmatic and *ad hoc* expedience rather than by political dogma.

Furthermore, Göring also managed to establish a virtual monopoly in German-Spanish trade. This he did through the two above-mentioned firms, ROWAK and HISMA; within the framework of these, a parastate apparatus originated which in turn came to serve as a vehicle for Göring's ascendant power.[354] It has been suggested that engagement in the Spanish Civil War contributed significantly towards the acceleration of efforts to direct the economic development in Germany towards autarchy. In this connection Göring's influence on the development of the Four Year Plan and his crucial role in the conduct of Germany's economic engagement in Spain have been singled out as an important link.[355]

On 18 October 1936, Göring was appointed to head the Four Year Plan. This strengthened his position further and in a number of ways. In his capacity as Commissioner of the Four Year Plan and because personnel from IG Farben joined the Plan's managing committee, Göring forged new and important alliances. In relation to this it is important to bear in mind that during this period IG Farben was given the control of productive units important for rearmament, such as local oil production and the manufacture of Buna rubber and explosives.[356] In addition the Plan strengthened Göring's say in economic and military matters considerably.

Göring primarily used the Four Year Plan as a platform for propaganda and as a vehicle to extend his political power in the ongoing strife which raged among the highest strata of Germany's political hierarchy. Furthermore, within the framework of the Plan, Göring developed new parastate institutions and functions to strengthen his position towards existing government departments, such as the Ministry of War, *Auswärtiges Amt* and the Ministry of Economy.

Göring soon clashed with Schacht over economic matters. In contrast to Schacht, who emphasized the importance of expanding German exports, Göring stressed that the most urgent task for Germany's international transactions was to safeguard the procurement of strategic resources and armaments related supplies.[357] By the turn of 1936/37 Göring had begun to penetrate the domain of the Ministry of War, and succeeded in gaining a decisive influence over *Ausfuhrgemeinschaft für Kriegsgerät*. On 5 December 1936 he decreed that armament export was to take place only "if fully approved by the staff of Colonel General Göring and *Wehrwirtschaftsstab* [The Army Economic Office]."[358] The latter was headed by George Thomas, who at that time held the rank of colonel. Shortly afterwards, *Wehrwirtschaftsstab* and Schacht joined forces as a response to Göring's infiltration.[359] In the same period Blomberg began to stress that the extensive exports of German arms posed a certain danger to Germany's rearmament programme. In December 1936, as a response to this, Göring emphasized that the import of raw materials for armaments was to be assigned the highest priority in Germany's international transactions. As Germany's currency reserves were scarce, he continued, arms exports remained an indispensable source for financing the import of raw materials.[360] By mid-1937 Blomberg decided to join Thomas and Schacht in an attempt to counteract Göring's influence.[361]

At the same time Göring extended his sphere of authority further. On 13 April 1937 he established the *Auslandsreferat des Vierjahrplan* (Foreign Department of the Four Year Plan) to secure supplies of raw materials and to tackle political problems abroad. To staff this institution, Göring hand-picked various people who then worked under his personal protection. In this way he also bypassed the influence of *Auswärtiges Amt*.[362] Furthermore, in April 1937, Göring decided – in secrecy – to establish what was later to become Reichswerke AG "Hermann Göring". His intention with Reichswerke was in line with the spirit of the Four Year Plan: to exploit low grade German metal ore as a substitute for imports of this material. By such *Ersatz* production Göring intended to secure Germany a higher degree of self-sufficiency in this field. These efforts can be seen as a counterpart in the realm of internal economy to Göring's maxim that the principal goal for Germany's international transactions was to secure the procurement of raw materials important to armament and currency.

Concurrently, Göring launched a campaign against Schacht, accusing the latter of "foul economic perceptions" which, according to Göring, meant that Schacht's thinking was solely dominated by considerations of profitability. In this period *Wehrwirtschaftsstab* began to notice that inquiries and applications to the Ministry of Economy brought no results. Reacting to this, Thomas decided to go through the administration of the Four Year Plan rather than through the Ministry of Economy in matters relating to quotas and exports. In this way Schacht lost an ally in his struggle against Göring. In July 1937 Göring made his plans for Reichswerke AG "Hermann Göring" public and decided to use this as a spearhead in his propagandist campaign against Schacht.[363]

By August 1937 Göring had finally succeeded in outmanoeuvring and sidetracking Schacht for good. After a long period of leave Schacht handed in his resignation, which, on 26 November 1937 Hitler accepted. Göring took over the Ministry of Economy on 10 October 1937 with a term of office until 31 January 1938.[364]

In the same period Göring entered on a course of confrontation with Hitler. Göring was at that time responsible for German-Chinese trade. By mid-October 1937, Hitler ordered a ban on sales of German arms to China in response to an urgent request from Ribbentrop. Officially Göring complied with Hitler's decree. However, on 20 October 1937 orders were issued by Göring to continue the arms traffic to China as usual.[365] This trade went on until at least June 1938.[366] Göring's decision constituted a significant departure from Hitler's foreign policy, which, since November 1937, had aimed to ally Japan with Germany and Italy.[367] However, it is important to note that this took place at a time when Göring's power was reaching its apogee. Furthermore, the episode illustrates clearly the fact that during this period Göring was acting with a huge degree of autonomy even at the risk of circumventing Hitler's explicit decisions. This is particurly important, because (as will be demonstrated later) Göring played a crucial and decisive role in the development and intensification of Greek-German relations, not least within armaments trade.

Göring, Germany and Italy

During the first half of the 1930s, German and Italian interests clashed over central and south-eastern Europe on several occasions. In 1931 German plans for the establishment of a German-Austrian customs union foundered as a result of international, not least Italian, opposition.[368] German and Italian interests collided again at the Stresa Conference. The conference was convened in order to mobilize international co-operation in stabilizing prices and markets in south-eastern Europe. Such efforts, however, did not correspond well with the basic guidelines of Germany's policy towards the area, a policy based on bilateral relations. The conference failed to produce any palpable results; nevertheless, the principles of international cooperation regarding the area later reappeared in Mussolini's so-called Danubian Memorandum dated September 1933.[369]

Hitler's and Göring's assessments of German-Italian relations differed substantially. Hitler primarily regarded Italy as a potential ally. Göring, whose foreign policy was deeply rooted in the traditional German nationalism widely accepted in the Army, preferred to emphasize south-eastern Europe as an important area for German expansion and in this context to see Italy as a rival.[370] To Hitler, south-eastern Europe was an arena of French-Italian rivalry, and the area had little significance in his long-range objectives.[371] German claims for a union between Austria and Germany, *Anschluss*, and Italy's ambitions for hegemony over the Alpine republic, however, complicated the prospect of immediate German-Italian cooperation. Hitler regarded Austria as a strictly German, i.e. national, issue, whereas Göring approached the problem of Austria in the context of wider German ambitions in south-eastern Europe.[372] For a long time Göring, more than anyone else, was the one person in the German hierarchy to pursue a fairly clear policy towards south-eastern Europe.[373] Among many of Göring's unofficial commissions, Hitler appointed him as his special envoy to Austria and the Balkans with the specific purpose of establishing informal contacts in that area.[374]

In the wake of the National Socialist's seizure of power, German propaganda against Austria increased. On 17 February 1934, as a response to this, Britain, France and Italy agreed to a joint declaration stating that Austria's independence was of vital importance to the three signatory powers.[375] Shortly after, on 17 March 1934, Italy, Hungary and Austria signed the so-called Rome Protocols. This was a consultative treaty, which partly served to underline Italy's interests in the Danube region, and was partly directed against German claims for *Anschluss*.[376] Moreover, the treaty was intended to form a framework for mutual economic assistance on the basis of preferential trade agreements, meaning that Italy was willing to pay prices above those on the world market for a number of products of Hungarian and Austrian provenance.[377] The Rome Protocols thus ran patently counter to German economic and political interests. Shortly after the conclusion of the Rome Protocols, Italy offered Germany her cooperation in south-eastern Europe. While *Auswärtiges Amt* declined the Italian proposal, Hitler declared himself ready to meet Mussolini.[378] Göring was convinced, however, that there was no way of combining Germany's policy of revisions and Italy's ambitions in south-eastern Europe.[379]

In May 1934 Göring set out to visit Belgrade, Athens and Budapest, i.e. countries within the Italian sphere of interest. Göring's visit to Belgrade was not announced until the last minute before his departure and the news of his tour caused indignation in Italy.[380]

German-Italian antagonism reached a peak during the summer of 1934. Germany's meddling in Austria's internal political affairs and the assassination of the Austrian Chancellor, Engelbert Dollfuss, by local Nazis on 25 July 1934 provoked Italy to concentrate troops at the Brenner Pass and Mussolini to declare himself protector of Austria's independence. This was an unmistakable massage to Germany that Italy would have nothing to do with a German-Austrian union, and marked the beginning of a period when Italy was closer to an understanding with Britain and France than with Germany: this lasted until Italy's attack on Abyssinia in October 1935. On 7 January 1935 Italy finalized an agreement with France which included a concorde on French-Italian cooperation in the Danube area. On 3 February the same year the agreement was confirmed in a joint French-British declaration. In April 1935, shortly after the German unilateral abolition of the armament clause in the Treaty of Versailles, British, French and Italian government delegates met in Stresa. The three powers reiterated their interest in Austria's independence and condemned the unilateral abolition of international treaties. Furthermore, they suggested an early conference concerning the Danube. Finally, the three powers took cognizance of Austrian, Bulgarian and Hungarian applications for revised limitations on their armaments.[381] These efforts, seen from a German point of view, threatened to reduce Germany's influence over traditionally friendly states in central and south-eastern European countries in favour of competing Great Powers.

On 5 December a violent exchange of fire between Italian and Ethiopian forces on the border between Abyssinia and Italian Somaliland marked the culmination of several encounters earlier that year. This so-called Wal-Wal Incident triggered a development which made war between Abyssinia and Italy seem increasingly likely. Italy now overtly escalated her military presence in the East African states Somaliland and Eritrea. Finally, on 3 October 1935, Italian forces launched an attack on Abyssinia against the last independent state on the African continent, in what was to become the largest colonial war in history.

In the period between the Wal-Wal Incident and Italy's attack in October 1935, Germany attempted to promote any development that could lead to war. The Germans assured the Italians that they would take a benevolent neutral position if war broke out. At the same time Germany tried to boost the morale of the Abyssinians and to strengthen their resolve to resist Italian aggression. Accordingly, in December 1934, Hitler promised to supply Abyssinia with arms. Subsequently, *Aussenpolitisches Amt der NSDAP* (the Foreign Political Office of the National Socialist Party) commissioned Major H. Steffen to go to Addis Ababa and there to use "any means to promote a development towards war".[382] Steffen was an expert on the Middle East and was well versed in its regional issues. Furthermore, he had been an adviser to Iraq's King Feisal and was an old friend of the Emperor of Abyssinia, Haile Selassi. In this respect it is significant that Haile Selassi states in a later account that Germany continued her arms deliveries to Abyssinia during the war with Italy, and later, when the Italians had defeated organised resistance, to supply Abyssinian guerilla forces.[383]

The motive behind this dual German policy seems to have been an interest in bringing Italy into conflict with the Western Powers. Concurrently, Germany hoped that this would make Britain and France exert less solid resistance against Germany's rearmament. Moreover, war in Abyssinia, it was hoped, would divert Italian resources from Europe to the Red Sea and in this way erode the material basis of Italian resistance to German advances towards Austria and south-eastern Europe.[384] German support of Abyssinia would serve such purposes well. First of all, it was important in the sense that a protraction of the war would tie Italy to a theatre which was only peripheral to German interests.[385] Italy's attack on Abyssinia in October 1935 and the weak reaction on the part of the League of Nations, certainly strengthened Germany in her political struggle for power in south-eastern Europe. The Abyssinian campaign isolated Italy internationally. Furthermore, due to the sanctions imposed by the League of Nations she lost her export markets, especially in south-eastern Europe. Simultaneously, she became increasingly dependent on her exports to Germany, and consequently, Germany became the most important market in Italy's foreign trade.[386]

Concurrently, Germany succeeded in a major breakthrough *vis-à-vis* Austria by the conclusion on 11 July 1936 of a German-Austrian agreement. Germany declared that she would refrain from interfering in Austria's internal affairs, while Austria declared herself a German state and agreed to pursue a policy corresponding to this fact. Mussolini recognized the agreement. This constituted a significant Italian retreat concerning the Austrian issue and it seems reasonable to conclude that Italy was forced into this because of her isolated international position and weakened economy. At the same time it removed an essential problem in German-Italian relations and paved the way for an intensification of a German-Italian connection. On 21 and 22 October 1936 the Italian Minister of Foreign Affairs, Count Galeazzo Ciano, and his German counterpart, Neurath, entered into discussion about various political and economic problems. The results of these negotiations were registered in a protocol as declarations of intent. On 1 November 1936 Mussolini declared that the German-Italian relationship constituted "an axis around which all European states who lived in the spirit of peace and cooperation could work together".[387] This so-called Berlin-Rome Axis became a symbol of the closer relationship between Germany and Italy.

Immediately before Ciano's visit to Berlin, Neurath made it clear that he regarded economic issues to be an important part of the negotiations. In relation to this, the German Minister of Foreign Affairs wanted a precise clarification of German and Italian intentions in the Danube area. For Germany it was important not to be tied by the Stresa Conference, the Rome Protocols or by Mussolini's memorandum dated September 1933. Germany got her way. In the protocol drawn up at the meeting, Neurath and Ciano agreed to resist international economic and political cooperation in the region unless Germany or Italy were participants: i.e. to resist the kind of cooperation that Italy had earlier been advocating. Ciano stressed that he expected Britain to be hostile towards Italy in the future. Regarding the situation in the eastern Mediterranean, he saw Greece, Turkey and Egypt as potential British allies in case of war.[388] The protocol says nothing about Italy's special interests in the Mediterranean. These, however, were emphasized by Mussolini when he proclaimed the formation of the Axis: while for other nations the Mediterranian was merely a road (*via*), he claimed, to Italy it was a matter of life (*vita*) [or death].[389] It is important to stress that the Axis did not lead to a formal agreement or declaration of intent about separate German or Italian spheres of interest nor to any official cooperation in the region. It would probably have been very difficult for Italy to make Germany accept such a schedule. Due to her weak economic position and international isolation Italy in fact possessed very few means to exert pressure on Germany, who at that time had clearly gained the upper hand in relations between the two powers. This state of affairs became quite evident during the Civil War in Spain. During this conflict Germany, and basically that means Göring, pursued German political and economic goals seemingly irrespective of Italian interests and often in conflict with these to the extent that Göring did not abstain from arms sales to the Republicans.

A further indication of Germany's aversion to formal cooperation with Italy in areas within Germany's sphere of interest is the fact that in 1937 the Germans rejected a proposal from Mussolini to form a four-power treaty between Germany, Italy, Austria and Hungary.[390]

Italy's involvement in the Spanish Civil War turned out to be a severe drain on her resources and made her increasingly unpopular with the Western Powers. Nor did the establishment of Italian sovereignty over Abyssinia do much to boost Italy's already strained economy, as Mussolini had originally hoped. On the contrary, Italy's colony on the Horn of Africa had a draining effect on her economy. In 1938 Mussolini reached the conclusion that the economic benefits from the extension of the Italian Empire in Africa were rather limited. Hereafter Italy redirected her attention towards the Balkans.[391]

In conclusion, German-Italian relations underwent several significant changes in the period. At the beginning of the decade and until 1935 the two powers confronted each other over a number of issues relating to their ambitions for influence over central and south-eastern Europe. In this period Italy managed to obstruct several German bids for power over Austria. Until her attack on Abyssinia, Italy was steadily moving in the direction of closer cooperation regarding central and south-eastern Europe with the Western Powers. Her war in Africa and the military engagement in Spain, however, interrupted this process and resulted in Italy's international isolation. This and the fact that Italy's main political and military occupations were now in Africa and Spain diverted her resources away from central and south-eastern Europe. This weakened Italy's power to resist the enhancement of Germany's economic and political position in the area, most conspicuously in the case of Austria. Concurrently, it led to a political *rapprochement* with Germany resulting in the declaration of the Berlin-Rome Axis, in which, however, Germany seemed to be the senior partner. Germany's policy towards Italy during this period was characterized by a certain duality. Hitler on the one hand strived for German-Italian cooperation, while Göring primarily perceived Italy as a serious competitor and an obstacle to German ambitions for hegemony in central and south-eastern Europe. By his actions, Göring also showed himself ready to realize this policy. Following the German-Italian clash over Austria in 1934 and also during the period of rising Italian-Abyssinian tension Hitler proved himself ready to counteract Italian interests, primarily by giving his support to Abyssinia secretly by supplying the African state with arms. The main objective in this seems to have been to promote a rift between Italy and the Western powers, as well as to contribute to furthering any development that could lead to war, and, as soon as war had broken out, to prolong it. In this way, Göring hoped that Italy's aggression in Africa would divert international attention from Germany's infringement of the Treaty of Versailles as well as protract the engagement of Italy's military and political resources in a region outside Germany's sphere of interest. This, he hoped, would reduce Italy's strength in areas central to German interest.

GREECE AND GERMANY

Increase in Greek-German trade

The establishment of Greek-German clearing and the increasing German purchase of Greek tobacco led to a significant growth in the total Greek-German trade. Greek exports to Germany exceeded German exports to Greece, resulting in an accumulation of credits on the clearing account in Greece's favour.

TABLE 16

Greece's outstanding account on Greek-German clearing, in million RM.[392]

	Current	Total
1932 (18.8. 1932 – 31.12. 1932)	1.7	
1933	12.0	13.7
1934	4.2	17.9
1935	12.8	30.7
1936 (1.1. 1936 – 30. 9. 1936)	13.6	44.3
old Greek debt		- 9.8
		34.5

Greek credits on the clearing account in Germany rose considerably in the period and reached 34.5 million RM in 1936, corresponding to 69.6 per cent of Greece's total imports from Germany in 1935 and 55.4 per cent of the exports of the preceding year.

In this way, Greece virtually financed a large part of her own exports to Germany at a time when she had been forced to suspend the service of her international financial obligations and was unable to obtain loans on the international finance market. The Bank of Greece acted as an guarantor for the clearing trade and in that way allowed generous commercial credits to Greek exporters, in particular to those engaged in the trade of tobacco. This placed a considerable strain on the Greek economy and was in terms of monetary politics equivalent to an increase in the banknote circulation. In addition, the expansion of Greek-German trade affected the Greek trade structure in regard to its composition as well as to its provenance. The following sections will examine these changes as well as the reactions to this from Greece's two other main trading partners, the United States and Britain.

American Reactions

Until the World Depression, Greece was the most important market in the Levant and south-eastern Europe for the United States. In the period between 1926-1930 Greece accounted for 58.3 per cent of total American exports to south-eastern Europe. In 1937 this figure had gone down to 18.6 per cent.[393]

The drop in US exports to Greece, which in 1937 had decreased by almost 40 per cent in relation to the preceding year, was, according to the Americans, a result of the discriminating effects of import quotas. MacVeagh informed Metaxas that the Americans were frustrated by the meagre US return from trade with Greece. At the same time he pointed out that Greece benefited substantially from her economic relations with the United States. In 1936, as much as 15 per cent of the total US deficit in her international trade stemmed from the commercial exchange with Greece, while emigrant remittances alone brought Greece a revenue of US$ 14 million, or 1.5 billion Dr..[394] This amounted to as much as 20 per cent of the total Greek revenues from exports, which in 1936 came to 7.4 billion Dr.[395] For Greece to preserve such economic advantages, the American Ambassador continued, it was a *sine qua non* that she seriously considered paying more attention to the commercial interests of the United States.[396] What the Americans wanted from Greece in this respect was a revision of Greek-US trade based on a so-called *modus vivendi* principle. By this, the Americans simply meant an organization of Greek-American trade based on the principle of most-favoured nation. In addition, they demanded that the quota system be based on trade figures from before the world crisis, that is from a period when the United States' trade with Greece fared better than it had in the 1930s.[397] The Greeks responded that this was impracticable without a total reorganization of Greek trade; however, Greece was willing to offer the United States all the practical advantages which the *modus vivendi* principle involved, but not, it was stressed, on the basis of an official concession.[398] The Greek attitude must undoubtly be explained by her reluctance to concede a similar arrangement to Britain, who also enjoyed a most-favoured nation agreement with Greece. In contrast to her commercial relations with the United States, Greece ran at a considerable deficit in her trade with Britain and in that way the economic risks of discriminating against British products could be expected to be significantly less than in discriminating against American ones.

A few months later, Metaxas specified how far Greece was willing to go in the reorganization of her trade relations with the United States.

The Greek dictator stressed that the decrease in American wheat exports to Greece was due to the high price of wheat produced in America and should not be seen as the result of discrimination. Furthermore, he stated that the purchases in Germany made by the Greek state should be excluded from the calculations. These were made solely to reduce Greek credits on the clearing account in Berlin, and, because of Greece's limited liquidity, it would not possible to make such purchases in the United States.[399] In this way, the Greek dictator also clearly indicated that he was not willing to let Greek-German trade be affected by US commercial interests, and concessions to accommodate such would be made at the expense of countries other than Germany.

British reactions

During most of the 1930s Britain enjoyed a considerable surplus in her trade with Greece. However, the expansion of Greek imports from Germany during the second half of the 1930s adversely affected Britain's exports to Greece. This did not basically change the fact that British exports to Greece were substantially higher than those of Greece to Britain. In 1937, the recession in British exports to Greece, however, prompted a number of British businessmen in Athens to react furiously, accusing the British legation of neglecting British trade interests in the area.[400] The British trade surplus and poor prospects for the Greeks of raising new loans in Britain, meant that the British had few means of exerting economic pressure on Greece, leaving her little alternative but to accept Germany's commercial expansion into that country.

Officially Britain even saw the German trade drive into south-eastern Europe as an advantage to her own commercial interests in a broader

104

European perspective. Thus, a memorandum from the Southern Department of the Foreign Office dated 20 August 1936 concluded that in 1935 British trade with south-eastern Europe amounted to two per cent of her total trade. Her commercial relations with Scandinavia, the Baltic States and Poland produced significantly more interesting results and constituted 10.6 per cent of the total British trade. Moreover, the trade in this area had increased considerably since 1932, while German trade, in the same area, had diminished. Thus, trade with the countries in the Baltic region was far more important to Britain than her commerical exchange with south-eastern Europe. Furthermore, the Southern Department was prone to interpret the infiltration of German trade into the Balkans and central Europe as a sign of weakness in Germany's economy and as a substitute for devaluation of the German *Reichsmark*, a move that would pose a serious threat to British trade in north-eastern Europe. Thus, it was sound economic sense to allow Germany to continue her commercial drive into south-eastern Europe. However, what worried the Southern Department in this respect was that German trade policy in south-eastern Europe might result in the area becoming politically dependent on Germany.[401] Nevertheless, until *Anschluss* in March 1938, Britain believed that Greece's dependence on the Royal Navy worked as an efficient counterweight to her economic dependence on Germany.[402]

Italy's attack on Abyssinia increased the strategic significance of the eastern Mediterranean to the Great Powers. It unleashed fears in Britain that Egypt might also become a target for Italian aggression.[403] In addition, the outbreak in Palestine of the Arab Revolt in 1936 and a general growth in anti-British agitation in the Arab world,[404] especially escalating political unrest, largely directed towards Britain in Egypt,[405] made the eastern Mediterranean increasingly important to Britain's security policy. Strategic planners in Britain began to pay more attention to Greece's harbour and airfield facilities. In December 1935, due to her adherence to the League of Nations' sanctions against Italy, Greece gained a joint French-British guarantee.[406] However, the combination of internal instability in Britain's Empire in the Middle East, the presence of substantial Italian military forces in Libya, west of Egypt, and in Abyssinia, east of the Anglo-Egyptian Sudan close to straits between the Red Sea and Aden, and Germany's reoccupation of the Rhineland in March 1936 inclined Whitehall to put a high priority on a *détente* with Italy.[407]

In relation to Germany's penetration of Greece, Sidney Waterlow, the British Minister in Athens, believed that the King, about whose pro-British inclinations he had no doubts, was fully in control of internal and external political affairs in Greece. In contrast to suggestions put forward in the British press, Waterlow did not believe that Metaxas was Germanizing Greece nor remodelling her into a Nazi-style police state. Such perceptions originated, according to the British Minister, from a superficial knowledge of the regime and from the fact that the Greek government sometimes had to bend to German economic pressure. In this connection Waterlow was convinced that: "...it should be remembered that the present German economic tyranny is universally detested here...". Moreover, the British Minister optimistically emphasized that: "...My own view is that in the end the Greeks will probably find some way of cheating Dr. Schacht..."[408]

In spite of this, British consular and diplomatic authorities watched the increasing German influence very closely. Thus, the legation in Athens would receive information from a local consul: this might be, for example, notification that two German professors had arrived in a certain village to teach ju-jitsu to the local gendarmerie, or that on a certain island the number of visiting German governesses had been unusually high during the summer vacation.[409] Although the reports from the British legation during 1937 do not reflect any unequivocal assessment of German intentions, they do betray a growing British anxiety about the increasing German penetration of Greece. Rumours that the Germans were about to take over the Aircraft Factory at Phaliro caused Waterlow to mention this to the King. The Greek monarch, however, assured the British Minister that neither he nor Metaxas would allow German influence in this field.[410]

German participation in the extension of the Greek coastal defence made fertile soil for rumours. It was claimed that German officers attached to the Greek Ministry of Naval Affairs were planning to establish bases for German submarines along the Greek coastline. Such rumours were rejected outright by Metaxas, but he confirmed that German officers were working as advisers to the project of extending the Greek coastal defence.[411] German influence at the Greek Ministry of Aviation was generally regarded as rather comprehensive.[412] In relation to this, it is significant that aviation was a common channel of German intrusion and that Göring used the Air Attachés as his secret information service.[413]

Britain followed the development of Germany's aviation agreements closely. In a 1937 agreement with Greece, Lufthansa obtained permission

106

to fly the Berlin-Athens route, which included several south-eastern European capitals. The British legation, however, succeeded in making the Greeks refuse German requests to use the route between Athens and the Italian dominated Rhodes.[414]

Greek plans to establish an air route between Athens and Alexandria in Egypt provoked immediate reaction from the British, who feared that, if the Greeks were granted this concession, the Germans would soon claim permission for a corresponding route. The last thing in world Britain wanted in this respect was German infiltration of Egypt, a country regarded as very responsive to German propaganda. The British High Commissioner in Egypt, Miles Lampson, succeeded in persuading the Egyptian government to shelve the Greek application.[415]

Thus, British fears of German influence in Greece were especially easily provoked by issues in which Greece might serve as a spearhead for German penetration into the Middle East, that is, by issues related to what one could call the "oriental facets" of Greece's economic and geopolitical structures.

Although in his 1937 reports Waterlow at times claimed that Germany's penetration into Greece served to promote her hegemony in the country,[416] he concluded in his annual report for 1937, dated 19 February 1938, that there were no indications that Germany had obtained such goals and stressed that Greece continued to depend on Britain in matters of foreign policy.[417]

Greece, Italy and Germany

Germany's violations of the Treaty of Versailles in 1935 and 1936, as well as Italy's war in Africa and the proclamation of the Berlin-Rome Axis, affected regional development in south-eastern Europe considerably. German rearmament and the march into the Rhineland dealt a hard blow to the confidence of the *status quo* states in the willingness of France to stand up to revisionist Germany. Moreover, it led to intensified demands from the two revisionist powers in the region, Bulgaria and Hungary, to change the provisions of the peace treaties. This in turn caused anxiety in Yugoslavia and Romania as well as in Greece and Turkey. The two Mediterranean states now began to emphasize their neutrality towards central Europe.

The Abyssinian Crisis also made way for a *rapprochement* between Turkey and Britain and this constitutes an important element in the development which, on 20 July 1936, resulted in the Montreux Agreement. Turkey was granted the right to fortify the straits and to control the traffic of warships in and out of the Black Sea. This strengthened Turkey's role as the guardian of the straits and consequently her military and political significance in the region. As a result of this, Greece's initiation of a rearmament plan made it attractive to Turkey to establish a closer coopera-tion with her western neighbour.[418] Such trends were further strengthened when Bulgaria and Yugoslavia concluded an agreement of friendship on 24 January 1937, as this nourished fears that the creation of a Slavic bloc in the Balkans might come under German leadership and thus strengthen the political might behind territorial demands on Greek and Turkish land.[419] Shortly afterwards Yugoslavia concluded a friendship and peace agreement with Italy.[420] The combination of these factors furthered Greek and Turkish desires to stay out of the problems in central Europe and must be seen as an incentive to negotiations between these two countries for an extension of the Greek-Turkish defensive alliance in October 1937.[421]

In spite of the Greek-Italian agreement of friendship drawn up in 1928, substantial problems in the relationship between the two countries still existed. First and foremost, the Dodecanese constituted a matter of dispute. In the 1930s the Italian colonial authorities launched a ham-fisted attempt to "Italianize" the islands, which led to resistance among the local population that had repercussions all the way to Athens. Italian plans of expansion and dreams of dominating the trade stations along the old Genoese and Venetian trade routes to the Levant, the so-called *Mare Nostro* doctrine, created nervousness in Greece. In addition, Greece feared Italian claims on Albania and thus the prospect of a Greek-Italian conflict over land claimed by both Albania and Greece.[422] The Italian annexation of Abyssinia also constituted the foundation for a clash of interests between the Greek diaspora in the East African state and the newly established Italian authorities.[423] Twenty-five years of constant colonial warfare in Libya, 1911-1932, and since then in Abyssinia indicated that Italy was ready to use military power to reach her goals. Moreover, Italy took a liberal view of the League of Nations' ban on gas warfare, used extensively in both Libya and Abyssinia.

According to the German legation, the conflict in Abyssinia made Greek security policy totally dependent on Britain. The development of the Greek coastal defence could, however, be seen as an attempt to prevent

Greece from submitting totally to British interests. Greek wishes to acquire German assistance, according to the legation, could be explained by the fact that the Greek government saw Germany as an impartial Great Power without direct political interests in the Mediterranean.[424] Periodically this Greek perception of Germany's intentions was clouded by the German-Italian *rapprochement*. The above-mentioned aviation agreement between Italy and Germany, which gave Lufthansa landing rights on Italian Rhodes, was depicted in the Greek press as an extension of ambitions concerning the Berlin-Baghdad railway project. In a conversation with Metaxas, the German legation had the impression that the Greek Prime Minister was seriously concerned about close cooperation between Italy and Germany in the eastern Mediterranean. In order to reassure Metaxas, the German Councellor of Legation, Theo Kordt, was at great pains to stress that German interests in the eastern Mediterranean were purely economic. Furthermore, Kordt underlined the fact that there were no contractual political bonds between Germany and Italy and that Germany would abstain from participating in any combination that might militate against Britain.[425]

Kordt believed that the British feared close German-Italian cooperation in the eastern Mediterranean. In order to serve German interests in Greece in the best possible way, he considered it necessary to convince Britain that this was not the case. He thought that if he succeeded the British would breathe a sigh of relief and leave Germany to have a free hand, from an economic point of view, in Greece.[426]

In May 1937 the German Minister to Greece, Prinz Victor zu Erbach-Schönberg, reached the conclusion that Germany's position in that country had strengthened since 1935 at a speed that no one in Germany would have dared to hope two years earlier. The German Minister emphasized to *Auswärtiges Amt* that Germany's impartial position in the eastern Mediterranean meant that she [still] had the confidence of the Greek government and, in particular, of Metaxas. However, this did not give Germany a decisive influence on Greece's foreign policy. In this realm, Britain was still seen as a kind of protector of Greece and especially so in case of conflict in the eastern Mediterranean.[427]

Regarding Greek foreign policy and his own relationship with Germany, Metaxas explained, off the record, in an interview with the *Sunday Times* on 24 June 1937: "...How could it be possible to let feelings influence my foreign policy in a direction that would come into conflict with the interests of our countries? Between Greece and Germany lies central

Europe. Germany is not a Mediterranean Power. [Foreign and security political] interests connect Greece to Britain".[428] Metaxas undoubedtly wished to stress that, although he was known to have strong inclinations towards Germany in the realm of philosophy and political organization, he intended to serve Greek national interests and there were no practical contradictions involved in this, as Germany was not a Mediterranean Power.

In conclusion, Greece first of all feared Italy and her ambitions in the Mediterranean. This was also obvious to the Germans, who were at great pains to emphasize that Germany was an impartial power in this part of Europe and that German-Italian relations (especially after the declaration of the Axis) were guided by no contractual bonds. Furthermore, the Germans went to great pains to emphasize that Germany had no intention of antagonizing Britain. Finally, the German legation in Athens believed that, if it were possible to convince the British of this, Germany would be left with a free hand to expand her economic presence in Greece.

In the following pages, the development of Greek-German relations will be investigated further. There will be a particular focus on the ways in which these relations developed and the goals that Greece and Germany pursued in the process.

German Political Pressure to Reorganize Greek Imports

In May 1934 Germany was represented in Greece at the highest levels. In the days between 17 and 23 May Göring was in Athens as part of a tour to the south-eastern European capitals Belgrade, Athens and Bucharest. According to Waterlow, neither the Greek Minister of Foreign Affairs nor the German legation had been officially informed about Göring's arrival, nor the purpose of his visit.[429] Göring was attended by various prominent people from German state and business circles. Among these were Julius Dorpmüller, General Director of the German Railways, with four of his employees, plus Prince Philipp of Essen, Erhard Milch, Secretary of State for Aviation[430] and Paul Körner, Secretary at the Prussian State Ministry.[431]

Despite the unofficial character of the visit, Göring had a reception which, according to the British Minister, was worthy of a king. Göring met Prime Minister Tsaldaris.[432] It has not been possible to ascertain the purpose of Göring's stay.

His trip has primarily been seen as political reconnoitring and the visit to Athens depicted as an indication of the fact that Göring's interests stretched as far as to the Aegean Sea.[433] Waterlow was of the same opinion and characterized Göring's visit to Greece as: "... not entirely unconnected with a desire to show the flag in the Balkans and suggest to the public that a rejuvenated and renascent Germany is a power which will sooner or later have to be reckoned with in the Near East".[434]

In the foreign press and within diplomatic circles, Göring's visit to south-eastern Europe gave new life to the old horror felt by the Western Powers since before the First World War of German *Drang nach Osten*.[435] Rumours were circulating that Göring had come to Athens to investigate the possibility of running the German Autobahn net via Italy and Greece and onwards in the direction of Constantinople and India.[436]

A few weeks after Göring's departure, Waterlow received information that the visit had been arranged by Prime Minister Tsaldaris' wife. She was known as an ultra royalist and pro-German, and had, according to rumours, arranged the visit through her sister in Hamburg, who was married to a Greek businessman with the rank of unofficial trade attaché in Germany. Waterlow concluded that the whole affair might only have been: "...A straw in the wind, perhaps; but interesting, I think, as an indication of possible future developments of German policy [towards Greece]..."[437]

The British Minister mentioned in his annual report of 1934 that Göring should have offered to renovate the rolling stock of the Greek railways. In his annual report the following year Waterlow wrote, on the basis of information from a Greek source, that Göring had also made an attempt to ensure German participation in Greek production of ammunition.[438]

As will be shown below, the Greek railways actually placed considerable orders with Germany during 1935. In the same year, Bodosakis concluded an agreement with German firms concerning delivery to the Greek ammunition industry.

In June 1934, shortly after Göring's visit, Kiriakos Varvaresos, the deputy-governor of the Bank of Greece, went to Berlin to meet the leader of the German Ministry of Economy and the German Reichsbank. The Greeks wanted to be paid the outstanding balance on the clearing account in convertible currency. This was rejected by the Germans with reference to their own currency problems.[439]

When the *Neuer Plan* came into force on 24 September 1934, German purchases in Greece rose considerably. This led to a substantial increase in the value of the total tobacco export from 1.7 billion Dr. in the years 1933-1934 to 2.9 billion Dr. in 1934-1935.[440] At the end of the tobacco season the Germans made it an indispensable condition for the continuation of their tobacco purchases that Greece seriously begin to place orders with German industry, a condition wholly in the spirit of the *Neuer Plan*. In March 1935 the Greek press reported that the German authorities would stop imports from Greece unless Greece increased her imports from Germany considerably. On 29 March, Varvaresos and the director of industry in the Greek Ministry of National Economy went to Berlin.[441] Varvaresos promised the German authorities a substantial extension of the German import quotas.[442] Moreover, he held out the prospect that the National Bank of Greece, extraordinarily, would provide 10 million RM to finance import from Germany.[443]

A Private Greek-German Clearing

The Bank of Greece and the German Reichsbank took the above-mentioned opportunity to accept the conclusion of a private clearing agreement between the National Bank of Greece and the German Dresdner Bank.

The National Bank of Greece was by far the largest bank in the country, holding a share of about 60 per cent of all deposits. It was also the most important creditor to the state.[444] Dresdner Bank was one of largest banks in Germany. Gradually, throughout the 1930s, members of the National Socialist Party began to occupy positions on the board of directors and Göring began to use it as an instrument against the German Reichsbank.[445]

The private clearing system was to work alongside official Greek-German clearing from 1932. The aim was to reduce Greek outstandings and promote German industrial exports to Greece by demanding that German purchases in Greece be immediately followed by Greek repurchases of German industrial products for twice the amount.[446]

On 19 April 1935 a special Greek law was passed "to promote the import from Germany",[447] and, finally, in May 1935 the two banks agreed to the creation of a private clearing system.[448] Subsequently, the German tobacco house Reemtsma offered to buy a consignment of Greek state tobacco at a total value of about 5 million RM by means of the private clearing account.[449] The condition for this was that Greek orders for twice the amount, 10 million RM, or 400 million Dr., were placed with German industry. This led to hectic lobbying of the Greek authorities by the National Bank of Greece to make the deal go through. It also resulted in increased German diplomatic pressure on the government in Athens to the same effect.

In the same month, on 31 May, Emanuil Tsouderos, Governor of the National Bank of Greece, handed in his resignation, ostensibly on the grounds of ill-health. However, according to the daily newspapers, among these the Venizelist *Athinaika Nea*, Tsouderos did this as a protest against the government's plans to subjugate the Bank of Greece and the National Bank of Greece to a joint management.[450] Tsouderos feared that short-term trade interests would dominate the bank of issue's activities and warned against this in a long memorandum, which exists in an English translation:

"...It would have been a catastrophe if the Bank of Greece were to be put in the shade instead of being strengthened by giving to it the necessary authority for the sake of currency and the national economy of the country. If the Government follows the policy of commercial banks against the Bank of Issue a catastrophe is certain to ensue and the responsibility of those who sacrifice the general interests upon the altar of the private ones will be immense..."[451]

In 1935, after a protracted period of time, both the board of directors at the Bank of Greece and the government accepted Tsouderos' resignation. The resignation was discussed eagerly in the press and headlines stated that the Greek bank of issue had fallen into the hands of a gang of criminals situated in and close to the National Bank of Greece and Bodosakis. Under the headline "Pesmazoglou, Loverdos, Bodosakis & Co." the newspaper *Anexartitos* stated that: "it is scandalous to leave the country's economic life in the hands of a group of plutocrats and their predatory tendencies. We are talking about a band of capitalists who use men like Loverdos and Bodosakis in a quest for their illegal, criminal and speculative ends."[452] (Loverdos had been appointed Tsouderos' successor).

The National Bank of Greece, Lobbyism and the Growth of Import from Germany

From D. N. Philaretos' letters to the National Bank of Greece, to Varvaresos and to various Greek ministries, it is possible to scrutinize the ways in which the interests of German industry were represented in Greece. Philaretos worked as a middleman for the National Bank of Greece as well as for German industry by unofficially representing their interests at the Bank of Greece and at various ministries. It appears from Philaretos' letters that he was very discreet about his connection with the National Bank of Greece. Thus, he avoided using the name of the bank in his communication with the Greek authorities. If he met difficulties in persuading the latter, he informed the bank and advised it to put pressure on the authorities.

Philaretos' personal interest was to activate the trade between Greece and Germany, as he received a two per cent commission on this.[453] As a middleman to the National Bank of Greece Philaretos tried to settle as much of the Greek import of German products as possible through the private clearing account. However, Philaretos' letters do not reveal political decision-making at close range.

Reorganization of Imports

In either 1934 or 1935 Philaretos informed the Greek government that the country's demand for quinine could be met by German industry. At that time quinine was imported from the Netherlands. According to an international cartel agreement between the Dutch, French, British and Swiss quinine industries, the Quinine Salt Producers Organization in Amsterdam, the Greek market was reserved from 1931 onwards for the Dutch industry.[454] In 1935 the Greek Ministries of Economy and Foreign Affairs and the Dresdner Bank intervened jointly with the cartel to the effect that the Greek medical industry won permission to import quinine from Germany.[455]

The cartel, however, only reluctantly yielded on this point and refused to grant the German quinine producers the right to offer Greece a so-called "state discount" which made it less expensive to import from the Netherlands. Thus, Greece had to pay considerably more for her import of German quinine.[456]

This clearly illustrates that the Greek government sometimes had to accept that price had only a secondary role in Greek-German trade

114

relations. This state of affairs undoubtedly made it more difficult for other countries to compete with Germany on the Greek market.

In September 1935, shortly before the start of the tobacco season, Greece had still not placed sufficient orders for repurchases via private clearing. This made the German authorities reluctant to approve Reemtsmas' purchase of Greek state tobacco. Furthermore, they had not yet decided to permit import of Greek tobacco the following season.[457] Accordingly, Philaretos was at great pains to initiate the import from Germany.

In a letter to Alexandros Korizis, Vice-President of the National Bank of Greece, Philaretos pointed out that the Greek Railways, the Salonika Railway, the Piraeus Gas Company, the Athens Sewerage System and the two British dominated companies, the Peloponnese Railway and Power and Traction, must place prospective orders with German firms. According to Philaretos, this would be possible if the Bank of Greece and the National Bank of Greece underwrote the financing of the purchases in Germany. Philaretos requested Korizis to put pressure on the Greek government to force the Greek Railways to place orders in Germany and on the Bank of Greece to finance this, but the bank was obviously reluctant to do so.[458]

At the same time Philaretos asked Korizis to solicit the President of the National Bank of Greece, Ioanis Drosopoulos, to use his power as chairman of the board of directors in Power to force the company to place orders in Germany.[459]

During 1935 the Greek Railways, the Piraeus Gas Company and the Athens Sewerage System finally decided to place orders in Germany for about 5 million RM.[460]

As previously noted, Philaretos had pointed out that the Peloponnese Railway was an obvious customer for German material. At the end of 1934, Siemens-Schuckert asked *Auswärtiges Amt* to assist them in winning a concession to deliver twelve engines to the railway. This created a substantial conflict of interests between the British dominated company on the one hand and the Greek state and German trade interests on the other. 65.2 per cent of the shares in the railroad was in the hands of the British company, (Hellenic and General Trust Ltd.: 34.8 per cent,[461] Hambros Bank Ltd.: 30.4 per cent), while the remaining 34.8 per cent was owned by the National Bank of Greece.[462]

115

The order had already been placed with a foreign competitor but the final approval had to be issued by the Greek Ministry of Traffic and had not yet been authorized.[463]

As a result of German appeals to the Greek authorities, the Greek Ministry of Traffic decided to force the railway to postpone the decision by delaying approval of the trade.[464] Subsequently, Philaretos tried to persuade the Prime Minister to withdraw his support for the original trade.[465] The representative of British shareholders, Hambros Bank, believed that purchases in Germany would be against the interests of the shareholders. The bank explained to Drosopoulos, who was also Chairman of the Peloponnese Railway, that this would tie the railway to the German market and in that way result in relevant British companies, in which Hambros Bank had vested interests, being ignored.[466]

In the second half of 1935, despite British opposition, the so-called Superior Council of the National Economic Defence[467] agreed to the order being placed in Germany.[468] Accordingly, the Peloponnese Railways office in London was closed on the grounds that the Greek state had taken over the actual control of the company.[469]

On 14 November 1935 Ernst Eisenlohr, the German Minister in Athens, informed *Auswärtiges Amt* that the concession had been placed with German industry as a result of active engagement by German diplomats. This took place, Eisenlohr went on, in full agreement with the railway's largest shareholder, the National Bank of Greece; it was on condition, however, that the demand attached to the private clearing regarding Greek repurchases for double the amount be withdrawn. In the future, purchases in relation to state tobacco were to be settled via general clearing. Eisenlohr supported the request because the principle of repurchases for twice the amount was impossible to realize.[470] On 30 November 1935 the German Ministry of Economy agreed to abandon the demand.[471]

This successful encroachment on the Peloponnese Railway seems to have encouraged the National Bank of Greece and the Greek authorities to test British capital interests again. In 1935 the largest foreign-controlled firm in Greece, the British dominated 'Power', was, as noted above, about to make new investments. These amounted to £305,000 or about 192 million Dr. (4.8 million RM). The company wished to place the orders with British firms, in which Whitehall Securities Corporation, the biggest shareholder in Power, had its interests. Nevertheless, Philaretos appealed to the Minister of Economy and Varvaresos to force the company to place orders

116

in Germany. According to Philaretos, Drosopoulos, chairman of the board of directors at both Power and the Peloponnese Railway, was willing to make purchases in Germany provided that he could explain to the British parent company that this was necessary due to state interference.[472]

Consequently, the Greek authorities denied Power hard currency, thus leading to lengthy negotiations between Power and the Greek government. After repeated intervention from the British legation, the Greek authorities decided, in 1936, to restrict demands for purchases in Germany to 33 per cent of the total orders placed abroad by the company.[473] In addition the firm was granted the right to move funds out of the country to settle debts and to pay dividends.[474]

Studies concerned with the power relations between foreign dominated public utilities and the state authorities in Latin America have shown that the former were often in a weak position. This was due to the fact that the politicians of the host country had to heed demands from the local workforce and consumers or gave priority to the national economy rather than to the companies.[475]

Similar power relations were apparantly present in Greece. Under pressure from Germany, the Greek state forced the Peloponnese Railway to place orders in Germany against the will of the British shareholders. The British legation was informed about the case but refrained from taking action against the Greek authorities. The reason adduced in support of this was the advisability of waiting until a more clear case was at issue.[476]

Moreover, under pressure from Greek middlemen serving the Germans, the Greek authorities tried to force Power to order turbines, buses and trams from Germany. However, in 1936, after repeated intervention from the British legation, the Greek authorities decided to limit demands for purchases in Germany. It is important to stress, however, that the Greek authorities did not reduce the demands on Power until the British interfered officially.

In summary, it can be concluded that there is no indication that the Greek government surrendered to British capital interests to any considerable extent. In this respect it is important to note that the British were in no position to threaten the Greeks, as they could offer neither capital export nor loans of any significance. In addition, direct investments from Britain primarily occurred within fields of poor developmental dynamics and little technological intensiveness, such as insurance, banking, trade, etc.

Regarding transport and electricity supply, the necessary technology had already been installed in Greece and daily operations were performed by locals. The equipment's technological stage of development was at a level which made it possible to maintain it or replace it from countries other than Britain.

The case of the Peloponnese Railway and Power is an example of the way in which the Greek government was willing to and succeeded in forcing firms to buy German equipment out of regard for the importance of trade relations with that country.

Metaxas and Germany

The mere circumstance that Metaxas was a radical anti-Venizelist of strong anti-French inclinations and known as a loyal friend and adviser to the late King Constantine would doubtless have ensured him a reputation both inside and outside Greece as notoriously pro-German.

On 29 September 1936 the German Minister of Propaganda, Joseph Goebbels, met Metaxas during his visit to Athens. The Greek dictator expressed admiration for the achievements that the National Socialist government had accomplished in Germany. Metaxas also told Goebbels that he would like to achieve something similar in Greece, but that Greece had to maintain friendship and peace with both Britain and Germany.[477]

At the time of the establishment of the dictatorship, Metaxas' position of power was mainly dependent on the pro-British King. For that reason Metaxas had to avoid allegations of copying Nazi Germany in his programme and government and it was in his interests that all publicity regarding the latter be toned down both inside and outside Greece, and particularly in Britain. It was therefore an embarrasment when Konstandinos Zavitsianos, the Minister of National Economy, erroneously stated on 18 January 1937 in connection with the announcement of the rearmament programme that the Greek government had obtained credits in Germany of no less than 100 million RM for purchases of German war equipment. On 22 January Metaxas relieved Zavitsianos of his duties and used the occasion to explain the facts of the matter.[478] Apparently, Waterlow felt confused and, even though he was assured by very reliable sources that the reality corresponded with Metaxas' official denial, the whole affair planted doubt in the mind of the Minister.[479]

These matters may be connected with the fact that on 25 January 1937 Metaxas told his Ambassador in Berlin to avoid any steps that might expedite Hitler's plans to visit Greece:[480] shortly before, the Embassy in Berlin had provided information that the German leader was planning a visit to Greece the same spring.[481]

However, it important to bear in mind that it was also in the interests of Germany that Metaxas kept a low profile regarding his pro-German inclinations. On their part the Germans were keen to underplay and tone down Metaxas' pro-German attitude. On 9 March 1937 the leader of the Press Department at the Greek Ministry of Foreign Affairs showed the German legation in strict confidence a telegram to Metaxas from the Greek Ambassador in London. The telegram explained that certain circles in Britain were unhappy with Metaxas's policy, which, they felt, was turning Greece into a National Socialist state. The German legation believed that it was the large orders for armaments placed in Germany that caused such worries. Other sources of discontent were Greek-German cultural relations (such as the excavations at Olympia, financed by the Germans on the occasion of the Olympic Games in Berlin), frequent visits by German statesmen to Greece and German aviation policy.

The legation had the impression that it was at Metaxas' own request that they were shown the telegram. The legation underlined the fact that: "...Prime Minister Metaxas feels a very strong inner sympathy towards Germany...", and did not doubt that Metaxas intended to pursue this as a policy. For that reason, the legation deduced that the Greek dictator was trying to warn the German authorities not to display too much cordiality regarding the Greek-German relationship.[482]

This corresponds with Goebbels' view of the matter. In connection with the inauguration of the German archaeological excavations at Olympia by the German Minister of Education, Bernard Rust, Goebbels wrote in his diary that the Greek government was very grateful, but the cordiality in relations between the two counties must be toned down, otherwise Metaxas could encounter trouble with Britain.[483]

On the occasion of the preparations for the anniversary of Metaxas's dictatorship, Kordt emphasized to the German press that they must avoid any comments indicating that Metaxas should favour Germany in particular. The German Counsellor of Legation knew from sources in Metaxas's inner circle that the Greek dictator had to protect himself against accusations from Britain. For that reason Kordt preferred the German press to stress the pro-British tendencies in Metaxas' policy.

Furthermore, the German Counsellor of Legation believed personally that Metaxas was first and foremost a Greek patriot.[484]

Ideologically Common Features and Differences

The fight against Communism was the area in which the shared ideological interests of the two regimes were most significant and successful for both parties. The oppression of political opponents, and in particular of the Communists, during the Metaxas regime was in terms of determination and efficiency without precedent in Greek history. In November 1936, on the initiative of the Gestapo[485] and as the result of an inquiry from the German legation in Athens, Metaxas declared that he approved the Greek Security Police and the Gestapo joining forces to exchange information as a defence against "Bolshevik agitation."[486] According to a German assessment, it was the merit of Metaxas that only about one year after the establishment of his regime, the Communists lost their most important stronghold in the Near East.[487] At the end of 1937 the British legation acquired an item of correspondence dated May the same year between Heinrich Himmler and Konstandinos Maniadakis, the Secretary of Security. This stated that Maniadakis accepted an invitation on behalf of the Greek police to participate in a congress about methods to fight Communism.[488]

In this way German assistance also played a certain part in Metaxas's fight against internal enemies. It is notable that the British Foreign Office learned from sources in Germany that ten per cent of the value of the German arms trade to Greece went to Metaxas. The money was used for the establishment of Metaxas' party organization and propaganda for the regime.[489] The British legation in Athens did not doubt the validity of the information, and in their eyes the crucial question was whether Metaxas would finally manage to claim supremacy and thrust the King into the background. Waterlow believed that even, with moral and economic support from Germany, Metaxas would not succeed in this.[490]

On certain occasions the propaganda used by the regime copied the methods of Mussolini and Hitler. Metaxas gave himself symbolic titles, such as 'First Worker' (*Protos Ergatis*) and 'First Peasant' (*Protos Agrotis*), founded the national youth organization EON (*Ethniki Organosis Neoleas*) which resembled *Hitler Jugend*, and introduced the so-called "Roman salute". However, observers inside and outside Greece agreed that Metaxas failed to generate genuinely popular support.[491]

Moreover, these were not symbols of unity rooted in an original mass movement, and Metaxas's road to power was very different from both Hitler's and Mussolini's. The fact alone that the regime was not based on a mass movement indicates that it would be wrong to call the dictatorship Fascist.[492] Moreover, the regime did not have any plans for territorial expansion: these had been buried in the wake of Greece's disastrous campaign in Asia Minor in 1920-1922.

The regime identified the modern, and culturally heterogeneous, Greece with the image of classical Hellas and Byzantium and introduced a cultural and national policy of integration. Metaxas ascribed paramount symbolic significance to the militaristic and oligarchic Sparta, archrival of the democratic Athens, and depicted Sparta as the first of three Greek civilizations. The two others were Byzantium and Metaxas's own regime, portrayed as "the Third Greek Civilization". The Germans tried to use this nationalism as a platform to pursue for own interests. During his visit to Greece in 1936, Goebbels went to Sparta, although there were few archaeological remains there from Antiquity beyond the name itself. The choice of Sparta was a demonstration to the regime that Germany regarded modern Greece as the true descendant of ancient Greece and accordingly that she saw Sparta as the most outstanding representative of the latter.[493]

The German Archaeological School in Athens was used as an instrument to gain goodwill.[494] On the occasion of the Olympic Games in Berlin, Hitler donated 300,000 RM for excavations in Olympia, on the Peloponnese, where the classical Olympic Games had been held. In addition, Goebbels donated 150,000 RM following his visit the same year.[495] This German coquetry with the Greek regime's identification with a classical image was pursued in tough competition with France and Britain. As a result, Erbach warned against a historical thesis questioning this perception being included in a large new German encyclopedia, even though this was intended only for the German market. Briefly the thesis suggests that modern Greeks have no relationship to the ancient Greeks, but are descended from immigrant Slaves.[496] Moreover, the Germans tried to strengthen their position in Greece through state as well as cultural activities and to stress the ideological spirit of community between Germany and Greece. At the Goethe Institute in Athens the Germans tried to arouse interest in German culture, and teachers and students received grants to go to Germany on exchange agreements. Furthermore, Germany sent doctors and other experts to Greece.[497] In this way Germany used official state organs to increase her goodwill to Greece by underlining modern Greece's connection to ancient Greece, by disseminating knowledge about German culture and by sending German expertise to Greece to give her population an opportunity to see the wonders of Germany with their own eyes.

Nevertheless, German admiration for Greek antiquity seems to have been more than just a publicity campaign directed towards the Greeks themselves. It is important to emphazise that classical antiquity had been at the forefront of Europe's intellectual life since the advent of Classicism. It had held a prominent position during Romanticism and the period that followed. An indication of this was the Philhellenism of the period and the number of volunteers from Europe who travelled the long and troublesome road to Greece during the Greek War of Independence to participate in the liberation of Plato's and Pericles's distant native land. As a result of the influence of art and of the curricula at schools, classical Greek antiquity represented the refinement of taste to generations of Europeans. This gave modern Greeks an opportunity to recall emotions mirrored in the ideal images of an admired antiquity, and to bypass 2000 years of Eastern Roman and Turkish influence. This was an easy way to reach the hearts of the Europeans and one peculiar to Greece. According to Waterlow the National Socialists saw an intellectual affinity between the ancient Greeks and the modern Germans, or, as he expressed it, between Pericles and Hitler.[498] Speer notes that Hitler was primarily influenced by Greek architecture, and regarded Greek culture as an expression of the highest imaginable perfection.[499] From the diaries of Goebbels it is possible to discern the feelings that were aroused in the German Minister of Propaganda during his first visit to Greece. In the following notes he describes how the dream of his youth came true in the air space above Mount Olympus: "...There towers Mount Olympus and there Parnassus. It makes one warm. Old memories from my youth emerge. A dream comes true. The sun sets beautifully. Over eternal Greece...."[500] On the second day of his visit, Goebbels went to the Acropolis. The Minister describes it as the happiest morning of his life: "...Yesterday: one of the most beautiful and most significant mornings of my life. On the Acropolis. Only a few people. And I wandered about for hours in these noble places of Nordic art..."[501]

122

It is interesting that Goebbels depicts Greek antiquity as a part of the pre-Christian nordic world. Impressions of "blessed antiquity" fill Goebbels soul with beauty: "...My soul is filled with beauty. Blessed antiquity, which lived in eternal joy free from Christianity. An evening stroll through the town. This joyful highest life. This smell of happiness. How pleased the Führer would be if he were here with us!..."[502]

His joy at seeing the Acropolis again in 1939 inspired Goebbels to describe it as the cradle of Aryan culture: "...On Acropolis. O, this shattering view! The cradle of Aryan culture..."[503]

Germany's ideology and her political attitude towards the 4th of August Regime was well received by the Greek government and helped to advance German interests in various fields. German newspapers were, unlike the foreign press generally, freely distributed in Greece. Kordt saw this as a result of Germany's warm welcome to Metaxas's assumption of power.

An exhibition in Athens arranged in 1938 by *Kraft durch Freude* enjoyed the full support of Metaxas, who was present when the exhibition was opened by the head of the German Labour Front, Robert Ley. The latter presented German orders of honour to Metaxas, Kostas Kodzias, Minister of the Capital, and Nikolaos Mavroudis, Deputy-Secretary at the Greek Ministry of Foreign Affairs.[504]

It is important to note that Metaxas made it clear from early on that he did not hold anti-Semitic views. On 9 September 1936 he stated in an interview that he had no intention of making any distinctions between the citizens of his country. He expected that the Jews in Salonika would be more than happy to cooperate in the reconstruction of the mother country. According to Kordt this reverberated in the censored Greek press, which stressed that the Jews in Greece had the same status as any other citizen and anyone in Greece who entertained anti-Semitic feelings was a bad Greek.[505]

This contradicts the impression Goebbels gained from his talks with Metaxas in September 1936.[506] However, this conversation was private and Metaxas might have attempted to please Goebbels by expressing such views. It is a fact that (at least officially) Metaxas distanced himself from anti-Semitic views. This stance was also noticed abroad. Thus *The Jewish Cronicle* in London printed a short article in September 1937 which praised Metaxas for prohibiting the publishing of anti-Semitic writings.[507]

There were, as previously noted, several common features in Greek and German state ideology. However, it is important to stress that this resemblance was far from complete. The regime was more closely comparable with various national conservative governments which came to power in large parts of the less developed, raw material producing countries in Europe, Latin America and the Middle East. The world crisis, and the transition from free trade to protectionism that followed, caused political reactions, when policies to surmount the crisis, based on national efficiency and economic modernization, took priority over parliamentarian principles.

In this connection, the "New Germany", controlled by the National Socialists, became a desirable image of successful modernization, and a symbol of a new era in which the old liberal order and its domestic and foreign exponents seemed to have failed.

Metaxas's Assumption of Power and Greek-German Trade

It is possible to detect a considerable increase in Greek-German trade which coincides in a spectacular manner with the assumption of power by Metaxas.

TABLE 17

Greek-German clearing trade 1933-1940 in millions of RM.[508]

	Imports	Exports
1933	22,7	36,5
1934	38,0	42,2
1935	49,5	62,3
1936	95,2	93,4
1937	92,7	84,2
1938	101,3	97,1
1939	85,2	84,5
1940	61,2	68,7

Imports from Germany grew from 49.5 million RM in 1935 to 95.2 million RM in 1936 and in the years 1936-1939 amounted to an average of 93.6 million RM. The latter represented a trebling compared with the period 1933-1935, when the average was 36.7 million RM.

Exports to Germany grew from 62.3 million RM in 1935 to 93.4 million RM in 1936 and averaged 89.8 million RM between 1936-1939, about double the amount averaged between 1933-1935, 46.9 million RM.

124

The German breakthrough in exports to Greece helped to balance Greek-German trade with a tendency towards higher exports from Germany to Greece than the other way around. The result was that the Greek outstanding on the clearing account was settled relatively quickly and the clearing account kept in balance until the outbreak of the war.

Table 17 shows a German trade surplus in the clearing trade in 1933-1936 of 29 million RM and a Greek surplus in 1937-1939 of 13.4 million RM, a total German trade surplus of 15.6 million RM. However, 9.8 million RM, which accumulated in favour of Germany in 1932, must be deducted from the above calculations. This brings the German surplus down to 5.8 million RM, a large part of which built up after the outbreak of war in September 1939.[509]

The increase in trade can be explained by a general worldwide economic recovery, but also by an expansion of the arms trade which was closely related to Metaxas's assumption of power. Between 1936 and 1939 Greek purchases of arms from Germany via the clearing account amounted to 39.3 million RM. However, it must be noted that, until the first half of 1938, 85 per cent of the arms trade was settled on the clearing account; the rest, 15 per cent, was paid for in hard currency. Subsequently, the exchange quota rose considerably. This means that the total value of arms bought in Germany was higher than indicated above. Finally, purchases for more than 34 million RM were financed by six-year Greek government bonds, which means that the arms trade was more extensive than it appears in table 18.

TABLE 18

The value of arms sold to Greece between 1936 and 1940, million RM, according to Ausfurgemeinschaft für Kriegsgerät:

	1936[510]	1937	1938[511]	1939	1940	1936-1940
Greece	23.5	16.5	9.8	7.0	1.8	58.6

As will be explained below, Greece placed orders for military equipment in Germany for at least 72 million RM between 1936 and 1940. Greek arms purchases in Germany were especially extensive in 1936 and 1937, when they amounted to 40 million RM. This corresponds with figures stating that Greece placed orders for about 60 million RM in the period December 1936 to December 1937.[512]

It is important to emphasize that Germany also delivered production equipment to both the armed forces and the Greek armament industry. Sales to the latter have not been listed under defence expenditures, as industrialization related to armaments was carried out on a private basis. It has not been possible to reach a precise assessment of the size of these transactions but figures from the Powder and Cartridge Company indicate that such purchases in Germany were of a significant size. In the period between September 1935 and March 1937 the Powder and Cartridge Company bought equipment worth 11 million RM and placed additional orders for 20 million RM.[513] Between March 1937 and March 1939 purchases in Germany amounted to between 35 and 45 million RM.[514] According to Walter Deter, Managing Director of Rheinmetall-Borsig in Athens, the Powder and Cartridge Company purchased equipment for a total sum of 55 million RM.[515] This means that the total value of arms and production equipment sold to the Greek armament industry amounts to more than 100 million RM, namely somewhere between 117 million (72 million RM for arms + 45 million RM for production equipment) and 127 million RM (72 million RM for arms + 55 million RM for production equipment), i.e. more or less the equivalent of the total increase of exports after 1935 (1936-1940: 116 million RM).

Greek Industrialization and *Grossraumwirtschaft*

On 30 October 1936 the interest organization of the German iron producing industry, *Wirtschaftsgruppe Eisenschaffende Industrie*, complained to *Auswärtiges Amt* about the opening of a rolling mill at the Greek metal company SA. Métallurgique D.& A. Stavrianos. According to the German steel industry this was a breach of Greece's current industrialization policy. The complaint referred to a declaration made in June 1934 by the Greek Minister of Economic Affairs, Georghios Pesmazoglou, to the German Legation "[that he would] use all means to prevent the rise of a Greek industry that could affect the import of foreign industrial products", on the grounds that Greek agricultural exports could be threatened [as a result of retribution].

The German steel industry tried to prevent the construction of the rolling mill through the cartel *Zentraleuropäische Gruppe der Internationalen Rohstahlgemeinschaft* ZEG (the Central European Group of the International Steel Community), the German Ministry of Economy and *Auswärtiges Amt*.[516] Although Greece was not included in the cartel agreement,[517] the German steel industry succeeded in persuading the other members of *Internationale Rohstahlgemeinschaft* to deny Stavrianos sales of semi-manufactured articles. Ultimately, however, the Greek rolling mill managed to ensure its production through imports from the United States.[518]

According to Erbach, the case in point was not a matter of Greece changing her industrialization policy. The rolling mill had been set up to supply the Greek demand for armaments and, for that reason, the German Minister considered it futile to file a complaint to the Greek government.[519] Erbach's belief that the mill was founded to meet the need for armaments seems reasonable. In this connection it is important to remember that, as early as May 1936, the 6th Office of the Greek General Staff for Economic Mobilization had stressed the significance to the defence of the country of the metal and chemical industry and underlined the point that the import of necessary raw materials was not seen as a hindrance.[520] This was a clear contradiction of the credo affirmed by the Greek Minister of Economic Affairs in 1934, but the situation had changed since then, and, by 1936, a large-scale rearmament programme was under way.

Nevertheless, in July 1937 Erbach apparently changed his mind: he now was of the opinion that the establishment of the rolling mill and the setting-up of a Greek company for the production of saltpetre were in fact breaches of Greek industrialization policy.[521]

Erbach's change of attitude stemmed from the fact that during 1937 the results of Greece's armaments related industrialization policy became visible. The German Minister's new approach to the problem was probably also conditioned by the fact that, from 1937 and as a result of the Four Year Plan, the authorities in Berlin issued new and more rigorous directives to discourage industrialization on the periphery. Finally, a more determined pursuit of the objectives of the *Grossraumwirtschaft* plan also seems to have played a role in this respect.

In words that provide a textbook example of *Grossraumwirtschaft* philosophy, Erbach reported that, instead of relying on German industry, Greece was industrializing within areas which were earlier met by import from Germany: "...Furthermore, the Greek economic policy seems increasingly to be abandoning the long observed and sensible rule, according to which local industry was set up only when based on local raw material and local labour..."[522]

Erbach tried in vain to persuade the Greek government to stop this policy, referring to the fact that it affected German exports to Greece negatively. His lack of success convinced the German Minister instead that the German saltpetre industry would have to participate in the establishment of such a Greek industry, as otherwise foreign competitors would do so: "...All references from the Legation, that this policy will reduce demand on the Greek market for certain goods of interst to Germany, have led to nothing. The German saltpetre industry, for example, has only one thing to do: namely to participate in the construction of a new plant, in order at least to protect itself from foreign competitors..."[523]

According to Erbach it was the Greek Minister of Economic Affairs, Andreas Chadzikiriakos, who was responsible for this new Greek policy.[524] The German Minister was also of the opinion that business and Varvaresos were "less mercantilist" than Chadzikiriakos. For this reason he suggested that the German authorities support this group and teach a lesson to those responsible for, as he expressed it in a phrase characteristic of the spirit of the time, "Hellenic business egoism". The Greeks must understand, Erbach went on, that Chadzikiriakos's policy must end if they wanted to maintain the exports of tobacco, wine, etc., to Germany.[525] Consequently, Erbach suggested that Germany stop the purchase of figs and dried grapes and turn up late for the tobacco season. In this way he hoped to put a knife in Chadzikiriakos's mercantilist ambitions.[526]

On 22 July Kordt informed *Auswärtiges Amt* that Chadzikiriakos had resigned. From Greek press announcements the German Legation had the impression that the resignation was due to a sharp disagreement between Metaxas and the Minister of Economic Affairs. Furthermore, Kordt was also sure that a complaint made by Erbach to Metaxas against Chadzikiriakos had an impact to this effect.[527]

A few days before Chadzikiriakos's resignation was made public Metaxas informed the King that the resignation of the Minister of Economic Affairs was due to a constant growth in prices of locally produced industrial products and because Chadzikiriakos only looked after the interests of the industry.[528] Like Erbach, Metaxas believed that the Minister of Economic Affairs was responsible for supporting the vested interest of the industry.

It is possible, however, that Metaxas found it convenient to "sacrifice" Chadzikiriakos: the dictator had previously disagreed with the Minister of Economic Affairs, and it may be that Erbach's complaint offered a welcome opportunity for Metaxas to show the Germans that he was attentive to their wishes.

Nevertheless, the growth of the metal and saltpetre industries and German discontent at these trends in Greek industrialization policy can hardly be conceived of as merely a result of Chadzikiriakos's policy. It was rather an expression of a more fundamental conflict between Metaxas's industrial rearmament policy and German *Grossraumswirtschaft* ambitions. Greek compliance with German demands would have posed a serious threat to the execution of the main point in Metaxas's policy: a national efficiency policy. In this respect it is notable that, according to the King, this policy was pursued to an extent that came close to chauvinism and xenophobia. In March 1937 the King entrusted the British Legation in Athens with the following message: "...Apart from the financial difficulty, he [the Greek King] had to cope with an exaggerated and childish chauvinism in all spheres, and he could not yet afford to antagonise this nationalist and anti-foreign exaltation, with which he indicated that General Metaxas was somewhat bitten [...] For instance there was the scheme for building [ships] for the navy in Greece, rather than buying abroad; he knew very well that this was a wholly uneconomic proposition, but he thought it better not to discourage it, as national pride was involved..."[529]

Seen against this background it is hardly surprising that plans concerning the construction of a local steelworks, already mentioned in a memorandum dated 11 May 1938,[530] were continued in spite of protests from the German steel industry. Reacting to this, *Wirtschaftsgruppe Eisenschaffende Industrie* asked *Auswärtiges Amt* to do everything in its power to stop the construction of the plant.[531] The German Legation recommended stopping the delivery of semi-manufactured goods.[532] The international steel cartel also tried to obstruct the project. However, at the end of the day the national German Steel Cartel came to the conclusion that retaliatory measures regarding prices would have no effect on the Greek government because of the high political priority of the plant.[533] In this respect it is important to note that investigations of German industry in the 1930s have demonstrated that attempts to fight industrialization on the periphery, when carried out under political protection, seldom succeeded. In most cases German industry ultimately joined the process instead.[534] This strategy corresponds with the concept previously mentioned, "*Export-*

steigerung durch Einschaltung der Industrialisierung der Welt", of which Max Ilgner was the spokesman.

German Rearmament and Greek Exports to Germany

As a result of the implementation of the Four Year Plan and Göring's increasing influence on Germany's trade policy, a wide range of Greek products, like bauxite, chrome and other metals, not to mention cotton[535] and olive oil, became all the more important to Germany.

In the period of international economic recovery, mid-1936 to August 1937,[536] Greece experienced a rise in her sales of products on the international market. This led to restrictions on the export to Germany. Plans to export cotton[537] were abandoned to avoid demands for sales to Germany on the clearing account. As a result, the export of olive oil to Germany fell from an average of 337,000 tons in the period 1934-1936 to only 57,539 tons in 1937.[538] The German share of the total Greek export fell from 36.4 per cent in 1936 to 31 per cent in 1937.[539]

On 7 July 1937 Erbach notified the economic department in *Auswärtiges Amt* that he had been informed that the Greek Minister of Economic Affairs had made it clear to a group of Greek exporters that realization of currency was more important than price. As a result of this, a prohibition was instituted against selling products to Germany that could bring in hard currency elsewhere; furthermore, the exportation of almost all products had to be approved by the Greek authorities. The German Minister concluded that the perspective for German trade with Greece was that Germany was going to trade valuable manufactured goods in return for Greek agricultural products like tobacco, currants and figs, while products important for the rearmament would go elsewhere. This, according to Erbach, was intolerable from a German point of view.[540]

On 22 July 1937, and in connection with the announcement of Chadzikiriakos's resignation, the German Legation adhered to its proposal to refrain from the purchase of figs and grapes and to arrive late for the tobacco season.[541] The German Ministry of Economy approved this as a means to make the Greeks conclude a contractual agreement defining the structure and size of quotas for both import and export between the two countries. This was considered the only way to meet future problems within Greek-German economic relations.[542]

The German goal was reached on 24 September 1937 when an agreement valid from 1 October the same year, regulating the Greek-German exchange of goods, was signed. This was an amendment to a trade and shipping agreement dated 24 March 1928 and was the first official agreement, in relation to the total exchange of goods, since the clearing trade was launched. The agreement created a basis for future trade, in that government commissions had to meet at least once a year to chart the course of trade for the following year.[543]

The objective was to settle the price, amount and type of trade between the two countries. Thereafter, it was up to the Greek and German authorities to ensure that the quotas were fulfilled. Finally, trade was to be organized in such a way that a repetion of the accumulation of a Greek outstanding on the clearing account could be avoided in the future.[544]

The trade agreement did not resolve all the problems arising from Greek-German trade, however. During a meeting held on 8 December 1937 Varvaresos expressed concern about the way in which Greek-German trade had developed since the agreement was brought into force, i.e. since 1 October 1937. In October 1937 Greece imported German goods to the value of about seven million RM, while Greek exports to Germany in the same period virtually stopped. This left Varvaresos with the impression that the German authorities had tried to force the price of, in particular, currants and tobacco to a lower level than that negotiated in the September agreement. Varvaresos urged the German authorities to ensure that trade went ahead smoothly, as otherwise it would be hard for him to enforce his pro-German

policy in the face of other political currents in Greece.[545]

Erbach emphasized to *Auswärtiges Amt* that Greek worries were well-founded. The German authorities had on several occasions made political use of Greece's dependence on the German purchase of tobacco. According to Erbach this policy was dangerous. Forcing the price of Greek agricultural products to a level below that of the world market included a risk of removing the incentive to buy German industrial products at a price higher than they would be on the international market. Moreover, the German Minister believed that the trade policy of the Greek government, especially because Varvaresos was aiming to make Germany the pivotal point in Greece's trade, had given Germany advantages transcending the sphere of trade policy. Erbach stressed that the Greek government had held on to this policy in spite of external and internal pressure that sought to direct Greek trade towards British markets: in this connection Erbach mentioned Chadzikiriakos's resignation. However, if the German outstanding on the clearing account accumulated [i.e. primarily by decreasing

131

Greek export to Germany], it would be hard to persuade the Greek government to maintain this course and similarly in matters regarding the armed forces. This could weaken Germany's position in Greece considerably.

To stress his point the German Minister referred to a speech given by Metaxas a few days earlier. The speech, held on 5 December 1937, was directed at farmers in Larissa, and Metaxas had stated that Germany was unwilling to import Greek products in the same quantities as before. For this reason, farmers had to limit the area under cultivation or produce crops saleable on markets other than the German one.[546]

The start of the tobacco season in 1937/38 showed that Metaxas's fears were not without foundation and that the Germans indeed tried to put pressure on Greek tobacco prices. Contrary to the situation in previous years, German buyers arrived late, thus creating great instability in Greek business circles and pushing the Greek economy as a whole into a state of crisis.[547] In a statement of affairs concerning the tobacco season 1937-1938 the German Vice Consul in Kavalla noted that the average price of tobacco had fallen from 65 Dr. the previous year to 57.75 Dr., representing a decrease of about 11 per cent.[548]

In conclustion, the agreement from 24 September 1937 must be seen as an attempt to realize Göring's economic policy within the framework of the Four Year Plan. It is possible to trace Greek acquiescence to German pressure in relation to the structure of the export: this is demonstrated in Table 19.

TABLE 19

Greek export to Germany of the most important products to supplies and armament.[549]

	Olive oil	Bauxite	Chrome
1934-36	337,000		
1937	57,539	80,670	
1938	1,123,433	67,964	18,160
1939	769,671	89,622	22,278
1940	245,338		1,449★

★ German sources state that the figure was considerably higher.[550]

132

ARMS TRADE I: GREEK-GERMAN NEGOTIATIONS

Rearmament and Import of German Arms

The problems related to a Greek demand for German supplies occurred simultaneously with the decision to rearm Greece. As a consequence of this, influential people in both Greece and Germany insisted on the Greek purchase of German military equipment. The first attempt to involve Germany in Greek rearmament seems to have come from Kondilis at the beginning of 1934. In January 1934 Bodosakis took over the Greek Powder and Cartridge Company from the National Bank of Greece. However, the deal was not made until Bodosakis had consulted Kondilis, who informed him that his ambition was to privatize the war industry so as to side-step control by the army.[551]

Kondilis's motives are not clear; however, it is important to note that the army was under the control of the Venizelists and that Bodosakis, shortly after taking possession of the Greek Powder and Cartridge Company, started to cooperate with the German explosives company Köln-Rottweil Powder Factory.[552]

At the beginning of February 1934, a few weeks after the establishment of the Balkan Entente, a Greek middleman with good connections to the Greek General Staff and the Ministry of War paid a visit to the German armament firm Rheinmetall-Borsig to buy arms for Greece. It was an extensive order which the German Ministry of War had already approved. The German arms company thus only lacked permission from *Auswärtiges Amt* for the export of this order. Major Pabst,[553] representing the armament company, promised that the delivery would be carried out under cover, i.e. through Rheinmetall-Borsig's shadow company Soloturn in Switzerland.[554] Apart from a single objection,[555] the arms trade with Greece was seen as healthy to German interests. State Secretary Bernhard W. von Bülow was believed that it was wrong to make arms deliveries only to Germany's friends, and he considered the suggestion to be attractive because Greece was a former enemy of Germany: "...In my opinion it would be wrong to deliver arms only to friendly nations. In this way we would only make ourselves appear more suspicious. On the condition that it is conducted under cover, for the time being, I consider delivery to a former enemy to be especially attractive..."[556]

In July 1934 *Auswärtiges Amt* decided to encourage the delivering of arms to Greece by means of export subsidies.[557]

It must be remembered that, about a year previously, the anti-Venizelists had ended more than a decade of Venizelist dominance in parliament and that, for the Germans, the anti-Venizelists symbolised Greek resistance to joining the First World War allies against Germany. In this context it is interesting to note that *Aussenpolitisches Amt der NSDAP* (APA) (the foreign department of the Nazi party) regarded the avoidance of a return to power of the Venizelists as being important for long-term German interests in Greece. For that reason the APA recommended cautious German support for the royalists.[558]

It has not been possible to trace any resistance from Venizelist officers to the planned purchase of arms from Germany; nevertheless, it is evident that the Greek-German negotiations did not take place until the anti-Venizelists had assumed control of the army. From the summer of 1935, this event was closely linked to Kondilis's ascendant power.

In September 1935 Admiral Wilhelm Canaris, head of the German intelligence, *Abwehr*, visited Greece to discuss the situation regarding Cyprus and the Dodecanese.[559] As will be noted below, Canaris had a close relationship with Ioanis Theotokis, the Greek Minister of Foreign Afairs. Available sources do not indicate when this relationship started. However, it appears from German sources that the Legation in Athens was giving confidential infomation to the German government through a person whom *Auswärtiges Amt* considered reliable and whom Canaris knew. According to this source the Greek government decided, at the beginning of September, to take all precautions to protect Athens against attacks from both air and sea.[560]

At the same time, on 19 September 1935, the Powder and Cartridge Company concluded a so-called agreement of friendship and cooperation with Rheinmetall-Borsig which paved the way for a massive expansion of the Greek armament industry but also made it increasingly dependent on German know-how and technology.[561]

On 30 September 1935 the Greek Minister of Finance informed the German government that, "Greece is in dire straits regarding war material"[562] and that the Greek government planned to omit the public tenders required by Greek law. The Greek government wished to negotiate with a commission headed by German government officials and interested German firms. This was an attempt to leave out middlemen and save the usual, and often very expensive, so-called "Orientalia", i.e. extraordinary payments such as provisions to middlemen as well as bribes and gifts, etc. to officials.[563] Moreover, the Greek government wanted the deal to be made in secrecy, a desire which, of course, was irreconcilable with the acceptance of public tenders.

On 30 September, the day that the Greek Minister of Finance addressed the German government, a commission from the Greek Navy, headed by the Chief of the General Staff, arrived in Germany on a secret visit. Rheinmetall-Borsig's Greek representative in Athens asked the German authorities not to comment on the visit, even to the Greek Embassy in Berlin.

The purpose of the naval commission was to inspect shipyards and Rheinmetall-Borsig's production facilities with an eye to the future purchase of war equipment. Orders were expected to be in the range of 75 to 100 mill. RM, but would not be placed until a final decision had been taken by the Greek government.[564] On the same occasion the Greek Navy commission asked for advice about the enlargement of the Greek coastal defence.[565] The secrecy of the visit, however, miscarried: on 4 September 1935 the Greek press announced that Greek officers had gone to Germany.[566]

The Abyssinian Crisis and Forced Greek Rearmament
The Italian attack on Abyssinia in October 1935 produced an immediate Greek mobilization and resulted in prompt negotiations over arms deals. In the week following Kondilis's *coup*, Kondilis and Theotokis turned to Britain and Germany to obtain an urgent delivery of 50 modern fighter aircraft.[567]

On 17 October 1935 Theotokis had a meeting with the German Minister in Athens about German arms deliveries to Greece, and, on the following day, 18 October, Theotokis contacted Canaris urging him to expedite the matter. In a personal letter, the Greek Minister of Foreign Affairs asked Canaris to do what he could to hurry up deliveries and offer cheap prices.

In return for this he held out prospects of improvements in the relationship between Greece and Germany. Theotokis concluded by asking Canaris to return his answer outside the usual diplomatic channels and to reply by airmail to his (i.e Theotokis's) wife's address.[568]

The confidential nature of the exchange shows that the Greek government still considered it necessary to keep the arms affair as secret as possible, perhaps because of competition between the Great Powers, but also because of internal Greek politics, i.e. the conflict between Venizelists and anti-Venizelists.

On 19 October Theotokis turned up at the German Legation with a list of new orders for arms; he also used the occasion to inform the Germans that the French Ambassador in Athens had told the Greek government that France would regard Greek purchases of German war equipment as a violation of the Treaty of Versailles. Theotokis told the Germans that he had chosen to ignore this. He went on to stress that it was important to the Greek government that the bombers were of the most recent type, because the rearmament was of "great importance" to the country, as he expressed it. In this connection Theotokis also asked whether Germany was fundamentally interested in supplying Greece with war equipment.[569] On 24 October Eisenlohr confirmed to Theotokis that Germany was indeed interested. The Greek Minister of Foreign Affairs then asked for immediate delivery and informed the German Minister that the Greek government was ready to stake a tremendous amount on rearmament: "...the total financial power of the country will be put at the service of the concept of rearmament..."[570] In return Theotokis offered to give information to *Abwehr* and to see that all military information related to the crisis in Abyssinia and sent to the Greek government was forwarded to Abwehr under cover of a private address in Athens.[571] In this way the Greek Minister of Foreign Affairs offered cooperation that extended further than just the arms trade. The Greek government clearly feared for Greece's security as a result of the crisis in Abyssinia and was therefore ready to concede much to ensure supplies of modern arms. In this respect it is important to stress that Germany was seen as impartial in relation to the other Great Powers *vis-à-vis* military and power political interests in the Mediterrannean; furthermore, the critical situation arose at a time when the power in Greece was wielded by a group of anti-Venizelists who had good connections with Germany.

A week later, on 1 November 1935, further steps towards increased military cooperation between Greece and Germany were taken, when Erich Raeder, the Commander-in-Chief of the German Navy, appointed Vice Admiral Walther Kinzel as expert to supervise the strengthening of the Greek coastal defence.[572]

A few days later the Monarchy was restored. This made the German Legation in Athens, as well as *Auswärtiges Amt*, exert increasing pressure to complete the arms deals before the King returned. This pressure perhaps resulted from the fact that Theotokis, whom the Germans regarded as "a warm friend of Germany", had expressed fears that foreign influence, especially British, could hamper the Greek-German arms negotiations if the return of the King resulted in the formation of a new government.[573]

Subsequently, on 8 November 1935, the leader of the above- mentioned *Ausfuhrgemeinschaft für Kriegsgerät* decided to establish an *Ausfuhrgemeinschaft zur Durchführung von Waffenlieferungen nach Griechenland* – referred to as *Greichenland-Konsortium* (Greece Consortium) – and had technical and financial advisers sent to Athens to discuss the matter in detail with senior military personnel and the government. The consortium was controlled by the armament company Otto Wolff, with the Dresdner Bank responsible for its financial management. In this way the Germans intended to meet the Greek request to leave out middlemen from the arms trade, while creating a formal framework for specific negotiations.[574] At the same time, the German Ministry of Aviation declared that it was unable to fulfil the Greek request for delivery of aeroplanes of the most modern type.[575] A similar answer was received from Britain on 14 November.[576] The following day the Greek government decided to turn down the British offer and send a delegation to Germany to try to persuade the Germans to change their decision.[577] Furthermore, Theotokis contacted Canaris in a personal letter in which he expressed the hope that the German Ministry of Aviation would revise its decision in return for extensive economic cooperation.[578]

Simultaneously, Britain learned of Greek plans to purchase war equipment in Germany. Waterlow warned Theotokis that Greek purchases of German military aircraft would have a negative impact on the good relations which Britain had with Greece. Theotokis defended the Greek government's conduct by stressing the fact that the purchases were very attractive due to Greek assets on the clearing account.[579]

On 18 November 1935 Waterlow informed the Foreign Office that: "...As a result of the German stranglehold on the Greek economy, reinforced by the corrupt influence of tobacco interests on the gang at the Air Ministry and on the entourage of General Kondylis, everything points to [the] greater part of [the] new aircraft being ordered from Germany..."

However, Waterlow promised that he would do anything to avoid this tendency, which, in his opinion, could have serious and undesirable political consequences. Subsequently, the British Minister asked the Foreign Office for further instructions and urged that the British authorities make it clear to the Greeks that they were taking a huge moral, and legal, responsibility upon themselves if they bought war equipment in Germany: "...such action by an ex-allied Power is to be strongly deprecated..."[580]

On 19 November the French Embassy warned the Greek government once again that German arms deliveries would constitute a violation of the Versailles Treaty. Theotokis repudiated the charge flatly. On the same day Waterlow came to the conclusion that the Greek request for urgent delivery of modern British aircraft had only served to illuminate the problem that Britain had in delivering at short notice.[581] According to Waterlow the above-mentioned "gang" had played tricks on the British to show that Britain could not fulfil the demands of public tenders: "...gang at the Air Ministry combining with personal entourage of General Kondylis, who is influenced by tobacco interests to which he looks to profit indirectly.[...] Minister of Foreign Affairs [Theotokis] (whose personal integrity I do not question) is obsessed by argument about tobacco and blocked credits..." [582]

Generally speaking, Waterlow felt that in relation to aircraft, the Greeks had been making fools of the British for a long time. For that reason, Waterlow suggested to the Foreign Office that the Greeks be informed that future requests for help would be given a stony reception unless the Greek government changed its present methods radically: "...Probably best time to do this will be after the King is in the saddle. Meanwhile I am doing what I can to gain time [until the King returns on 25 November]..."[583] The British Minister thus advised using the King to oppose the pro-German policy of the Kondilis government.

The Return of the King and Arms Negotiations with Germany
Shortly before his departure from Britain, the Greek King, George II, said in a conversation with Permanent Under-Secretary at the Foreign Office,

138

Sir Robert Vansittart, that he was interested in rearming Greece while at the same time he wanted to limit her dependence on France in military matters. The King regarded Britain as the most important alternative to France and wanted British advisers to all three Greek military services, mainly because the French mission destroyed discipline in the Army.[584]

The comments from the King may indicate that he was more interested in British than in German material. However, it is important to note that he was speaking to his British connections and that he had been out of Greek politics for about 12 years. From a conversation between the German Minister and the King, held later in Athens, it is clear that the latter had a very limited knowledge of Greek-German relations and especially the economic aspects of these, one of the most essential and urgent problems in Greek politics. In addition, at the time of his conversation with Vansittart, the King did not possess sufficient information about the development of Greek-German arms negotiations and related technical considerations.[585]

As the British could support the King only morally and were in no position to offer material aid[586] Germany would almost automatically maintain her central role in the field of arms delivery.[587]

When Kondilis resigned, Greek-German arms negotiations came to a standstill. On 11 December 1935 the issue of armaments orders was on the agenda at a meeting of the so-called Greek Superior Council for the National Defence. The council was headed by the King. On the same day, just before the meeting, the German Minister sought for and obtained a private audience with the King. His purpose was to persuade the King to buy German war equipment.[588]

During a two-hour audience with the King, Eisenlohr put forward the German point of view. He underlined the economic power relations between the two states and hinted that future German purchases of Greek tobacco would be dependent on whether or not the Greeks placed orders for war material with Germany. Moreover, he referred to the "tobacco nerve" and threatened the all important economic and political significance of the trade with Germany to Greece, making it clear to the King: "...that Greece could not live without her German customers and that, in particular, a reduction or cessation of our purchases of tobacco must lead to the impoverishment of the Macedonian peasants and to grave disturbances in Greek domestic politics. Careful fostering of the these [trade] relations was therefore as much an economic as a political imperative..."[589]

Thus, Eisenlohr used Greece's economic and political dependence on the tobacco exports to Germany as a tool to put pressure on the King. In the same breath he mentioned the clearing problem. The German Minister admitted that there were structural problems connected to Greek-German trade but on the other hand the active balance enabled Greece to acquire products from Germany which would otherwise have to be paid for in hard currency: "...It was therefore God-given that Greece should obtain her war material requirements from Germany; there she was able to pay for the major portion of her purchases by her own exports of goods..."[590]

Eisenlohr put forward a central dilemma to Greece regarding her trade with Germany: the choice between a decrease of the export or an increase of the import. The German Minister had proposed a way in which to guarantee the tobacco export and liquidate the outstanding balance on the clearing account: purchase of German war equipment. Furthermore, Eisenlohr took the liberty of mentioning that presumably it was also a matter of paramount importance to the King himself to build up an efficient Greek defence. The German Minister connected this with the prospect of strengthening Greece's international position and in this way the loyalty of the Army towards the King. Thus, Eisenlohr also recommended the purchase of German war equipment for motives related to the King's own political position.[591]

George II replied that it was impossible for him to reach a decision that day; however, he was very grateful to the German Minister for his elucidation, as until then no one had given him a clear explanation of the matter. He intended to bring up the matter in the Defence Council later that day. Subsequently, the King asked Eisenlohr, with astonishing frankness, whom he thought would be suitable to head the reorganization of the Army. At the same time the King complained about a serious lack of expert knowledge in certain people, whom he mentioned by name, within the Greek officer corps. The King described the politicians as a bunch of sick old men but praised Kondilis for his loyalty. He then asked Eisenlohr for an assessment of Theotokis and Varvaresos, both men playing a crucial role in the development of Greek-German relations. The King was displeased with the former because of his independence. However, the German Minister praised both of them and assured the King that he could trust them. Eisenlohr finally took the opportunity to warn the King against a *rapprochement* between the Balkan Entente and the French dominated security system, the Little Entente, which the Romanian Minister of Foreign Affairs was attempting to negotiate at the time. This, according to

Eisenlohr, would in the long view commit the Balkan Entente politically to Central Europe and thus lead to conflicts between Greek and German interests.

No decision to buy German war equipment was reached at the meeting of the Defence Council later that day.[592] Eisenlohr, nevertheless, had the opportunity to give the King a thorough explanation of the German points of view. In addition, the King had betrayed a remarkable tendency to seek advice from foreign advisers; however, it is impossible to know whether he followed Eisenlohr's advice.

Be that as it may, the King immediately disputed the policy of conciliation and informed the German Minister accordingly. During an audience held on 6 January 1936 the King told Eisenlohr that for him the policy of conciliation with the Venizelists was against the grain, although fear of Venizelos's personal power had forced him to undertake this. The German Minister saw this as a positive political turn.[593] Eisenlohr was further encouraged by the fact that during the same period the King had the strength to resist British pressure. The Admiralty in London regarded the Chief of the Greek Naval Staff, Ikonomou, as pro-German, and managed be means of pressure from Waterlow to force Ikonomou to hand in his resignation. However, the King would not accept this and ordered Ikonomou to keep his appointment.[594] Although the King was pro-British, he apparently would not accept British interference in Greece's military affairs. Such interference would probabaly also have met strong opposition from the anti-Venizelist army. Furthermore, Ikonomou had headed the Greek Navy commission which visited Berlin in the second half of 1935, so it is reasonable to presume that he had valuable knowledge about the material that the German armament industry could offer the Greek Navy.

During a meeting held on 8 January 1936 between Rambow, the representative of the German *Ausfuhrgemeinschaft für Kriegsgerät*, the Greek Minister of War, the Greek Minister of Finance and members of the Greek General Staff, the Greek party expressed their continued interest in meeting the acute demand for armaments by means of German equipment. Nevertheless, negotiations could not start until the political situation in Greece was settled, and they asked Rambow to return to Greece after the election on 26 January.[595]

The Greek representatives obviously feared that they would be compromised with an ingoing Venizelist government by ordering war material from Germany. Two days after the election, Kordt considered the consequences to the German interests if a Venizelist government were formed. The situation, he maintained, was "not disadvantageous", as the social stability and economic welfare of the political strongholds of Venizelism, Macedonia and Thrace, were heavily dependent on Germany: the Venizelists had every reason to avoid ruining the good relationship with Germany. An embargo on the German import of tobacco from northern Greece would, according to Kordt, lead to revolution: "...Now it is precisely these provinces that have a vital interest in our purchases of tobacco, i.e. Thrace and Macedonia, and on the 26th voted for the Venizelists by a majority. The Venizelists have to summon all their strength to please these provinces. It is not an overstatement to say that if our purchases of tobacco were cancelled it would soon result in a revolution. Venizelism therefore has every reason to stay on friendly terms with us..."[596]

Kordt saw certain dangers to German interests in the arms trade because of the pro-French Venizelists. After the formation of the caretaker government, German arms dealers had met far less willingness to cooperate in the various ministries than they had under Kondilis. According to the Counsellor, this situation arose because none of the leading personalities in politics or the army would risk making decisions that might tie them to any promises that could destroy their careers if the Venizelists came back into power. In addition, Demerdzis did not show the same personal interest in the purchase of German war equipment that Theotokis and Kondilis did.[597] The report from the German Legation was characterized by dismay and irritation, as even the most elementary procedures created problems, for example the interpreter employed during the negotiations was not able to translate a word like "saddle blanket" into intelligible German. Kordt could not therefore see how they were going to discuss technical details concerning sophisticated anti-aircraft equipment.[598]

The Tobacco Industry, the Clearing Problem and the Arms trade
By early 1936 the political climate in Greece had changed considerably since the time of Kondilis's dictatorship. Furthermore, the arms trade with Germany had become an issue for public debate. This happened at a point

when Greek politics had reached a deadlock and the anti-Venizelists and Venizelists were, at times, manoeuvring in unusual directions to gain power. Furthermore, Greek middlemen were annoyed with plans to organize the arms trade from government to government, as this would ruin their chances of making a profit on commissions. This plan also dissatisfied officials of middle rank in the state administration, who would then lose the prospect of cash payments and other kinds of bribery from enterprising middlemen who wanted to approach civil servants or ministers. According to Kordt this led to a regular "conspiracy" between dissatisfied middlemen and the bureaucracy.[599]

As a consequence of this situation, a large-scale public debate ensued. The above-mentioned 'Greece Consortium' was depicted as a price cartel, trying to sell as expensively as possible. An assessment by *Ausfuhrgemeinschaft für Kriegsgerät*, made at a later date, cited this public criticism as the main reason for the slow progress in Greek-German arms negotiations during the early part of 1936.[600]

Furthermore, it was maintained that some of the tobacco sold to Germany via clearing was resold by Germany on other markets where the price was settled in hard currency.[601] Regarding the 32 million RM which had accumulated on the clearing account in Greece's favour, the press wrote that Germany would try to reduce the purchasing power by devaluation of the Reich Mark, and that a point would come when Greece was in danger of losing her total outstanding in Berlin. The Bank of Greece feared the latter too.[602]

On 20 February the clearing problem was brought before the so-called Superior Council of the National Economic Defence. Shortly before the meeting, Varvaresos told Kordt that, as the representative of the Bank of Greece, he would suggest that Greece placed orders for German war equipment to a total value of 15 million RM.[603] In his statement to the council Varvaresos stressed that the blocked outstandings in Germany posed a threat to the Bank of Greece and the Greek currency reserve. The increasing trade with Germany had a negative effect on hitherto good political and economic relations between Greece and Britain and the United States. Of the 32 million RM on the account, 10 million was in liquidation [i.e. stemming from private clearing]; the planned purchases of German arms to the value of 15 million RM [earlier these purchases were planned to be on a level of some 75-100 million RM] would reduce the outstanding to seven million RM. Varvaresos noted that if the outstandings were to rise again, the state must guarantee the credits. (In this way Varvaresos underlined the fact that the Bank of Greece, as the Bank of issue, could not offer commercial credits: Tsouderos had issued exactly the same warning shortly before his resignation the previous year). However, at the request of government representatives, the council finally decided to stop the further accumulation of credits by refraining from giving guarantees.[604]

This decision would mainly affect tobacco exports and provoked an immediate reaction in northern Greece. The same day all tobacco trade came to a standstill. Representatives from the tobacco industry held a meeting at which they agreed to send a delegation to Athens to persuade the government to alter its decision. Their demands were supported by the National Bank of Greece: the government must withdraw its resolution and continue to guarantee the outstanding: any other decision would be damaging to the tobacco sector.[605]

This combined pressure bore fruit. On 1 March 1936 the government announced that – contrary to its former decision – it would guarantee the outstandings. Waterlow, who was informed of this by Finlayson,[606] announced to the Foreign Office that the altered policy had been decided during a meeting of the Council of National Economic Defence on 29 February. On the same occasion it was decided to raise the value of arms purchases from 15 to 20 million RM. In addition to the permanent members of the Council, the leaders of the political parties and the presidents of the chambers of commerce in Athens and Piraeus were present. Waterlow reported that the meeting was a result of comprehensive protests from chambers of commerce and agricultural organizations affected by the decision announced on 20 February.[607]

The decision called for an extensive increase in the import from Germany, thus requiring considerably more reorganization of the Greek import than had been case in previous years. The British Minister was worried about the implications of the decision: "...If a non-party government [the Demerdzis government] has been prevented by the vested interests which the system [clearing] has fostered from checking a process which is generally recognised as an increasing national danger, what prospect is there that a party government will do any better when those interests have time to entrench themselves still more deeply? [...] the probability seems to me to be that the present course of economic debauchery will continue indefinitely. The forces behind it are powerful; German policy [...] and the cupidity of sectional interests against which no

Greek politician can stand. If the bank is powerless to resist these forces, I see no factors here that can."

Finally, Waterlow concluded: "The future of United Kingdom trade with Greece is not bright if this diagnosis is correct..."[608]

Metaxas's Assumption of Power and the Breakthrough in Greek-German Arms Negotiations

On 5 March 1936 Metaxas was appointed Minister of War and vice-president of the Council of Ministers. The rising political power of Metaxas coincides in a spectacular manner with a substantial breakthrough in Greek-German arms negotiations. As the incarnation of radical anti-Venizelism and an admirer of Germany (especially of German arms) and fiercely anti-French, Metaxas had little to lose.

In connection with Germany's termination of the Locarno Agreement and the German march into the Rhineland the Greek press announced on 12 March 1936 that the Balkan Entente and the Little Entente had agreed to a French and Belgian condemnation of these German acts. However, the Greek government was at pains to stress that Greece was neutral in the Locarno dispute.[609] The Greek government was anxious to show Germany that Greece intended to remain uninvolved in Central European affairs and distance herself from the French-dominated Little Entente. A few days later Kordt told *Auswärtiges Amt* that, among other things, Metaxas was an asset to German interests and one of Germany's reliable friends. Referring to the Greek government's refusal to make the Balkan Entente dependent on the Little Entente, Kordt concluded: "...We have several important friends in the cabinet who will not allow the Balkan Entente to be taken in tow by the Little Entente, that is, by France..."[610]

The attack in the press on the Greece Consortium meant that the Demerdzis government had to give up its plans to make arms deals without inviting public tenders. This resulted in renewed German pressure on the government. *Reichsgruppe Industrie* stressed in a note to Demerdzis that the 'Greece Consortium' was a result of Greek desires to conduct the arms trade on a "government to government" basis, without middlemen.[611]

On 19 March 1936 the Greek General Staff met extraordinarily to discuss the issue of purchases of war equipment from Germany. The discussions were headed by Metaxas.[612] Demerdzis was seriously ill at the

145

time, so Metaxas also functioned as Prime Minister. By the end of March, Metaxas and Kordt were meeting daily to discuss the arms deals.

On 31 March 1936 *Ausfurgemeinschaft für Kriegsgerät* asked State Secretary von Bülow to inform Metaxas that the prolongation of the negotiations was most unsatisfactory.[613]

On the same day Metaxas met Kordt and told him that, as the Minister of War, he was going to place as many orders for war equipment with Germany as possible. Nevertheless, in compliance with public demand he had to compare the German offers to those from other countries, or else he said, referring to the earlier attack from the press, his position would be seriously threatened. In reply, Kordt commented that, if this were the case, several months of work to meet the Greek desire to trade on a "government to government" basis would be wasted. Metaxas replied that he would demand a legislative framework providing special attention to offers from Germany.[614] Kordt then asked Metaxas to meet representatives from the 'Greece Consortium' but Metaxas refused because of its poor reputation. If he started to negotiate with representatives from the Consortium, Metaxas told Kordt, the government would face charges of corruption and of putting aside public interests. Moreover, he feared being personally compromised. Metaxas agreed, albeit reluctantly, to a meeting if Kordt promised to participate in this himself and thus tincture the meeting with an appearance of being concerned with governmental affairs.[615]

The meeting was held on 7 April 1936. According to Kordt Metaxas was still affected by severe public criticism claiming that Germany was trying to "fleece" Greece in the arms trades. Metaxas explained to Kordt that he himself did not believe this and excused public outspokenness by referring to Greece as a parliamentarian state with an inordinate freedom of speech.[616]

About two weeks later Demerdzis died and the King appointed Metaxas as Prime Minister. Kordt believed that the King had made the right decision because Metaxas commanded general trust in the Army. Moreover, Metaxas had the strength to take proper action in case of parliamentary chaos. Kordt even felt that Metaxas would be a better support for the King than Kondilis had been and saw the new premier as the "King's strong man". The Germans also considered it helpful that Metaxas had always been on good terms with the German Legation. Kordt illustated this by mentioning that Metaxas both spoke and wrote German, unlike any of his predecessors.[617]

On 6 May 1936 the government decided to extend Germany's import quota at the expense of other countries.[618] At the same time northern Greece became the scene of the largest ever rising of workers in modern Greek history, culminating on 9 May 1936.[619] On 12 May the trade unions declared a general strike for the following day. *Auswärtiges Amt* immediately asked the Legation in Athens to inform the Greek government that German business circles wanted to see an end to the strike as soon as possible. Moreover, the Germans wanted to know whether the Greek government had any precautions in mind for appropriate handling of the tobacco, should the strike continue.[620]

Due to increasing internal and external pressure to restore social and political peace in the area, the government chose to meet all the tobacco workers' demands.[621] However, by doing this, the need to have a stable market for tobacco exports became ever more urgent. According to Waterlow the Greek government had no other solution to the clearing problem than to increase imports from Germany: "...Recent labour unrest, particulary in the tobacco-growing districts, renders it practically impossible for the Government to impose any solution which [...] would imperil tobacco exports;..."[622]

Indeed, the labour unrest seems to have made Metaxas act quickly in order to further an arms deal with Germany. On 14 May, Kordt and representatives from *Ausfuhrgemeinschaft für Kriegsgerät* met Metaxas, Tsouderos, the Minister of Finance and three officers from the Greek General Staff. Kordt noticed that Metaxas seemed exhausted as a result of the recently ended strike, yet the Greek Prime Minister was quite prepared to discuss arms matters even down to the finest details. According to Kordt the mere reduction of the outstanding on the clearing account was enough to make Metaxas interested in German war equipment. At the Greek Ministry of War there still seemed to be some opposition towards the trade. Some Greek officers feared that Germany would deliver worn-out and old-fashioned weapons. However, Kordt noted that Metaxas was impatient with comments of this kind: "...The Prime Minister [Metaxas] who solely for economic reasons (in order to reduce the Greek assets) is ready to place the orders [for war equipment] with Germany, apparantly wanted to reduce resistance from the specialists in the Ministry of War ad absurdum [...] The questions from the officers were sometimes so poorly founded that Mr. Metaxas [...] became unmerciful. Just to give an example: a colonel attempted to prove that German prices had gone up by referring to a

German tender for pistols in 1930 [...] The Prime Mininster silenced the objection of this uninformed man by the following remark in Greek: 'shut up, you don't understand any of this'..."[623]

Metaxas's reaction made the officers noticeably more cautious. After the meeting Metaxas told Kordt that this was the way to avoid problems, both now and in the future. The German Counsellor left with the impression that the meeting had furthered the matter considerably.[624] On 28 May emergency legislation was put in force that gave the government full authority to place orders for war equipment in Germany:[625] this gave Metaxas a legal entitlement to bypass public tenders. The law also gave the government the option to place state orders where Greece had clearing assets even though the expenses were higher.[626]

From 13-15 June 1936 Hjalmar Schacht, President of the Reichsbank, visited Greece as part of a tour of different capitals in south-eastern Europe. He had meetings with Metaxas, Tsouderos, Varvaresos, the Minister of Finance, the Minister of Economic Affairs and various business people. On 14 June he discussed problems with Tsouderos and Varvaresos arising from the Greek-German trade. The Greeks mentioned with appreciation that the extensive German import of Greek tobacco had raised prices, not only on the German market, but globally. This had stabilized the Greek tobacco market and had made the high prices of German imports easier to accept. The worst hindrance for increased imports from Germany was the low standard of living in Greece which limited the demand for German industrial products.[627]

For this reason, the Greek government was interested in settling the outstanding on the clearing account through the import of war equipment. However, in order to do this a number of problems had to be solved. First, German equipment seemed expensive compared to the prices offered by other countries. Moreover, Greece did not have interpreters to translate technical German into Greek. Finally, the Greeks feared that Germany would sell them old-fashioned equipment. Schacht promised Tsouderos a list of German prices compared to those offered by other countries, and suggested that Greece have a military commission sent to Germany to resolve the two remaining problems. Both Varvaresos and Tsouderos approved Schacht's suggestion.[628]

On the following day, 15 June, Metaxas met Schacht. Metaxas declared that he would expedite the orders for German arms and send a Greek military commission to Germany as soon as possible. Details concerning prices and orders would be settled by negotiations at governmental level. Finally, Metaxas stated that under no circumstances would he negotiate with the 'Greece Consortium'.[629]

Schacht's visit marked a progress in Greek-German arms negotiations, but his presence gave rise to another series of attacks from the press depicting the German Minister's stay in Athens as part of a German economic and political conquest of the Balkans. Shortly after Schacht's visit, Metaxas met von Lupin, managing director of *Ausfuhrgemienschaft für Kriegsgerät*, in Athens.[630] According to Lupin, Metaxas was still very sensitive to public criticism. He was obsessed with guarding himself against possible public attack, fearing that this might bring about his downfall, as he was expecting strong political opposition when the arms deal was concluded.[631]

It is important to bear in mind that Metaxas, with only seven seats out of 300, was undoubtedly in a weak parliamentary position and it is reasonable to assume that he was trying to settle the arms negotiations before parliament sat again in October, in order to be able to present a *fait accompli* to the opposition, primarily the Venizelists. It is perhaps against this background that Metaxas decided to make use of the decree promulgated at the end of June 1936 to purchase German war equipment without inviting public tenders.[632]

Further negotiations were to be held in Berlin. A central issue in these negotiations was the proportion of the total price to be paid by Greece in hard currency. The Germans wanted 25 per cent in hard currency while the Greeks preferred to settle the entire deal by clearing. On 11 July Tsouderos went to the German Legation in Athens. He recommended that the Germans agree to Metaxas's proposition. Tsouderos mentioned, confidentially, that Metaxas's internal political position was weak and that his downfall might well be imminent. This would cause difficulties and delays similar to those which had occurred when Theotokis [and Kondilis] lost their influence in the wake of the return of the King. Moreover, Tsouderos explained that the arms negotiations with Germany had met strong opposition from the public and resulted in attempts to hamper or totally obstruct purchase of arms in Germany. The driving force behind the latter opposition comprised not only discontented businessmen but also, according to Tsouderos, foreign diplomats.[633]

Three days later, on 14 July, Metaxas appeared in person at the German Legation: he announced that he was unable to comply with German requirements concerning a partial currency payment and threatened to resign. This, he said, would mean that all confidential negotiations would be wasted and that Greek public opinion would without doubt be turned against [Greek] connections with Germany.[634]

It is true that Metaxas's position was very weak at the time. However, it is interesting to note that he apparently tried to turn this to his own advantage by giving the Germans the impression that his own political survival was a preliminary condition for, not only a swift and safe conclusion to the armaments deal, but for Greek-German relations as a whole. This must be seen as part of a negotiation strategy adopted to make matters easier for Varvaresos, who was due to arrive in Berlin the following day.[635]

On 22 July the Greek and German representatives agreed that 15 per cent of the price was to be settled in hard currency for purchases up to a value of 60 million RM.[636] In a letter dated the same day, the Greek Minister in Berlin confirmed to Neurath that the Greek government was ready to accept these terms of payment.[637]

Also on 22 July the leaders of both the anti-Venizelists and the Venizelists announced that they were ready to form a government. The agreement was based on the reinstatement of purged Venizelist officers. Waterlow described the agreement as unnatural and saw it as an attempt to prevent Metaxas from winning credit for the forthcoming (and quite sizeable) arms contracts with Germany.[638] This explanation is plausible. Purchase of German arms would enable the rearmament to begin. This would please the army, who, on several occasions recently, had interfered in politics. At the same time it would make possible the liquidation of clearing assets in Berlin, the existence of which had been a political issue for some years. This in turn could also improve prospects for tobacco exports to Germany for some time to come and in that way bring stability to the tobacco world.

On 8 December 1936 Deutsche Golddiskonto Bank[639] and the Greek state concluded a formal agreement concerning financial conditions related to Greek arms purchases from Germany: this is the so-called Schacht-Tsouderos Agreement. The assets on the clearing account enabled Greece to pay cash for purchases up to 34 million RM; the remaining 60 Million RM was to be settled in six-year government bonds. This provided a framework agreement and it was the task of the Greek government to make contracts with the German arms firms. Deutsche Golddiskonto Bank guaranteed the credits and the agreement was declared valid until 30 June 1937.[640]

The breakthrough in the Greek-German arms negotiations on 22 July 1936 and the agreement between the anti-Venizelist and the Venizelist politicians must be seen in relation to the decisions that led to the Metaxas dictatorship, and against the background of Italy's plans for expansion. It must also be seen in the light of the clearing trade and German trade policy. The fact that Greek exports to Germany exceeded Greek imports from Germany made it necessary to increase these imports. To accomplish the latter, comprehensive state intervention during 1934/35 was imperative. However, the initial orders from state and business were not enough to balance Greek-German trade, so it was obvious that the large-scale rearmament project must be based on German equipment. By 1935/36 this left Greek governments a choice between reducing the export to Germany or carrying through an extensive rearmament programme based on German material. A decrease in exports would hit the tobacco industry and threaten the already unstable political and social situation in the tobacco provinces. This made the import of German arms an obvious and urgent solution. Nevertheless, arms cannot be considered a neutral product, but are, on the contrary, an item of high political voltage. The establishment of the dictatorship on 4 August 1936 can be seen as the result of an interaction between traditional conflicts in Greek policy and society and new conflicts created by the world crisis, the latter originated especially by the shift from multilateral trade based on the world market to bilateral exchange of goods without the use of hard currency. Finally, the breakthrough in arms negotiations must also be seen against the background of Germany's trade policy and Italy's assault on Abyssinia.

Hard Currency as a Condition for the Arms Trade

When Göring assumed direct control of *Ausfuhrgemeinschaft für Kriegsgerät*, he ordered, on 5 December 1936, that all exportation of war equipment be settled in hard currency or raw materials essential to the armament production. Nevertheless, it was possible to depart from this rule if "politically desirable".[641] This was a considerable departure from previous conduct regarding trade and currency. *Reichsgruppe Industrie* felt that the

151

regulation should be more subtle if the German industry was not to lose its recently acquired customers. They pointed to Turkey as an example: Germany had just lost a Turkish order valued at 40 million RM because *Ausfuhrgemeinschaft für Kriegsgerät* had insisted that six per cent of the price be settled in hard currency. This, according to *Reichsgruppe Industrie*, was regrettable because the German armament industry was on the brink of establishing itself in south-eastern Europe and it was therefore very important, initially, to ensure Germany a position on the market. This was most easy to achieve in countries where political opposition to arms purchase in Germany was minimal. In this connection Greece was mentioned.[642] In an annual report for 1935/36, *Ausfuhrgemeinschaft für Kriegsgerät* stressed that arms deliveries to Greece would be important to German employment and valuable as an experiment.[643] It was considered that the lessons learned in Greece could be used on other markets. The country was therefore seen as an important part in the bid to expand German arms trade.

In a memorandum to Göring, *Reichsgruppe Industrie* emphasized that arms exports constituted a valuable political tool, as delivery of war material served both as a way to bolster [good] connections and to establish new ones. The relationship with Greece resulting from the arms trade had helped to maintain good political connections. Furthermore, war equipment was valuable as merchandise *per se*. The reorganization of Germany's import from overseas trade to a clearing trade with south-eastern Europe [i.e. the implementation of the *Neuer Plan*] meant that the latter had built up huge outstandings on the clearing account. However, the trade in arms had helped to stop such accumulations on the account at a time when the assets seemed to threaten the [overall] trade. In this way, the arms trade had also helped to ensure Germany's dominant commercial position. Finally, initial deliveries of arms created a demand for future deliveries. To keep these advantages, *Reichsgruppe Industrie* recommended that the demand for 100 per cent of the price to be settled in hard currency be withdrawn.[644]

Thus, it is possible to speak of different objectives within Germany's arms trade policy. Göring tried to secure an immediate supply of hard currency and raw materials essential to armament production, whereas *Reichsgruppe Industrie* saw the delivery of arms in the light of broad and long-term politics and trade. Nonetheless, an agreement between *Reichs-*

gruppe Industrie and Göring was reached, namely that the demand for total settlement in hard currency be repealed when it was "politically desirable".

In March 1937, negotiations between the German armament companies and the Greek authorities reached a deadlock. The disagreement was partly technical and partly military. Regarding the former, the Greeks refused to 1) guarantee the German companies' currency risk; 2) cover the expenses related to financing the credits; 3) pay more than the cash price.[645] The military disagreement arose because the Greeks wanted German artillery equipment delivered with firing tables.

On 29 March 1937 Tsouderos approached Schacht and asked him to intervene to the advantage of Greece. Following a meeting with *Ausfuhrgemeinschaft für Kriegsgerät*, the German Minister of Economic Affairs decided to give in to Greek pressure and call back the representatives from the 'Greece Consortium'. To the Greek authorities Schacht described the episode as a regrettable misunderstanding.[646] In a similar way, the disagreement about firing tables was solved when superior German authority took action, by Blomberg ordering that the tables be delivered to the Greeks.

This rift delayed the orders considerably and, on 1 June 1937, a month before the Schacht-Tsouderos agreement expired, the President of the Bank of Greece applied for an extension of the agreement with Deutsche Golddiskontobank.[647] The German Legation recommended that the Bank comply with Greek wishes on the grounds of the existing good relationship between the Legation and the Bank of Greece and the significance of a successful arms deal to Greek-German trade connections. On 8 July 1937 the German Ministry of Economy announced that the agreement had been extended until 31 October 1937.[648]

Two weeks later, on 22 July 1937, Göring issued a decree that, in future, trade in arms be settled 100 per cent in hard currency.[649] In the same month the Dornier factories presented their latest model, the bomber Dornier Do 17, at an international competition for military aircraft held in Zürich. The qualities of the aircraft aroused enthusiasm among military experts and the Dornier factories received many orders,[650] including some from the Greek Air Force.

Permission to export the aircraft had to be obtained from the German Ministry of Aviation, which was controlled by Göring. The head of the General Staff in the Greek Air Force, Colonel Ghaziz, was very interested in the aeroplane. He informed Dornier that if exports of the bomber were

153

permitted he would abandon public tenders and place the order directly with the German aircraft company.

At the beginning of September 1937 permission was given for the aeroplane to be exported. However, at the same time, Göring's demand for settlement in hard currency was announced. This came as a great disappointment to the Greeks. The purchase of the German aircraft was a matter of prestige to Colonel Ghaziz and the failure threatened his position seriously.[651] As a response to this, the Greek authorities refused to buy the bomber on the new conditions; at the beginning of October, Dornier's managing director decided to go to Athens hoping to persuade the Greeks to revise their decision, but he returned to Germany shortly after without having achieved any success. The German Legation then asked Rheinmetall-Borsig to put pressure on the German authorities to waive their claim for 100 per cent settlement in hard currency. Not only did the Legation see the demand as impracticable, but it also feared that the Greek authorities would see it as a hostile action.[652] It is important to note that the German representation in Athens expressed its discontent at the demand through one of Görings's parastate companies, Rheinmetall-Borsig.[653]

On 19 October 1937 the German Ministry of Aviation offered to trade the Dornier Do 17, settling for 30 per cent in hard currency and 70 per cent on the clearing account.[654] However, Greece would not accept the offer and instead an order for Potez planes was placed in France.

The problems connected to the purchase of the Dornier aircraft undoubtedly made it difficult to finish the Greek armament orders before the Schacht-Tsouderos agreement expired on 31 October 1937. With reference to this the Greeks applied for a further extension of the agreement, so that the deadline would be 31 December 1937.[655]

On 8 December 1937, the anniversary of the Schacht-Tsouderos agreement, Varvaresos and Mavroudis had a meeting with Erbach. Varvaresos complained that the German authorities were unwilling to extend the Schacht-Tsouderos agreement beyond the 31 December 1937 and that they were also demanding renegotiation of the exchange quota. Varvaresos believed that the exchange quota was independent of the Schacht-Tsouderos agreement and hence the German wish to renegotiate the quotas was unacceptable. Erbach warned *Auswärtiges Amt* that a breaking-off of the arms deliveries could have serious consequences for German trade with Greece as well as for the German position in the country as whole.[656]

Erbach stressed that the arms deliveries were a preliminary condition for a strong German position in Greece. He felt that the cancellation of the terms of credit and payment agreed upon in the Schacht-Tsouderos agreement involved a serious and realistic risk of breaking-off the trade: this would give both Britain and France the opportunity to regain their positions.[657]

Erbach's fear was not a figment of his imagination: it was mirrored in disagreements about the financial conditions attached to the trade of the Dornier aircraft and in the mere fact that the Greek Air Force placed orders in France. The German Minister was anxious for the German authorities to understand this, and, in consequence, to accept the Greek terms. In a personal letter dated 10 December 1937 Erbach addressed Hans Georg von Machensen, State Secretary in *Auswärtiges Amt*.[658] Erbach referred to his letter from the previous day and stressed that German participation in the Greek rearmament had given several profitable advantages to German interests. Erbach mentioned the role of German officers as advisers in the enlargement of the Greek coastal defence and the participation of German experts in the improvement of the Greek railroads. As Erbach put it, "our by the British, French, Italians and Americans equally envied position" would be seriously threatened if Germany insisted on terms of payment prescribing 100 per cent of the price in hard currency.[659]

Erbach's letter resulted in a debate at the German Ministry of Economy headed by Spitta, the director. He stressed that the Schacht-Tsouderos agreement and Göring's demand for total settlement in hard currency constituted a problem for Greek-German trade. Greece had at that time spent the 60 million RM (with the exception of one million RM) included in the Schacht-Tsouderos agreement.[660] In the light of the above- mentioned problems, Spitta suggested that production equipment need not be characterized as arms and could therefore be deducted from the total orders for German arms placed hitherto (these orders amounted to 10-15 million RM). This would give Greece the opportunity to purchase arms for an additional 10-15 million RM on the terms of 15 per cent in hard currency and 85 per cent through clearing. According to Spitta this would be sufficient to cover Greek arms purchases in the forthcoming year, 1938. The German government decided in favour of this proposal.[661]

In this connection it is significant that, apart from Scandinavia and Argentina, with whom arms were settled 100 per cent through clearing, Greece had the most easy terms of payment among Germany's customers. Furthermore, the Greek exchange quota was considerably lower than the exchange quota in the rest of south-eastern Europe.[662] This indicates that Germany, at least until the turn of the year 1937/38, was eager to maintain good political relations with the Metaxas government and one could say that the Germans exchanged arms for political goodwill. In addition, the arms trade with Greece was seen as pioneer work to enhance German trade interests overall: these interests had experienced a veritable boom in Greece since Metaxas assumed power.[663]

The Expansion of the Powder and Cartridge Company and Increasing Dependence on German Technology and Know-How

The expansion of the Powder and Cartridge Company began immediately after Bodosakis took over the firm in 1934. In the same year he made an agreement with the German explosives company, the Köln-Rottweil Powder Factory.[664] The latter was controlled by IG Farben through a cartel agreement,[665] which shortly after gained a monopoly of the German explosives production. As a consequence, the value of Greek ammunition production increased from 8.3 million RM (332 million Dr.) in 1935 to 35.4 million RM (1.42 billion Dr.) in 1936, a growth factor exceeding four.[666]

On 19 September 1935 Bodosakis concluded a so-called friendship agreement with the German armaments company Rheinmetall-Borsig.[667] The company had played an important part in the international arms trade since the early 1930s as a result of deliveries to China. Moreover, Rheinmetall-Borsig occupied a leading position during the Spanish Civil War as a result of deliveries to the export monopoly ROWAK. Accordingly, Rheinmetall-Borsig became a part of Göring's parastate apparatus. The firm was export oriented: thus in 1938 and 1939 sales abroad amounted to about 25 per cent of the total sale of arms.[668]

The company's affiliation to Göring's complex was strengthened even further in June 1938, when Reichswerke Hermann Göring purchased the majority holding in Rheinmetall-Borsig from Vereinigte Industrieunternehmungen AG (VIAG).[669] Moreover, Hellmuth Roehnert, managing director of the company since 1938, held several important appointments within the German armament industry[670] and was appointed to head the so-called "Arms Bloc" in Reichswerke Hermann Göring after *Anschluss* and the occupation of Czechoslovakia.[671]

In a strictly confidential letter dated 8 April 1937 from Rheinmetall-Borsig to the German export control agency, *Überwachungsstelle für Eisen und Stahl* (Control Office for Iron and Steel),[672] the company outlined its role in relation to the Greek Powder and Cartridge Company. The agreement signed in 1935 committed Rheinmetall-Borsig to continuous delivery of steel products and steel semi-manufactures for the Powder and Cartridge Company. In return, the Greek firm had to deliver a certain amount of scrap metal.[673] By means of technical know-how and delivery of machinery, Rheinmetall-Borsig controlled the technical organization of production and the development of production facilities.[674]

During a ceremony held on 18 March 1937, attended by the King, Metaxas and representatives from the German company, a number of new engine shops, capable of producing artillery ammunition ranging from 75 mm to 155 mm, were opened: previously the factory had only been capable of producing calibres of up to 75 mm. This enabled the factory, technically, to supply most of the calibres used in the Greek army. Rheinmetall-Borsig saw this as a significant step forward for German interests because it would ensure continuous orders for the German engineering industry. Moreover, the German company saw prospects of additional orders being placed for German war equipment.[675] In October 1937, after a meeting with Papagos, the German firm noted that it virtually enjoyed a monopoly in the Greek army.[676]

On 7 October 1937 the Greek company purchased the licence to produce 20 mm and 37 mm anti-aircraft grenades at Rheinmetall-Borsig. These were used for Rheinmetall-Borsig's anti-aircraft and anti-tank guns, which, along with Krupp 88 mm, constituted the backbone of this section of the Greek artillery. The licence was approved by Göring, who insisted that 100 per cent of the price be paid in hard currency.[677]

Rheinmetall-Borsig noted that Metaxas was well disposed towards Germany and that he also asked the company to provide the Powder and Cartridge Company with technical assistance and know-how in the future to ensure Greece's self-sufficiency within ammunition production. According to Rheinmetall-Borsig this would further safeguard its own position within Greece's military and industrial rearmament.[678]

Rheinmetall-Borsig saw the cooperation with the Powder and Cartridge Company as part of a strategy, best characterized by Max Ilgner, as "*Exportsteigerung durch Einschaltung in die Industrialisierung der Welt*", i.e. expansion "without currency" based on the technical and scientific superiority of German industry and, in this particular case, a Greece dependent on exports to Germany.

Consequences for International Competition: French Influence is Weakened

Until the agreement of 1935 the French company Schneider-Creusot enjoyed a monopoly in Greece. For several years Rheinmetall-Borsig had tried to take over Schneider-Creusot's position on the Greek market. Greece's internal political development, the restoration of the Monarchy and Metaxas's assumption of power helped Rheinmetall-Borsig to enter the Greek market and to take over contractual undertakings with the Greek Powder and Cartridge Company form Schneider-Creusot.[679]

This has a clear connection with the rearmament programme: if the Powder and Cartridge Company had remained dependent on Schneider-Creusot it would have been difficult to finance the Greek rearmament plans, due to the limited export from Greece to France.

Greek-French trade was settled on a clearing account,[680] the average value of Greek exports to France in the period 1935-1937 being 228 million Dr. a year.[681] In the period September 1935 to August 1940 the Powder and Cartridge Company purchased equipment to the value of about 45 to 55 million RM in Germany or 1.8 to 2.2 billion Dr., an average of approximately 360 to 440 million Dr. a year. Bewteen 35 and 45 million RM (1.4-1.8 billion Dr.) was spent between March 1937 and March 1939, an average of 700 million Dr. to 900 million Dr. a year.[682]

Given the small French demand for Greek products it would have been impossible to extend the Greek export to France sufficiently to cover Greek rearmament demands from France.

In addition, Rheinmetall-Borsig had the technical know-how needed to deliver the necessary production facilities to manufacture the German 88 mm, 37 mm and 20 mm anti-aircraft and anti-tank guns which had a high priority in Greek defence policy.

Bodosakis mentions that one of the reasons for breaking off cooperation with the French armament firm was that it was unable to deliver production facilities of a sufficiently modern standard.[683] This, added to the fact

158

that the French armament industry could not deliver arms of a recent date, would have obstructed the implementation of Metaxas's large scale and ambitious rearmament programme.

Furthermore, Rheinmetall-Borsig believed that cooperation between the Metaxas regime and the French armament industry was politically impossible unless a radical political change in Greece took place. In this connection Rheinmetall-Borsig felt that Metaxas's political success was dependent on a good relationship between the Powder and Cartridge Company and the German firm.[684] This assessment was probably designed to put pressure on the German authorities, who saw Metaxas as an asset to German policy. It must be stressed, however, that military and industrial rearmament, as well as self-sufficiency, was of paramount importance to the Metaxas regime.

This is corroborated by the fact that in 1937 the Greek king told the managing director of Rheinmetall-Borsig during an audience that the Greek defence would be left helpless without German deliveries of arms and, in particular, of semi-manufactures. In addition, the Powder and Cartridge factory was ready, and obtained permission from the Greek government, to pay 15 per cent of the price of steel deliveries and 50 per cent of the price of machinery and tools in hard currency. The latter (50 per cent) was considerably higher than the 15 per cent quota that the Greek government had been willing to pay earlier for arms which held a high priority in Metaxas's programme.[685] Furthermore, as already noted, the Powder and Cartridge Company paid 100 per cent of the price in hard currency for Rheinmetal-Borsig patents.

Rheinmetall-Borsig's cooperation with the Powder and Cartridge Company was the first German encroachment on the position held by the French steel industry in south-eastern Europe. Schneider-Creusot served as France's industrial spearhead in the area. The French firm controlled Skoda, the leading Czechchoslovak company within steel and armament production: by this means, France also controlled the industry in both Romania and Yugoslavia.[686] An agreement made by the International Steel Cartel assured the Czechoslovak steel industry a share of 70 per cent of the south-eastern European markets in Albania, Yugoslavia, Bulgaria and Romania through the trade cartel Zentraleuropäische Gruppe der internationalen Rohstahlgemienschaft. This agreement provides one of the best examples of power policy put forward by the Treaty of Versailles.[687]

Greece was not included in this agreement. Nevertheless, Rheinmetall-Borsig saw cooperation with the Powder and Cartridge Company as an advantageous step in its competition with French industry in south-eastern Europe. Consequently, Rheinmetall-Borsig considered it important to maintain the relationship with the Greek firm in order to prevent Schneider-Creusot from regaining its former position; if this were not done, the newly established German stronghold in the Balkans, as Rheinmetall-Borsig put it, would be endangered.[688]

In the second half of 1937 Rheinmetall-Borsig judged that it had no stronghold in the world to compare with its position in Greece.[689] This must be explained by the fact that the French steel and armament industry still had a firm grip on the rest of south-eastern Europe, especially on Yugoslavia and Romania, and that it was not until Germany's conquest of Central Europe in 1938 by *Anschluss* and by the Munich Agreement that she achieved a major breakthrough in these countries. Furthermore, it is important to note that the trade with the Powder and Cartridge Company produced considerably more hard currency in Germany's favour than previous arms trade with south-eastern Europe had done. Finally, cooperation with the Powder and Cartridge Company was expected to guarantee long-term sales.

According to an assessment by Rheinmetal-Borsig, the breakthrough of the German armament industry in Greece and the subsequent consolidation of its position was primarily due to internal political factors: the restoration of the Monarchy in 1935 and the establishment of the Metaxas dictatorship in 1936.[690] This seems plausable. At the same time it implies that it was above all the internal political development in Greece that had enabled the German armaments industry to gain a stronghold in Greece much earlier than in any other south-eastern European country and thus to establish itself in a country which was allied with Romania and Yugoslavia, members of the anti-German Little Entente. According to Rheinmetall-Borsig this made the Metaxas regime a most important asset to German political and economic interests in that part of the world. In addition, Greece could also provide access to the Mediterranean and a platform to the Orient. In order to investigate further these aspects of Greek-German relations, the following chapter will focus on Greece's exports of war material and Germany's response to these activities.

160

ARMS TRADE II: GREEK EXPORT OF ARMS

Greece and the Trade in Arms

The Greek arms trade received so much international attention that the American journalist Frank Gervasi started an investigation and published the results in the American weekly magazine *Collier's* in 1940. In an article entitled "Devil Man", featuring Bodosakis as the main character, Gervasi depicted the owner of the Powder and Cartridge Company as one of the most important arms dealers in the Mediterranean area. Trade was conducted in close collaboration with the Greek government. Bodosakis sold redundant weapons from Greek military depots and ammunition from the Greek Powder and Cartridge Company in order to bring hard currency to Greece. Gervasi states that Greek export of arms to Turkey in 1940 amounted to 1.2 million US$ (about 250 million Dr.) and trade with China amounted to 0.3 million US$ (about 70 million Dr.). According to Gervasi the arms trade was Greece's second largest source of income, after tobacco.[691]

Greek national statistics show the export value of arms in the years 1937 and 1938 as 400 million Dr. and 176 million Dr, respectively. These figures, however, make up only 4.2 and 1.7 per cent of total exports in those years.[692] It is therefore important to bear in mind that the figures do not include the illegal arms trade or any trade that the authorities did not wish to make public. For this reason it is likely that the trade was considerably more lucrative than the official figures suggest.

According to Hill, Greece entered into large-scale agreements for arms deliveries to Republican Spain, Turkey, Romania and China in the second half of the 1930s, and, after the outbreak of the war, Britain was added to the list.[693] In this connection it is important to stress that the Powder and Cartridge Company relied mainly on private finance to support plans for expansion. Until the second half of 1939, investments in new plants and machinery were, except for one order in 1937, for the production of bombs for the Greek Air Force, and were financed by loans and the international arms trade. A report for the year 1937, dated 15 July 1938 and addressed to the company's Annual General Meeting, states that: "...Our plants and technological progress have given the firm a world-wide reputation and made it an important factor on the international market..."[694]

Considering the dramatic and costly expansion of the Powder and Cartridge Company in the period 1936-1939, it is reasonable to assume that part of its production was used for export. To elucidate Greece's role as supplier of arms, we must now to turn to Spain, where the Civil War created a flourishing market for illegal trade in arms during the 1930s.

Greek Export of Arms to Spain
In February 1937 the American Ambassador claimed that the Greeks re-exported to Spain a huge quantity of the arms they received from Germany. According to information he had obtained from British intelligence officers, this partly explained an increased Greek arms import from Germany.[695] Gervasi claims that Bodosakis conducted a systematic "two-way trade" with both sides involved in the Spanish Civil War, and the annual report by the British Minister in 1937 made the same point: that Greece was selling arms to both warring factions in Spain. The Greek government had already decreed a law prohibiting trade of this kind, yet, as noted in the above-mentioned annual report: "... the main occupation of the government appears to have been to make as much money as possible by selling war material to both sides, and chiefly to the Republicans. In this they [the Greeks] were thoroughly successful. Exports of arms and munitions rose by leaps and bounds, and proved a fruitful source of foreign exchange. They were financed through a Paris bank, and the emissary of the Spanish government in charge of the negotiations, one [Moses] Rosenberg,[696] visited Athens more than once during the year. ..."[697]

According to rumours which the Greek Ambassador in London judged to be reliable, Greek ships were willing to be captured by the Nationalists if the price was high enough and thus the cargo fell into the hands of the rebels.[698] This was very profitable because the Republicans had already paid for the arms before embarkation. Gervasi mentions that Bodosakis had a central role in this trade. He was joint owner of a shipping company whose only route was to Spain.[699] A German report, dated 1940, concerning Greek shipping confirms that Bodosakis and Theophanidis, a notorious gun-runner,[700] owned the shipping company Davaris, which had its head-quarters in Piraeus.[701] According to his own account, Bodosakis started selling to the Republican government soon after the beginning of hostilities in 1936. His terms for dealing with the Republicans were that the shipments should be paid for in gold or in hard cash and in advance, a so-called "100% irrevocable credit". Bodosakis in turn would arrange all the practical details necessary for war materials to get through the international blockade of Spain. All shipments to the Republicans were declared bound for Mexico. As soon as the ship was loaded in Piraeus it would head for a desolate island in the Greek archipelago. When the name and papers of the vessel had been changed the ship would sail for Spain; if stopped en route the captain would claim that he was bound for Mexico.[702]

Furthermore, Bodosakis stresses that he procured huge quantities of grenades, mines and powder from Germany. This was achieved with the help of the Greek government, which officially assured Germany that the equipment was meant for the Greek army. Bodosakis explains that the demand from Spain was so great that he suggested to Metaxas that redundant weapons arms in the stores of the Greek army be resold. The Greek Ministry of War opposed this, so Bodosakis's trade with old military equipment was limited to a small scale.

Moreover, Bodosakis explains that the Powder and Cartridge Company made an agreement with the Republicans in September 1936, just after the outbreak of the Civil War, to deliver 5 million cartridges. Metaxas was enthusiastic about the trade because the Republicans paid in hard currency and in advance. Even before the original order was settled, a new order for 20 million cartridges was received. This created a demand for larger production facilities at the plants, a demand met by the above-mentioned orders for machinery placed in Germany.[703] These facts correspond very well with the impression that the trade secretary at the British mission obtained during a visit to the Powder and Cartridge Company at the end of 1937. Bodosakis made no secret of the fact that the factories were working at high pressure to meet the orders from Spain and told the British visitor quite openly that he was interested in stepping up the company's international activities in the Far East as well as in the Middle East. The trade secretary reported: "...The factory, which has been working on a 24 hour schedule for some time past chiefly to supply orders received from Spain, is being considerably enlarged [...] great activity was visible on all sides and new machinery was being installed in every available space in the existing factories.[...] the managing director [Bodosakis] drew his [the trade secretary's] attention to the advantageous geographical position of Greece and her facilities for supplying any Mediterranean country and even the Far and Middle East. He stated that so far he had received no orders from China for small arms ammunition but that the factory was working full-time on orders from Spain..."[704]

Koliopoulos mentions that ten aircraft had been assembled under German supervision at an annexe to the Powder and Cartridge Company and afterwards flown by German pilots to unknown destinations, most probably Spain;[705] this, at least, was what MacVeagh believed.[706]

Bodosakis explains that, in November 1937, he flew via Paris to Barcelona in a Soviet aeroplane to sign a contract with the Republicans for a delivery of ammunition to a total value of £ 2.1 million (about 1.2 billion Dr.): this alone would have constituted about 12 per cent of the total Greek export that year.[707]

Spanish Nationalists held Metaxas and Bodosakis responsible for the arms deliveries to the Republicans. This is made clear by the contents of a box in the Metaxas archive which includes a photograph, stamped by the Nationalist Ministry of the Interior, of four dead men. On the back is written: "Objectivos militares – Obreros gente pacifica asesinada por la metralla rusa" (Workers, peaceful people murdered by Russian grenades), and in French: "Il y a sur la place centrale de Salamanca, un cadre en fer forgé pour exposer un jour la peau bien tendu du soi-disant Président du Conseil, M.Metaxas, et de ses associés, Diakos, Bondozakis [Bodosakis], et Cie." (On the main square of Salamanca [the headquarters of the National-ists] stands a plaque in cast iron to display at some date the skins of Mr. Metaxas – who calls himself Prime Minister – and his companions Diakos [close friend and assistant to Metaxas], Bodozakis [Bodosakis] and Co.).[708]

With the photograph is a personal and confidential letter to Metaxas dated Burgos 30 May 1938 and signed by the head of the Greek Legation, M. P. J. Arghiropoulos.[709] The letter refers to material collected by the Nation-alist intelligence and passed on to the Greek representative in Burgos to prove that Greece delivered arms to the Republicans. The following are extracts from the letter, translated into English:

1) Photograph of coded telegram from Admiral Sakelariou [vice secretary to the navy] to Mr. Politis in Paris [Greek Ambassador to France] and a photograph of the confirmatory document, a request to support Theophanidis, Bodosakis's representative, and the purchase of 30 155 mm canons on the Powder Company's account. To this I [Arghiropoulos] said that it was to be used to fortify the Saronic Bay.
2) Photograph of Bodosakis – Plastiras – Alexandris [middleman for Bodosakis] [...] in Paris discussing arms deliveries etc.
3) Photograph of written authorization from the political office with signature "Metaxas" [...] to the port authorities in relation to shipments [of arms.] etc.
4) Photograph from Dr.Lorandos's[710] house (Bucharest Street [in Athens] where Mr. Diakos is present. Conversation about orders, shipments etc. [of arms])

Bodosakis confirms points one and three, as he explains that he supplied the Republicans with guns. The latter were bought in third countries under the pretext that they were for the Greek army. Metaxas fully supported this trade and the Greek authorities helped to obtain the equipment, declaring that it was meant for the Greek armed forces.[711] Papagos states that the Greek army found the French 155 mm guns unsuitable and thus excludes the possibility that these weapons were bought for Greece.[712] However, the collected material does not reveal whether the guns were actually purchased.

According to Koliopoulos, whose figures are based on Tsouderos, Greece made £ 600,000 in 1937 (300 million Dr.) from trade with Franco. The money was transferred to an account in the British and French Discount Bank:[713] this was probably Bodosakis's own account.[714]

A conservative estimate of the aggregate value of exports of war material to the Republicans in 1937 would be £ 2.1 million (1.2 billion Dr.) This figure alone would make the arms trade the second most important commodity in Greek exports. However, the estimate is based on an agreement concluded in November 1937 and does not cover substantial deliveries during the preceding year, nor does it cover the deals Bodosakis made with the Nationalists.

It is reasonable to conclude that the Powder and Cartridge Company received substantial orders from Spain, at least in 1936 and 1937, and that the earnings from this trade were considerable, not least because payment

165

was settled in hard currency. This income was apparently used to expand the Powder and Cartridge Company and therefore fulfil one of Metaxas's most important objectives: the provision of facilities to ensure self-sufficiency within ammunition production.

Germany and the Powder and Cartridge Company's Deliveries of Arms to the Republicans

Transactions between the Powder and Cartridge Company and the Republicans in Spain constituted an essential element in the financial basis for the company's expansion and in that way also for its demand for machinery and steel from Germany, mainly from Rheinmetall-Borsig. The total German sales to the Powder and Cartridge Company between 1935-1940 amounted to somewhere between 45 million and 55 million RM. In the period between March 1937 and March 1939, that is during the Spanish Civil War, sales peaked to between 35 and 45 million RM, i.e. an average of 17.5 – 22.5 million RM per year.[715] As 50 per cent of the payments for machinery and 100 per cent for patents were settled in hard currency this meant that the Powder and Cartridge Company's trade with the Republicans constituted a source of hard currency for Germany, and, in effect, a very important one. German reserves of hard currency and gold had fallen dramatically since the beginning of the Depression and in 1937 they reached a low ebb of 70 million RM, threatening to dry up completely in 1938.[716] In this way hard currency and gold, stemming from trade with the Greek Powder and Cartridge Company, would represent somewhere between 13 per cent and 16 per cent of total reserves in Germany. This must have made transactions between the Powder and Cartridge Company and the Republicans very attractive to Göring, at least in a strictly economic sense.

In addition, Germany and Italy were competing for influence in central and south-eastern Europe. Although Italy had fewer economic resources at her disposal than Germany, her military and economic involvement in Spain was considerably greater. This also meant that while substantial economic earnings were related to Germany's engagement in Spain, Italy's involvement in Spain had a draining effect on her economy.[717] As a result, scarce Italian resources were channelled away from central and south-eastern Europe. It has been suggested that Hitler saw Spain as another opportunity to advance German policy in Eastern Europe.[718] Supplying the Republicans would tie Italian resources to the south-western periphery of

Europe and in that way indirectly help Germany to fulfil the above-mentioned plan. It is also worth recalling that Germany had previously sought to keep Italy busy in Africa through arms deliveries to Abyssinia in order to strengthen her own position in Austria and south-eastern Europe.

In February 1934, Pabst, president of *Waffen- und Verkaufszentrale* (The Main Office of Arms and Sales) in Rheinmetall-Borsig, was contacted by a Greek citizen who wanted to buy arms. He claimed to have good connections with the head of General Staff and the Ministry of War in Athens, and said that he was involved in negotiations for extensive arms deliveries to Abyssinia. At this early stage Pabst could only treat the proposal as "music from the future";[719] however, in 1935 Bülow told Neurath that arms deliveries to Abyssinia had to be conducted through shadow firms abroad in order not to disturb good relations with Italy. In this connection Rheinmetall-Borsig was mentioned as a possible supplier.[720] Bülow must be referring to already existing or planned arms deliveries arranged behind Italy's back.

In June 1935 a German delegation visited certain Greek factories. According to Waterlow the Germans used the occasion to obtain interests in the Powder and Cartridge Company and a textile factory. The latter supplied the Greek army and worked at high pressure to meet demands from the Abyssinian army.[721] This does not verify Greek-German cooperation concerning arms delivery to Abyssinia, however, although it makes it possible to speak of common Greek-German interests in this field. The Greeks were in possession of the means and connections to conduct secret shipments to Abyssinia. The Greek colony in Abyssinia constituted an important link between internal and external trade, while several of the Greeks in the country occupied prominent positions: for example, the Greek Consul-General in Addis Abeba was the personal doctor and close friend of Haile Selassi.[722] Furthermore, Rheinmetall-Borsig was aware that Greek arms dealers with good connections to the Greek government were willing to cooperate over the export of war material.

In the summer of 1935 Göring started negotiations with the Spanish government for arms deliveries in return for raw materials or hard currency.[723] As usual, economic interests were of paramount importance to Göring and his policy towards Franco echoed this.

In March 1938 *Wehrwirtschaftsstab* in *Oberkommando der Wehrmacht* asked Rheinmetall-Borsig to reply to rumours that the firm was participating indirectly in arms deliveries to the Republicans. The Nationalist Ambassador to Germany told Göring that the Greek Ministries of War and of Marine as well as the Powder and Cartridge Company were re-exporting German war material and ammunition to the Republicans. *Wehrwirtschaftsstab* ordered Rheinmetall-Borsig to investigate the case in strict confidence and inform no other [German] authorities of the results. One of the allegations was that Bodosakis had delivered 70,000 rifles to the Republicans.[724]

Rheinmetall-Borsig announced that it was ready to investigate the allegations in relation to the Greek Ministries of War and of Marine. Nevertheless, concerning the Powder and Cartridge Company, the German firm denied everything, explaining that it only delivered know-how and machinery. The outcome was that Rheinmetall-Borsig maintained that the accusation against Bodosakis had very little to do with the firm, and the only connection between them was related to his function as president of Rheinmetall-Borsig Athens, a branch of the German firm in Greece. Nevertheless, the German firm continued to deny the accusations categorically and maintained that the cooperation between Rheinmetall-Borsig and the Greek military commission, the Greek administration, and the army, was so close that it would be impossible for the Greeks to keep such activities hidden. Moreover, Rheinmetall-Borsig's participation in the Greek rearmament extended to even the smallest detail. This, according to Rheinmetall-Borsig, would make it impossible [for the Greeks] to conceal any so-called "dirty tricks", i.e. the re-sale of German arms to the Republicans.

As a further argument that the rumours were false, Rheinmetall-Borsig pointed to the Greek regime's goodwill towards the German firm and National Socialist Germany. It was stressed that both the King and Metaxas recognized the achievements of the Third Reich and its philosophy. Rheinmetall-Borsig therefore considered it impossible for Greece to act "hypocritically" and ship as much as a single consignment of arms to the Republicans: "...It appears unthinkable that all these people – if the rumours are true – could have hypocritically shipped a single load of arms to Soviet-Spain, – the more so, as his Majesty, the King of the Hellenes, in particular, and Prime Minister Metaxas have expressed their special recognition of the achievements of the Third Reich and declared themselves friends of National Socialist thinking..."[725]

As demonstrated above Rheinmetall-Borsig did any time possible to deny the rumours. Colonel Rohde, the German Military Attaché in Athens and Ankara, was subquently commissioned to conduct an additional investigation into the rumours. Rohde attempted to trace and register all arms delivered to the Greek army by Rheinmetall-Borsig. However, his work can hardly be seen as a full-scale investigation: thus, on Greece's national day, Rohde attended the military parade in Athens and counted the German-manufactured guns as they rolled by. The German Military Attaché reached twenty-six 20 mm cannon and eight 37 mm cannon while he saw no 88 mm ones.[726] These figures are quite disparate from those stated in other sources.[727] Although he had not inspected the area personally, Rohde stated that the rest of the guns were in northern Greece, where [Rheinmetall-Borsig] specialists were preparing them for use. This brought him to the conclusion that the rumours were pure imagination. However, he could not repudiate the accusations concerning the delivery of rifles. Rohde regarded it as possible, but not certain, that the Greek army had sold redundant rifles to arms dealers who had then resold them to the Republicans. Nevertheless, he maintained that the Greek government knew nothing of this. He did not state whether Bodosakis was the supplier or not.

The German Military Attaché suspected that a certain Likourgos Sarsentis had started the rumours. Sarsentis already had a bad reputation and Rohde was surprised that anyone believed him at all.[728]

Sarsentis had been working as Rheinmetall-Borsig's representative until 1937/38 when the German firm got rid of him, probably due to disagreements about commissions. Thereafter, the German firm established a branch in Athens on the initiative of Bodosakis, who was also appointed chairman of the board of directors. Furthermore, in 1936 Sarsentis became involved in a dispute with Metaxas because, Metaxas felt, he seriously threatened on-going arms negotiations between Greece and Germany.[729]

In February 1937 Sarsentis informed Rheinmetall-Borsig that the Powder and Cartridge Company delivered arms to the Republicans.[730] His information was discussed at the highest level of the firm during a meeting held on 27 May 1937 between Luther, managing director at that time, and the board of directors. They concluded that Sarsentis's allegation was ill-founded and Luther declared that he was ready to take full responsibility for the trade with Greece [i.e. with the Powder and Cartridge Company] in the future.[731]

On 26 September 1937 Sarsentis repeated his allegation in writing.[732] This time Rheinmetall-Borsig informed Clodious from *Auswärtiges Amt*, APA, and *Abwehr* that the Powder and Cartridge Company was delivering war material to the Republicans.[733] This possibly came about because Sarsentis threatened to inform the German authorities about the case.[734] Meanwhile, the German firm investigated the possibility of a lawsuit against Sarsentis for defamation.[735]

From talks between Rheinmetall-Borsig and the German Legation in Athens in October 1937, it is clear that the official German line was to refrain from taking any action as long as the Greek government supervised deliveries by the Powder and Cartridge Company. The Legation approved of the official German decision, and felt that it was impossible to prove that Bodosakis delivered arms to the Republicans.[736]

Shortly after, on 12 October 1937, Kordt received information from Berlin that substantial proof had been revealed that Bodosakis [spelled Vodosakis in the text] and Sarsentis [!] were behind arms sales to the Republicans.[737] Nevertheless, neither Rheinmetall-Borsig nor the German authorities felt called upon to take action of any kind: official German opinion was that it was a matter between the Greek authorities and the company.

This leaves the impression that the arms deals were conducted with the implicit recognition of the German authorities and not least Göring's, because Rheinmetall-Borsig, as noted above, was connected to Göring's parastate complex. In addition, the high priority Göring gave to hard currency and raw materials must be borne in mind. In this connection it is interesting to recall that Veltjens, the arms dealer who sold arms to the Republicans, enjoyed Göring's protection.

Some time near the end of 1937 or the beginning of 1938 Bodosakis contacted Göring[738] for permission to buy a patent to manufacture Krupp 88 mm grenades. Friends of Bodosakis had informed him that Göring already knew of his role as supplier of arms to the Republicans. However, when Göring mentioned this, Bodosakis claimed that he was selling to Mexico and not to Spain. Furthermore, he told Göring that companies in Poland and Finland were selling arms to the Republicans and supported this claim with a list of the companies concerned.

Bodosakis explains that Göring was both surprised and angry; on the other hand, he did not take further steps in the matter, except that Bodosakis failed to obtain the patent to manufacture 88 mm grenades.[739]

A meeting held on 2 May 1938 between the German Ministry of Aviation, *Oberkommando der Wehrmacht, Auswärtiges Amt, Ausfuhrgemeinschaft für Kriegsgerät* and the Ministry of Economy, decided to stop arms export to Greece and Mexico due to the suspicion of resales to countries on the German blacklist.[740]

Thus, Göring officially decreed that trade in arms with Greece be stopped on the grounds of the above-mentioned suspicions. It is worth noting, however, that production equipment and know-how were not mentioned, and that the ban on arms sales to Greece would give the Germans bargaining power in the forthcoming renegotiations of Greece's payment terms for German war material. This latter point is underlined by the fact that, as early as May 1938, Greece and Germany entered into a new agreement concerning the arms trade, in which the Greeks accepted an increase of the exchange quota from 15 to 35 per cent for purchase of war material.[741]

The ban on arms sales can also be seen as Göring's reaction to the pressure put on his unique position within the German power hierarchy. This meant that he had to show certain consideration, at least officially, for Germany's overseas political interests, as corroborated by the fact that the same meeting decided to stop sales of arms to China, i.e to Chiang Kai-shek, in the interests of Japan. Accordingly, *Ausfuhrgemeinschaft für Kriegsgerät* stopped exports to China.

In the same period Bodosakis established contact with Chiang Kai-shek through a certain Frau Hirscheimer during a meeting with her in Paris. Later the Powder and Cartridge Company received orders from China.[742]

The sources do not reveal whether this connection was made in cooperation with Göring. It is clear, though, that Göring continued to deliver arms to China by channels other than *Ausfuhrgemeinschaft für Kriegsgerät*. The trade was conducted in secrecy through the Ministry of Economy and other channels. Apparently Göring received Japanese complaints that German arms were still finding their way into China through third countries. Göring responded to the Japanese Embassy by saying that he endeavoured to stop the resale of German arms from third countries; however, he "did not have the situation well in hand yet".[743] Greece was evidently one of those countries that was "not yet in hand".

Greek Export of Arms to the Middle East

In 1936 Palestine became the scene of clashes between Jews, Arabs and the British Mandatory Authorities. This civil war-like conflict, known as the Arab Revolt, raged until 1939. So far, scholars on the subject have not been able to identify the sources from which the Palestinian Arabs purchased their arms: Italy has been mentioned among other possibility.[744]

In 1938 the Iraqi authorities confiscated a considerable quantity of Greek ammunition.[745] The illegal character of the delivery rules out the possibility that it was meant for the Iraqi army. It is much more likely that the arms were destined for Palestine, and that the confiscated freight was only one of many consignments. At that time Iraq provided a well-used route for smuggling arms to the Arabs in the troubled British mandatory area.[746] Furthermore, the British Minister in Athens informed the Foreign Office that Bodosakis was conducting arms trade in Palestine.[747] Whether he was selling to the Jews, the Arabs or both sides is not clear, however.

In 1938 a British agent, sent to Greece to investigate the routes of illegal transportation of Jews to Palestine, reported that Jews and arms to supply the immigrants in Palestine were shipped from Piraeus. The agent also believed that Bodosakis was responsible for the arms deliveries: " ...there is a great move now on in Athens for the purpose of smuggling arms to Jews in Palestine. Richard, the well-known smuggler of arms, is now in Athens and this coupled with the presence of Stavsky, Dr. Perl and confederates and the large sum at the disposal of Krivoshein[748] tend to confirm the view that with the next shipload of immigrants or perhaps by special chartered ship, arms will be smuggled to Palestine.[...] The arms will in all probability be supplied by the firm of Bodosaky, the notorious smuggler of war materials to Spain. He is a powerful person and un-crowned King of Greece. He is the managing director of almost all the important enterprises in Greece, and has been decorated by the Greek Government for his contribution to the economic welfare of the country."[749]

Apparently knowing nothing of the above-mentioned report the British had turned to Bodosakis and asked him to help with the investigation into the confiscated arms in Iraq. A minute from Foreign Office pointed out that: "it is amusing to see, that [...] M. Bodosakis, [...helping] to trace the smuggled arms discovered in the Iraqi customs [...], is himself described as a notorious smuggler."[750]

However, in 1938 Waterlow could report that the Greek King had succeeded in putting an end to the traffic.[751] It has not been possible to make an assessment of the extent of this arms traffic, and it has been equally difficult to draw any conclusions as to whether it was conducted in cooperation with the Germans.

Shortly after the outbreak of war in 1939, British Embassy officials expressed their fear that the Powder and Cartridge Company was working for German interests in the Middle East. Rumours that Theophanidis, who had a leading position in the Powder and Cartridge Company and had been middleman in several arms negotiations, was in Egypt gave rise to anxiety. Ultimately the British authorities concluded that he was not in the country anyway. However, it was maintained that representatives of the Greek armament industry had been to Egypt. Two ex-colonels [probably from the Powder and Cartridge Company, as Bodosakis employed some of the purged Venizelists after the March Revolt of 1935] had contacted the Egyptian head of General Staff, Aziz Ali al-Masri, offering to sell Czecho-slovak Bren guns.[752]

Al-Masri and Prince Nabil Abbas Ibrahim Halim, cousin of the Egyptian King Fuad, were involved in arms negotiations with the Germans from mid-1938.[753] Both were well-known for their anti-British symphathies. Prince Halim had served, among other things, as a pilot under Göring's command during the First World War.[754] Al-Masri ma-sterminded a strong pan-Arab and anti-British faction in the Egyptian army.[755] By the end of the 1930s al-Masri had established close connections with the Muslim Brotherhood, the most powerful anti-British movement in Egypt. The Brotherhood was deeply engaged in the Arab Revolt in Palestine and had strong links with the Grand Mufti of Jerusalem. In this way the Brotherhood served as an important link between anti-British and pan-Arabic movements inside and outside Egypt.[756] In a letter to the Axis dated April 1941, the Grand Mufti of Jerusalem explained that al-Masri was planning a riot against the British authorities.[757] Following the assumption of power by anti-British insurgents in Baghdad in May 1941, al-Masri tried in vain to flee from Egypt with the help of the German secret service in order to join the rebels in Iraq.[758]

Greek-German Cooperation within Arms Export to the Middle East

There is a consensus of opinion among researchers investigating Germany's policy towards the Middle East that the only German interests in the area were economic, and that trade was conducted with an eye to avoiding a conflict with Great Britain. The Middle East was seen as a British sphere of interest. This was clear from the Arab Revolt: Arab requests for moral and material support and recommendations by German diplomats were not met by the German government. This meant that the Arabs in Palestine did not obtain German support and that Germany abstained from criticizing the so-called Peel Plan, put forward in 1937. The plan advised that the Mandatory Area be divided between Jews and Arabs. According to Francis Nicosia, the only departure from this policy arose from the September crisis of 1938, in which Germany conducted a so-called "policy of limited interference" in Palestine. Nevertheless, as Nicosia stresses, this policy was primarily maintained to keep Britain from taking action against Germany in Czechoslovakia and to avoid undermining the British position in Palestine, or promoting the Arab cause.[759] German intervention in Palestine was chiefly related to her own interests in Central Europe.

Referring to German negotiations for arms deliveries to Iraq, Egypt and Saudi Arabia, Heinz Tillmann, a German scholar from the former GDR, underlines the point that the deliveries were made with British acquiescence. Until her march into Prague in 1939, Germany avoided making arms deals that might transgress British interests.[760] Accordingly, representatives from Rheinmetall-Borsig went to London to obtain British agreement to the delivery of German arms to Arab states. On 9 December 1937 the first of three arms deals was made with Iraq. The two latter deals were signed in September 1938 and April 1939 respectively.[761] An additional plan, to deliver arms to the Egyptian army, failed as a result of British opposition.[762] However, the German scholar, Helmut Mejcher, has recently pointed out that Germany's Middle Eastern policy was subtle and ambiguous. He pinpoints what he refers to as the "dual aspect" in Germany's policy, meaning simply that the official state foreign department, *Auswärtiges Amt*, and the Nazi party's foreign political office, *Aussenpolitisches Amt der NSDAP*, were rivals pursuing different objectives.[763] Unlike *Auswärtiges Amt*, *Aussenpolitisches Amt* endeavoured to let German interests "join hands" with anti-British Arab Nationalism and with a general antipathy to the presence of the Great Powers in the area. Within Arab

Nationalist circles Germany was seen as an impartial Great Power without ambitions in the Middle East. Moreover, many Arabs in the newly established Middle Eastern states saw Germany as a victim, like themselves, of the "unfair" peace agreements made by the Great Powers after the First World War.

The Germans made the condition of arms sales to independent Saudi Arabia a promise by that country to conduct a neutral policy. Mejcher's work offers an opportunity to interpret these arms negotiations in a perspective that goes beyond economic considerations and illuminates German political interests in the Middle East.[764]

In order to conduct the arms deliveries to Iraq, leading German armament companies established a consortium. This was made up of Friedrich Krupp AG, Otto Wolff, Berlin-Suhler Waffen- und Fahrzeugwerke, Rheinmetall-Borsig and Waffenfabrik Solothurn AG. Rheinmetall-Borsig headed Untergruppe I, which undertook delivery of artillery ammunition, while Otto Wolff headed Untergruppe II, which delivered other kinds of ammunition and war material.[765]

On 17 June 1937 Waterlow informed the Foreign Office that, according to Bodosakis, Otto Wolff had invited the Powder and Cartridge Company to participate in exports of cartridges to Iraq for a total value of 500 million Dr. and cooperation in arms exports to Egypt and Afghanistan: "...German firm [Otto] Wolff has asked Manager [Bodosakis] whether he will accept order for one million pounds' worth [about 500 million Dr.] of cartridges to be supplied by Germany to Iraq as part of a credit of between 6 and 7 million sterling for war material which Germany are negotiating with Iraq Government. Germans had also suggested that Greek firm should collaborate with them in supplying Egyptian and Afghan Governments. Manager [Bodosakis] is shortly leaving for Berlin for further discussions..."[766]

In a detailed letter dated the same day, Waterlow stressed that Bodosakis had stated that his company could be very useful to the British government and that he would prefer to be connected with Britain than with Germany: "...The line which M.Bodosaki took up with Sir Gerald, as a representative of British armaments firms, was that possibly the services of his factory might be useful to His Majesty's Government, and that he would much prefer to be connected with British interests than to do business with the Germans"...[767]

Bodosakis's message is clearly marked by an attempt to persuade the British to cooperate with the Powder and Cartridge Company and we must view his statement with scepticism. In reality, Bodosakis doubtless wanted to cooperate with both the British and the Germans.

The Middle East was at that time a disputed market. By the end of July or the beginning of August 1937 German arms dealers in Egypt called for Greek help. The representative for Rheinmetall-Borsig, Sarsentis, complied with the German request and went to Cairo to establish contacts with prominent Egyptian circles. After several weeks of negotiations Sarsentis arranged a meeting with Nahas Pasha, the Egyptian Prime Minister.[768]

During a meeting between Bodosakis and Rheinmetall-Borsig, held in October 1937, the former mentioned the possibility of export cooperation with the German firm: the Powder and Cartridge Company could serve as a platform for exports to neighbouring states. Bodosakis stressed the low wages in Greece and her geopolitical position as important assets: "...The president of the firm, Mr. Bodosakis, as well as his directors, often point out that their plant is especially well geared for exports to the neighbouring states, because salaries in Greece constitute only about one tenth of what we have to pay in Germany. It is obviously the wish of the management of the Powder and Cartridge Company to negotiate seriously one day about cooperation in exports..."[769]

Whether such cooperation was established or not is impossible to deduce from the available sources. However, it is clear that in August 1938 Bodosakis negotiated with the Egyptian government for the delivery of 2 million gas masks at a total value of £E (Egyptian Pound) 350,000. The negotiations were made in strong competition with the German gas mask company, Auergesellschaft.[770] As a result of the Czechoslovak crisis, the German authorities prohibited Auer from supplying British dominated Egypt.[771] Subsequently, Bodosakis and Auer established a gas mask factory in Athens, thus giving the German firm a platform for export.[772]

In conclusion, it is clear that the Powder and Cartridge Company was involved in extensive and profitable arms trade with Spain. Weighty arguments suggest that this trade was conducted in collusion with Rheinmetall-Borsig and Göring. Furthermore, Bodosakis's deliveries to Spain constituted an important precondition for the company's expansion, at least in 1936 and 1937, and thus for increased purchases from Germany.

It is certain that Rheinmetall-Borsig regarded the deliveries to the Powder and Cartridge Company as attractive in an economic as well as a political sense. Accordingly, it is likely that Rheinmetall-Borsig, and quite certainly Göring as well, turned a blind eye to the Powder and Cartridge Company's exports to the Republicans. This also seemed to be Göring's attitude to the trade with China.

As noted above, Greek arms found their way illegally into the British mandatory areas, Palestine and Iraq. Moreover, Bodosakis cooperated with German companies in the practically and politically awkward export of war materials to Egypt. These transactions could hardly have been conducted without the knowledge of the Greek government, given its determination to exercise control of such exports. It is tempting to conclude that the export of arms was part of an innovative, but politically risky, Greek strategy to surmount an internal crisis: innovative because increase of the ammunition production was to a certain degree financed by tobacco export to Germany and made it possible to convert frozen assets on the clearing account in Germany into hard currency: risky because this could make Greece dependent on Germany and create conflicts with Britain.

In this connection MacVeagh made an interesting comment on 27 September 1938: "...On the financial side, the Government is still performing the same miracle of keeping the ship of state afloat that has been accomplished now for years by other and even more bankrupt countries, and which, so far as I know has never been explained..."[773]

An explanation of the "miracle" could be the considerable "grey income" resulting from arms trade. Bodosakis played a central role in the arms trade, and the following section therefore investigates his political position and contacts within Greece.

Bodosakis's Political Position and Contacts in Greece

Prodromos Bodosakis-Athanasiadis was born an Ottoman Greek in Cappadocia, Asia Minor, in the last decade of the nineteenth century. He established his fortune as a contractor in the period around the First World War. In Asia Minor and the Middle East, he worked primarily on the fronts in Mesopotamia and Palestine, supplying the Turkish army as well as the units working on the Berlin-Baghdad railway.[774] The latter were in close cooperation with the German building and development company,

Philipp Holzmann, which had Deutsche Bank as the main shareholder.[775] Bodosakis's connections to leading business and military circles in Germany were further strengthened through his marriage to the daughter of an Austrian engineer who had worked on the Berlin-Baghdad Railway[776] and was related to Otto Liman von Sanders, the head of the German military mission in Turkey before and during the First World War.[777] During the war Bodosakis became personally acquainted with Mustafa Kemal. From the early days of his career, Bodosakis therefore had close contacts with the prominent figures in Germany and with the future leader of the Turkish Nationalist movement.

By the end of 1918 he had bought Pera Palace, one of the most exclusive hotels in Constantinople, and the "Jockey Club".[778] Both places were venues for high society, including important people from political circles. In the same period Bodosakis became politically engaged on the side of the Venizelists. He financed a building for the Greek Embassy in Constantinople and a sporting club in Smyrna for the Greek Officers Club.[779] The anti-Venizelists' victory in the elections in November 1920 seriously affected the attitude of the Ottoman Greeks towards Athens and played a significant part in the split between the predominantly Venizelist diaspora and the anti-Venizelist Greek state. In the same spirit that had led to the foundation of Venizelos's Salonica government in 1916, *Ethniki Amina*, the Organization for Constantinople's National Defence (*Ethniki Amina Konstandinoupoleos*) was founded in 1920. The latter, which was supported by Venizelos, sought to ensure British recognition and financial aid to establish an autonomous Ionia, independent of Greece: in this the organization was unsuccessful.[780]

The split between Venizelists and anti-Venizelists culminated in a conflict between the Venizelist Patriarchate in Constantinople and the government in Athens. The result was that the latter stopped its financial support of the Patriarchate. This made the economy of the church dependent on private funds for a time and in this respect Bodosakis played an important role.[781]

Pera Palace became the domicile of leading Venizelist officers who had deserted Constantine's army, as well as of organizations which worked for the Great Idea. Bodosakis financed arrangements of this kind and became a member of the board in the Organization for Constantinople's National Defence.[782]

Bodosakis also housed Mustafa Kemal and became personally acquainted with Venizelos in the same period.[783]

178

According to a later account, Bodosakis delivered arms during the campaign in Asia Minor to both the Greek army and the Turkish Nationalists.[784] It has not been possible to establish what – if any – connections he had with the politically influential Basil Zaharoff, the most powerful arms dealer of the period.[785] It is clear, though, that the latter was also strongly engaged politically and economically in the realization of the Great Idea in Asia Minor.

Immediately before the catastrophe in Asia Minor, Bodosakis went to Greece and had to leave his landed property behind.[786] He was able to raise money through outstandings in Germany and shares in the Berlin-Baghdad Railway. He invested some of the funds in commodities like coal and wood and in this way avoided the impact of hyperinflation in Germany; as a result Bodosakis was able to bring a considerable fortune with him to Greece.[787]

Bodosakis became Venizelos's adviser during the negotiations concerning the exchange of populations in 1923. Moreover, he supported the Venizelists financially in their plebiscite about constitutional reform in 1924.

First and foremost he was concerned with the refugees, however, and not least with the issue of compensation for abandoned property.[788] To reinforce their claims, the refugees established a pressure group called "commission exécutive chargée de la defence des Grecs, sujets turcs, établis à Constantinople et sejournant provisoirement en Grèce." (The Executive Commission charged with the Defence of Greeks, [who] are Turkish subjects, established in Constantinople and staying temporarily in Greece).[789] The organization was particularly dissatisfied with the so-called Ankara Agreement drawn up on 21 June 1925 between the Greek and Turkish governments. In effect, the result of the Agreement was that the number of refugees entitled to compensation was reduced considerably.[790] According to Bodosakis, the Greek government's attitude towards the compensation issue caused him severe financiel losses, but it has not been possible to establish his connection with the above-mentioned pressure group.[791]

However, on 25 July 1925, four days after the Agreement was signed, General Pangalos seized power by a *coup d'etat*. Pangalos delayed the ratification of the Ankara Agreement while the pressure group persuaded the neutral members of the mixed commission, established to oversee the exchange of population, to disallow the Agreement.[792] According to British information Bodosakis was financing Pangalos.[793] Bodosakis mentions that the latter sent for him two days after the *coup* to ask him what he wanted in return for generous financial assistance.[794] Soon afterwards Bodosakis obtained the concession to establish the first public telephones in Greece. To help Bodosakis realize the project, Pangalos passed a special law which made it possible for Bodosakis to raise a loan from the state using as security the property he had left behind in Turkey.[795] However, as a result of a conflict between the Pangalos government and Turkey, the Turkish government passed a law March 1926 making it possible to expropriate property left behind by Greeks.[796]

Kondilis was prominent in activities that led to the denouncement of the republic in 1924. Politically he had established himself as a patron of the refugees and in August 1926 he toppled Pangalos by a *coup d'etat*.[797] Participating officers have stated that Bodosakis was responsible for the success of the *coup*.[798] The way in which Bodosakis helped is not clear, but it is likely that he bought the loyalty needed by bribing the right persons. According to Bodosakis's own account he backed Kondilis.[799]

At the same time Bodosakis established the Greek Telephone Company Inc. and assigned the work of installing automatic telephones in Greece to Siemens & Halske[800], on the recommendation of Deutsche Bank.[801] Siemens was the first major German company to enter the Greek market after the First World War. In this way, Bodosakis gained, from the very beginning, an important contact with leading industrial circles in Germany.[802] Kondilis broke with Venizelos over the ratification of the so-called Ankara Convention on 30 October 1930; thereafter, he became one of the most uncompromising of anti-Venizelists.

Kondilis's breakthrough in terms of power policy came, as noted above, when he was designated Minister of War in 1933. It was while Kondilis was in power that Bodosakis began to reconstruct the war industry in close cooperation with the German armament industry.

According to Gervasi, Bodosakis's name was often mentioned in connection with the *coup* that gave power to Kondilis on 10 October 1935.[803]

Bodosakis and Metaxas
Bodosakis and Metaxas met for the first time at the beginning of 1934 on the premises of the Greek Telephone Company, where they talked about the possibility that Bodosakis might employ Metaxas's son-in-law. Shortly

180

after, the latter started work for Bodosakis.[804] In 1934 Metaxas participated in negotiations with Bodosakis and Kondilis for a *coup* against Tsaldaris.[805] After the March Revolt of 1935 Bodosakis began to support Metaxas's political career financially. Metaxas tried to gain royalist votes and hoped to make a breakthrough at the parliamentary elections in June 1935. In this connection Metaxas made contact, through a middleman, with the German Counsulate in Geneva to ensure political and economic support in the building of a powerful army. The middleman informed the Consulate that Metaxas wanted Greece's military dependence on France to end and to loosen France's grip on the Balkan Entente.[806] Neither *Auswärtiges Amt* nor the German Legation in Athens questioned Metaxas's intentions.[807] Nevertheless, the election turned out to be a complete disaster for Metaxas, in that he won only 1.3 per cent of the seats in parliament.[808] The German Legation concluded that there was no reason to pursue the matter further.[809] It is important to note, however, that Metaxas's military and political objectives and Bodosakis's economic interests shared much common ground.

Shortly after the establishment of the 4th of August Regime Metaxas asked Bodosakis what he could do to return the favour. Bodosakis answered that he merely wanted "a little help" in getting his armaments industry going.[810]

Bodosakis gave employment to several purged Venizelist officers in the Powder and Cartridge Company during the same period, so as to ensure military know-how in the factories. The officers had been dismissed from the army without a pension, so Bodosakis doubtless received their greatest respect and loyalty. Furthermore, in doing this, he might also have contributed to the pacification of an extremely unstable political group of unemployed men who possessed dexterity and in other repects had every motivation to contribute to the toppling of Metaxas's regime.[811]

Part III

Recession and War:
1938-1941

GREECE

Metaxas, the King and Relations with Germany

The King's most important power base was the army. Firstly, because he held the formal position of commander-in-chief; secondly, because he played an important role for anti-Venizelists as the sovereign of the country; finally, because he had the support of Britain.[812]

By his establishment of a dictatorship in August 1936, Metaxas relied to a large extent on the goodwill of the King.[813] Metaxas had already taken charge of several important state institutions, however: the Prime Minister's department, the Ministries of the Armed Forces and the Ministry of Foreign Affairs.

Furthermore, Metaxas tried to extend his power base by appointing staff from outside the usual political circles, and by surrounding himself with loyal followers. Shortly after he became Prime Minister, he began to reappoint a number of local officials. In May 1936, he used the labour dispute in northern Greece to install a new Minister of the Interior, Theodoros Skilakakis, who was known to be in his confidence.[814]

After the installation of the dictatorship, Metaxas established several ministries and secretariats, which were either new or challenged the authority of those already existing. The most important of these were the Secretariats of Security, Press and Tourism and the Administration of the Capital.

The Secretariat of Security was given to Konstandinos Maniadakis. This secretariat included the Security Police, who soon comprised a state within a state; they did not constitute part of the Ministry of the Interior like the regular police and were therefore a very useful tool in Metaxas's personal struggle for power.

Theologos Nikoloudis, a former fellow partisan of Metaxas, was appointed to head the Secretariat of Press and Tourism, which included censorship and propaganda. This secretariat also served as a platform to propagate the ideology of the 4th of August Regime.

The Ministry of Administration of the Capital was handed over to another of Metaxas's old colleagues, Kostas Kodzias.[815] Kodzias had a friendly relationship with both Göring and Goebbels and was the only member of the Greek government to have met Hitler personally. The British saw him as the "Greek Göring", and Goebbels characterized him as a true friend of the German people.

Finally, it is important to mention Ioanis Diakos, who has been depicted as an extremely influential personal advisor to Metaxas and is often referred to as the dictator's "alter ego" and the *eminence grise* of the regime. He was present during most of the important government meetings and controlled significant industrial and financial interests; nevertheless, he did not hold any official appointments and avoided appearing in public. This makes it difficult to give a precise assessment of the true influence he had on the policy of the regime; however, a British report describes him as "an able, unscrupulous and aggressive schemer".[816]

By the establishment of a dictatorship, Metaxas thus had personal control of Greece's foreign policy, internal security, administration of the politically important capital and of the press. Moreover, he sought to influence coming generations by means of the paramilitary youth movement EON.

Varvaresos was offered the position of Minister of Economy, but preferred to keep his appointment as Deputy-Governor of the Bank of Greece. From this position he could continue negotiations concerning economic issues, not least with Germany. Furthermore, Varvaresos worked as Metaxas's personal economic advisor. Metaxas also obtained economic advice from Korizis, Vice-President of the National Bank of Greece, who was appointed to the newly established Ministry of Social Security. The National Bank of Greece was represented additionally when Arvanitis, an executive of the bank, was appointed Minister of Economy. The economic policy in Greece was thus decided by representatives from institutions which had previously been willing and able to pursue Greece's economic development and trade in a number of fields and in accordance with German demands. In this respect it is especially important to bear in mind that the National Bank of Greece, which worked as a bank of commerce, had direct economic interests at stake within Greek-German trade.[817]

In December 1936 Metaxas forced Skilakakis, Minister of the Interior, and Papachelas, State Secretary of the Armed Forces, to resign from their posts. The official reason was that the Minister of the Interior had openly declared that Metaxas was not sufficiently engaged in fighting the enemies of the regime. According to MacVeagh, Skilakakis even tried to mobilize military units in northern Greece so as to seize power.[818] It seems safe to conclude that this was primarily a struggle for power between Metaxas and the radical right within the government. This faction was generally of the opinion that Metaxas was too easy going with the enemies of the regime, in particular former politicians. According to Kordt, these people also created problems regarding the relationship between the King and the dictator, as they tried to undermine Metaxas's power. To this effect they recommended to the King the establishment of a coalition government. Although Metaxas was proposed as head of government, his other ministers, according to these suggestions, would have to resign. In particular, Kordt noticed that hatred of Metaxas's personal advisor, Diakos, provided a platform for joint action in the opposition and that the attack seems to have been mainly directed towards the people who had been appointed after Metaxas's assumption of power.[819] According to MacVeagh, Metaxas made an effort to exile the most vociferous of these politicians in order to neutralize the opposition, but had to give up such plans as a result of opposition from the King.[820]

In the following year a new trial of strength arose between Metaxas on one side and the King and the former politicians on the other. Several of the leaders of the pre-dictatorship parties were invited to the wedding of Crown Prince Paul and Princess Frederike on 9 January 1938. According to the German Minister, this was interpreted as a sign that the King was dissatisfied with Metaxas. Immediately after the ceremony, the former politicians issued a manifesto demanding Metaxas's resignation. However, the security police arrested the dissidents and deported them to islands in the Aegean Sea.[821]

Waterlow believed that the King was aware of Metaxas's unpopularity and for that reason was trying to establish a kind of representative administration. The most crucial dilemma for the King in this respect was that he had difficulty in finding an alternative to Metaxas among the former politicans, leaving him with the sole option of assuming the political control of Greece himself. This state of affairs made Waterlow expect that drastic political changes were under way in order to get rid of the most undesirable elements in the "gang of General Metaxas".[822]

Action against the regime, however, never materialized and instead Waterlow had to inform the Foreign Office that Metaxas had tightened his grip and officially announced that the regime was a totalitarian one. In addition, the dictator stressed that he had been soft until now, but, in the future, action would be taken against political agitation.[823]

On 29 July 1938 an armed uprising broke out on Crete. The rebels quickly seized control of Chania the principal city on the western part of the island. However, the government soon regained control of the area when the Navy and the Air Force were brought into action. Metaxas announced that the revolt had been launched by Plastiras from his place of exile in Paris.[824] Waterlow's opinion was that it was instigated by former politicians from both factions and that the uprising on Crete was a part of a planned nationwide revolt; be that as it may, Metaxas directed his revenge against this specific group. He ordered the arrest, especially in Thessaly and in the Venizelist tobacco province Macedonia, a number of former politicians and ex-officers.[825]

This limited yet more the alternatives open to the King and weakened his position considerably. On 27 September 1938, MacVeagh noted that the King's influence with the government was virtually nil and that he was no longer in control of the army. The latter difficulty and the fact that he was losing "that love of his people which (was) the strength of his house", reduced the King's significance to the dictator to that of a kind of buffer or "scapegoat". Moreover, the American Ambassador commented that the King had told the Brazilian Ambassador that he had been to Germany and Italy and was familiar with the kind of oppression they used there. For this reason he hated the position he was now in because he was seen as the one personally responsible for similar conditions in Greece. The King thought that Metaxas's announcement of the regime as permanent was "ridiculous". Nonetheless, according to MacVeagh, the King showed neither the ability nor the willingness to alter the situation.[826]

In November 1938 an internal power struggle in the government showed that Metaxas still had enemies. This situation was triggered by the election of a new Archbishop of Athens. The strong position of the church made the appointment of the spiritual leader of the country a matter of great importance. The late archbishop, Chrisostomos, had been chosen by Plastiras and was the last Venizelist to hold a leading post in the Greek state.[827]

Illegally, and in contravention of the usual practice, the government interfered directly in the election. Metaxas and his closest associates,

Nikoloudis and Maniadakis, supported the former Archbishop of Trapezunt, Christhanos, who was running against the Archbishop of Corinth, Damaskinos. The latter won the election; however, pressure from Metaxas forced another vote, with the result that his own candidate, the former Archbishop of Trapezunt, was elected. Metaxas's action makes it clear that he saw the election as a showdown between himself and the faction within the government that supported the King. He was equally convinced that he himself emerged victorious. It was for this reason, according to Metaxas, that the King decided to remain faithful to him after the election, a fact which, still according to Metaxas's own account, encouraged him to pursue his current and future aims to their furthest extent.[828] Erbach, too, was of the opinion that Metaxas's position was strengthened considerably by these events and the German Minister stressed that the Greek dictator had purged the royalists after the election. In order to replace these people, he appointed the vacant posts to himself or to men he trusted.[829]

In the last days of 1938 the British Minister tried to persuade the King to get rid of Metaxas. His attempt, however, was in vain. Waterlow presumably took action because the dictator was continuing to turn Greece into a Fascist state without the support of the people. At the same time, the King was exposing himself to the risk of losing the opportunity to mobilize popular support. In his annual report dated 1938 Waterlow described the situation in Greece as follows: "...This process of apotheosis did nothing to make him [Metaxas] popular, and it also marked a low ebb in the popularity of the King, whose destinies were now believed to be irretrievably bound up with those of the dictator. There was simultaneously a marked tendency to emphasise the fascist and totalitarian aspects of the régime..." [830]

Instead of listening to Waterlow's advice, the King began to manifest his support for Metaxas in public. MacVeagh described this change of course as a victory for the dictator.[831] In this respect it is notable that the American Ambassador did not regard the King as a central element in Metaxas's power base. In words more appropriate to a description of criminal circles, MacVeagh outlined the following persons and institutions as central to Metaxas's position: "...about and behind the Dictator, [are] – Drossopoulos of the National Bank, Kanellopoulos of the Youth Movement, Diakos, "the eminence grise", Maniadakis the sardonic reincarnation of Fouché, Bodossakis, the arms merchant et al..."[832]

In order to explain the obvious discrepancies between the reports from Waterlow on the one side and those from MacVeagh and also to a certain extent from the German Legation on the other, it is important to bear in mind that Waterlow was commenting to the Foreign Office in response to his fellow countrymen in Athens and certain members of the press in Britain complaining that Metaxas was turning Greece into a pro-German satellite. Waterlow, for his part, dismissed such allegations, at least until the end of 1938. In this period he stressed that the King stood as a guarantor of British interests. Assertions that Greece had entered on a pro-German course were linked by Waterlow to the fact that the British community in Athens consisted mainly of business people and that Britain's commercial interests in Greece were negatively affected by German trade policy. Waterlow's fixed impression of the King as a guarantor of British interests and his rejection of complaints by British businessmen about Greece's pro-German attitudes, suggests that he overestimated the power of the King and thus his own potential to influence the situation in Greece. This would also mean that, for some time at least, it would be in Waterlow's own interests to stress the significance of his relationship with the King.[833]

For such reasons, it also seems safe to conclude that in 1939, by means of cleverly spun alliances Metaxas had placed himself in a situation quite unlike the one that arose in 1936, in that he was stronger than the King in their relationship; it was now Metaxas who had become the most important guarantee in relations to Germany. In March 1939 MacVeagh stated that the King was now completely dominated by his "Fascist Frankenstein, the German-educated General Metaxas." According to MacVeagh, British attempts to liberate the King from this "monster" could be seen as endeavours to stop the influence that foreign totalitarian states [i.e. Germany] had gained during the dictatorship.[834] However, by putting pressure on the King, Britain only achieved the opposite: namely that the monarch was forced to turn to Metaxas.

In the summer of 1939 the Greek security police uncovered a conspiracy against Metaxas headed by Tsouderos. The Governor of the Bank of Greece was placed under house arrest and later deported. The outcome of the conspiracy, often referred to as the last serious attempt to get rid of Metaxas, made it even more difficult for the King to find an alternative to the dictator.[835]

190

At the beginning of June 1939 the Foreign Office replaced Waterlow with the considerably younger Michael Palairet: this was effected several months before it was scheduled. However, Koliopoulos argues that Waterlow was replaced because he had lost his influence with the King and had a poor relationship with Metaxas.[836] In the light of the observations noted above, this seems a perfectly plausible explanation.

Shortly before the outbreak of war in September 1939, Palairet told MacVeagh that he was worried about the two pro-German ministers, Kodzias and Nikoloudis, particularly because he was uncertain as to their stance in the event of conflict between Britain and Germany. Reporting this, the American Ambassador told the State Department that he was surprised at Palairet's worries, because these ministers had no influence on Greek foreign policy. Moreover, MacVeagh wondered why the British Minister did not know anything about "the vast underground power of the Diakos group"[837], i.e. the above-mentioned group which included Diakos, Maniadakis, the National Bank of Greece and Bodosakis.

It seems, therefore, that Metaxas had accrued substantially increased power shortly before the outbreak of war in September 1939. The King was apparently ready to accept this and to join forces with the dictator. This power balance seems to have been maintained until at least July 1940. According to the Italian Ambassador to Greece, Emmanuele Grazzi, it was Metaxas who held the real power in the country. Only fear of transgressing Turkey's policy and then standing alone against Bulgaria, plus consider-ations for the merchant fleet, kept Metaxas from supporting the Axis powers openly.[838] Commenting on this assessment, the Greek historian Kitsikis claims that it was the King who made the decisions. Kitsikis bases his argument on events in 1936, 1937 and the beginning of 1938, when the King wielded great power.[839] Kitsikis does not, however, mention the power struggle in November 1938. Furthermore, he does not seem to be familiar with Waterlow's, MacVeagh's and the German Legation's assess-ments: this prevents him from considering their interpretation of the situation, which indicates that Metaxas's power increased considerably in relation to the King from 1938. Kitsikis's reply to Grazzi's assessment must be rejected and it is reasonable to maintain that Metaxas, in the summer of 1940, was in a strong position *vis-à-vis* the King.

GERMANY

Recession, Centralization and Transition to an Aggressive Ideological German Foreign Policy

In the second half of 1937 the world economy experienced a recession.[840] This, the forced rearmament and the fact that the high priority given to rearmament weakened the international competitiveness of German industry, brought about a shortage of raw materials and hard currency. The German military economy faced a serious structural crisis and it became clear that the Four Year Plan could not fulfil its purposes.[841]

On 5 November 1937 Hitler summoned Neurath, Göring, Blomberg, the Commander in Chief of the Army, Colonel General Werner von Fritsch and Raeder to a conference. The occasion was the aggravated raw material crisis and the threat which this posed to the preparation for war. In a two hour monologue Hitler explained the foreign policy objectives of National Socialism, the current precarious economic situation and the chances of aggressive German expansion in the future. Moreover, Hitler established an ideological platform for his foreign policy. The aim of his policy was to ensure the maintenance of the German population and its reproduction. *Lebensraum* for a racially close-knit population of more than 85 million people was necessary to fulfil Hitler's visions. The alternative was sterilization of the German population. Germany's future depended on a solution to this so-called "space problem". According to Hitler, a strong Germany at the centre of Europe would be a thorn in the side of Britain and France. These nations would not approve of a stronger Germany, either in Europe or overseas. Nevertheless, both Britain and France were relatively weaker militarily than Germany and would therefore seek to avoid an armed conflict. This advantage to the Germans was to disappear in subsequent years and the last opportunity to solve the "space problem" came in the period 1943-1945. Hitler declared that he was ready to use this advantage and strike fast, "ein blitzartig schnelles Losslagen", as early as 1938 if necessary. To promote Germany's military and political situation it was important to bring both Czechoslovakia and Austria under German control. This would also improve Germany's economic situation in case of war.[842] Thus, Hitler outlined an ideologically based policy of expansion as the task of German foreign policy, although this included a risk of war against Britain and France.

Blomberg, Fritsch and Neurath raised a number of objections. The two officers were sceptical about Hitler's optimistic assessment of the possibility of avoiding a war against the Western Powers and stressed the necessity of keeping on good terms with France and Britain.[843] In a subsequent discussion about the rearmament, Blomberg and Fritsch criticized Göring's implementation of the Four Year Plan.

Three months later the opposition was crushed and Blomberg, Fritsch and Neurath were removed from their posts. Hitler took over the Ministry of War himself and the radical National Socialist Ribbentrop was appointed as Minister of Foreign Affairs. This strengthened Hitler's influence in the two National Socialist strongholds within the German state while he gained even greater control of foreign policy.[844] The result was that German foreign policy became more aggressive and directed against Britain. At the same time, domestic and foreign policy became centralized and ideologized and racial policy was sharpened (the "Reichskristallnacht"). This had consequences for the position of the more pragmatic Göring. On 15 January 1938 Göring agreed with Hitler that Walter Funk should take over the Ministry of Economy, previously headed by Göring himself. Göring accepted Funk, anticipating that he could use the new Minister of Economy as his own instrument. However, Göring's autonomous power[845] was further curtailed when Hitler passed him over for appointment as Commander in Chief, a post expected to be Göring's by contemporaries.[846] In this way, Hitler increased his own power over Germany's policy even further; this increase was accompanied by a conflict between Ribbentrop and Göring, who fought for the control of Germany's foreign policy and the goodwill of Hitler. Göring's pragmatic policy, not least in connection in the arms trade, cut across Ribbentrop's foreign policy programme which was based on ideological considerations.[847]

The Munich Agreement, Hitler, Göring and Ribbentrop

In December 1937 the German army changed its plans for the mobilization and deployment of troops. The so-called "Case Green" (Fall Grün) i.e. war in the south-east against Czechoslovakia acquired an offensive character: "...The war aim in "case green" is always the rapid capture of Bohemia and Moravia and the simultaneous solution of the Austrian question in the sense of the inclusion of Austria in the German Reich..."[848]

On 12 February 1938 Hitler presented Kurt von Schuschnigg, the Austrian Chancellor, with an ultimatum that forced him to concede Germany a considerable influence on the internal, foreign and military policy of the Alpine republic.

Hereafter, Göring's role was considerably augmented. His disappointment with the results of the arms trade with south-eastern Europe, the meagre results of the Four Year Plan, the vehement power struggle between rival ministries and leading figures within the German hierarchy of power and the fact that he was not appointed Minister of War made Göring eager to produce tangible results. As early as the middle of 1937, *Anschluss* began to gain increasing significance in Göring's plans.[849] Not only was Austria in possession of several raw materials essential to the armaments industry but she also provided an entrance to south-eastern Europe.[850]

Schuschnigg proclaimed a referendum, to be held on 13 March under the slogan of a free and independent Austria, in an attempt to escape the increasing influence of Germany. Hitler would not accept this and authorized Göring to do whatever he considered necessary. Schuschnigg was presented with an ultimatum demanding that he resign and that government and power be transferred to the Austrian National Socialist, Arthur Seyss-Inquart. On 11 March Schuschnigg resigned. On the night between 11 and 12 March, using the pretext that the demands of the ultimatum had not been met, Seyss-Inquart called Berlin for help. On 12 March German troops marched into Austria, which was annexed to Germany the following day, 13 March.[851]

On 30 May 1938 Hitler gave secret orders for "Zerschlagung der Tschechoslowakei", i.e. a military attack on Czechoslovakia. Göring was against a military solution, both because he believed that it was impossible to isolate a conflict with Czechoslovakia and because he did not think that Germany was ready to fight a large-scale war. Ribbentrop held the opposite opinion and was thus ready to launch an assault on Czechoslovakia.

Göring, however, succeeded in arranging an international conference by means of hectic diplomatic activity. However, by the Munich Agreement of 29 September 1938, Göring made Hitler agree to a solution that did not fulfil his goals. This disgraced Göring with the Fuhrer and weakened his influence, while Ribbentrop's position was strengthened.

The difference of opinion between Göring and Hitler over foreign policy matters was due principally to Hitler's willingness to risk armed conflict. Consequently, Hitler began issuing orders to Göring without prior discussion. In mid-October Göring was ordered to enlarge the *Luftwaffe* to five times its strength. Demands to enforce rearmament, combined with the so-called Z-plan dated January 1939, prescribing the construction of a special unit within the German fleet to fight in the North Sea, indicate that Britain was seen as a potential enemy.[852]

On 21 October, about a month after the Munich Agreement, Hitler ordered the liquidation of remaining territory in former Czechoslovakia: "Erledigung der Rest-Tschechei". On 15-16 March 1939 German troops marched into Prague. This intensified the conflict with Britain and increased the possibility of an armed conflict between the two powers. Hitler's new high-risk policy increased Germany's need for autarchy and in this way also stressed the importance of *Grossraumwirtschaft*.[853]

The New German Policy and South-Eastern Europe

While Göring's influence on German foreign policy was reduced, Reichswerke Hermann Göring's significance to German industry overall grew as a result of Germany's strengthened position in south-eastern Europe. This was especially true within the field of armament production. Immediately after *Anschluss*, Reichswerke Hermann Göring took over the Austrian iron and steel industry with support from the Dresdner and Deutsche Banks. In March 1939 Reichswerke assumed control of Österreichisch-Alpine Montangesellschaft after a long struggle with the privately-owned Vereinigte Stahlwerke. The main part of the Austrian industry was taken over by the state holding company Vereinigte Industrieunternehmungen AG (VIAG).[854] The role that Reichwerke Hermann Göring played in this connection demonstrates the way in which *Anschluss* strengthened state- and party-related industrial interests considerably *vis-à-vis* the private sector in Germany, while at the same time Göring's armament and industrial complex grew in size.[855]

German control within the Austrian steel and iron industry also entailed German dominance over certain industries in south-eastern Europe that had previously been controlled by Austrian interests. *Wehrwirtschaftsstab* believed that *Anschluss* had strengthened Germany's position considerably, not least towards south-eastern Europe: "...because of *Anschluss*, the German Reich is now bordering directly on south-eastern European space, which in its capacity as supplier of food- and raw stuffs, as well as its capacity as an outlet for industrial products, constitutes its natural hinterland. Austria also constitutes in the future, no matter whether in time of war or of peace, the important entrance of the Reich into south-east[ern Europe]..."[856]

During a meeting held on 5 April 1938 by the board of directors of the Four Year Plan, Göring pinpointed the fact that German economic control in south-eastern Europe emanated from Austria.[857]

According to *Wehrwirtschaftsstab* the effects of significantly increased German dominance in the forecourt to south-eastern Europe spread instantly. Thus, it was noted that *Anschluss* had altered the situation of Czechoslovakia's war economy considerably and caused a heavy reduction in the value of the armaments industry in Slovakia.[858] *Wehrwirtschafsstab* must have been considering the possibility of war between German and Czechoslovakia, in which case it would be easier to cut off Slovakia from Bohemia and Moravia. According to an assessment made by *Ausfuhrgemeinschaft für Kriegsgerät*, *Anschluss* had also weakened general confidence in the Skoda plants among the south-eastern European nations; this in turn had strengthened the position of the German armaments industry in the area,[859] and consequently of Germany's political position too. Following *Anschluss*, the Czech state increased its control over the Skoda plants. This led to a conflict between the Czechoslovak government and Schneider-Creusot. As a result a French banking consortium cancelled an agreement concerning substantial credits to finance Romanian arms purchases at Skoda, thus leaving Romania to look for supplies elsewhere.[860] In this way *Anschluss* constributed to a considerable strengthening of Germany's economic and political position in south-eastern Europe.

The annexation of the Sudetenland and the establishment of the Reich Protectorate, Bohemia and Moravia, also gave Reichwerke Hermann Göring control of leading companies within Czechoslovak industry, including the Skoda plants and the armaments plants at Brno. As had been

197

the case after *Anschluss*, Reichwerke gained control of essential companies within the Czechoslovak mining industry.[861]

Germany's conquest of Central Europe in 1938 and 1939 also meant that her steel industry took over the Austrian and Czechoslovak quotas in the cartel Zentraleuropäische Gemeinschaft[862] and thus assumed control of the militarily and politically important steel and armaments industry in south-eastern Europe. The result was that the dependence of the south-eastern European states on German armaments increased considerably. This was reflected in a substantial increase of Germany's arms exports to Romania and Yugoslavia, as shown in the Table below.

TABLE 20

German trade in arms with Antirevisionist states 1938-1940 in million RM:[863]

	1938	1939	1940
Yugoslavia:	11.6	72.7	18.6
Romania:	9.6	107.9	69.7

Moreover, *Anschluss* and direct German political and economic dominance in Czechoslovakia led to a considerable increase in the commercial dependence of south-eastern Europe on Germany as a result of those countries' trade with the old centres in the Habsburg Empire. It is noteworthy, though, that Greek trade with Central Europe was limited compared with that of Romania and Yugoslavia.

TABLE 21

Pro rata share of Yugoslavia's, Romania's and Greece's trade with Germany, Austria and Czechoslovakia, export (X) and import (M).[864]

	Germany				Austria		Czechoslovakia			
	1937		1938		1937		1937		1938	
	X	M	X	M	X	M	X	M	X	M
Yugoslavia	21.7	32.4	42.0	39.4	13.5	10.3	7.9	11.1	7.9	10.6
Romania	22.3	28.9	26.5	40.0	6.8	8.5	8.2	16.1	9.6	8.5
Greece	31.0	27.5	38.6	29.0			4.0	1.8	2.9	1.6

198

Furthermore, *Anschluss* and German control over Czechoslovakia meant that Germany confiscated the gold reserves of the two states, amounting to 295 million RM and 500 million RM respectively.[865]

Following the German occupation of Poland, Holland, Belgium and France, Reichswerke Hermann Göring assumed control of several important steel and armaments companies including Schneider-Creusot, which was soon placed under the control of Rheinmetall-Borsig.[866]

New German Trade Agreements with South-Eastern Europe

On 23 March 1939 Germany concluded a trade agreement with Romania, the so-called Wohlthat Agreement, named after the German chief negotiator, Helmuth Wohlthat. This was a framework agreement ensuring Germany supplies and raw materials, especially oil, necessary for the armaments production, from Romania. Moreover, the agreement included certain measures aimed at adjusting the Romanian economy to German demands. One of these measures demanded that Romanian industry be developed within the framework of a joint German-Romanian plan.

Wohlthat suggested to Göring that Germany made similar agreements with the rest of south-eastern Europe, Yugoslavia, Bulgaria, Hungary and Turkey.[867]

A further German objective was to use the agreement to prevent industrialization in Romania and thus realize important objectives within the *Grossraumwirtschaft* concept. A comment added to the agreement of 26 May 1939 stated that: "...the industrialization of Romania generally has to be limited to the delivery of simple consumer goods..."[868]

However, the unstable political situation in the spring and summer of 1939 and the outbreak of war, combined with British and French attempts to launch an economic counter-offensive against Germany, meant that a number of Romanian products, and especially oil, were directed to the British market for a while.

Germany countered this by using the trade in arms as a means of putting pressure on Romania. As a result, in mid-July Göring cancelled a German-Romanian protocol regarding delivery of German war material in return for Romanian oil deliveries to Germany.

By the end of July, Hitler had ordered that German arms could only be delivered to countries where such transactions would be of benefit to German [political] interests, or at least would not harm these.[869] At the same time Hitler ordered that a large consignment of arms meant for Yugoslavia be delivered to Germany's ally, Italy, instead.[870] However, on 24 August Göring bypassed Hitler's orders by offering Yugoslavia the arms that Hitler had promised the Italians. In return Göring wanted Yugoslavia to supply Germany with raw materials essential to armaments production.[871] This was fully in line with Göring's previous conduct, namely the use of the trade in arms to acquire essential raw materials. Furthermore, as in the case of Romania, he used this as a means of pressure or punishment.

In the first half of 1940 the Romanian government nationalized French and British interests in the country.[872] On 29 May 1940 Romania signed the so-called *Öl und Waffenpackt* (Oil and Arms Pact) with Germany. As a result Germany's influence on Romania's economy was strengthened considerably. On the previous day, 28 May 1940, Yugoslavia had made a similar agreement with Germany and in October Hungary followed suit. In the period from October 1940 to May 1941 Bulgaria signed several agreements with Germany which ensured German influence on the internal economic development of the country.[873]

Germany's success in imposing her demands on Romania has been ascribed to political factors, or political dynamics, to use Karl-Heinz Schlarp's terminology. Using Yugoslav as a parallel, Schlarp pinpoints the fact that Germany had to use political pressure to gain a larger share of Yugoslav copper production.[874] Schlarp's opinions support Milward's thesis that it was political factors that ensured Germany's dominance in south-eastern Europe.[875] However, it is questionable whether Germany could have activated the same political dynamics without the powerful economic position she had already constructed in the area. In addition to Germany's commercial dominance in south-eastern Europe, her steel and armaments related industry established a dominant position in the areas during 1938 and 1939 by taking over Austrian and Czechoslovak firms, including their network of cartel agreements, within this field.

Growing German-Italian and German-Soviet Competition in South-Eastern Europe

The annexation of Austria and the Munich Agreement constituted substantial readjustments of the Treaty of Versailles and caused a change in the balance of power in eastern and south-eastern Europe. This development first and foremost weakened France's political and military position as a result of the dissolution of the Little Entente. Secondly, both France and Britain lost international prestige. Finally, the Italians neither wished nor were able to react to the German annexation of Austria, as they had done in 1934 at Brenner. This led to a destabilization of the status quo on the eastern periphery of Europe, from the Baltic in the north to the Mediterranean in the south. The situation was characterized by increasing demands for revisions and competition between the Great Powers to win the race for influence and control in an area in which the old balance of power was in the process of rapid change. This also meant that the rivalry between Germany and Italy in south-eastern Europe intensified.

The German annexation of the Sudetenland, as well as the establishment of an autonomous Slovakia on 6 October 1938 and Carpatho-Ukraine on 8 October, led to Hungarian demands for readjustments with Slovakia. On 2 November 1938 Hungary was entrusted with Carpatho-Ukraine by the Axis Powers at the so-called First Vienna Award. In this way Hungary also accepted *de facto* the hegemony of the Axis Powers in the area.

The establishment of the protectorate in Bohemia and Moravia and Germany's takeover and control of Memel on 23 March 1939, as well as German demands for revisions directed against Poland on 23 March 1939, were followed on 25 March 1939 by an ultimatum issued by Mussolini to the Albanian King Zog. Italy claimed the establishment of a formal protectorate in Albania and the right to station troops in the country. The Italian ultimatum was rejected and on 7 April 1939 Italian troops marched into Albania.[876] This action took place without prior notice to Germany, just as Germany had marched into Prague without consulting the Italians, and must be seen as an Italian countermove to the German campaign. In this way, the Italians gained control of the strategically important Otranto Strait, the entrance to the Adriatic, and therefore crucial for the control of navigation to and from Yugoslavia. In addition, Italian troops were now placed immediately north of Greece.

At a meeting held on 15 April the same year Göring informed Ciano that Yugoslavia fell completely within the Italian sphere of interest, yet Germany would continue to claim her "normal" economic interests in the country.[877] On 22 May 1939 Germany and Italy concluded an alliance and friendship agreement, the so-called Pact of Steel. At the first meeting between Hitler and Ciano, held on 12 August 1939, Hitler stated Germany's geostrategic and defensive position. Regarding the eastern borders of Germany, the best method of defence was attack, Hitler claimed, and added that he planned to act before 15 October 1939. In response to this, Ciano stressed that Yugoslavia constituted the problem to Italy that Poland did to Germany. Hitler called upon Ciano to react [militarily] at the first opportunity and to split the country into Croatian and Dalmatian states.[878]

On 23 August 1939 the Soviet Minister of Foreign Affairs, Molotov, and his German colleague, Ribbentrop, signed a non-aggression pact, the so-called Hitler-Stalin Pact. In a secret protocol recognized in 1988 by Soviet historians, the eastern and central European area was divided into German and Soviet spheres of interest.[879] Hitler allocated Eastern Poland, Finland, Estonia, Latvia, Lithuania and Bessarabia, the latter being part of Romania, to the Soviets. This triggered a new surge of revisionism with consequences for the states throughout the whole area, from Finland in the north to Greece in the south. On 1 September 1939 Germany attacked Poland from the west. On 17 September 1939 Soviet troops moved into eastern Poland. On 28 September 1939 Germany and the Soviet Union made a so-called border and friendship agreement. On 30 November 1939 the Soviet Union invaded Finland, starting the first Winter War which ended on 12 March 1940 and resulted in Soviet territorial expansion at the expense of Finland.

On 11 February 1940, following protracted negotiations, Germany signed a trade agreement with the Soviet Union. The agreement prescribed Soviet delivery of raw materials to Germany in the period February 1940 to August 1941 amounting to a total value of 1 billion RM (in 1938 Soviet deliveries to Germany amounted to 50 million RM). German counter-deliveries were to be settled within 27 months. From a German perspective the agreement was important because of the British blockade of Germany.[880] The agreement marked the beginning of a long-term cooperation between the two states. At the same time, it was soon revealed that the Soviet Union intended to join the competition with Germany for influence in south-eastern Europe, a fact which created steadily escalating tension between the two powers.

Following the German campaign in Denmark, Norway, Holland, Belgium and France, the Red Army occupied the three Baltic states of Estonia, Latvia and Lithuania. Meanwhile, German policy in the Balkans aimed to preserve peace, i.e. the status quo, or at least to isolate conflicts in the area.[881] On 26 June 1940 the Soviet Union presented Romania with an ultimatum prescribing the surrender of Bessarabia, which had been ceded to the Soviet Union in the secret protocol between Hitler and Stalin, and Northern Bukovina. Hitler advised Romania to surrender, and offered German protection in return. As a result, Germany's grip on south-eastern

Europe was further strengthened. On 1 July 1940 Romania renounced the British guarantee but had to leave Southern Dobrudscha to revisionist Bulgaria in August. This intensified Hungary's claim for Transsylvania, thus creating fear in Germany of a Hungarian-Romanian war. At the Second Vienna Award, signed on 30 August 1940, the two "Axis Powers of law and order" ceded Transsylvania to Hungary and guaranteed the rest of Romania its inviolability.[882]

The Soviet Union had not been informed about the Second Vienna Award, a fact that caused dissatisfaction in Moscow. Furthermore, Soviet claims for Southern Bokuvina would cut across German interests in the future. Accordingly Romania rapidly became dependent on Germany. On 6 September General Antonescu became head of a dictatorship and shortly afterwards asked Germany for help in reorganizing the Romanian army. In the period 11 September to 8 October 1940 German troops, including fighter and anti-aircraft personnel, arrived in Romania to protect the oilfields producing supplies for Germany, to train the army and to prepare German and Romanian troops for a common effort against the Soviet Union.[883] This left Greece and Yugoslavia as the only anti-revisionist states in former Russian, Austro-Hungarian and Ottoman lands who were not confronted with demands for revision.

On 13 September Italian troops from Libya attacked British dominated Egypt and seized control of Sollum and Sidi Barrani. About three days after the establishment of Germany's *de facto* control of Romania, Italy called for the right to march into and seize certain strategic places in Greece. On 28 October Metaxas rejected the Italian ultimatum and Italy and Greece were at war.

Germany, Italy and the Attack on Greece

It has been claimed that the Italian attack on Greece was part of an overall German-Italian strategy. This thesis was launched by Martin van Creveld, who believed that the so-called German-Italian "peripheral warfare" was formulated after aborted plans to land German troops in Britain.[884]

MacGregor Knox has since firmly rejected Crevelds's thesis. Knox stresses the competition between Germany and Italy and underlines the fact that Mussolini tried to conduct a policy which made Italy Germany's equal partner. Industrial circles in Italy and Ciano himself believed that Italy would never be recognized on equal terms in German plans for a redefined Europe: Neuropa.[885] These plans left room for only one industrial nation: Germany.[886] This did not correspond with the Italian Fascists' plans for modernization[887] and Great Power status. Mussolini visualized Italy taking part in a so-called "parallel war", in which Italy drove British forces out of the eastern Mediterranean and Egypt single-handed, while Germany fought Britain in Western Europe.[888] Knox bases his thesis on extensive unpublished material of Italian provenance, point-ing out several important fields in which Germany threatened Italy's Great Power dreams and thus rejecting Crevelds's narrow military strategic approach.

Today the consensus of opinion is that Hitler did want "peace in the Balkans" and that the Italian assault on Greece was part of a parallel war.

The German march into oil-rich Romania infuriated Mussolini.[889] He had expected a joint Italian-German move against Romania, not least because previous problems between Romania and her neighbours had been settled within the framework of German-Italian cooperation. The Italian dictator decided to attack Greece without giving prior notice to Hitler, in order "to pay him [Hitler] back in his own coin"; moreover, Il Duce thought it would be appropriate for Hitler to read in the papers that he [Mussolini] had marched into Greece.[890]

As a result of a meeting between Mussolini and Ciano, held on 15 October 1940, it was decided that two of the Ionian islands, Northern Epiros and Salonika, should be occupied. This would improve Italy's position in the Mediterranean *vis-à-vis* Britain's. The second phase of the action was aimed at the total occupation of Greece, thus ensuring both economic and political control. Mussolini intended to seize Mersa Matruth in Egypt[891] just before the assault on Greece to avoid British relief action. According to the Italian schemes, an Egypt under Italian control would result in the British Empire being as good as lost.[892] It is also possible to see the Italian plans for the attack on Greece as part of a large-scale design which included an attack on Egypt to drive the British from the eastern Mediterranean, thus constituting an important step towards the establish-ment of an Italian Empire in the Mediterranean, Middle East and Africa which would make Italy a Great Power on a par with Germany.

German-Italian relations during the first years of the war were character-ized by strong competition in south-eastern Europe. In the period between the outbreak of the war and the Italian entrance into the conflict, Italy tried to use her *non beligeranza*, i.e. "non beligerent" status, to take a lead-ing position in a neutral Balkan bloc.[893] Grazzi described the German-Italian trade competition in the Balkans and in the Levant as very tough and was of the opinion that Italy could have won the Levant trade, had she not entered the war: "...The Balkans were an area in which the competition between European nations was most severe, and it goes without saying that the closest competitors we found in our way were always the Germans. Without our entrance into the war, we could have conquered the whole of the Levant...[894]

Grazzi may have been over-optimistic, however; a German overview of the situation dated 19 September 1940 stresses that Italy's share of south-eastern Europe's total trade rose after the outbreak of the war. In Turkey and Greece this happened at the expense of German trade.[895]

Grazzi explains how a concession for a nickel mine in Lokris, Greece, in this period was just about going to be transfered from German control to the Italian firm Azienda Minirali Metallici Italiani.[896] The mine in Lokris was the only nickel mine in south-eastern Europe[897] and had been administered by the German firm Krupp until then. MacVeagh stated that he detected growing German jealousy of Italian success during this period.[898] Furthermore, direct Italian control of Greece would have threatened Germany's economic position in the country even further, so from this point of view an Italian occupation of Greece would clash with German interests.

As late as 24 October 1940, four days before the Italian assault on Greece, Hitler recommended that Greece be persuaded to join the Axis.[899] The following day Hitler was informed that Mussolini planned an attack on Greece. To avoid this he insisted on a meeting with Mussolini, yet the meeting was not set until 28 October, that is after the war between Greece and Italy had broken out.[900] Hondros argues that Hitler had the chance to veto the Italian action before the campaign started and concludes that Hitler accepted the Italian action.[901] However, this does not mean that the Italian attack was part of a shared German-Italian plan. According to Hitler's aide-de-camp, Major Gerhard Engel, the German dictator regarded the Italian campaign as "revenge for [Germany's occupation of] Norway and France" and linked it to the fact that Mussolini was worried about Germany's dominant economic position in Greece.[902] Accordingly, Hitler interpreted the Italian move in the context of German-Italian competition.

Following the German occupation of Greece in April 1941 Germany forestalled the Italians by ensuring German control of the most important

economic interests. When the Italian authorities laid claim to the administration of the Powder and Cartridge Company, the Germans simply took
over the firm.[903] Negotiations between the Greek owners and Krupp in
May 1941 ensured Germany all-important mining products in Greece.[904]

A circular from IG Farben dated 22 May 1941 describes the way in
which Germany and Italy had each sent a financial delegation to Greece
following the occupation, to confiscate, purchase and administer Greek
companies. This led to German-Italian competition and created, according
to the report, an "unfortunate situation" which harmed the prestige of the
two countries. As a result of this, the German government suggested that
the above-mentioned commissions be withdrawn and that the two Axis
Powers make a so-called "economic truce" (wirtschaftlicher Waffenstill-
stand) until the governmental committees of Germany and Italy had
divided Greece into zones of interest.[905]

Germany and the Greek-Italian War

The Italian invasion encountered powerful Greek resistance. In mid-
November 1940 the Greek forces launched an offensive and were victorious
on a broad front; suddenly the war threatened to be a prolonged one.

Hitler wanted the war to be short and limited, because he feared that the
rest of the Balkans would be involved and would give Britain or the Soviet
Union an excuse to interfere. German diplomats in Sophia, Belgrade and
Ankara made an immediate attempt to persuade the three neighbouring
states to stay out of the conflict.[906]

In addition, the German government tried to divert the Soviet Union's
interest away from the Balkans. At a meeting held in Berlin on 11 and 12
November 1940 Hitler offered Molotov a free hand in the British
dominated areas south of the Soviet Union's borders in the direction of the
Indian Ocean. Moreover, Hitler wanted Soviet participation in an anti-
British continental bloc. On 25 November 1940 the Soviet Union declared
that she was ready to join the Tripartite Pact and thus participate in the
creation of a continental bloc. However, in return, Stalin called for German
acceptance of a Soviet-Bulgarian pact of mutual assistance and the
establishment of certain Soviet strongholds along the Dardanelles and
Bosporus. Such demands made it clear that the Soviet Union was unwilling
to give up its ambitions in south-eastern Europe.[907]

Immediately following the Italian assault, Metaxas turned to Britain for help. At the beginning of November, British troops and anti-aircraft artillery were sent from Egypt to Crete, while aircraft were sent to the mainland.[908] Hitler feared a British attack on the Romanian oilfields. To prevent this, he issued orders on 12 November 1940 to prepare for the occupation of northern Greece and an attack against British airfields within flying range of which British bombers could reach the Romanian oilfields.[909] At a meeting held in the Reich Chancellery on 5 December, Hitler stressed the neccesity of a campaign against Greece. The only way to avoid this was for the Greek army to bring the war with Italy to an end and force the British troops to leave Greek soil.[910] On 13 December 1940 Hitler issued the final orders in preparation for an attack on Greece, the so-called Marita Plan. Five days later, on 18 December, Hitler called for the preparation of an attack on the Soviet Union, the so-called Barbarossa Plan. In the planned war against the Soviet Union, it was imperative that Germany's southern flank be secure, i.e. that the British had left Greece. The only way to avoid an armed conflict between Greece and Germany was for the British armed forces to be evacuated from Greek soil before Operation Barbarossa was launched.

In January 1941 German troops marched through Hungary and were concentrated in southern Romania, just north of Bulgaria. On 17 February 1941 Turkey and Bulgaria exchanged friendship and non-aggression declarations.[911] On 1 March 1941 Bulgaria joined the Tripartite Pact and, on the following day, German troops marched into the country.[912] After German assurances that their movements were not directed towards Turkey, the government in Ankara opted to stay out of the conflict.[913] The German entry into Bulgaria clashed with Soviet interests and was further-more viewed with disapproval in Greece and Britain. On 5 March 1941 three British divisions and an armoured brigade were transferred from North Africa to Greece. On 25 March Yugoslavia joined the Tripartite Pact, but two days later the government was overthrown by pro-western Serbian officers. On 6 April German troops moved into Yugoslavia from Austria, Hungary and Bulgaria; these were followed by Hungarian and Italian troops and on 17 April Yugoslavia surrendered unconditionally.

Concurrently with the attack on Yugoslavia, German troops moved from Bulgaria towards Greece. On 27 April German tanks rolled into Athens and on 29 April the British Expeditionary Force had to leave the Greek mainland and head for Crete. Following a German parachute operation, the British subsequently withdrew from Crete as well.[914]

On 18 June 1941 Turkey signed a friendship pact with Germany. In this way, order was restored in the Balkans and the British dislodged. These were the preliminary strategic preconditions for a German attack on the Soviet Union and three days after the agreement with Turkey had been signed, Germany launched Operation Barbarossa.

Informal Negotiations with Greece

Shortly after British aircraft arrived in Greece, Erbach made it clear to Metaxas that it would be seen as *casus belli* if the Greek government granted permission for the Royal Air Force to use the airfields in Macedonia. However, the German minister also declared that the German government was ready to accept that a limited number of British aeroplanes might participate on the frontlines.[915] Consequently, the Greek government ordered the Royal Air Force to be stationed at Athens airport and to call off assaults on Italian positions in Albania. Moreover, the Greek government banned attacks on Romania and the participation of British troops on the frontline.[916] This indicates that it was of urgent importance to Metaxas not to provoke the Germans and to limit the war as much as possible.

On 4 December 1940 Greek forces broke through the Italian lines. For a while Hitler considered the use of German tanks, but unfavourable weather conditions made such an operation impossible. Concurrently, Hitler stressed to the *Luftwaffe*, about to enter the war in the Mediterranean, that Germany was not at war with Greece and it was of paramount importance to avoid any operations directed against Greece.[917] At about the same time informal negotiations between Greece and Germany were initiated. On 5 December 1940 the Greek Ambassador to Germany was told to make his government contact Berlin to arrange the suspension of hostilities with Italy.[918] Shortly afterwards, Rizo-Ragavis told the German security police that he was willing to accept a truce with Italy on the basis of the status quo.[919] The Greek Ambassador was clearly expressing Metaxas's opinion, as in mid-December 1940 the dictator sent the same message through a middleman to Canaris. Maniadakis subsequently received a German compromise proposal through the German cultural attaché. According to this proposal German troops were to go between the Italian and Greek armies to enforce the conclusion of an armistice. In return Greece must declare her neutrality in the Great Power conflict and compel all British troops to leave Greece.[920] The proposal was repeated to the Greek Ambassador to Spain on 17 December 1940.[921]

208

The Greek government replied that the compromise must be delivered through regular diplomatic channels if it were to be considered: the reason for this was that the Greek government wanted the British to be informed officially as well.[922]

On 20 December 1940 Metaxas met Erbach for the first time since the Italian invasion. The German Minister asked Metaxas if the Greek alliance with Britain was also directed at Germany, to which the Greek dictator replied that it was not: this would only be the case if Germany became involved in Balkan matters.[923] Furthermore, Metaxas informed the German government that he intended to prevent the landing of British troops on the Greek mainland as long as German troops remained north of the Danube, i.e. out of Bulgaria.[924]

That Greece still wanted to avoid provocation of Germany became clear once more when the Greeks refused to participate in British-Turkish talks, held in January 1941, about the formation of a common Balkan front directed against both Axis Powers.[925]

In January 1941 the conditions of the German proposal put forward in December were altered, as the Germans now also demanded control of the airports in Macedonia.[926] The availabale sources do not reveal whether the Greek government commented on this. However, Koliopoulos mentions that, shortly before his death on 29 January 1941, Metaxas planned to take over from Papagos as head of the general staff, a move which would have met German wishes expressed in May 1940.[927]

After the death of Metaxas on 29 January 1941, the King proposed the formation of a national government with the participation of leading Venizelist politicians, a move which would be appreciated by Britain.

On 21 February 1941 Franz von Papen, German Ambassador to Turkey, contacted the Greek Ambassador in Ankara. Von Papen offered guarantees for the inviolability of Greek territory. Greece could keep what she had won in the war against Italy if the Greek government agreed to allow German troops to dislodge the British forces.[928] At the same time, several Greek officers were planning a *coup* in order to form a government that was willing to conclude a peace with the Axis Powers.[929] On 6 March Pangalos informed Erbach that he represented influential military men who planned the establishment of a pro-Axis government. The condition for this was that Germany would guarantee peace on the basis of the status quo.

In the following week and a half, both the Greek armed forces and the Greek government contacted the German government. On 18 March 1941 the Greek Ambassador to Germany, Alexandros Rizo-Ragavis visited

Weizäcker. The Greek Ambassador admitted that Greece had made a mistake in accepting the British guarantee and indicated that the Greek government was ready to oust the British forces if the war in Albania - ceased. However, the Greek *demarches* did not receive an answer from Germany. On 17 March 1941 Hitler issued a new order concerning Operation Marita, and on 24 March Erbach received orders to discontinue all talks with the Greek government.[930]

The main difference between the German and Greek proposals concerned the presence of British troops in Greece. German demands became increasingly rigorous in the period December 1940 to February 1941, in that Germany finally demanded the right to use her own troops to dislodge the British Expeditionary Force. Originally, the demand was that the Greek government should resolve this problem.

In conclusion, Greek-German negotiations indicate that Germany preferred to avoid going to war with Greece and that she was ready to sacrifice Italian interests to this effect. However, the landing of British troops in Greece posed a serious threat to the forthcoming German attack on the Soviet Union and made a peaceful solution with Greece impossible.

GREECE AND GERMANY

Changes within German Policy and the Growing Conflict

The aggressive and militant turn in Germany's policy, its centralization and ideologization as well as its efforts to create autarchy, had serious consequences for Greek-German relations.

Taught by the experience of the previous season, the Greek government tried to peg tobacco prices for 1938-1939 by limiting the cultivated area to a maximum of 86,000 hectares, considerably less than in previous seasons.[931]

In turn, the German tobacco company Reemtsma made efforts to establish itself in a monopoly position as buyer in Germany by persuading other importers of Greek tobacco to change commodities through subsidy schemes.[932] Reemtsma's share of the total German purchases of Greek tobacco amounted to 68 per cent in 1938-1939.[933] In addition, German purchases became yet more dominant when the Austrian clearing was incorporated into the German one on 14 April 1938. Thus, 1938 was marked by a clear indication that both Greece and Germany were attempting to gain control of the movement of prices on the tobacco market.

At the same time an increasing number of Greek businessmen expressed their wish to have Britain in the market, in order to reduce dependence on Germany. By the end of July 1938 a so-called Anglo-Greek committee was established to investigate the possibility of extending the trade between Britain and Greece.[934] Although the motive for this was ostensibly business related, MacVeagh explains that fear of war played a role too, and that it was becoming a widely-held opinion in business circles that Greece should trade with a country [like Britain] which controlled the oceans.[935]

In this connection, it is important to note that the largest Jewish community in Greece lived in Salonika. 86 per cent of all Greek Jews were inhabitants of this city and made up about 20 per cent of its total population prior to 1940.[936] Many Jews in this area were traditionally employed in the tobacco industry.[937] Germany's severe race policy and her efforts to impose this on business partners appears to have made an impact on the development of the tobacco trade in 1938-1939. It is telling that Jewish merchants who had been working for the Austrian tobacco monopoly were dismissed and had to find new customers after *Anschluss*.[938] Voivodas, a family business dealing in tobacco, lost Reemtsma as a customer due to a complaint from the German Vice-Consul in Volos that a Jew was employed by the family.[939]

Against German expectations Greek tobacco prices rose by 15 per cent in 1938-1939 in relation to the previous year and almost all of the crop was sold. This trend the German Vice-Consul in Kavalla ascribed to mutual competition among the German buyers, who unwillingly drove up prices. Furthermore, the trade, according to the same source, was marked by expectations that the British were to enter the market.[940]

This relative success, seen from a Greek point of view, was mirrored by cautious optimism regarding legislation. The upper size-limit of the cultivated area was increased from 86,000 to 92,700 hectares. All other legislational activities displayed an interest in encouraging Britain to enter the Greek tobacco market. Thus, the government granted 2 million Dr. for farmers to experiment with growing Virginia tobacco, which was preferred on the British market.[941]

The preliminaries to Greek-German trade negotiations in the autumn of 1939 included a proposal put forward by the German cotton company Bremer Baumwoll-Aktiengesellschaft (BREBAG) dated August that year. It is worth considering this proposal in detail, as not only was it in line with *Grossraumwirtschaft* concepts, but it also corresponded with efforts to establish *Lebensraum* and autarchy, both of which had strong affinities with Nazi ideology.[942] BREBAG had been established with an eye to extending the cotton production in what it called "the eastern cotton-producing countries, to the mutual interest of both parts", that is Germany and Greece in this particular case.

BREBAG's aim, in close cooperation with the Greek government, was to increase Greek cotton production and make it more effective. The German firm offered to deliver the required know-how and agricultural technology. Thereafter, a Greek company was to be established to organize the export of cotton to Germany. BREBAG argued that the project would lead to rising Greek employment as well as to an increase in the cotton export; additionally, prices would be higher than on the international market and protected from fluctuations on the world market.

BREBAG stressed that Germany's *Raum* policy, namely an expansion of German-dominated land in Europe, would guarantee this happening.

It is important to bear in mind that an increase of cotton import from Greece would make Germany less dependent on overseas markets and in that way allow her to move a step further towards basing trade on commercial exchange with continental Europe, rendering her immune to a blockade.[943] In many respects, BREBAG's proposal resembled plans for a German-Romanian extractive oil project, included in the above-mentioned Wohlthat Agreement, as well as plans proposed by IG Farben and *Mitteleuropäischer Wirtschaftstag* to increase the soya bean production in Romania and Bulgaria to meet German demand.[944]

The cotton plan, however, was never realized. This must partly be attributed to the outbreak of war, which, in particular during its first six months, hampered the development of Greek-German trade. However, the failure should also be seen against a background of increasing conflict in Greek and German interests regarding commercial exchange between the two countries. In this respect, and especially regarding the proposal from BREBAG, it is revealing that on 5 September 1939 Varvaresos told a British representative of the international finance committee that he feared substantial German demands in Greek-German trade negotiations and that he had the connection with the recently concluded German-Romanian agreement, namely the Wohlthart Agreement, especially in mind. According to Varvaresos, he had made it clear to the German delegation from the beginning that the government in Athens would not be willing to adjust the development of the Greek economy to the demands of another country.[945] Finally, the Greek attitude should probably also be seen against the background of growing British pressure on Greece to resist Germany's infiltration.

In conclusion, the Germans did not succeed in controlling the develop-ment of the Greek tobacco market. Threats to cut off trade were never realized, and it is questionable whether such interruptions to commerce would have been possible at all, if the demand of German consumers were taken into account.[946] In addition, it would probably also have been expensive to place the same orders on another market, making a sudden reorganization of the import from Greece unlikely.[947] However, this does not alter the fact that the tobacco industry, as already demonstrated, was very sensitive to prospects of and actual changes in Greek-German trade relations, and it is important to stress that the Greek government was vulnerable to German demands: this in turn resulted in Greek dependence on Germany. Furthermore, it seems safe to say that Germany continued and stepped up her attempt to control the Greek economy and to draw Greece into an economic orbit in which Germany was also trying to include a number of other south-eastern European countries. Greece responded to this by internal reorganization, as well as by trying to persuade Britain to relieve Greece of the mounting German economic pressure. This subject is investigated in the following section.

British Countermoves in Greece

Anschluss forced Britain to see her positions threatened in Europe well as in the Middle East. Consequently, the Foreign Office began to see Turkey as the last bulwark against German aggression towards the British Empire in the Middle East and India. Lord Halifax, Foreign Secretary, expressed his anxiety as follows "...Beyond Turkey...lie the lands of the Middle East (Syria, Iraq, Palestine, Saudi Arabia, Egypt) through which run our sea or air communications with India [...] It is therefore scarcely too much to say that Turkey has become, not the main, but the only obstacle to the Drang nach Osten..."[948]

However, Greece was also regarded as an important hindrance to German progress towards the eastern Mediterranean. According to the Foreign Office: "...a friendly Greece is essential, while a Greece subservient to Berlin would constitute a menace to be avoided at all costs. If the defence of Egypt be a criterion, then first in importance comes the consolidation of British influence in Turkey and Greece..." [949]

This gave rise to a re-evaluation of the Ministry's policy towards the German penetration of south-eastern Europe. To meet the latter threat the British government decided to give Turkey a £16 million credit for industrial products and arms.[950] The Foreign Office hoped that this departure from regular practice would provide a model for thwarting further German penetration of the Balkans.

214

Simultaneously, Greece was looking for new methods to limit her dependence on Germany as a result of increasing conflicts of interest in Greek-German relations. The Greek economy was largely dependent on imported fuel, i.e. primarily coal and coke. Between 1934 and 1938 Germany's share of this import grew from four to 37 per cent: the result was that Germany had replaced Britain as Greece's main supplier.

At the end of the tobacco season, in April 1938, Andreas Apostolidis, the Greek Minister of Finance, launched a proposal that might benefit both British industry and the Greek economy. He suggested that Greece buy British coal in exchange for Greek state bonds.[951] The proposal won the support of the Foreign Office. Halifax underlined the fact that *Anschluss* made British assistance necessary and that the coal proposal could be realized if export guarantees were granted.[952] Nevertheless, the Department of Export Credits rejected the proposal, referring to the Greek debt.[953] The Miners Department, responsible for the coal industry, reacted promptly. The Foreign Office was asked to make another attempt[954] and the Ministry of Trade was mobilized to pursue the possibility of regaining the lost market: Greece.[955]

However, the Department of Export Credits' decision remained immovable[956] and the proposal fell on stony ground. The decision was based upon Greece's poor reputation as a debtor: this seemingly also prevented the support of the British coal industry. Furthermore, Britain was at this point concentrating on the Scandinavian market and therefore did not want to challenge Germany on the south-eastern European market, which had lower priority in British trade policy.[957]

Concurrently, the British government decided to create an institutional framework to establish a systematic and continuous economic strategy against the German push forward in south-eastern Europe. In June 1938 the so-called Interdepartmental Committee on Economic Assistance to Central and South-East Europe was established. The committee was often referred to as the Leith-Ross Committee, after the senior economic advisor to the British government, Sir Frederick Leith-Ross. The committee operated at the highest inter-ministerial level and included, among other people, representatives from the Foreign Office, the Chancellor of the Exchequer, the Ministries of Trade and Overseas Trade, and the Bank of England.[958]

To effect an efficient blockade of the German penetration of Greece, the committee decided, on 27 June 1938, that Greece's credit-worthiness must be revalued. First, Greece and Turkey must be treated equally and, secondly, an increasing proportion of Greek tobacco must be directed towards the British market.[959]

The first suggestion met resistance from both the Ministry of Trade and the Treasury. The latter saw the Greek national debt as an insuperable obstacle, a point of view shared by Neville Chamberlain.[960]

The committee suggested that British purchases of Greek tobacco be increased by 110 per cent.[961] This would constitute only two per cent of the total German tobacco purchases and must therefore be seen primarily as a political signal to Greece. The proposal was criticized by the Ministry of Trade, who stressed that the import of Greek tobacco clashed with American interests. In addition, Britain had to consider her relations with the Commonwealth countries and the Dominions. The import of cigars from India and tobacco from Southern Rhodesia would suffer from competition with Greece.[962] This illustrates clearly that it was not only imperial preferences, as outlined by Wendt, but also more general British trade interests that hindered a considerable increase in imports from south-eastern Europe.

Following the September crisis and the Munich Agreement, uncon-firmed reports claimed that Germany would not guarantee the purchase of tobacco and other Greek agricultural products. Guarantees would only be issued if the Greeks complied with German demands. Among other things, Germany wanted the right to establish air bases on Greek soil, the Greek government's official support of Nazi propaganda intended for educational purposes, Metaxas's cooperation in creating close diplomatic relations between the Balkan states and Germany and information about all kinds of financial support that Greece might obtain from France or Britain. The reports came from the British Legation in Athens; the information was supplied by secret, but usually reliable, sources. Furthermore, additional confidential sources confirmed the reports. Nonetheless, the British Legation doubted their correctness.[963] Leith-Ross himself tended to believe the information, however, as he had previously heard of similar German demands on Romania. He believed that this might be an official in-struction issued by the German government to all the embassies in central and south-eastern Europe. For this reason, according to Leith-Ross, it was time for Britain to help Greece.[964] Ingram from the Foreign Office was inclined to believe that Leith-Ross was right, yet would not ignore the possibility that the reports were constructed by the Greeks to ensure British help.[965] Later it was revealed that the Romanian document was a forgery circulated by the Romanian authorities.[966]

The relationship with Greece was brought before the Foreign Policy committee in November. On that occasion Lord Halifax proposed British purchases of Greek tobacco to the value of £ 500,000. Moreover, he insisted that the Prime Minister put pressure on the British tobacco companies, as neither Leith-Ross nor himself had been able to persuade them. Even so, it proved impossible to convince Chamberlain; instead the committee decided to investigate the possibility of offering Greece non-commercial credit intended for arms purchases. Finally, at a meeting held in December, the tobacco proposal was rejected and instead a £2 million credit was granted for arms purchases in Britain. The decision was reached in spite of resistance from John Simon, the Exchequer, who wanted to include in the agreement the problem of the Greek national debt.[967]

Meanwhile, Greece's economic dependence on Germany grew. The British Minister described the situation as follows: "...The strength of Germany's stronghold over Greece became ever more evident in the course of the year [1938]. Greek shops overflowed with poor quality German goods, and importers wishing to import more saleable articles from other countries were informed by the Bank of Greece that they could only import from Germany. To this visible economic domination, the events of the year in Austria and Czecho-Slovakia added increased fear of Germany's might..."[968]

On 24 March 1939, the day after the conclusion of the Wohlthat Agreement, Orme Sargent, the head of the Southern Department, expressed his fears about the negative psychological effects that the agreement might have on Greece: "... the psychological effect of Germany's economic success in Romania, following upon her political successes elsewhere, is bound to have a very depressing effect upon the Greek Government. In fact, this is obviously the right moment for Germany to strike: it is for this reason I expect she will.[...] ... personally I am bound to assume, after what we have experienced, that H. M. Government will be in this matter too slow and too cautious to take any effective measure to prevent Germany from achieving her economic objectives in Greece if she makes a push to do so..."[969]

The defeatist attitude of the Greek administration is reflected by S. Simmonds, trade secretary at the British legation, in his description of a meeting with Apostolidis, the Greek Minister of Finance, on 28 March

1939: "...I went to see Monsieur Apostolides this morning about commercial affairs and found him in a state of great depression.[...] He asked me not to mention the question of British buying of Greek tobacco as he was sick of hearing about it – he knew it would lead to nothing but more talk.[...] He referred to the recent German economic arrangement with Romania and said that, as far as he could see, Romania had given away almost everything. What was more, he added, was that Greece's position was as hopeless as that of Romania and she might be called on to make a similar or worse agreement..."[970]

In 1938 and 1939 Leith-Ross and Lord Halifax had regular contact with the Imperial Tobacco Company (ITC), the largest tobacco company in the world. The Foreign Office suggested three different ways to introduce Greek tobacco onto the British market. Greek tobacco belonged to the Oriental type and was mainly used in cigarettes. One way of marketing the tobacco was to produce a pure Oriental blend. Another way was to mix Virginia tobacco, which dominated the British market, and Oriental tobacco, as in the American cigarettes Chesterfield, Camel and Lucky Strike. Finally, it was suggested that a small quantity of Oriental tobacco be added to all British brands.

In a memorandum dated 16 March 1939, Lord Dulverton from the Imperial Tobacco Company informed Sargent that all three methods had been rejected with reference to the so-called "Virginia Clause". The latter simply indicated that 99 per cent of British smokers were willing to smoke pure Virginia tobacco.[971]

A report from the Anglo-Hellenic League, which worked to promote the sales of Oriental tobacco in Britain, states that it was not until after the First World War that Oriental tobacco lost its share of the British market. The export of Greek tobacco to Britain amounted to seven per cent of the total tobacco export in 1919. Thereafter it fell and had settled at one per cent since 1927. This was a strange development, since Greek tobacco was used for cigarettes and the consumption of cigarettes throughout Europe grew rapidly in the 1920s and 1930s. The proportion of tobacco used for cigerettes in Britain increased from 41.5 per cent in 1912 to 73.5 per cent in 1935. American tobacco made up between 70 and 80 per cent of the British market in the 1930s while 20 per cent came from the Empire.[972] The explanation for the decrease in Oriental tobacco was attributed to improved methods of cultivation in the United States. The latter ensured

218

standardization and quality. The blend became much simpler and cheaper to produce than Greek tobacco, which varied in quality. The import of tobacco from the imperial countries was promoted by means of the so-called Imperial Preferences from 1919 onwards and by the Empire Marketing Board, established in 1926 to persuade British consumers to buy products from the Empire.[973]

In a report from the British Ministry of Trade concerning the cartellization of the tobacco market in Britain, it appears that, in the case of the Imperial Tobacco Company, the connection between importer and producer was very close. The company owned tobacco plantations and shipment facilities in the United States. Moreover, the tobacco company had invested huge sums in marketing Virginia tobacco in Britain. In 1939, 75 per cent of the tobacco consumption in Britain was supplied by the Imperial Tobacco Company. Furthermore, the firm largely controlled the retail stage through bonus agreements.[974]

The Imperial Tobacco Company was therefore hardly powerless against the Virginia Clause, indeed the case in point indicates that its interests were intimately knit with those of Virginia tobacco. Consequently, the problems arising from negotiations between the Foreign Office and the Imperial Tobacco Company can best be characterized as a conflict of interests between two types of tobacco, Oriental and Virginia (ITC's interests were linked to the latter, while the Foreign Office pursued the interests of the former).

A letter from the Treasury to the Foreign Secretary dated 31 March 1939 stressed that arms credits were insufficient to protect Greece from German pressure. For this reason the problem related to purchases of Greek tobacco should be handled as a political issue.[975] The answer from the Foreign Office was long in coming. Sargent used the guarantee declaration as an excuse to repeat his request. He feared that the Greek acceptance of guarantees would lead to a German trade embargo of Greece.[976] Nor did this initiative lead to any results. At the end of May, Leith-Ross went to Athens to discuss the tobacco and debt problem, once again without reaching a solution.

While plans for British purchases of Greek tobacco in this pre-war period were futile, an Anglo-Greek agreement offering arms credit amounting to £2 million was signed on 12 July 1939.[977]

In contrast it is notable that British policy towards Romania managed to unite state and private economic interests. A British-Romanian clearing arrangement made on 2 September 1938 led the way to an increase of Romanian exports of oil and grain to Britain. A similar agreement with Greece was obstructed by the limited possibilities of marketing Greek export products in Britain. Export of Greek tobacco to the British market was incompatible with the interests of the British tobacco firms to an extent that tempts one believe that the smoking habits of the British jeopardized Britain's security policy in the eastern Mediterranean. Nonetheless, the problem illustrates the complex nature of the interaction between different states and supports Wendt's focus on the multiple forms of interaction between them.

In the light of the Greek example, we must agree with Wendt that Britain was not able to combine foreign policy interests with a determined commercial effort. Britain was then, and had long been, in a situation whereby her security and foreign policy interests were inconsistent with private economic ones.

The outbreak of war, however, and Greece's geopolitical position led to increased Greek-British cooperation, especially in the field of trade policy. Greece concluded war trade agreements with Britain in October 1939 and January 1940. In accordance with the agreement of 26 January 1940 Britain committed herself to buying £500,000 worth of Greek tobacco (about six per cent of the total Greek tobacco production).[978] In return Greece had to service her debt at a rate of 43 per cent, instead of 40 per cent, for the duration of the war; this was still considerably less than the bondholders had demanded.[979] Britain also offered free passage through contraband control of oil, sugar, wheat, coal, iron, copper, etc., destined for Greece.[980]

That Greece agreed to participate in Britain's economic warfare against Germany must be attributed to the Greek shipping trade, which operated mainly in British dominated waters and was producing hard currency. In 1939 international shipping brought in £2 million, or 1.1 million Dr.; this doubled the following year, to £4.7 million, or 2.6 milllion Dr.[981] Further-more, Greece was dependent on supplies of various important foodstuffs and raw materials from overseas, and, in addition, a good relationship with the wealthy Greek colony in Egypt was also of great importance. This is clearly indicated by the fact that Nikoloudis went to Egypt to promote the Metaxas regime to the Greek population there, a large majority of whom were known to be Venizelist.[982]

Finally, Greece obtained a loan of £2.4 million in 1939 and another of more than £13 million in 1940.[983] In his review of 1939 Palairet described the temporary war agreement as a manifest sign of goodwill and benevolent neutrality from Greece.[984] Koliopoulos, however, doubts whether Greece's attitude could be described as neutral,[985] a plausible reservation if we consider the period before the German campaign in Denmark and Norway. However, it is important to stress that, when the war escalated in Europe during the summer of 1940, Greece began to violate her war trade agreement with Britain.[986]

The American Reaction and the Strengthening of Greek-American Trade Connections

On 15 November 1938 the United States and Greece signed a trade agreement. It was not published but was based on the so-called *modus vivendi* principle.[987] MacVeagh believed that Greece signed the agreement due to fears of war and saw it as a Greek surrender. From a subsequent German report, it appears that the agreement gave the Americans a virtual monopoly in Greek import of vehicles, radios, refrigerators and electrical kitchen equipment. This had only a minimal impact on imports from Germany.[988]

The trade agreement with the United States was doubtless the result of a softening of the Greek attitude towards the American demands as they were stated in 1937. This makes it plausible that MacVeagh was right when he claimed that it was the fear of war that made Greece depart from her previous attitude. The agreement did not clash with German trade interests and the Greek export to the United States expanded considerably in 1938 and 1939. In addition, emigrant remittances continued to flow into Greece. Overall Greece managed to met the American requests without affecting German interests.

Both Teichova[989] and Nilson[990] underline the fact that the United States had feared a British-German front against American interests since the Munich Agreement. The United States might well have felt pressure from the latter in concluding the agreement with Greece: Greece was still one of the most important markets for American products in German-dominated south-eastern Europe and the British-dominated Levant. In 1939 and 1940 the Americans boosted their participation in Greek trade. Greek exports to the American market grew from 17.1 per cent of total Greek exports in 1938 to 21.6 per cent in 1939 and 25.0 per cent in 1940.

Greek imports from the United States fell from 7.3 per cent in 1938 to 7.0 per cent in 1939, only to rise to 11.4 per cent in 1940. Consequently, imports from the United States were exceeded only by imports from Germany. Emigrant remittances continued to stress the United States' importance to the Greek economy still more.[991]

The Advance of the Axis Powers and Changes in Greece's Security Policy

Extended Cooperation with Turkey and Efforts to Ally with Britain

Germany's conquest of Central Europe in 1938 meant that considerations of security policy became yet more important to Greece and played an increasingly significant role in her foreign policy.

On 27 April 1938, shortly after *Anschluss*, Greece and Turkey signed an additional protocol to the friendship agreement of 1930, this time regarding military and political cooperation.[992] While Greek security policy became increasingly dependent on a good relationship with Turkey and was vulnerable to developments in the eastern Mediterranean, Greece tried to distance herself from Romania and Yugoslavia as a result of Germany's advance into Central Europe.

Anschluss also created a basis for a British-Italian understanding. The high priority given to a status quo in the Mediterranean by both Britain and Italy led to a British-Italian agreement on 16 April 1938.[993] In this way, British endeavours to turn Turkey and Greece into a bulwark against German advances into the area were necessarily combined with a *detente* with Italy.

In May 1938, Metaxas and the King asked the Foreign Office to guarantee Greece against aggression from Bulgaria. However, the Foreign Office was not willing to engage in such an undertaking and concluded that economic aid was the best help Britain could offer Greece.[994]

At the same time MacVeagh received information from the Egyptian Ambassador in Athens that Britain planned to unite the three Levantine states, Greece, Turkey and Egypt, to form a bloc.[995] These plans were never carried out. However, the proposal can be seen as an attempt to form a pro-British security system without direct participation by Britain. It also indicates that Britain gave high priority to defending imperial trade routes by means of the British-Italian *detente*.

The September crisis unleashed fears in Athens of a European war. Immediately after the signing of the Munich Agreement, Metaxas informed Waterlow, at a meeting on 3 October, that he wanted an alliance with Britain. He stressed the importance of the Greek islands and harbours to the British fleet in case of war in the Mediterranean. Neither Waterlow nor the Foreign Office were willing to answer Metaxas. On 16 October Metaxas addressed Waterlow again. The Greek dictator was at pains to stress that his government had to prepare the country for a war between Britain and Italy, as such could easily involve Greece. For this reason, he wanted an alliance with Britain or at least British support for the development of a strong coastal and air defence. If this were not possible, Greece would have to observe a strictly neutral attitude in case of a conflict between Britain and Italy. Furthermore, an alliance with Britain would make it possible for Greece to escape from Germany's economic stranglehold. Waterlow interpreted the latter to mean that if Britain did nothing to support Greece, Athens would have to accept the "German stranglehold". In his report to the Foreign Office, the British Minister added that influential official Greek sources had confirmed this.[996]

Koliopoulos rejects Waterlow's interpretation and points to Metaxas's general readiness to meet British wishes.[997] Kitsikis argues that Metaxas submitted the proposal by order of the King, and that the Greek dictator himself was against an alliance with Britain out of consideration for Germany.[998] The latter argument is based on a note in Metaxas's diary, made on 20 October 1938, in which the dictator writes that he is certain that the British will not accept the proposal, but that he is relieved. This does not prove that he was acting on royal orders; however, it is important to stress that during this period Metaxas was working to strengthen his position *vis-à-vis* the pro-British King. This made it important to manoeuvre tactically; the above-mentioned note indicates that Metaxas was aware of this.

Koliopoulos mentions the note as well but does not analyse it thoroughly. Neither does he mention the conflicting interests or the power struggle between Metaxas and the King. Finally, he does not consider the political consequences of Greece's economic dependence on Germany, which was the central point in Waterlow's interpretation. In fact during this period the Greek government was exposed to increasing German pressure to adjust the economic development of the country to German demands.

Throughout this time every indication is that the Greek government paid an increasing political regard to Germany. In a note from Metaxas's diary dated 20 October 1938 it appears that the Greek dictator had a meeting with Erbach just after the meeting with Waterlow, apparently in order to explain the situation to the German Minister.[999] About a week earlier, on 13 October, Metaxas had been informed that Walther Funk had told the Turkish Minister of Foreign Affairs that Germany did have interests in the Mediterranean, though they were not direct. In the same period Metaxas asked the King, who was on a private visit to Britain, to meet Hitler. However, the meeting was not set up because the King succeeded in preventing it discreetly.[1000] Nevertheless, this shows that after the September crisis Metaxas attached great importance to emphasizing the closeness of Greek-German relations in public as well as privately. This poses a contrast to Metaxas's attitude in 1937, when he sought to tone down the close relations between Greece and Germany in his confrontations with the public, the King and Britain. It is therefore possible to detect a change in Metaxas's policy towards Germany. This can be explained by Germany's advance into central Europe, by Greek fears of a growing economic state of dependence on Germany and by the strengthening of Metaxas's position of power in relation to the King.

The reason given for the rejection of a Greek alliance by the Foreign Office was consideration for Italy. Furthermore, there was widespread opinion in the Foreign Office that Greece would pursue an active benevolent and neutral policy towards Britain in case of war in the Mediterranean.[1001] In respect of this, it is important to stress the reasons for Waterlow's urging the King to get rid of Metaxas at the turn of the year 1938/1939. According to the British Minister's own account, the King was becoming Metaxas's political hostage. At the same time the regime was in danger of collapsing due to its lack of popularity, and, with such a scenario, the King, according to Waterlow, would quite probably be swept away.

These circumstances made Waterlow fear that the British government would risk losing its influence on Greek politics. MacVeagh depicted Waterlow's intervention as a reaction to the fact that Metaxas was slowly assuming control of Greek foreign policy and the American Ambassador felt that the British government wanted Greece to take a less neutral attitude in the growing Great Power conflict by assuming certain responsibilities in order to support Britain: "...Traditionally England has not exerted any pressure of this kind on Greece in times of peace, trusting to her naval superiority to force Greek compliance once the war is on. But times have changed [...] Mr. Metaxas is not only a German sympathizer personally, but politically a confirmed believer in the advisability of neutrality for his country vis-à-vis the Great Powers. Current rumors as well as the logic of the international situation as springtime approaches make this interpretation a possibility..."[1002]

Waterlow's abortive interventon with the King shocked the Foreign Office because it demonstrated that the British Minister had seemingly lost his influence in that direction. The Foreign Office feared, like Waterlow, that the regime's lack of popularity could lead to its fall and that this would give Italy or Germany better opportunities for infiltration. The Foreign Office believed that a liberalization of the government could serve as a means to reduce such risks. However, it was important that Metaxas should not feel that this was a British attempt to unseat him, as that would provide a perfect incentive for him to turn pro-German.[1003] Thus, Metaxas's improved position in relation to the King from the end of 1938 created British fears that Greece might enter on a pro-German course. This is in line with MacVeagh's suggestion that Britain wanted Greece's support more openly, and that she disliked the prospect of Metaxas opting to keep Greece strictly neutral in the event of a conflict of the Great Powers.

Greek Neutrality and Germany

Immediately after *Anschluss*, Metaxas expressed to Erbach his understanding of the German policy in Austria. The Greek dictator severely criticized the League of Nations and thus the French and British collective security systems. With an out-spokenness unusual for a head of government in a member country of the League of Nations, the German Minister went on, Metaxas expressed his deep indignation that the League of Nations only focused on the interests of the three Great Powers. According to Metaxas, Greece had not received any help during Italy's attack on Corfu in 1923. This had made Greece choose, like Germany, to take necessary precautions and to maintain an armed neutrality.[1004] It must have been near to Metaxas's heart to express his criticism of the League of Nations because the Italians actually did not leave the Greek island until Britain and the League of Nations threatened to start a war in the Mediterranean.[1005]

Shortly after the signing of the Munich Agreement, Metaxas met Erbach. Metaxas declared that in the event of a Great Power conflict he would try to keep Greece neutral as long as possible. The German Minister told *Auswärtiges Amt* that in his opinion this would be impossible on a long-term basis, as the central point in Metaxas's foreign policy was an understanding with the countries in the eastern Mediterranean and mainly with Turkey. Erbach believed that it was quite likely that Greece would join Britain in case of war.

Erbach stated that any official move during the September crisis would have caused the fall of Metaxas. If, and the German Minister saw this as most unlikely, he had supported Germany, the King would have taken action against this and the result would have been revolution. On the other hand, if Metaxas had declared himself in favour of Britain, the Venizelists might well have taken over governmental power.[1006] For this reason, according to Erbach, Greek neutrality was the most that Germany could hope for in case of conflict with Britain.

On 6 March 1939 Goebbels asked Kodzias, who was in Leipzig at that time, to clarify the Greek attitude to the international situation, especially towards Germany's Axis partner Italy. Furthermore, Goebbels told the Greek visitor that Berlin held the view that the Greek King was ill-disposed towards Germany and that Greece had submitted herself to Germany's enemies. With this in mind Goebbels had asked Kodzias to meet him the same day to discuss these issues. Kodzias then asked Metaxas to decide whether he should attend the meeting at all, and, if so, what to say.[1007] Metaxas told Kodzias to meet Goebbels and reject the German assessment of the King. Kodzias was to present the following case: foreign policy was the responsibility of the Greek government [and not the King]. Greece had friendly relations with all Great Powers and intended to remained strictly neutral. In addition, Greece did not want to become involved in non-Balkan issues and had not made any political commitments outside the Balkans.[1008]

Metaxas repeated these points to Goebbels at a meeting held in Athens on 1 April 1939. From Goebbels's diary it is clear that he believed that Metaxas intended to keep Greece on a neutral course and that he was convinced that the Greek dictator wanted friendship and peace with Germany.[1009] The German Minister did not assume that Britain had turned to Greece to participate in a collective security system.

Metaxas therefore stressed to the German government that Greece intended to adhere to her strictly neutral course. Metaxas's proposal for a Greek-British alliance, put forward to Britain both before and after he told Erbach that he intended to keep Greece on a neutral course, must be ascribed to tactical manoeuvring. This is especially true if we consider that

226

Metaxas might well have expected a negative British reply anyway. The British answer prior to the meeting with Erbach indicates that this is a possibility. Another British rejection of the Greek proposal would only make it easier for Metaxas to defend a strictly neutral course against opposition to this policy. An alternative explanation could be that Metaxas's proposal of an alliance on 16 October was ordered by the King, and that Metaxas himself had not anticipated this during his meeting with Erbach. Furthermore, in March 1939 German-British relations had been considerably strained in comparison to the immediate aftermath of the Munich Agreement. This means that, from a Greek point of view, an alliance with Britain – contrary to the situation that pertained during the Abyssinian Crisis and to a certain extent during the September crisis – risked the Germans perceiving it as an act, not only against Italy, but also against herself. Moreover, it was clear that Britain had not managed to limit Greece's dependence on Germany by the spring of 1939.

In any event, the course of action taken by Metaxas can be interpreted as an attempt to keep on good political terms with Germany too, as a strictly neutral course would be of considerably more interest to Germany than to Britain.

Italian Advances in the Balkans and Greek Security Policy

On 7 April 1939 Italian troops crossed the border into Albania. Shortly after midnight between 8 and 9 April, Metaxas told Waterlow that the Greek Military Attaché in Rome had been informed from a reliable source that Italy would attack Corfu in the period 10-12 April 1939. Metaxas also informed Waterlow that he was prepared to resist the Italians with every means, no matter how high the price. The Greek dictator did not ask for British help however.[1010]

On the evening of 8 April Halifax met Crolla, the Italian Chargé d'Affaires in London. The British Foreign Secretary informed Crolla that the British government had defended the British-Italian Agreement dated 12 April 1938 against strong opposition for a long time. Nevertheless, Mussolini had made the position of the British government very difficult. In all circles it was voiced that: "...the Germans invaded Czecho-Slovakia three weeks ago, the Italians now walk into Albania, where is it going to end? And I [Halifax] could not accordingly conceal from him the grave anxiety that His Majesty's Government felt..."

Halifax stated that the British government would view an occupation of Corfu with the utmost seriousness.[1011] On the following day the British Ambassador in Rome gave Ciano a summary of the conversation between Halifax and Crolla.[1012] On 10 April Mussolini ensured Metaxas that Italy intended to respect Greece's territorial integrity.[1013] Metaxas asked Britain to make it clear that the Italian assurances had been due to British efforts only, and were not a result of a previous agreement between the Greek and British governments.[1014]

British officials debated whether the Italian assurances to Greece were sufficient to avoid provoking Italy any further. However, Halifax felt that it was desirable to give a guarantee out of consideration for public opinion at home and in the United States. Halifax's proposal was adopted.[1015]

However, Turkish pressure also seems to have had an impact on Britain's decision. On 10 April Halifax received information from Ankara that the Turkish Minister of Foreign Affairs was "extremely disappointed" that Britain had not taken a firmer stand against Italy.[1016] The British Ambassador to Turkey believed that the outlook of the Turkish Minister of Foreign Affairs could be altered if France and Britain gave an unambiguous and categorical guarantee to Greece in the event of an Italian threat. On the following day, Halifax asked the British Ambassador to Turkey to inform the Turkish Minister of Foreign Affairs that the British government was considering the option of giving a guarantee to Greece.[1017]

On 12 April Ribbentrop informed several German representations that the German attitude to the forthcoming British guarantees was that Germany did not expect other nations [i.e. other than Greece and Romania] to accept such. If this were the case it would be seen as an act against German interests.[1018] Apparently, the German prohibition was not addressed to Greece and the German government seemed willing to allow relations with Greece to remain unaffected in spite of the British guarantees. Shortly before the British government gave the guarantee, Erbach told the Greek Ministry of Foreign Affairs that a British guarantee would displease the German government. Mavroudis replied that the Greek government knew nothing about British guarantees.[1019] Waterlow could confirm the latter because the Greek government had not been informed about the British decision at that time. About a week after Britain had given her guarantee, Mavroudis stressed to Erbach that Greece had not asked for British help and that the guarantee was merely a result of unilateral British conduct. Furthermore, Mavroudis underlined the point that the Greek government would defend the Greek harbours against any aggressor in case of war.[1020] The Greek government was thus anxious to declare its neutrality to the German Minister.

On 12 May 1939 a British-Turkish declaration of mutual assistance in case of war in the Mediterranean was made public. Turkey seemed to be moving towards an alliance with Britain. On 15 June 1939 Metaxas announced to Erbach that the British-Turkish declaration did not alter Greece's strictly neutral position.[1021] In this connection the British Minister noted that the Greek government exercised caution and refrained from making political moves that could be seen as a breach of the country's neutrality. Among other things, the Greeks abstained from opening talks on a staff level with Britain in connection with the implementation of the British guarantee.[1022]

Nevertheless, on 21 August 1939 Metaxas told MacVeagh that Greece was on the side of the Western Powers because this was in the interests of both Greece and Turkey. However, an open declaration of such would provoke Italy and irritate Germany. Metaxas informed MacVeagh that the Turkish government understood the Greek need for caution, and that the Greek government would only maintain this attitude during times of peace.[1023]

The First Six Months of the War. Benevolent Greek Neutrality towards Britain and France

The Italian decision concerning *non belligeranza* and a neutral Balkan bloc headed by Italy resulted in her withdrawing her troops from the Greek border in Albania;[1024] thereafter, Italian-Greek relations improved considerably. Following an exchange of notes in September, Greece and Italy confirmed their wish to cooperate, inspired by the above-mentioned Greek-Italian friendship agreement dated 23 September 1928. The Italians did not succeed as planned, however, in turning Greece into an Italian satellite through a non-aggression and consular pact, thus moving the country away from Britain.[1025]

The Hitler-Stalin Pact and the German-Soviet division of Poland created fears of German-Soviet cooperation in south-eastern Europe, not least apprehensions of bellicose Soviet intentions directed at Turkey. On 18 October 1939, Britain and Turkey concluded an alliance based on mutual assistance. During the same period the Powder and Cartridge

Company began delivering ammunition to the Turkish army. In January 1940 Bodosakis was invited to Turkey by the head of the Turkish General Staff with an eye to reorganizing the Turkish war industry.[1026]

By means of this cooperation Greece assisted one of Britain's non-belligerent allies from shortly after the outbreak of war. The Greek army also participated in secret talks about an allied landing in Salonika. In respect of this the Greek General Staff discreetly supplied the French with sketches of harbour facilities in northern Greece. Furthermore, two French officers were allowed to investigate field conditions in Greece. Finally, the Greek government declared that it was ready to receive supplies for the preparation of an allied landing.[1027] This, combined with the fact that Greece participated in the British trade war against Germany makes it difficult to depict Greece as strictly neutral in the first six months of the war. This policy can be explained by Greece's geopolitical position, the Royal Navy's control of the Mediterranean and consideration for the Greek merchant fleet.

Germany as Protector? Greece, Germany and Italy from 9 April 1940

The German campaign in Denmark, Norway, Holland and France changed the balance of power in Europe; this was also reflected in the Greek attitude to the belligerents.

Grazzi noted that the Greek armed forces began to strengthen coastal defences on the Peloponnese and in Salonika. Moreover, Grazzi stated that the Greek government no longer took security precautions along the Greek-Albanian border. Grazzi concluded that Greece was determined to maintain her neutrality and was ready to defend it against any violation, even by Britain.[1028]

On 25 May 1940 the German State Secretary, Ernst Woermann, noted that the Greek Ambassador in Berlin had expressed fear to his government in Athens that Italy was about to enter the war and an Italian assault on Greece was to be expected in the near future. Rizo-Ragavis should have suggested that the government in Athens make Germany provide a guarantee against Italian occupation.[1029] Notes in Metaxas's diary from 24 and 28 May reveal that the Greek dictator did indeed receive "frightening predictions" from Rizo-Ragavis. Following Belgium's surrender on 28 May and the advance by German troops towards the British expeditionary forces along the Channel coast, Metaxas wrote in his diary that it was only by the help of God that plans for a landing in Salonika were never implemented. On the following day, 31 May, he noted that the only thing that could save Greece [now] was competition between the three dictatorships [Italy, Germany and the Soviet Union] over influence in the Orient.[1030]

At about the same time Metaxas confided to Deter from Rheinmetall-Borsig that Britain had assured him that she had no plans to occupy Greek territory and that he believed this; nevertheless, according to the Greek dictator, the British Minister had [also] asked Metaxas how he would view a temporary [British] occupation of Greek territory. Metaxas told Deter that his answer was that he would not give up the smallest island or piece of land even to Britain or France without fighting. Metaxas contacted Deter to make Roehnert ask the German authorities to force Italy to stay out of the Balkans and refrain from violating Greek territory. Metaxas's explanation for this unorthodox procedure was to avoid British reprisals that were likely to have been the result of an open and official request to this effect. Through Maniadakis and Metaxas's nephew, the Greek dictator asked Deter in a more casual tone to point out that he was "dying for" Germany to guarantee the Greek borders: "...As a matter of fact, in this fatal hour for Greece, he [Metaxas] is dying for Germany to guarantee the Greek borders immediately. The German government can be assured that such a guarantee will be received with enthusiasm by the Greek government as well as by the majority of the Greek people..." [1031]

On 4 June 1940 Deter and Roehnert passed on Metaxas's unofficial request to State Secretaries Keppler and Woermann, heads of the *Politische Abteilung* in *Auswärtiges Amt*. *Auswärtiges Amt* authorized Deter to tell Metaxas that Berlin did not anticipate an Italian assault on Greece, and that the Greek government would be better off to declare her adherence to the Axis powers openly.[1032]

A few days later *Auswärtiges Amt* rejected the case as "amateur politics". It appeared that Metaxas only wanted the guarantee to be implemented in connection with an Italian attack, not with a British one.[1033]

At the beginning of July 1940 the leader of the German trade mission in Athens, Morath, informed the Greek General Platis that Germany would appreciate it if certain pro-British Greek officers, including Papagos, were replaced. The Germans wanted Platis to be the new head of the general staff.[1034] Platis and a group of officers around him then suggested to Metaxas that he change his foreign political course radically and make Greece join the Axis Powers. Furthermore, it was recommended that various pro-British ministers be replaced. Papagos had Platis arrested and later deported from Athens. According to the Italian Ambassador to Greece Metaxas was anything but pro-British. However, the Greek dictator did not dare to make [such] a decisive change in Greece's foreign policy out of considerations for the Greek merchant fleet. Furthermore, such a change would clash with Turkish interests and leave Greece alone to confront Bulgarian demands for revision.[1035]

On 29 July 1940 Metaxas received information from the Greek Ambassador in Berlin concerning the Axis Power's reaction to [Bulgarian and Hungarian] demands for revision in Romania. According to the same information, the general attitude in Germany was that Greece would [only] obtain [German] support against Bulgarian demands for revision if she adjusted to the "new situation" [i.e. joined the Axis].[1036] Nevertheless, Metaxas could hardly believe these reports. He referred to the peace treaty of 1913, signed after the Second Balkan War, in which Greece, with German support, had been granted Kavalla at the expense of Bulgaria. Metaxas regarded Germany's support of Greece as emotionally conditioned and was therefore convinced that Hitler's love of ancient and modern Greece meant that Germany would never support such demands by Slavic Bulgaria.

Moreover, Metaxas was sure that an "honest and sincere" Greek neutrality was appreciated by the German government and that there was an understanding of the difficulties which Greece's geographical position entailed. For these reasons Metaxas refused to abrogate the British guarantee.[1037]

When Italy entered the war on 10 June, Greek-Italian relations became tense once again. On 12 July Greece complained to the Italian Ministry of Foreign Affairs that Italian aircraft had attacked units from the Greek fleet north-west of Crete.[1038] The Italians pointed out that on several occasions the British fleet had received fresh supplies in Greek ports and was therefore violating Greek territorial waters. On 30 July Italian aircraft attacked a Greek destroyer anchored in the Gulf of Corinth and two days later a Greek customs vessel only a few nautical miles from Piraeus.

According to Ciano, Mussolini decided, on 11 August, to occupy the northern part of Epiros – called Ciamuria in revisionist Italian jargon. On the following day, 12 August, the political and military aims of a campaign

232

against Greece were outlined: if Greece gave up Ciamuria and Corfu without fighting, Italian aims would be fulfilled. On the other hand, in case of resistance Italy would go "all the way".

Thereafter a deceased Albanian sheep thief became the focus of attention. The thief – Daut Hodja – was found dead, murdered by unknown perpetrators. In August the Italian authorities described him as an Albanian patriot. Mussolini approved of this move and said that he had an old score from the Corfu affair in 1923 to settle with the Greeks.[1039] On 13 August the state controlled Italian press launched a campaign which made Greek agents responsible for the murder of Daut Hodja. The Greek government immediately denied the accusations to Weizsäcker, who nevertheless believed the Italian version.[1040] On the same day, Metaxas told Erbach that he expected an Italian assault on Greece in the near future. Nevertheless, if Italy thought that she could use the same ploys that the Soviet Union had used in the Bessarabian conflict with Romania she was making a great mistake: Greece planned to use military power against any aggression.[1041] The tension culminated on 15 August when an Italian submarine torpedoed and sank the Greek battle cruiser "Elli".[1042] This dramatically increased the risk of war in the Balkans.

On 16 August Ribbentrop told the Italian government that it was not in the common interests of the Axis Powers to start a war in the Balkans, either in Yugoslavia or in Greece.[1043] The next day Ciano asked the Italian Ambassador in Berlin to tell Ribbentrop that the Italian government planned to resolve Greek-Italian problems through diplomacy, and that Italy would abstain from taking action without giving the German government prior notice.[1044]

In a note to the Greek Ambassador in Rome, Ciano declared that Italy was now representing Albania and was therefore supporting ancient Albanian claims on the areas Yannina and Preveza in the northern part of the province of Epiros. Ciano asked the Greek Minister to tell his government in Athens that Italy was ready to solve the conflict in the same way that analogous problems in the Balkans and the Danube area had found a solution. This could be a first step on the way to a complete and continuous definition of the relationship between Greece and Italy.[1045] In other words, Ciano suggested that Greek concessions to Albania might settle the Greek-Italian dispute.

On 18 August 1940 Metaxas noted in his diary that he had been informed by sources at home and abroad that Italy had abstained from attacking Greece at the very last minute. The Greek dictator wondered whether this was a result of interference by Hitler.[1046]

On 19 August Ribbentrop summoned the Italian Ambassador in Berlin. The German Minister of Foreign Affairs warned the Italian government against exerting even diplomatic pressure on Greece. If the Greeks rejected the Italian pressure it might lead to either British or Soviet intervention.[1047]

On 20 August 1940 the Greek Ambassador in Rome reported that he had been informed by a reliable source that the German government had told the Italians that under no circumstances would it agree to peace in the Balkans being disturbed. However, Germany promised to give Italy diplomatic support in questions that the Italian government saw as vital.[1048]

This insight was important for the Greek governmennt, as it was then possible for it to adopt an uncompromising attitude towards Italian diplomatic pressure.

From a conversation on 20 August between Erbach and the Greek Minister of Justice, whom the Germans regarded as pro-German, Erbach had the impression that the Greek government still believed that Germany would not allow Italy to "play the same game as the Allies did in 1916", i.e. to violate Greek territory. The Greek Minister of Justice said that Italian provocation made it difficult for the Greek government, from a internal political point of view as well, to give in to Italian demands [about revisions].[1049]

On 22 August 1940 Metaxas turned to Britain to ascertain the kind of help that Greece could depend on in case of an Italian attack. On 24 August the British government replied that the Greek government should prepare the country to defend herself against the Italians without help from Britain. The only help Britain could offer was to "knock Italy out of the war".[1050]

At about 2 a.m. the same night the Greek Ambassador in Berlin telephoned *Auswärtiges Amt* to inform Ribbentrop that Italy had concentrated troops on the Greek-Albanian border and that a mobilization of the Greek armed forces was necessary. Woermann explained that he would not rouse Ribbentrop for that reason but that he would inform him in the morning.[1051] In the morning, Ribbentrop asked Woermann to contact the Italian Embassy and to refer to the conversation of 16 August. Woermann was to emphasize that Ribbentrop was of the opinion now, as then, that peace in the Balkans must be preserved. Woermann delivered this message to the Italian Embassy.[1052] On the same day Mussolini informed Hitler that the Italian concentration of troops on the Greek-Albanian border was a precautionary measure against Greek or Yugoslav aggression.[1053] On 26 August the German Minister of Foreign Affairs met Rizo-Ragavis. Ribbentrop pointed out that Greece, from a German point of view, had chosen to ally herself with Britain by accepting the British guarantee, by letting the mercantile fleet sail in British service and by delivering arms to Britain. For this reason, he advised Greece to comply with Italian claims. Finally, Ribbentrop referred to Romania, who had also been relying on British guarantees.[1054] Like Ciano, the German Minister of Foreign Affairs stressed the necessity of Greek compliance to Italian demands for revision. In addition, he hinted that Greece must denounce the British guarantee.

Nevertheless, Ribbentrop stressed to the Italians that a disruption of peace in the Balkans was against German interests. Thus, Greek appeals to the Germans worked to the extent that the German government intervened against Italy in order to avoid an attack on Greece, and in this capacity Germany functioned as a kind of protector to Greece.

A few days later Metaxas learned from foreign sources that Hitler had taken measures against Italy.[1055] This gave Greece good reason to regard Germany as a protector.

Subsequently, Italy's bellicose behaviour was directed towards North Africa. At the beginning of September Italian troops in Libya launched an attack on Egypt; however, this action came to a halt in mid-September. Later, after the concentration of German military forces in Romania, Mussolini made the decision to attack Greece.

On 22 October 1940 German intelligence acquired information for the first time about Italian plans for an attack on Greece.[1056] Whether the Greek government was informed at the same time it is not possible to deduce from the available sources.[1057] However, on 23 October 1940 Mavroudis told Erbach that Greece would understand [Italian] demands to base strongholds [in Greece] to support an attack on Egypt; nevertheless, Greece would defend herself against an Italian attack designed to conquer Greek territory.[1058] The Greek government was in this way offering passage to the Italian troops. According to Erbach this was the first time the Greek government had voiced any such intention.

On 25 October Erbach informed Grazzi about his conversation with Mavroudis. The German Minister stressed the Greek will to resist but added that Greece would not refuse to investigate the possibility of joining an anti-British bloc if it included all other countries in the Mediterranean. Erbach was not certain that Greece would keep that promise or whether Mavroudis himself believed that Turkey should also to be included in such a bloc.[1059] It has not been possible to obtain information about the Italian reaction to the latter. The fact remains that on 28 October 1940 Italy claimed the right to occupy certain strategic points in Greece until the war with Britain was concluded and that the Greek reply to the Italian ultimatum was "no". Thereafter Italy and Greece were at war.[1060]

The points set out above demonstrate that the Greek government was still manoeuvring to avoid conflict and that Greece was willing to discuss cooperation with the Axis Powers, in this particular case, in order to make a common front against Britain on the condition that all other nations in the Mediterranean join too. It is hard to tell whether this was simply a negotiation strategy. However, if we consider that the Italian assault on Greece was part of an Italian parallel war, the above-mentioned cooperation would hardly have helped Greece to stay out of conflict with Italy anyway, in so far that Greece wanted to maintain her sovereignty. Nevertheless, the Greek government tried to use Germany as a protector and mediator against Italy, a role that the German government actually performed. Germany was not able to stop the Italian assault on Greece because the Italian conduct was part of a bellicose race with Germany to gain the best possible starting point for future negotiations about a division of Europe, the Middle East and Africa.

British Control in the Mediterranean obstructs Greek-German Trade
The outbreak of war intensified the security, military and political conditions under which Greek foreign trade was conducted. The Royal Navy's control of the Mediterranean forced Greece to organize her trade in accordance with the British blockade of Germany, thus hampering Greek-German trade considerably. The main part of the traffic between Greece and Germany was by sea and went from Greek harbours to Antwerp, Rotterdam or Hamburg, i.e. though the Straits of Gibraltar. As part of the British contraband control, initiated on 28 November, the Royal Navy established control posts at Port Said in Egypt, the entrance to the Red Sea and the Indian Ocean, and at Haifa in Palestine. Moreover, surveillance was established along the Turkish coast to intercept traffic through the Dardanelles, in and out of the Black Sea and through Gibraltar, the entrance and exit of the Mediterranean to the Atlantic Ocean.[1061] This gave Britain control of the most important seaways connecting the Mediterranean with the oceans. The only Greek product that the

236

British would allow to pass on to Germany was tobacco, out of consideration for the Greek economy.[1062]

On 9 October 1939 Greece and Britain made a temporary war trade agreement. This agreement limited the annual Greek exports to Germany so that they did not exceed the average in the period 1934-1938. Moreover, the agreement prohibited the export of minerals essential to the war industry, first and foremost chrome. In return, Britain was obliged to supply Greece with certain essential raw materials like oil, wheat and coal.[1063]

The Germans investigated the possibility of sailing to Trieste and then using the railway: the cost of this was a hindrance in itself.[1064] Another problem was that the Greek authorities in the ports of disembarkation and at the loading berths of the freight trains normally needed British approval of the exporter.[1065] A letter from a Greek company in Patras shows that companies exporting to Germany without a British certificate were blacklisted by the British authorities, meaning that the contraband control would hold back goods meant for neutral countries as well.[1066] Rumour claimed that Britain paid out prizes to captains who could identify illegal goods intended for Germany in their cargo.[1067]

The trade with Germany was obstructed even further by a temporary Greek ban on exports to Germany. The Bank of Greece refused to finance German purchases, referring to the accumulation of Greek outstandings on the clearing account in Berlin; these were ill-timed as Greece was facing an acute need for hard currency.[1068] Meanwhile, the German authorities disallowed pre-war contracts due to the *force majeur* situation triggered by the war. The result was that most agreements, especially the ones concerning sales of German war material, had to be renegotiated.[1069]

The Germans acknowledged that, following the outbreak of the war, the Greek position was a special one. In October 1939 it was reported that the Greek shipowners were about to charter a huge part of the mercantile fleet to Britain. This caused repercussions among the authorities in Berlin and on 28 October 1939 State Secretary Ernst Weizäcker told Erbach to inform Metaxas that such a move would be seen as a serious departure from Greece's neutrality.[1070] Metaxas rejected the proposal that the Greek government could take any measures against shipowners, as the question of allowing Britain to charter their ships was a private one.[1071] On 22 January the Greek shipowners made a so-called shipping agreement with the British government which ensured Britain 500,000 tons of extra capacity. To confirm the temporary war trade agreement dated October

1939 the Greek government signed a final war trade agreement with Britain on 26 January 1940.[1072]

As a result, Germany's sea warfare was also directed against Greek shipping. Between October 1939 and February 1940 *Auswärtiges Amt* received at least ten complaints[1073] from the government in Athens about the German Navy's capture or sinking of Greek vessels sailing from a neutral port and a under neutral flag. According to the Greeks, this could hardly be accidental.[1074] The German Navy trailed about 90 per cent of the Greek tonnage in the first six months of the war and came to the conclusion that 40 per cent was sailing on behalf of Germany's enemies and 20 per cent was sailing for Holland and Belgium, countries presumably serving Germany's enemies as well; this was the reason for the Greek merchant fleet suffering relatively large losses, according to a note from the German Navy.[1075]

In spite of the British engagement in trade war, Germany nominally remained Greece's most important trade partner in both 1939 and 1940, and the Greek economy was therefore still largely dependent on Germany.

Increasing German Control over Continental Europe Strengthens German Demands on Greece

Shortly after the Scandinavian campaign the Greek authorities approached the British Legation in Athens for permission to increase exports of chrome to Germany.[1076] The fall of France and Italy's entrance into the war changed the trade situation in the eastern Mediterranean radically. Greek trade with Britain and France decreased considerably and the exchange of goods with neutral states overseas became increasingly difficult because of the war in the Mediterranean. For this reason, Greece had to reorganize a huge part of her trade with continental Europe, thus only increasing her own dependence on Germany.[1077]

On 14 June 1940 Wiehl asked the German Legation in Athens to inform the Greek government that Italy's entrance into the war meant that the only outlet for Greek exports was the German market and that Greece was therefore almost totally dependent on the Axis Powers.[1078]

Germany exerted similar pressure on Greece during new trade negotiations in the autumn of 1940. To prepare themselves for these negotiations, Kirou, head of the trade political department at the Greek Ministry of Foreign Affairs, and Clodius met on 20 August 1940. Clodius was dissatisfied because he felt Greek chrome deliveries were too small. Kirou promised to provide a satisfactory explanation to the Germans at the forthcoming trade negotiations. Clodius stressed that the most serious complaint from Germany was that the main part of the Greek merchant fleet served British interests. He would accept no excuse for the latter, not even the danger of Britain confiscating the Greek vessels. Clodius noted that Kirou left the meeting "rather depressed". Shortly after, Clodius called on Kirou and stated that the Romanian government had published a statute prohibiting Romanian ships from sailing in British waters. Clodius had the impression that a sufficiently stubborn German attitude in this respect would force the Greek government to draw up a corresponding law.[1079] In connection with subsequent Greek-German trade negotiations, Varvaresos told the German representatives that Greek trade was dependent on Germany to the extent that it would be necessary to reorganize the Greek economy totally if Germany stopped her purchases in Greece. Varvaresos would therefore do anything he could to satisfy Germany. His readiness to meet German wishes had no limits and could not be "influenced from outside" [i.e. by Britain]. He was acting purely out of consideration for the Greek economy.

Nevertheless, Varvaresos hoped that the negotiations would concentrate on economic matters. The Germans replied that politics were indeed at the forefront in Berlin, not least because the German administration had several matters with which to reproach Greece that were of an economic nature but interfered with political issues. The British chartering of the Greek merchant fleet was then mentioned, as well as the sale of Greek arms to Britain. The Germans not only demanded a ban on exports of war material to Britain but also wanted to put an end to fuel supplies to the Royal Navy. Varvaresos believed that the Greek government could go no further than it had already done; otherwise Greece would risk British counter-measures, like confiscation of the Greek merchant fleet and a suspension of currant purchases. Varvaresos appealed in vain for German understanding and ended by expressing the view that the logical conclusion to the German position was that Greece was forced declare herself in agreement with the Axis. The German answer was that "this was close to reality".[1080]

On 20 September 1940 Greece signed a new trade agreement with Germany. This was a violation of the Greek-British war trade agreement entered into in January of the same year. Koliopoulos believes that the latter was only applied in theory because in practice the Greek government succeeded in hindering delivery to Germany of raw materials essential to the war industry.[1081] However, this is denied by German calculations concerning deliveries of chrome. Germany came into possession of a copy of the Greek-British war trade agreement following the occupation of France. The German authorities concluded that Greece had complied with the agreement in the period between January 1940 and 1 September 1940 and had delivered only 1,073 tons of chrome to Germany in spite of the 15,730 tons agreed upon. On the other hand, it was apparent that the agreed tonnage was delivered to Germany in the period from August 1940.[1082]

On 26, 27 and 28 September 1940 Metaxas's diary notes that the Greek government held meetings concerning the Greek merchant fleet. The result is not mentioned; nevertheless, a note from 26 September indicates that growing irritation characterized Greek-British relations.[1083] It is a fact that German dominance in south-eastern Europe and pressure from the German government forced the Greek government to violate her war trade agreement with Britain, just as Yugoslavia and Romania had done earlier.[1084]

ARMS TRADE

Continued Greek Dependence on Germay

Greek arms procurement from Germany between 1938-1940 amounted to considerably less than it had in the previous two years.[1085]

First of all, the new policy in Germany increased the need for war material for her own rearmament; secondly, Greek credit for arms purchases granted in the Schacht-Tsouderos agreement had been completely expended. In March 1939, Papagos turned to Roehnert to acquire additionally 40 to 50 million RM credits in Germany.[1086] In a letter to *Auswärtiges Amt* dated 30 April 1939 Erbach, who was not well-informed about the matter, states that he had the impression from Rheinmetall-Borsig that a decision had been made to offer Greece an armaments credit of 50 Million RM.[1087] On 5 May Clodius replied that the decision had yet not been made.[1088] Whether this was a misunderstanding on the part of Erbach or Rheinmetall-Borsig or a result of the tense situation in the Mediterranean due to Italy's invasion of Albania in April 1939, is difficult to deduce from the available material. Nothing indicates that the Germans met Papagos's wishes. Nevertheless, the issue shows that the Greek authorities still wanted to base the country's rearmament on German material.

Shortly after *Anschluss*, on 22 April 1938, the Greek authorities made an agreement with the German aircraft company, Henschel, to deliver 16 Hs.126 aeroplanes:[1089] 35 per cent of the price was to be settled in hard currecy and 65 by clearing.[1090] This was an increase of the previous currency exchange quota of 15 per cent and is thus an indication that the ceiling of the above-mentioned Schacht-Tsouderos agreement had already been reached. It also shows that the Germans no longer insisted on 100 per cent payment in hard currency.

In April 1939 the Greek Air Force bought a licence to produce the Henschel Hs. 126 aircraft.[1091] The production was to take place at the aircraft factory in Phaliro and was to be carried out with the participation of German specialists. It is important to note that to some extent this appears to contradict the King's previously mentioned assurance to Britain that neither he nor Metaxas would allow Germany to assume control of the factory.

Almost simultaneously, one of Germany's leading companies in the practical application of scientific research and development, Auergesellschaft, was granted a contract on delivery for gas masks to the Greek army and the construction of a factory for local production of these items.[1092] The latter was established in cooperation with Bodosakis's gas mask factory, EKAP. The total value of the orders amounted to 3-4.5 million RM. The German penetration of Greece's primary armaments industry therefore intensified considerably in 1939, principally by means of know-how and patents.

German Attempts to assume Control of the Powder and Cartridge Company

Shortly after the signing of the Munich Agreement, Rheinmetall-Borsig attempted to take over the majority of shares and thus the direct control of the Powder and Cartridge Company.[1093] In January 1939 Roehnert went to Athens to investigate the possibility of a takeover, but had to return without success.[1094] Rheinmetall-Borsig's efforts must be seen in the light of the forced German rearmament. The Powder and Cartridge Company had production capacity within certain types of ammunition used in the German army and was therefore useful for the German rearmament. In addition, Germany had allowed deliveries to Greece's neighbouring countries in the same period. In this context the Powder and Cartridge Company could operate as a sub-supplier. Finally, the company could be used for "politically difficult exports" in line with earlier plans to use the company in order to reach the market in the Middle East. According to Bodosakis, he and Metaxas rejected the German offer.[1095]

This makes it clear that Germany, and Göring in particular, made efforts to assume control of the Powder and Cartridge Company and thus to extend German control in south-eastern Europe so that it also included the most important armaments company in Greece.

Politicization of Armaments Deliveries

On 25 July 1939, as a response to the rising international political crisis, Göring decreed a general reduction of the German arms trade with the Balkans. On 30 July 1939, *Ausfuhrgemeinschaft für Kriegsgerät* ordered that the trade in arms with Greece was to be handled in a dilatory way; the trade was not to be stopped, but preferably suspended for a few years.[1096]

On 7 November, i.e. after the outbreak of war, *Ausfuhrgemeinschaft für Kriegsgerät* ordered a halt to all deliveries to Greece of armaments related material and tools.[1097] This was perhaps a reaction to the Greek government's rejection of German demands to intervene in the British chartering of the Greek merchant fleet.

The German arms embargo led to a reaction from the highest Greek authority. On 18 November Metaxas asked the German Legation in Athens for a quotation for 12 Messerschmitt Bf.109 fighter aeroplanes. He did not use the Greek Embassy in Berlin because Rizo-Ragavis was investigating the possibility of buying Italian Fiat aircraft at the same time. Metaxas said that he would prefer the German aeroplanes to the Italian ones and that Fiat had only been taken into consideration due to the German embargo on arms deliveries to Greece.[1098] In this way, Metaxas made it clear that Italy, if necessary, constituted an alternative to Germany but that he preferred German war material.

In January 1940, Papastathis, Metaxas's nephew, addressed Rheinmetall-Borsig on behalf of the Powder and Cartridge Company and as Metaxas's special emissary: he delivered an urgent request to Roehnert to persuade the German authorities to permit Rheinmetall-Borsig to resume its deliveries to the Powder and Cartridge Company. According to Papastathis, the Powder and Cartridge Company would be unable to meet demands from the Greek army in the event of a negative German reply. On 31 January 1940 Rheinmetall-Borsig contacted *Auswärtiges Amt*. The German armaments firm stressed that the delivery of tools and machinery to the Powder and Cartridge Company was of "vital importance" to the Greek government and thus of great significance to Greek-German relations overall. For that reason it was essential not to disappoint the pro-German Metaxas: "...this transaction [is] not just a transaction between Rheinmetall-Borsig and the Poudreries & Cartoucheries, but is rather of vital importance to the Greek government [...] so that even the Prime Minister [Metaxas] has taken a personal interest in it and has sent his nephew on a special mission to us [...] it also seems to be desirable to the *Auswärtiges Amt* to keep good relations intact, and in particular, not to disturb the friendly attitude of the Prime Minister his Excellency, Prime Minister Metaxas..."[1099]

This informal procedure might also have been a result of Metaxas's wish to keep these negotiations secret in order to avoid confrontation with other political forces within the Greek government and in Britain. It is also an indication of the close relationship between Metaxas and the Powder and Cartridge Company.

On 12 February 1940, the German Ministry of Economy gave permission for arms deliveries to Greece, provided that 50 per cent of the value be paid in hard currency and the remaining per cent in so-called "lebeswichtige Rohstoffen" (vital raw materials), i.e. nickel, chrome, iron ore, leather and furs.[1100]

The Greek Ministry of Aviation also asked the German authorities for German fighters: 32 Henschel aeroplanes, material for the production of an additional 40 Henschels under licence, 12 Fieseler-Storchs and the licence to produce this type of aeroplane in Greece. The German Air Attaché stressed to *Auswärtiges Amt* that the Greek government planned to build up the Greek Air Force as quickly as possible and by all available means. However, in spite of British pressure, the Greek government preferred German material.[1101]

The German Air Attaché added that, as a matter of principle, the Greek government was ready to meet German demands and settle the price in raw materials essential to armament and in hard currency as far as possible. Nevertheless, it was important that Germany was aware that Greece was exposed to strong pressure from Britain which could make it difficult for Greece to enter into contracts regarding the above-mentioned commodities [and in relation to earlier, strenuous,] conditions.[1102]

On 28 February the finance department in *Auswärtiges Amt* made an appeal to Ribbentrop. It stressed that arms deliveries were a crucial precondition for Germany's good connections with Metaxas and thus a vital element in the maintenance of German interests in Greece. Rearmament based on German material was even depicted as one of Metaxas's "favourite ideas". Furthermore, *Auswärtiges Amt* underlined the point that Metaxas had put all his personal political prestige at stake to achieve this. It was also in German interests that Metaxas did not lose face in this matter because the dictator stood as guarantor for Greek neutrality. It was therefore imperative, *Auswärtiges Amt* continued, that Germany meet

Metaxas's wishes, because this would strengthen his internal political position and indirectly help to bolster his [neutral] foreign policy.[1103]

Auswärtiges Amt thus recommended arms deliveries to Greece as a means to secure the neutral status of that country. This must have served Hitler's interests at that time because of his desire to maintain peace in the Balkans. Three weeks later, on 21 March 1940, Hitler gave approval for arms deliveries to Greece. The result was permission for a delivery of 30 Henschel 126 aeroplanes, 24 Avia fighters, and 72 pieces of 20 mm anti-aircraft cannon, including machinery and tools to manufacture 20 and 37 mm ammuniton.[1104]

On 22 March 1940 Wiehl stressed in a note on "arms deliveries to foreign countries" that trade in arms was of special importance to foreign policy. Delivery of war material had to be seen from a perspective of foreign policy and should be estimated from the point of view of the political and economic advantages that Germany could gain from it. Arms deliveries to neutral countries were seen as a special concession.[1105]

The note was transmitted to Wilhelm Keitel, head of *Oberkommando der Wehrmacht*, under Ribbentrop's signature and dated 26 March 1940. In this connection it appears that Hitler, after a meeting with Göring, withdrew permission to deliver 88 mm anti-aircraft batteries to Italy and claimed *quid pro quo* in the shape of military support to free the guns for delivery.[1106] It is significant that Italy possessed no modern anti-aircraft guns, so procurement of the German guns was of the highest priority.[1107] In the second half of April permission was granted for delivery of the guns. Ribbentrop was not told of this until later. He regarded the decision as "very important to our relationship with Italy" and complained to Göring about not having been notified immediately about a decision of such importance for Germany's foreign policy.[1108] Apparently, however, the guns were not delivered until Italy entered the war.[1109]

It is significant that Greece obtained permission from Hitler to buy 88 mm guns from Germany before Italy did. It is also significant that neutral Sweden had ordered 120 20 mm Flak guns from Germany. However, while the deliveries to Sweden made slow progress, permission to deliver to Greece was granted as early as 21 March 1940. On 11 May 1940 Göring announced categorically that "as long as no proof was produced of Sweden's benevolent neutrality, not a single cartridge would be delivered". It seems safe to conclude that Germany used the deliveries of arms as a means of political pressure in this period.[1110]

When we compare the German policy towards Sweden and Italy with her procedure in dealing with Greece, it is clear that arms deliveries to Greece resumed quickly and without any German counter demands. The explanation may be that Germany was aware that Greece was dependent on Britain and therefore under heavy British pressure. This made it important to support Metaxas, who was seen as favourably disposed towards Germany and a guarantor of Greek neutrality. In other words, an enhancement of the political position of Metaxas was the political compensation that the Germans hoped would result from the arms deliveries to Greece. These efforts must be seen in the light of the German Balkan policy, aiming at a status quo in the region.

This assessment of the situation seems to be corroborated by the fact that on 27 June 1940 a self-contained point in the Greek-German trade agreement for 1940-1941 stipulated that trade in arms, including the purchase of licences, was to be settled 50 per cent in hard currency and 50 per cent through clearing.[1111] This happened after Italy entered the war and indicates that the "peace in the Balkans" priority played a considerable part in Germany's overall foreign policy. Moreover, it suggests that Italian interests and ambitions were subordinated to this policy, even to the extent that Germany was ready to arm one of Italy's potential enemies. A further explanation may be that German-Soviet relations were marked by a growing conflict of interests and that it had become obvious to the Germans that the Soviet Union had ambitions in the Balkans. A strengthening of the Greek defence could be expected to have a deterrent effect on a potential aggressor like Bulgaria, traditionally friendly with Russia, and thus to contribute to maintaining peace in the Balkans. Finally, the agreement also showed that Greece, to a far greater extent than hitherto, was willing to settle the payment in hard currency: this would achieve another German goal.

The Powder and Cartridge Company and Cooperation with Britain

British Rejection of Trade and Cooperation with the Powder and Cartridge Company
In 1937 the British Ministry of War rejected an offer of arms deliveries from Bodosakis with the explanation that Greece was an unstable supplier of arms both in times of peace and war.[1112] Distrust in the War Office

mainly emanated from the fact that the British authorities were suspicious of Bodosakis. In December 1937 Bodosakis visited London to deliver his offer personally to the British government. Immediately upon arrival he was pulled aside and interrogated only to be released shortly after.[1113] Whatever the reason for this treatment, the Ministry of War rejected his proposition.

Following the Munich Agreement, Bodosakis told the British Legation that Germany had tried to obtain interests in the Powder and Cartridge Company, but that both he and Metaxas had turned down the German offer. Bodosakis said that he was interested in British investments in his plants because close Greek-British relations, in his opinion, would lead to Greece aligning herself with Britain in the event of war. Thereafter, Bodosakis invited the First Secretary and the Naval Attaché of the British Legation in Athens to visit the plants of the Powder and Cartridge Company: "... M. Bodosakis informed Mr. Hopkinson [First Secretary] and Captain Packer [Naval Attaché] confidentially that the Germans have been making strenuous efforts to obtain an interest in the [Powder and Cartridge] company. As he is convinced that, once they get a foothold in the firm, they would eventually succeed in getting complete control he has refused to have anything to do with their proposals. His attitude, he said, had been warmly approved by General Metaxas.[...] He said that, in view of the close political ties between Great Britain and Greece, which would inevitably result in Greece aligning herself with Great Britain in the event of war, he would have no hesitation in accepting British capital in the business, with whatever measure of control it might give..."[1114]

Leith-Ross emphasized the political and economic aspects of British co-operation with the Greek firm. In a minute dated 26 October 1938 he stressed that an increase of ammunition exports to Britain would strengthen Greece's economic position. In addition, a British manifestation of interest in Greek ammunition would influence the Greek government's attitude towards Britain positively.[1115]

However, the Ministry of War still refused to place orders with the Powder and Cartridge Company. This increased the danger of German control and Leith-Ross stressed the necessity of injecting British capital into the firm. In a minute dated 19 December 1938, Leith-Ross stated that he knew that the Greek firm earned hard currency by means of illegal business; nevertheless, this trade would not last forever. Hence, if it were possible to make Vickers[1116] cooperate with the Powder and Cartridge

Company it would probably safeguard British control of the firm. This could also be a way to ensure that Bodosakis's actvities would not harm British interests: "...The more important objective is keeping the factories occupied and the company solvent, since only if financial difficulties arise need German offers have any attraction. Since, however, we can apparently do nothing to increase orders we ought seriously to try to secure the second objective of obtaining British control of the factories. I therefore suggest that we press the War Office to examine the question urgently in the light of the above and if possible approach Vickers themselves...[1117]

However, Vickers refused to cooperate.[1118] There is no explanation available for this rejection, but Vickers was probably deterred by two decades of disappointing results in Romania where it had liquidated its interests only two years earlier.[1119] Cartel agreements may have constituted a hindrance as well.

On 8 March 1939, in reaction to Vickers' rejection, the British Legation in Athens stressed Greece's significance as a link with the Middle East, partly due to her geographical position in the eastern Mediterranean and partly because of Greek experience and skill in trade with the Levant: "...it would not be possible to supply the requirements of the British forces in Egypt, Palestine and Cyprus and the anti-aircraft shells required by the fleet in the Eastern Mediterranean from the United Kingdom *in time of war*. [...] Even if our fleet were not in complete control of the Eastern Mediterranean there is no doubt that the Greeks, who, as we know to our cost, are adepts at smuggling, would have no difficulty in arranging for the shipment of these supplies to Egypt, Palestine or Cyprus, when the time came. [...] The company is certainly short of business as a result of the virtual cessation of its profitable trade with Spain, and, to a lesser extent China..."[1120]

On 29 March 1939 the British Ministry of War declined to resume talks on Greek arms deliveries to Britain.[1121] In reality, the British government accepted the risk that the largest armaments company in the Near East, just north of the important British sphere of interest in the Middle East, came under German control. Furthermore, after the German march into Prague in March 1939, the Powder and Cartridge Company also became the most important ammunitions factory outside direct German control in south-eastern Europe.

248

Change in the British Attitude after the Outbreak of War

After the outbreak of war and the conclusion of a temporary Greek-British war trade agreement on 15 November 1939, the Ministry of Supply asked for an investigation into the possibility of a £1 million purchase of ammuniton from the Powder and Cartridge Company.[1122] On 9 January 1940 Palairet received information that the Ministry of Supply planned to place a huge order with the Powder and Cartridge Company. The Ministry needed information about possible German interests in the company and whether it supplied Germany with war material. In addition, the Minister was asked to state his personal opinion of the plans.[1123] As far as Palairet knew, Germany had received no war material and had no interests in the Greek company. However, he knew that the Powder and Cartridge Company was equipped with German machinery. Palairet added: "...Although the character of the owner [Bodosakis] is not all that could be desired, this Legation has incidentally recommended that the concern should be given orders for United Kingdom interests and I see no reason to revise this opinion at the present time..."[1124]

At the same time, the Ministry of Economic Warfare had acquired a telegram containing information that Bodosakis had offered to produce gas masks for Germany. In addition, the telegram stated that financial transactions were taking place between Germany and the Powder and Cartridge Company.[1125]

This, however, did not lead the Ministry to discourage the placement of orders with the Greek company. On the contrary, it seems that the Ministry planned to make use of Bodosakis's personal experience and contacts within the international arms trade.

On 16 January 1940, the Ministry of Economic Warfare informed the Ministry of Supply that Bodosakis was to be used as a middleman in the trade between the Hungarian armaments industry and Britain: "...I understand that your reason for employing an intermediary is that the firms are unable to export war materials to the U.K. on account of official instructions, and we suspect that the Hungarian Government's objections to permitting export will be likely to disappear if this were done under cover. Moreover, even if the infringement of Hungarian regulations were found out and objected to, the odium would fall, not on us, but on the Hungarian and Greek firms concerned,..."[1126]

While Metaxas's nephew tried to persuade the Germans to deliver production material to the Powder and Cartridge Company, Bodosakis negotiated with the British authorities in London about the purchase of basic products for ammunition production and sales of Greek war material to the British army. Bodosakis, however, soon began to lose patience with the slow progress of negotiations between the British ministries. He was used to the quick decision-making of dictator states and was irritated by democratic routine. His attendant observed that Bodosakis was about to leave London and go back to Greece.[1127] Nevertheless, a contract between Britain and the Powder and Cartridge Company was eventually signed. It has not been possible to obtain information about the exact date of this agreement, but on 11 April 1940 a group from the Chief Inspector of Armament's Department at Woolwich went to Athens to inspect products at the Powder and Cartridge Company.[1128] Furthermore, a secret letter from the Ministry of Supply to the Southern Department dated 12 June 1940 states that the first of several orders had been placed with the Greek firm.[1129]

A Weakened British Position and the Advance of Heavy Demands by Greece

France's defeat, Italy's entry into the war and the altered trade situation in the Mediterranean to Britain's disadvantage placed the Powder and Cartridge Company in a position from which it could advance new demands concerning delivery to and payment by Britain. A letter dated 13 July 1940 indicates that commercial motives played a considerable role in this connection. In August 1939, the Powder and Cartridge Company accepted that the arms trades with Britain be settled through counter trade agreements.[1130] Nevertheless, in July 1940 the Greeks increased the conditions and claimed payment of the full price in advance and in dollars.[1131] The Ministry of Supply described the situation as follows: "...The Greeks have steadily been putting up the terms against us. We have to some extent been forced to give way to them because we are in very urgent need of small arm ammunition, and the factory at Athens is one of the few places actually in production which can give immediate or reasonably early deliveries..."[1132]

According to the Southern Departmant, German pressure on Britain and the state of war in the Mediterranean made British concessions to the Greeks imperative. In addition, it was important that the Powder and

Cartridge Company worked for Britain and not for Germany; this was, according to the Southern Department, the alternative.

The Southern Department could agree to most of the terms but the demand for 100 per cent irrevocable credit when the order was placed was seen as "a piece of blackmail".[1133]

On 16 August the Ministry of Supply stated that the Greek authorities had stopped the loading of the vessel "S.S. Destro" which was to bring a cargo of war material to Egypt. The Ministry of Supply suggested putting pressure on the Greek government to get the shipment under way.[1134] On 17 August 1940 the Legation in Athens claimed that the explanation, according to the Greek Minister of Communication, was that the Greeks needed the ammunition for themselves in case of war. However, the Greek Minister said that if the situation relaxed in the following months the cargo could be released. Palairet blamed the Ministry of Supply for the failure.[1135] The Ministry of Supply offered an excuse by claiming that the Powder and Cartridge Company had refused to load the ship until Britain offered "irrevocable credit".[1136]

The Southern Department and the War Office expressed their full understanding of the Greek point of view and added that the Ministry of Supply was to blame for the temporary ban on the cargo.[1137]

Blunt, the British Military Attaché in Athens, believed that it was the political situation that hindered the shipment. For that reason he had let the Powder and Cartridge Company know that Britain contemplated placing new and large orders with the company mainly in order to supply the Middle East. According to Blunt, the Greek company had declared itself ready to execute such orders, whether they were to be shipped openly on board British vessels or in secrecy by Greek sailing boats. The Military Attaché also believed that the Greek government would soon lift the ban on the shipment as a result of Greece's financial crisis and the size of the orders. Furthermore, Blunt regarded the Powder and Cartridge Company, and not least Bodosakis, as important to British warfare: "...The importance of Greece as a source of ammunition supply is clear.[...] and the Managing Director, who was prominent in the supply of arms to Spain during the civil war, is adept at securing stocks of ammunition from neighbouring countries to make up any deficiencies which he cannot fill himself..."[1138]

On 9 October 1940 the British were informed by a secret source that the reason for the non-delivery of the ammunition was due to a Greek agreement with Berlin prohibiting Greek exports of ammunition.[1139]

German Reactions to Greek Sales of Arms to Britain

On 10 August 1940 the German authorities received information about the Powder and Cartridge Company's agreement with Britain. Clodius told Metaxas that this trade should be stopped immediately. The Germans also complained about a delivery of ammunition to Turkey, Britain's ally (50 million cartridges in 1939 and 21 million in 1940). All German firms in business with the Powder and Cartridge Company were ordered to terminate their transactions with Bodosakis's firm. Metaxas replied that as far as he knew the shipment had not yet taken place and that he would do everything to stop it.[1140] On 17 August 1940 the Greek government banned all exports of ammunition and war material. This affected all material included in previous agreements[1141] and thus also the contract with Britain.

Neither Metaxas nor Papagos denied that the Powder and Cartridge Company had made an agreement with Britain, but asked the Germans not to break off connections with the firm because of the precarious employment situation in Greece. Rheinmetall-Borsig's German representative supported the Greeks and referred to the fact that both Italy and Germany had previously been offered Greek ammunition deliveries but that Bodosakis had never received an answer.[1142]

On 27 August 1940 Clodius said that the boycott against the Powder and Cartridge Company could be lifted as Greece had met German demands and stopped the delivery of arms to Britain; this could not be effected immediately, however, due to the strained relations between Greece and Italy.[1143] In a response to this, Göring stated that he considered it improper to lift the boycott, out of consideration for Italy.[1144] *Sonderstab für Handelskrieg und wirtschaftliche Kampfmassnahmen* (HWK) doubted Metaxas's assurances. HWK felt that the Greek dictator's worries about rising unemployment as a result of the German boycott of the Powder and Cartridge Company were irrelevant as the firm could direct its attention towards the Italian market instead. Furthermore, if Bodosakis's factories were placed under German or Italian control, HKW had no difficulty in accepting that Rheinmetall-Borsig and other German companies should resume deliveries to the Powder and Cartridge Company.[1145]

HKW began to investigate the possibility of cooperation between the Greek company and German or Italian interests. This task was undertaken by the German Military Attaché who made a report and presented it to the Italian authorities.[1146] However, on 7 September 1940 Morath informed HKW that the Greek government had issued a general ban on exports of arms and ammunition.[1147] This led to increased fears in HKW that the German boycott might negatively effect employment at the Powder and Cartridge Company. The latter was in the interests of neither the Greek nor the German government, and HKW considered it quite natural that everything should be done to avoid such a situation arising.[1148]

Mass unemployment would cause social instability and put an end to Greek production of war material; this in turn would lead to loss of prestige for Metaxas and a weakening of his position, not least in relation to the army. Because the Germans saw Metaxas as the best guarantee of Greek neutrality, this situation would also work against the German policy of "peace in the Balkans".

Accordingly, the German authorities in Berlin suggested to the Italian Trade Attaché that Italy place orders at the Powder and Cartridge Company. On 17 October 1940 Morath said that he doubted whether the Greek government would agree to sell war material to Greece's "mortal enemy", Italy. According to Morath, the Greek government was determined to comply with the export ban.[1149] From the available sources there is no indication that Greece contemplated selling to Italy. Furthermore, the ban on exports seemed to work satisfactorily and it was not until after the Italian assault on Greece that ammunition was released for delivery to Britain.[1150]

In conclusion, by the autumn of 1940 Metaxas was on the point of facing new demands for arms delivery from the belligerent Axis Powers. The German authorities were in a position to impose strong pressure on Greece, as the Powder and Cartridge Company was dependent on deliveries from Germany. A long-term suspension of deliveries would hit Greek rearmaments hard and thus also affect Metaxas's political position. The sources available do not reveal Metaxas's attitude to this, and Metaxas's plans remain mere speculation, as the Italian attack on Greece changed the whole situation considerably. However, several circumstances indicate that Germany was interested in the continuation of the production of the Powder and Cartridge Company, not least out of consideration for Metaxas's political position and his importance as a guarantee of Greece's neutral position. This suggests that Germany still believed it possible to combine German and Greek efforts within this field of production less than a fortnight before Italy's attack on Greece and after the Germans had been informed that Greece had been planning to deliver war material to Britain.

SUMMARY AND CONCLUSION

Greece faced various developmental and modernization problems in the interwar period. The integration of more than a million refugees was the most pressing issue. This process drained resources considerably and threw Greece into a state of dependence on foreign countries. In the 1920s this dependence was characterized by capital import. In the 1930s the political and social instability in northern Greece, combined with the dependence of the Greek economy on tobacco exports and the closing of the international capital market, made Greece increasingly reliant on Germany. This reliance was intensified by the fact that Greek industrialization and rearmament, which had the highest priority on the political agenda during this period, had to be financed by export revenues and thus primarily by the sale of tobacco to Germany.

The development of Greek-German relations between 1929-1941 has been divided in this book into three phases, 1929-1933, 1934-1937 and 1938-1941.

The first of these three phases was characterized by the world crisis and a recession in the Greek-German trade. The closing of the international credit market, increasing protectionism on the world market and the decrease in prices of raw materials created an acute shortage of currency in Greece. The result aggravated internal structural and modernization problems, especially in connection with the integration of refugees. A huge fall in tobacco prices threatened this integration, first and foremost in northern Greece, where the population was almost totally dependent on tobacco production. Accordingly, Greece became even more sensitive to fluctuations on the tobacco market and therefore increasingly dependent on Germany as the most important market for Greek tobacco.

Lack of hard currency in both Greece and Germany constituted a serious problem to Greek-German trade, which reached a low ebb in 1932. The signing of a Greek-German clearing agreement in mid-1932 led to a slight increase in Greek-German trade the following year.

Simultaneously, German export-orientated industry strengthened its global position in respect to its main international competitors. This resulted from its supremacy in science and technology and through international cartel agreements. The German chemical industry attained a dominant position on the Greek market by means of such methods. The German electrotechnical industry gained a hegemony over the low-voltage sector in Greece, while British industry managed to keep its dominant position within the high-voltage sector.

In the second period, from 1934 to 1937, Greek-German trade increased rapidly. In September 1934 the so-called *Neuer Plan* (New Plan) was launched, followed by increasing German purchases, especially of tobacco, from Greece. The value of Greek exports to Germany more than doubled in the following two years. As Greek imports from Germany could not keep pace with exports to Germany, huge Greek credits soon built up on the clearing account in Berlin. Germany turned down Greek requests to have the assets liquidated in hard and convertible currency which could be spent on purchases from third countries and thus give Greece more room for manoeuvre. Germany made it a *conditio sine qua non* for further German purchase of Greek tobacco that Greece increased imports from Germany substantially.

Germany began to exert diplomatic pressure on the Greek government. The National Bank of Greece, as well as Greek tobacco producers and private German finance and business, started lobbying for Greece to place more orders in Germany. The Greek government channelled large orders from state and private business to Germany and forced foreign – primarily British – controlled firms to shift their imports from other countries to Germany. However, these measures did not substantially reduce Greek assets in Berlin. It was not until the conclusion of a Greek-German arms deal in late 1936 and after huge Greek purchases of German war material that the Greek clearing credits were finally reduced.

In the third period, from 1938 onwards, Greek-German relations became more complicated. This was due to a new and more aggressive German policy, rising international tensions and Greek political attempts to make

Greece economically less dependent on Germany while at the same time her actual dependence on Germany rose.

During the tobacco season of 1937-1938 the Germans succeeded in exerting pressure on the prices of Greek tobacco. At the same time Germany demanded that Greece export more raw materials important for the German war economy. Attempts were also made to force Greece to give up her industrialization in areas where this clashed with German economic interests. The aim was to serve the German rearmament programme and at the same time to fulfil long-term aspirations of establishing a larger economic bloc in south-eastern Europe under German domination, the *Grossraumwirtschaft* concept.

Germany succeeded in acquiring more raw materials from Greece. On the other hand, it was not possible to prevent the establishment of a Greek metal industry as part of an import substituting policy. However, this Greek policy led the way to cooperation between the Greek and German armament industries in spite of disagreements within German industry concerning this development.

With blatant affinity to the *Grossraumwirtschaft* concept the German cotton firm BREBAG tried to assume control of the production and export of Greek cotton; nevertheless, the Greek government was not willing to yield this field of production. Furthermore, in the tobacco season 1938-1939 Greece even managed to raise the prices of tobacco.

Greek-German relations were further complicated after the outbreak of the Second World War. The Royal Navy ruled the seas and the geopolitical position of Greece forced the Greek government to participate in Britain's economic warfare against Germany. The total value of Greek-German trade in the years 1939-1940 was lower than in 1938. In spite of this, Germany continued to be Greece's most important trading partner.

Germany's successful invasions of Denmark and Norway, as well other parts of Western Europe and Italy's entry into the war put Greece under mounting pressure from the Axis powers. Greece was forced to infringe her War Trade Agreement with Britain. At the same time Germany began to demand Greek participation in economic warfare against Britain. This was followed by Greek-German negotiations to prohibit Greek vessels sailing in British national waters. However, these negotiations were interrupted by the Italian attack on Greece on 28 October 1940.

The German attitude to the Italian attack on Greece is not clear. Growing fears in the Greek government urged the Greek dictator Metaxas to make an unofficial petition to the German government to obtain a German guarantee for Greece. The German government declined this and advised Greece openly to declare herself on the side of the Axis powers. In spite of this, Germany intervened twice in August 1940 to prevent an Italian attack on Greece. In this manner Germany *de facto* behaved as a protective power for Greece. This must be explained by the general German policy of "peace in the Balkans" and by the fact that Italian hegemony in Greece would run counter to German interests. Germany's attitude during the Greek-Italian war in 1940-1941 also shows that she was ready to sacrifice Italian interests to re-establish "peace in the Balkans". Hitler's decision to launch an attack on Greece seems to have been a result of the British threat to the German southern flank in the planned attack on the Soviet Union. However, the German action against Greece must also be seen against a background of rising competition between Germany and Italy as well as between Germany and the Soviet Union.

The increase of Greek import from Germany clashed mainly with French and Italian interests. The decrease of the Greek import of American products from 1933 must primarily be ascribed to the redirection of Greek wheat import from the United States to Argentina combined with a rise in wheat production in Greece, so in this case the expansion of German export products to Greece played only a minor role. Additionally, the Americans saw the Greek import quotas from 1937 as discriminating in favour of German exports.

British exports to Greece were not affected until 1937 and then only very little. This situation never led to official reactions from Britain. The trade with Greece constituted more in the 1930s until 1937 than before the crisis; thereafter it fell slightly.

However, Britain followed the German penetration of Greece carefully. British interests in Greece were mainly strategic and financial. Greece's geographical position in the eastern Mediterranean and her relatively close connections with Egypt created British fears that Germany would use Greece as a platform for infiltration into Egypt. British commercial interests in Greece were limited and by far outweighed in importance by her trade relations with the Empire, the United States and Scandinavia. The high priority of the Scandinavian market seems to have made Britain willing to abstain from a commercial push forward in south-eastern Europe. However, the growing political and military competition and the aggravated conflict between Germany and Britain made it imperative for

Britain to take up the fight with Germany within the field of economy as well.

The British-Italian appeasement made Britain attempt to withhold military and political guarantees to Greece. Instead, the Foreign Office tried in vain to establish to possibility of Greek tobacco exports to Britain to reduce Greek economic dependence on Germany and thus prevent further German penetration into the Mediterranean.

Three fundamental conditions stood in the way of Britain's efforts to reduce Greece's economic dependence on Germany. Greece's name was tainted in British business circles as a result of the unresolved Greek debt, so neither the City of London nor the Treasury was willing to offer financial support to Greece. Another hindrance resulted from British considerations of the Empire and the United States. Finally, the financial interests of the British tobacco companies, which were tied to Virginia tobacco, combined with a low level of cooperation between state and business posed an insurmountable obstacle to the sale of Greek tobacco on the British market. Similarly, it turned out to be impossible to reduce the dependence of Greece's armaments industry on Germany, as both the War Office and the armaments company Vickers were unwilling to deal with Greece.

Greece did not seem concerned that German penetration cut across Italian and French interests. On the contrary it appears that Metaxas was even ready to use Germany to reduce Greece's dependence on France. However, the Greek government did try to prevent the growing German penetration of Greece from interfering with British strategic interests, as became clear from 1937. Thus the Greek authorities prohibited Lufthansa from flying the route from Athens to Rhodes.

American complaints about Greek discrimination against exports from the United States were also taken seriously by the Greek government. Greece met the American demands and organized the trade according to the most-favoured nation principle, expressed in an American-Greek trade agreement on 15 November 1938. This Greek flexibility must be explained by the fact that Greece had a surplus from her trade with the United States and because she received huge emigrant remittances. Furthermore, both incomes were settled in hard currency.

The result of this investigation shows clearly the size and significance of the Greek-German arms trade.

Shortly after the conclusion of the Balkan Entente in February 1934, Greek requests for purchases of German arms were received by the German authorities. This was a departure from the usual Greek military policy which until then had been directed towards Britain and France. The German Foreign Office considered the idea of delivering arms to a former enemy power to be rather attractive. In May 1934 Göring arrived in Athens, thus suggesting that he believed that German interests stretched as far as Greece and the Aegean Sea. In the second half of 1935 secret Greek-German negotiations were initiated, but the uncertain political situation in Greece in 1935 and 1936 made any conclusion most difficult. The Germans missed no opportunity to let Greece know that they wanted her to buy German weapons and that they viewed this as an important preconditon for German purchases of Greek tobacco. This, combined with serious political and social upheavals in the tobacco growing provinces in Northern Greece during the winter and spring of 1936, made it clear that Greece was dependent on her tobacco trade with Germany.

Greek-German arms negotiations were resumed in 1936 but it was not until after the establishment of the dictatorship of Ioanis Metaxas that a Greek-German arms deal could be concluded, namely in December 1936.

An important German motive for selling arms to Greece was that Germany considered her dominant commercial position in Greece, as well as her cordial political relations with Metaxas, to be dependent on arms deliveries to that country.

For these reasons the agreement from December 1936 was extended and altered to give Greece the opportunity to continue her arms procurement in Germany.

The political motive in the arms trade became especially clear after the outbreak of the Second World War. Greek demands for German weapons in 1939 and 1940 were considered at the highest level of the German political hierachy. Hitler gave permission to resume the arms deliveries to Greece much earlier than for most other countries and without any political counter demands. Arms deliveries to Greece, it was emphazised, provided a way of strengthening the power base of Metaxas and thus enhancing the possibility that Greece remain neutral during the war.

Cooperation with the German armaments industry provided a base for extensive Greek arms exports, primarily to the Republicans in Spain, but also to the Middle East and China.

In this way Greece acquired important quantities of gold and hard currency. This was also the precondition for a considerable expansion of the Greek armaments industry based on German technology and know-how and made it possible for Greece to convert frozen assets on the clearing account into hard currency. It also made possible the fulfilment of one of Metaxas's important political goals, namely to maximize the degree of Greek self-sufficiency within the production of munitions.

It is important to emphasize that the Greek armament industry primarily cooperated with Rheinmetall-Borsig, part of the industrial complex controlled by Göring. Furthermore, the spectacular rise in the Greek arms trade coincides with the equally spectacular rise in Göring's power and autonomy within German foreign policy until well into 1938, when Göring even delivered arms to China in spite of Hitler's expressed ban on this trade.

In the same period the German armaments industry was planning to use Greece as a platform for exports to the British dominated Middle East. It is notable that such transactions would be both politically and logistically complicated for Germany to conduct herself.

Cooperation between the Greek and German armaments industries created an opportunity for the latter to use Greece as a platform for exports to "politically complicated" markets.

Moreover, as Greek trade in arms was an important precondition for Greek imports from Germany, business with the Greek armaments industry gave Germany revenues in hard currency. In this respect it is significant that Göring was even ready to accept the fact that Greece exported to Germany's enemies.

The establishment of the Metaxas dictatorship has to be seen against a background of the interaction between traditional conflicts in Greek policy and the impact of several external factors. The world crisis emphasized the precarious stability of the tobacco producing areas in northern Greece. In addition, the growing threat from Italy and the necessity of strengthening the Greek defence gave questions regarding the procurement of arms technology for armaments production a key role in Greek politics. The Metaxas regime's dependence on the army and the high priority of rearmament put the dictatorship in a position in which it was imperative that arms deliveries from abroad, mainly Germany, were maintained. This in turn also made Greek exports of arms and ammunition politically significant to Metaxas, as this trade proved a vital basis for the provision of arms and technology for the armaments industry.

In the light of the discussion between Bernd-Jürgen Wendt and Alan S. Milward regarding whether it was the south-eastern European states or Germany which capitalized on their mutual trade relations, one can at least conclude that Greece became increasingly dependent on Germany. At the same time the rise in Greek-German trade made it possible for Metaxas to maintain political and social stability in northern Greece and to pursue a policy that tended to make Greece less dependent on foreign powers by raising her degree of self-sufficiency and by rearming the country. In this connection, it is important to note that Greece was never unilaterally dependent on Germany like the rest of south-eastern Europe, because both the United States and Britain played a significant role politically, militarily and economically. Traditional and historical ties were also important in this context. Unlike the rest of south-eastern Europe, Greece had never formed part of the Habsburg Empire, but had belonged to the Ottoman Empire. In this way Greece maintained old connections with the Levant and Egypt, the latter having a rich Greek colony with substantial economic interests. In addition, several of the refugees from Asia Minor had personal and business networks with countries in former Ottoman territory in Anatolia, Northern Africa and the Arabian peninsula.

A unique example was Bodosakis, an Ottoman subject until 1922, who worked with a special kind of familiarity in Asia Minor and the Middle East. At his hotel in the former Ottoman capital Constantinople he gathered leading politicians, military men and other important persons from Greece, Turkey and the Middle East. This network combined with Greek skill and experience in international trade and with the strong cosmopolitan character of the Greek business world, can be seen as an important resource to Greece, especially in terms of trade with Germany.

Within various fields Greece functioned as a tool for Germany in the Mediterranean and the Middle East. This enabled Greece to pursue a balancing act, exploiting the rivalry between the Great Powers, and gave the country a certain freedom of manoeuvre. Accordingly, Greece managed to maintain her national independence towards Britain and Germany long after the outbreak of the war, initially by following a course of undisguised pro-British policy, later by increasingly adapting to German demands.

The question is whether this policy could have been pursued if the dictatorship had not been established. The dictatorship simplified the decision-making process and reduced the voice of the oppositon to a minimum, thus enabling the regime to take unpopular decisions. This helps to explain the successful resistance by the Greek Army when Italy attacked the country on 28 October 1940. Earlier Greek plans for re-armament were not as extensive as Metaxas's and it is doubtful whether it would have been politically possible to fulfil Metaxas's ambitious re-armament programme in a democratic climate. The persecution of the Communists and the ban on unions resulted in internal political and social stability; this was also the case within the Greek tobacco industry, a state of affairs previously unknown within that industry.

In this way the abolition of democratic principles and parliamentarism, as well as the brutal persecution of enemies of the regime, can be seen as part of the price needed to realize a policy that led Greece through the Depression in the 1930s. However, Metaxas's policy laid the foundation for a number of new political conflicts which were exacerbated by the Axis Occupation, 1941-1944, and the Civil War, 1946-1949, and which con-ditioned political developments in Greece well into the post-war period.

NOTES

1. Fritz Fischer, *Griff nach der Welt-macht: Die Kriegszielpolitik des kaiser-lichen Deutschland 1914-18*, Düsseldorf 1961.

2. Idem, *Krieg der Illusionen: Die deutsche Politik von 1911-1914*, Düsseldorf 1969.

3. For a recent discussion of the so-called "Fischer affair", see R.J.B. Bos-worth, *Explaining Auschwitz & Hiro-shima: History Writing and the Second World War 1945-1990*, London and New York 1993, pp.54-60.

4. Bernd-Jürgen Wendt, 'England und der deutsche 'Drang nach Südosten' Kapitalbeziehungen und Warenverkehr in Südosteuropa zwischen den Welt-kriegen', in Imanuel Geiss and Berndt-Jürgen Wendt, eds, *Deutschland in der Weltpolitik des 19. und 20. Jahrhunderts: Fritz Fischer zum 65. Geburtstag*, Düssel-dorf 1973, pp.483-511.

5. Ibid.

6. Alan S. Milward, 'The Reichsmark Bloc and the international Economy', in Gerhard Hirschfeld and Lothar Ketten-acher, eds, *'Der Führerstaat' Mythos und Realität: Studien zur Struktur und Politik des Dritten Reiches*, Stuttgart 1981, pp. 377-413; p.401.

7. Bernd-Jürgen Wendt, 'Südosteuropa in der nationalsozialistischen Gross-raumwirtschaft: eine Antwort auf Alan S. Milward', in Hirschfeld and Ketten-acher, pp.414-427. Wendt cannot accept Milward's interpretation of Germany's policy towards south-eastern Europe as an *ad hoc* solution. On the other hand, he accepts Milward's suggestion that the south-east European states be investi-gated individually regarding their relationship to Germany.

8. Antoine Fleury, *La pénétration alle-mande au Moyen-Orient 1919-1939: Le cas de la Turquie, de l'Iran et de l'Afghani-stan*, Leiden 1977. William S. Grenze-bach Jr., *Germany's Informal Empire in East-Central Europe: German Economic Policy toward Yugoslavia and Romania, 1933-1939*, Stuttgart 1988. Hans Joa-chim Hoppe, *Bulgarien – Hitlers eigen-williger Verbündeter: Eine Fallstudie zur nationalsozialistischen Südosteuropapolitik*, Stuttgart 1979. David E. Kaiser, *Eco-nomic Diplomacy and the Origins of the Second World War: Germany, Britain and Eastern Europe, 1930-1939*, Princeton 1980. Philippe Marguerat, *Le IIIe Reich et le pétrole roumain 1938-1940*, Leiden and Geneva 1977. Hans-Jürgen Schrö-der, 'Südosteuropa als 'Informal Empire' Deutschlands 1933-1939. Das Beispiel Jugoslawien', *Jahrbücher für Geschichte Osteuropas*, Bd. 23, 1975. pp.70-96.

9. This author has dealt with some aspects of Greek-German relations in various articles, see, Mogens Pelt, 'Bodosakis-Athanasiadis, a Greek Businessman from the East: A Case Study of the Interrelationship between State and Business', in Lars Erslev Andersen, ed., *Middle East Studies in Denmark*, Odense 1994 pp.65-86, idem, 'Germany and the Economic Dimension of the Metaxas Regime' *Journal of the Hellenic Diaspora*, Vol.20.2. 1994, idem, 'Greece and Germany's Policy toward Southeastern Europe, 1932-1940', *Epsi-lon*, No.2 1988, idem, 'Grækenland mel-lem Centraleuropa og Middelhavet' (Greece between Central Europe and the Mediterranean), in Carsten Due-Niel-sen, Hans Kierchoff, Carl-Christian Lammers and Torben Nybom, eds, *Konflikt og Samarbejde, Festskrift for Carl-Axel Gemzell* (Conflict and Co-operation,

Festschrift for Carl-Axel Gemzell), Copenhagen 1993 pp.89-106.

10. See especially, John S. Koliopoulos, *Greece and the British Connection 1935-1941*, Oxford 1977 and Dimitris Kitsikis, *I ellas tis 4s augoustou ke i megale dinamis* (Greece of the Fourth of August and the Great Powers), Athens 1974.

11. Alexis Alexandris, *The Greek Minority of Istanbul and Greek-Turkish Relations*, Athens 1983, pp.22-24.

12. For a discussion of the Great Idea and its significance in the early twentieth century, see, Michael Llewellyn Smith, *Ionian Vision: Greece in Asia Minor 1919-1922*, London 1973.

13. P.C. Ioakimidis, 'Greece: from Military Dictatorship to Socialism', in Allan Williams, ed., *Southern Europe Transformed: Political and Economic Change in Greece, Italy, Portugal and Spain*, London 1984, pp.33-60.

14. Ibid, p.34. The Greek nation state did not offer the same business opportunities that the more modern Ottoman trade centres did. In the period between the middle of the nineteenth century and the Balkan Wars (1912-13) a considerable number of people emigrated to the Ottoman urban centres. (Thanos Veremis and Kostas Kostis, *I Ethniki Trapeza sti Mikra Asia 1919-1922*, (The Greek National Bank in Asia Minor) Athens 1984, pp.46-47. In 1910 the Ottoman Greek population in Asia Minor was estimated to be about 2.5 million. This constituted about 20 per cent of the population in Anatolia.(Ibid, p.35), but 50 per cent of the industrial investments were Ottoman Greek. This was more than the total amount invested in industry in the Greek nation state. (Konstandinos Tsoukalas, *Exartisi ke anaparagoji: o kinonikos rolos ton ekspedeftikon michanismon stin Ellada (1830-1922)*, Athens 1981, p.309 (Interdependence and reproduction: the societal role of educational mechanisms in Greece 1830-1922, originally published in French, Paris 1975).

15. Annual Report 1935, Public Record Office (PRO), FO 371/20392.

16. A patron-client relationship should be understood as a personal relationship connecting two individuals or families. The relation is contractual but informal, i.e. an agreement can be made or broken, can be explicit or implicit, without any juridical sanctions. It relies on mutual favours, for example one gives with an expectation to receive, or receives and is expected to give. The relationship is asymmetrical and vertical, for example it is built on a relationship between a strong and a less strong party. This means that the "patron-client relationship" can assume the dimensions of huge and far-reaching social networks consisting of myriads of "patron-client relationships" in which the patron appears as client in another relaitionship and so on. Clientilism is therefore fundamentally different from, for example, a class society; this does not preclude coexistence, however. George Th. Mavrogordatos, *Stillborn Republic: Social Coalitions and Party Strategies in Greece 1922-1936*, Berkeley 1983, pp.5-14.

17. Thanos Veremis, 'The Officer Corps in Greece, 1912-1936', *Byzantine and Modern Greek Studies*, Vol 2 1976, pp.130-132.

18. Ibid, p.128.

19. John A. Petropoulos, 'The Compulsory Exchange of Populations: Greek-Turkish Peacemaking, 1922-1930', *Byzantine and Modern Greek Studies*, Vol.2, 1976, pp.135-160.

20. The number differs slightly in the sources. This has to attributed to inadequate methods of registration, to high death-rates and to immediate emigration upon arrival in the chaotic period after the exodus in 1922. See *Greek Refugee Problem*, League of Nations, Geneva 1926. p.15; p.93.

21. Michael R. Marrus, *The Unwanted: European Refugees in the Twentieth Century*, Oxford 1985, p.103.

22. This constituted 32.4 per cent of the population in 1928. *Statistiki epetiris tis Ellados* 1930, p.40.

23. *Greek Refugee Problem*, p.81. Mavrogordatos does not mention which month this refers to. Because an increasing number of refugees were established in the agricultural sector, this discrepancy suggests that his source used figures collected at another time of the year. Mavrogordataos, pp.187-188.

24. Ibid.

25. Between 1922-1938 the arable area was enlarged from 12,453 to 24,093 square kilometres. *Statistiki epetiris* 1939, anadromiki pinakes 16, p. 438.

26. Mavrogordatos, pp.187-189.

27. Ibid., p. 188.

28. Margarita Dritsa, *Biomichania ke trapezes stin Ellada tou mesopolemou* (Industry and Banks in Greece in the Inter-War Period), Athens 1990, pp.208-209.

29. Athanse G. Politis, *L'Hellénisme et l'Egypte moderne: Histoire de l'Hellénisme égyptien de 1798 à 1927*, Paris 1929-1930, Vol.II, pp.19-21.

30. Internally they were united by common traumas connected to the exodus and immediate loss of social status in Greece. Moreover, there was widespread hostility among the Greek population toward the refugees. Mavrogordatos, p.202.

31. This preference Mavrogordatos explains by the fact that the Ottoman Greeks regarded Venizelos's "liberation policy" as providing a rescue from the Young Turks. Moreover, the Venizelists conducted an active rehabilitation policy after 1922. Ibid., pp.198-201.

32. Ibid., pp.208-210.

33. It may seem odd that Venizelos accepted the Ankara Agreement, but it is important to point out that *détente* between Greece and Turkey took place at a time when Venizelos's modernization programme and the costs of Depression placed a heavy burden on Greece's economy. Thereby *détente* between Ankara and Athens would make it possible to release resources otherwise committed to the maintenance of the Greek armed forces. Indeed, military expenditures were reduced in the years following the Ankara Agreement and did not reach the pre-1930 level until the fiscal year of 1935/36.

34. *South-Eastern Europe: A political and Economic Survey*, The Royal Institute of International Affairs, London 1939, p.156.

35. Ibid., p.253.

36. Ibid.; see also Hermann Gross, *Südosteuropa, Bau und Entwicklung der Wirtschaft*, Leipzig 1937, p.91.

37. *Les conditions de l'agriculture mondiale en 1938-39*, Rome 1940, p.252; p.257.

38. Mark Mazower, *Greece and the Inter-War Economic Crisis*, Oxford 1991, pp.87-88.

39. Henry A. Hill, *The Economy of Greece: Prepared for the Coordinating Committee of American Agencies in Greece*, Vol.I-V, New York. (Published without information about year), p.28.

40. *Greek Refugee Settlement*, pp.148-153.

41. Mazower 1991, p.119.

42. Ibid., p.117.

43. Hill, Vol. III, p.25.

44. *Les conditons*, p.257.

45. *The Balkan States*, The Royal Institute of International Affairs, London 1936, p.65 table 23.

46. *Les conditions*, pp.257-258.

47. *Les grands produits agricoles: compendium international de statistiques 1924-1938*, Bureau régional européen de la FAO, Rome 1948, pp.125-130; 215-224.

48. Thanos Veremis, *Ikonomia ke diktatoria: i sinkiria 1925-1925*, (Economy and Dictatorship: The case 1925-1926), Athens 1982, p.46.

49. The earnings of the Greek merchant fleet between 1915-1919 is estimated to have been about 800 million gold francs. In comparison, the annual earnings before the war were between 25-30 million gold francs. Mazower 1991, pp.55-56.

50. Ibid., pp.91-100.

51. *Statistiki epetiris tis Ellados 1939* (Year Book of Greek Statistics 1939), p.454, table 22.

52. Mavrogordatos, p.146.

53. Ibid.

54. Christos Jecchinis, *Trade Unionism in Greece*, Chicago 1967, p.51.

55. Hill, Vol.III, p.29.

56. Mazower 1991, pp.127-128.

57. Mavrogordatos, pp.277-279.

58. Hill, Vol III, p.29.

59. Salonika 20 May 1936, report from the German Consul, Politisches Archiv des Auswärtigen Amtes (PAAA), Ha.Pol. IVa, Waren und Rohstoffe, Tabak Bd.1.

60. The victorious powers had the right to claim the same conditions as Germany in any trade agreement Germany made with a third country. This resulted in a general ban on German exports and imports. However, it was possible to obtain a dispensation from an institution set up for this purpose, the so-called *Aussenhandelsstellen,* which was composed of representatives of industry, trade, consumers and employees. This created an institutional framework for co-operation between state and business, as foreign trade belonged to a so-called *Sonderreferat Wirtschaft* under the *Auswärtiges Amt.* Harm G. Schröter, *Aussenpolitik und Wirtschaftsinteresse: Skandinavien im aussenwirtschaftlichen Kalkül Deutschlands und Grossbritanniens 1918-1939*, Frankfurt am Main, Berne, New York 1983, pp.23-28.

61. The point was made that supernational control of heavy industries would limit Germany's national sovereignty, because political self-assertion and conquest were dependent on military power, and for that reason also on a national heavy industry. Dirk Stegmann, 'Mitteleuropa, 1925-1934: Zum Problem der Kontinuität deutscher Aussenhandelspolitik von Stresemann bis Hitler', in Dirk Stegmann, Bernd-Jürgen Wendt and Peter Christian Witt, eds, *Industrielle Gesellschaft und politisches System: Beiträge zur politischen Sozialgeschichte: Festschrift für Fritz Fischer*, Bonn 1978, pp.208-209.

62. Ibid., pp.210-212.

63. Bernd-Jürgen Wendt, *Grossdeutschland: Aussenpolitik und Kriegsvorbereitung des Hitler-Regimes*, Munich 1987, p.51.

64. Verena Schröter, *Die deutsche Industrie auf dem Weltmarkt 1929-1933. Aussenwirtschaftliche Strategien unter dem Druck der Weltwirtschaftskrise*, Frankfurt am Main 1984, p.519.

65. Stegmann, pp.215-218.

66. Hans Jürgen Schröder, 'Deutsche Südosteuropapolitik 1929-1936: zur Kontinuiätet deutscher Aussenpolitik in der Weltwirtschaftskrise', *Geschichte und Gesellschaft* 2.Jg. Heft 1, 1976, pp.5-32.

67. Wendt 1987, pp.58-59.

68. Stegmann depicts it as an early counterpart to the *Neuer Plan* dated 1934, p.218.

69. The Tardieu Plan aimed at the creation of a customs union between the Danubian states. The plan received support from the British and French governments, while Germany saw it as an attempt to obstruct her economic expansion towards the Danube countries. Schröder 1976, pp.15-17. See also Wendt 1987, p.58.

70. Ibid. See also Stegmann, pp.216-218.

71. Schröder 1976, p.11; Stegmann, p.218. *Mitteleuropäischer Wirtschaftstag* (MWT or MEWT) had its headquarters in Vienna and aimed to create a united Central Europe. A German section of the organization was established in 1926.(Stegmann, pp.209-210). The President of the German sector was Tilo Freiherr von Wilmowski, member of the board of directors at Krupp; the Vice President was Max Ilgner, President of IG Farben.

72. Verena Schröter, p.507.

73. Stegmann, pp.216-217.

74. Alice Teichova, *An Economic Background to Munich: International Business and Czechoslovakia 1918-1938*, Cambridge 1974, passim.

75. Harm G. Schröter, 'Siemens and Central and South-East Europe between the two World Wars', in Alice Teichova and P.L. Cottrell, eds, *International Business and Central Europe 1918-1939*, Leicester 1983, pp.173-192; p.176.

76. In 1913 German industries accounted for 85.1 per cent of the global production of synthetic dyes and managed to maintain this position into the inter-war period. Harm Schröter, *Aussenpolitik*, p.250.

77. Wendt, 1987, pp.54-55.

78. Harm Schröter, *Aussenpolitik*, p.257.

79. Ibid., p.250.

80. German firms defended this position. To cite an example, IG Farben invested ten times as much as their main rivals, the British Imperial Chemical Industries (ICI), in research. ICI had the same share capital as IG Farben. Ibid., pp.250-251.

81. Verena Schröter, pp.448-455.

82. Clemens A. Wurm, 'Aussenpolitik und Wirtschaft in den internationalen Beziehungen: Internationale Kartelle, Aussenpolitik und weltwirtschaftliche Beziehungen 1919-1939: Einführung', in Wurm, *Internationale Kartelle und Aussenpolitik*, Stuttgart 1989, pp.1-31.

83. Ibid., p.10.

84. Charles P. Kindleberger, *The World in Depression 1929-1939*, Los Angeles 1973, p.172.

85. British exports to the Empire grew from 41.4 per cent of the total export in 1929 to 46.3 per cent in 1938. The imports from these countries grew from 29.4 per cent to 40.4 per cent in the same period. Bengt Nilson, *Handelspolitik under skärpt konkurrens: England och Sverige 1929-39* (Trade Policy during Increased Competion: Britain and Sweden, 1929-1939) Lund 1983, p.166, tables I and II. See also, Kaiser, pp.201-203.

86. Eckart Teichert, *Autarkie und Grossraumwirtschaft in Deutschland 1930-1939*, Munich 1984, p.10.

87. Verena Schröter, p.524.

88. Stegmann, pp.220-221.

89. Teichert, p.212.

90. Ibid., pp.85-86. From 1934 the German army gained more influence over trade policy, having been offered a say in such matters along with *Auswärtiges Amt* and the Ministry of Economy. (Ibid., p.53.) The army dealt with economic issues through the *Wehrwirtschaftsstab* (The Army Economic Office) which was established in October 1935. *Wehrwirtschaftsstab* had access to information about economic issues as a result of its close connections with research establishments.(Ibid., p.62).

91. Alfred Kube, *Pour le mérite und Hakenkreuz: Hermann Göring im Dritten Reich*, Munich 1986, p.79.

92. Teichert, p.198.

93. Grenzebach, p.135.

94. Hans-Erich Volkmann, 'Aussenhandel und Aufrüstung in Deutschland 1933 bis 1939', in Friedrich Forstmeier and Hans-Erich Volkmann, eds, *Wirtschaft und Rüstung am Vorabend des Zweiten Weltkriegs*, Düsseldorf 1975, pp.81-131; p.101.

95. "...Wie soll pol.[itische] Macht, wenn sie gewonnen ist, gebraucht werden? Jetzt noch nicht zu sagen. Vielleicht Erkämpfung neuer Export-Mögl.[ichkeiten], vielleicht – und wohl besser – Eroberung neuen Lebensraums im Osten u.[nd] dessen rücksichtslose Germanisierung..." Quote from 'Liebmann-Protokoll', Wendt 1987, pp.186-187.

96. Ibid., pp.51-52.

97. Ibid, pp.52-53.

98. Fleury, pp.57-58.

99. Greek-German relations in the period leading up to the First World War are discussed in Konstantin Loulos, *Die Deutsche Griechenlandspolitik von der Jahrhundertwende bis zur Ausbruch des Ersten Weltkrieges*, Frankfurt am Main, Berne, New York 1986.

100. From the end of the 1880s German capital started to flow into Turkey, and in 1888 Deutsche Bank established a branch in Istanbul. Loulos, pp.37-38.

101. In 1883 Major Colmar Freiherr von der Goltz was appointed to reorganize and modernize the Ottoman army in accordance with a German model. Fleury, p.15.

102. Kaiser Wilhelm II made several journeys to the Ottoman Empire. During a visit to Damascus in 1898 he proclaimed himself friend and protector of the 300 million Muslims in Asia Minor, the Middle East and Northern Africa. Fleury, p.18.

103. The railway was planned to connect Anatolia, Mesopotamia, the Levant and Hedjaz with the European continent through the Balkans and Central Europe.

104. Loulos, pp.170-171; pp.252ff.

105. Politis II, pp.270ff.

106. The German bank took over branches in Constantinople and Hamburg and established Deutsche Orient Bank in 1906 in co-operation with Dresdner Bank and Schaffhausen Bankverein. The initial investment was 16 million RM., (Loulos, p.130). The increasing significance of Deutsche Orient Bank can be seen from the fact that it expanded into British dominated Egypt. (Eric Davis, *Challenging Colonialism: Bank Misr and Egyptian Industrialization, 1920-1941*, Princeton 1983, pp.70-71; pp.75-76; pp.93-95).

107. In addition to army and navy officers the 'Little Court' included the President of the National Bank and several prominent intellectuals. Loulos, pp.82-84.

108. Ibid., pp.84-88.

109. *The Balkan States*, p.65, Table 23.

110. Letter from tobacco producers in northern Greece to the Minister of the Administration of Macedonia, 12 March 1937. *Istoriko archio tis ethnikis trapezas Ellados* (The Historical Archives of the National Bank of Greece. Henceforth the National Bank of Greece), XXVIII Proionda, A Kapnos, 7.

111. Vera Kacarkova, 'Handelsbeziehungen zwischen Deutschland und Griechenland in den 30er Jahren des XX. Jh.', *Études balkaniques* 12, 1976, 3 Sofia, pp.43-61; pp.52-53.

112. See, Introduction in Teichova and Cottrell.

113. *South-Eastern Europe*, pp.14-21.

114. Irvine H. Anderson, *Aramco, the United States and Saudi Arabia: A Study of the Dynamics of Foreign Policy, 1933-1950*, Princeton 1981, p.15.

115. The areas around Smyrna and Andalia were granted to Italy by the London Agreement in 1915 and the St. Jean de Maurienne Agreement, 1917, respectively. In March 1919 Italy landed armed forces in Andalia, from whence they moved towards Smyrna in May. This caused an immediate reaction from Greece, who landed her armed forces in the city in the same month. Llewellyn Smith, p.68.

116. France agreed to reconsider her rights to Cilicia, while Italy gave up the Andalia region. Richard Clogg, *A Short History of Modern Greece*, Cambridge 1979, p.117.

117. Ibid., p.179.

118. Ibid., p.181.

119. Grenzebach, pp.9-10.

120. *The Problem of International Investment*, Royal Institute of International Affairs, London 1937, pp.123-126.

121. Teichova 1974, pp.1-29; pp.377-378.

122. *The Problem of International Investment*, pp.126-128.

123. Ibid., Table 1, p.2.

124. Ibid., pp. 216-218.

125. Teichova 1974, pp.377-382.

126. L. Berov, 'Le capital financier occidental et les pays balkaniques dans les années vingt', *Etudes Balkaniques 2-3*, Sophia 1965, pp.139-169; p.145. *The Balkan States*, appendix IV, pp.142-143.

127. Berov, p.145 note 18. The corresponding figures for Bulgaria represent the years prior to 1914 and are distributed as follows: French, Dutch, British, Swiss capital: 77 per cent; German: 10 per cent; Austro-Hungarian: 13 per cent. In 1931 these amounts made up 80 per cent of the total of Bulgaria's public loans. Turkey did not take any loans after the foundation of the Turkish Republic in 1923. *The Balkan State*, appendix IV.

128. Berov, p.145. Public loans are included in the figures for Turkey. These made up 54 per cent of the total investments of foreign capital and the figures mainly describe the situation before the First World War. Albania was totally dependent on Italy.

129. Teichova 1974, p.8.

130. The establishment of the General Hellenic Trust was an attempt to channel British funds into Greek industry from the latter part of the 1920s. The original aim was to invest about £6 million, but in 1939 total investments were still only about £0.33 milion. Mark Mazower, 'Economic Diplomacy between Great Britain and Greece in the

1930s', *The Journal of European Economic History*, Vol. 17, No. 3, Winter 1988, pp.603-619; pp.604-607.

131. Ibid, pp.604-607.

132. *South-Eastern Europe*, p.164. The railway handled traffic between the Greek capital and the Peloponnese. The 842 kilometres of track made it the second largest railway, out of eight, in Greece.

133. Mazower 1988, pp. 604-608.

134. Griechenlands Seeschiffart u. Seehäfen, Kiel May 1940, Bundesarchiv-Militärarchiv (BA-MA), RW 19/3329. See also, Die griechische Handelsflotte im Frieden und im Kriege, BA-MA, WI/IC1./7B.

135. Hill, Vol.I, pp.42-43.

136. *Statistiki epetiris tis Ellados*, 1939, pp.434-435.

137. Hill, Vol. I, p.12.

138. Figures until 1938; see Mazower 1991, table A1. 5. Otherwise, see the annual report (1940) from The Bank of Greece, the Historical Archive of the National Bank of Greece, XXI, 13.

139. Politis, Vol.II, pp.266ff.

140. Tsoukalas, pp.297-298.

141. Politis, passim.

142. Alexander Kitroeff, *The Greeks in Egypt, 1919-1937: Ethnicity and Class*, London 1989, pp.192ff.

143. Robert Tignor, 'The Economic Activities of Foreigners in Egypt, 1920-1950: From Millet to Haute Bourgeoise', *Comparative Studies in Society and History*, Cambridge 1980, pp.416ff.

144. Hill, Vol.I, p.42. *The Balkan States*, p.142.

145. Report concerned with the development of the Greek Air Force 1930-1938, Genika archia tou kratous, Archio tou Metaxa (The Greek State Archives, Metaxas Archive) Henceforth the Metaxas Archive, fak.77.

146. *The Balkan States*, Appendix II.

147. Ibid., Appendix II; table 28, p.73; table 24, p.65.

148. *Statistiki epetiris* 1939, table 28, p.459. *The Balkan States*, Appendix II, p.138.

149. Mazower 1988, pp.610-611.

150. *Les conditions*, pp.252-255.

151. *The Balkan States*, table 22, p.64.

152. N.D. Mousmoutis, *The Estimate of the National Income of Greece: From the Production Side*, Athens 1950, p.13.

153. *The Balkan States*, table 23, p.65.

154. *South-Eastern Europe*, p.157.

155. *Statistiki epetiris*, 1931, 1936, 1939, V Emborion. The figures are taken from *Mineon deltion tou idikou emboriou tis Ellados meta ton xenon epikration*, December 1939, Athens 1939, Pinax II. Index numbers have been worked out on the basis of the above-mentioned statistics. The value of the total trade in the 1930s (measured in Gold Drachmas) never attained the 1930 level. The total value fell between 1929-1933, whereafter it grew until 1938. As a result of the war, the total trade fell in 1939-1940. The war also partly explains changes in the Germans, British and American share of the Greek trade. *Statistiki epetiris* 1939, p.458.

156. Including Czechoslovakia and Poland.

157. Excluding Czechoslovakia and Poland.

158. Memo from the German Vice-Consul in Kavalla, 29 June 1939, W III5640/39, PAAA, Ha.Pol.IVa, Rohstoffe und Waren, Tabak Bd.1.

159. Salonika 6 November 1938, memo from the British General Consulate, PRO, FO 371 22366/1360/17/6/16.

160. *South-Eastern Europe*, p.157.

161. *Les conditions*, p.255.

162. *Statistiki epitris*, 1931, 1936, 1939. V Emborion.

163. Ibid., 1935-1939, XI Dimosia ikonomia; *The Balkan States*, Table 30, p.78.

164. N. D. Mousmoutis, table 13; *Statistiki epiritis*, V, emborion; *Mineon detion*, October, November, December 1940, pinax II.

165. Harm Schröter, *Siemens*, p.179.

166. Idem, *Aussenpolitik*, p.264.

167. Bundesarchiv Abteilung Potsdam (BA Abt. Potsdam), 80 IG 1/IG Farben/B 6549/107.

168. Harm Schröter, *Aussenpolitik*, pp.275-276.

169. Dritsa, p.181.

170. IG Farben 8 March 1938, Entwurf zu einem Schreiben an das Dreier Kartel, BA Abt. Potsdam, 80 IG1/IG Farben/B 4006.

171. Verena Schröter, p.512.

172. On 4 December 1937 IG Farben made an agreement with ETMA according to which ETMA was to buy the chemical products necessary for their production at IG Farben. BA Abt. Potsdam, 80 IG1/IG Farben/1617. In 1932 an international artificial silk cartel was established. Schröter, *Aussenpolitik*, p.280.

173. Schröter, *Aussenpolitik*, pp.268-269. The 'Haber-Borch' method made it possible to establish large-scale production of synthetic saltpetre, a field in which Germany became dominant.

174. Mazower 1988, p.607.

175. Veremis 1982, pp.116-118.

176. Harm Schröter, *Siemens*, p.174. Griechenlands feinmechanische u. optische Industrie, Institut für Weltwirtschaft, Kiel, May 1940, BA-MA, RW 19/3329.

177. Harm Schröter, *Siemens*, p.174.

178. Ibid., pp.178-179.

179. Ibid., pp.183-184.

180. Griechenlands feinmechanische u. optische Industrie, Institut für Weltwirtschaft, Kiel, May 1940, BA-MA, RW 19/3329.

181. Schröter, *Aussenpolitik*, pp.322-354.

182. Mavrogordatos, p.46.

183. Ibid., pp.315-318; Veremis 1976, p.118.

184. Veremis, *I epemvasis tou stratou stin elliniki politiki, 1916-36* (The Intervention of the Army in Greek Politics 1916-1936), Athens 1983, p.190.

185. Kondilis planned to enforce the executive power with Metaxas as President, to reform the army and to introduce a labour market bill. Veremis 1983, pp.195-198.

186. Veremis, p.183; Mavrogordatos, p.318.

187. Annual Report 1935.

188. The Venizelists declared the election invalid, on the grounds that the state of emergency had been lifted too late.

189. Mavrogordatos, pp.48-51.

190. Hary Cliadakis, 'The Political and Diplomatic Background to the Metaxas Dictatorship, 1935-36', *Journal of Contemporary History*, January 1979 Vol 14, No 1, pp.117-138; p.127.

191. Everett J. Marder, 'The Second Regime of George II: His Role in Poli-

tics', *Southeastern Europe* II, 1, 1975, pp. 53-69; p.58.

192. Athens, 1 February 1936, Kordt to AA, Zum Tode des General Kondilis, Abschrift von II Balk 282 Gr. PAAA, AB. IIb Griechenland Pol. 11-4, Militär.

193. Mavrogordatos, pp.227-279.

194. Koliopoulos, pp.39-40.

195. Athens 15 April 1936, Kordt to AA, PAAA, Abt.II, Griechenland Politik 7, Ministerien Bd.2.

196. *Istoria tou ellenikou ethnous* (History of the Greek Nation), tome IE., p.378.

197. Griogrios Dafnis, *I Ellas metaxi dio polemon* (Greece between two wars), tome II, Athens 1955, p.432. Daphnis cites an interview with Diakos, one of Metaxas' intimate friends.

198. Metaxas, tome, IV, pp. 232-233.

199. Koliopoulos, pp.44ff.

200. Ibid, p.52.

201. Spiros Linardatos, *I 4e augoustou* (The Fourth of August) Athens 1966, p.77. Censorship made it illegal even to comment on foreign trade, a matter that had stirred public opinion earlier, see below.

202. The department consisted of 45 officers, 400 men, 30 political advisors and a motorcycle corps with 1,200 men (equipped with sub-machine-guns). Yannis Andricopoulos, 'The Powerbase of Greek Authoritarianism', in Hagtved and Larsen, eds, *Who were the Fascists?*, Bergen 1980, pp. 568-584; p.578.

203. Hill, Vol. II, p.45.

204. Annual Report 1938, PRO, FO 371/23777.

205. Athens 10 May 1939, Erbach to AA, der 1. Mai in Griechenland, PAAA pol IV po 5. Gr. Bd.1.

206. Linardatos, p.121 note 1.

207. Athens, 10 May 1939, Erbach to AA, der 1. Mai in Griechenland, PAAA, Pol.IV Po.5. Gr. Bd. 1. The first law regulating social insurance was passed in 1922 and became the basis of funds established by specific employees, e.g. the tobacco workers. In 1932 Law 5733 was passed introducing more general social insurances. The fall of the Venizelos government and the subsequent chaos obstructed the realisation of these plans, however. The Social Insurance Fund (*Idrima kinonikon asfaliseon* IKA) was founded at the end of 1936, yet did not operate in Athens, Piraeus and Salonika untill 1937. Throughout the rest of the country it was operative by the end of 1938. Linardatos, pp. 125-127.

208. Ibid.

209. Griechenlands nationale Wiedergeburt. Zum ersten Jahrestag der Einführung der autoritären Regierungsform, PAAA Pol. IV. Po.5 Gr. Bd.1.

210. Athens, 10 May 1939, Erbach to AA, der 1. Mai in Griechenland, PAAA, Pol.IV Po.5. Gr. Bd. 1.

211. See below.

212. Alexadros Papagos, *O ellinikos stratos ke i pros polemon proparaskevi tou, 1923-1940* (The Greek Army and its Preparation for War), Athens 1945.

213. *I pros polemon paraskevi tou ellinikou stratou, 1923-1940* (The Greek Army's Preparation for War, 1923-1940), General Staff, Directorate for Military History, Athens 1969.

214. Papagos was the military leader of the Greek National Army during the Civil War, 1946-1949. His military career ended in 1951, when he held the rank of field marshal. Thereafter he established the political party, 'Greek Rally', which was oriented towards nationalism and conservatism. In 1952 he was elected Prime Minister, an appointment he kept until his death in 1955. His rule was characterized by economic recovery and growth based on an austerity programme and ample aid from the United States. He maintained an uncompromising policy towards former members of the Resistance and the losers in the Civil War, the Communists and their supporters.

215. MacVeagh p.103. Athens 29 May 1937, MacVeagh to the State Department.

216. Papagos, p.130.

217. Ibid., p.131.

218. Ibid., p.130.

219. Ibid., pp.140-141.

220. 12 May 1936 (Confidential memo to the leaders of the General Staff concerned with the organization of Greece's war industry) Metaxas Archive, fak. 97.

221. The aim was to make Greece self-sufficient in terms of various modern weapons, ranging from machine-guns to aeroplanes, on the basis of a five or ten year programme. Ibid.

222. See below.

223. Papagos, p.134.

224. *Statistiki epetiris XI Dimosia Ikonomika*, 1930, p.377, 1936, p.344, 1939, p.321. If the figures for the Army are compared with those in Papagos's book, and the figures for the Navy and the Air Force with those in the British annual reports, the deviations are as small as 1.6 per cent for the Army, 0.8 per cent for the Navy and 1.3 per cent for the Air Force. However, the Greek national statistics do not contain the figures from 1939-1941. In this period Papagos, who only discusses the Army, states that the expenditures were higher because of the war. The ordinary appropriations to the Army between 1936-1941 amounted to 8.89 billion Dr. (i.e. 1.78 on average per year) The distribution was as follows: 1936-37, 1.45; 1937-38, 1.61; 1938-39, 1.73; 1939-40, 1.68; 1940-41, 2.42. Papagos, p. 202.

225. Ibid., p.9.

226. Ibid., p.143.

227. See below.

228. Papagos, p.202.

229. Ibid., p.190.

230. Ibid., p.181.

231. Ibid., pp.149-151.

232. The original orders were worth 1.37 billion Dr., whereas the actual deliveries were worth 1.02 billion Dr., Ibid., p.152.

233. *Ausfuhrgemeinschaft für Kriegsgerät* (AGK), Griechenland, Gemeldte Abschlüsse 1. 1. 1936 – 30. 6. 1938, PAAA, Ha. Pol, geheim, Handel mit Kriegsgerät, allgemeines Bd. 3.

234. Papagos, pp.162-164.

235. Ibid.

236. Annual Report 1938.

237. The Greek General Staff, p.50.

238. Papagos, p.157.

239. Ibid., p.156. The latter does not include the expenditures for tools, which amounted to 13.1 million Dr. Ibid., p.181.

240. The Saint Etienne machine-gun was a Hotchkiss product.

241. In 1897 Maxim Guns and Ammunition Company was sold to Vickers Arms Company. Jaroslav Lugs, *Firearms Past and Present*, London 1973, p.284.

242. After the First World War, the Belgian factory Fabrique Nationale d'Armes de Guerre in Herstal started to produce Mauser rifles. Ibid., pp.488-490; 501.

243. Papagos, p.154. The British annual reports state that the number was 25,000 Mauser rifles. Moreover, they also state that Greece bought 250 Brandt Stokes additional infantry weapons. The discrepancy in relation to the Mauser rifles must be ascribed to the fact that Papagos covers the whole period.

244. Papagos, pp.154-155. However, the guns had still not been paid for on 28 October 1940.

245. PRO, Annual Report 1938.

246. Papagos, p.156.

247. Ibid.,165-166.

248. Ibid., p.159.

249. Ibid., p.171.

250. AGK, Griechenland, gemeldte Abschlüsse 1.1.1936 – 30.6.1938.

251. Papagos, p.172.

252. Ibid., p.183.

253. Ibid., p.182.

254. 25 French Potez, 10 British Fairy and 12 British Atlas aeroplanes. A report on the development of the Greek Air Force 1930-1938, Metaxas Archive fak. 77.

255. Due to the antiquated condition of its material, the Air Force was, according to a British assessment, capable of raising only one operational squadron. Annual Report 1937, PRO, FO 371/23371.

256. Top secret report, 20 December 1935, Metaxas Archive, fak. 82.

257. Ibid.

258. The distribution was to be: 96 fighters, 72-84 bombers, 12 aircraft cooperating with the Navy, 16 aircraft cooperating with the Army, 118 (training) aircraft. In addition, 70 old-fashioned aircraft were to cooperate with the Army and the Navy (60 for the Army

and 10 for the Navy); Annual Report 1935, Belgrade 17 April 1935, the Greek Ministry of Foreign Affairs 1935, politiki AAK 36, fak. 8.

259. Report on the development of the Greek Air Force 1930-1938, Metaxas Archive, fak. 77.

260. The fighters were not delivered until the end of the fiscal year 1937-1938. Ibid. In this connection it is significant that Poland's import of Greek tobacco rose from 60 tons in 1936 to 923 tons in 1937, Kavalla 12 June 1938, the German Vice-Consulate, Tabaksproduktion und Tabakshandel in Mazedonien und Westtrazien, Kampagne 37/38, PAAA, Ha.Pol.IVa, Rohstoffe und Waren, Tabak Bd.1.

261. The Czechoslovak aircraft were donated by Kandarelis and the British ones by Sanakis; report on the development of the Greek Air Force 1930-1938, Metaxas Archive, fak. 77.

262. Annual Report 1938. FO 371/23777, PRO. A confidential special report from Germany, dated 1939, notes that the purchases of Spitfires, Blenheims and tanks from Britain were to be financed by a £2 million credit on weapons which the British Government gave the Greeks shortly before the outbreak of the war in 1939. Vertraulicher Sonderbericht 94. Griechenland – Wirtschaftsbesprechungen mit sir Frederich Leith-Ross, 21.7.39.

263. The Greek General Staff, p.82.

264. Athens, 17 October 1937, the German military attaché, Colonel Rohde, to the Reichsluftfahrtsministerium, PAAA, Gesandschaft Athen Nr. 21, Waffenlieferungen der Griechischen Regierung.

265. The deal was made on 22 January 1938, and the aircraft were to be delivered within the following twelve months. Report on the development of

the Greek Air Force 1930-1938, Metaxas Archive, fak. 77.

266. The Greek General Staff, p.82.

267. Report on the development of the Greek Air Force 1930-1938, Metaxas Archive, fak. 77.

268. Undated memo by the Greek Naval Attaché in Berlin, W 2160 40g, PAAA, Ha.Pol., Geheim, Handel mit Kriegsgerät, Griechenland Bd. 2.

269. Athens, 13 February 1940, Deutsche Gesandschaft, der Luftattaché, Betr. Deutsche Flugzeuglieferungen an Griechenland, PAAA, Ha.Pol., Geheim, Handel mit Kriegsgerät, Griechenland Bd.2.

270. The Greek General Staff, p.82.

271. Report on the development of the Greek Air Force 1930-1938, Metaxas Archive, fak. 77.

272. London, 21 October 1935, confidential letter from Simopoulos, the Greek Ambassador in London, Metaxas Archive fak. 80.

273. RPT Davenport-Hines, 'Vickers' Balkan Conscience: Aspects of Anglo-Romanian Armaments 1918-1939', *Business History*. Vol XXV 1983, pp.287-319.

274. Annual Report 1938.

275. Report on the development of the Greek Air Force 1930-1938, Metaxas Archive, fak. 77.

276. Ibid.

277. *Krigsfly 1939-1945*, Copenhagen 1970, p.153.

278. Berlin, 28 February 1940, Kriegsmaterial für Griechenland, PAAA, Ha. Pol. Geheim, Handel mit Kriegsgerät, Griechenland, Bd.2.

279. This appears in a report from a group under *Oberkommando der Wehrmacht* (OKW), which investigated various Greek firms and government institutions after the German occupation, in preparation for a German takeover. 31 May 1941, Bericht über die Tätigkeit der Abteilung Rohstoff-Allgemein, Unterabteilung Immobilien, Übernahme wichtiger Betriebe in Besitz und Eigentum, PAAA, Ha.Pol., Handakten Clodius, Griechenland, Bd.4.

280. Athens, 13 February 1940, Deutsche Gesandschaft, der Luftattaché, Betr. Deutsche Flugzeuglieferungen an Griechenland, PAAA, Ha.Pol., Geheim, Handel mit Kriegsgerät, Griechenland Bd.2.

281. In 1940 the Greek Navy consisted of: 1 armoured cruiser, 1 light cruiser, 10 destroyers, 13 torpedo boats, 6 submarines, 4 minelayers, 4 minesweepers; 1 June 1940, Orientierungsheft, Griechenland, Der Oberbefehlshaber der Luftwaffe, BA-MA, RLD 13/94.

282. See below.

283. Annual Report 1938.

284. Annual Report 1937 and 1938.

285. Sofia, 9 October 1937, Rheinmetall-Borsig, Aktennotiz, Imperial War Museum (IWM), Speer Documents, FD 790/46.

286. In German documents, the factory is called Poudreries et Cartoucheries Helléniques, and in British, the Greek Powder and Cartridge Company. In Greece it is normally referred to as Bodosakis's Weapon Factory.

287. Hill, Vol.II, pp.28-31.

288. I.e. 6.5 mm, 7 mm, 7.7 mm, 7.92 mm, 8 mm, 13.2 mm.

289. Hill, Vol.II, pp.28-31.

290. I.e. 20 mm, 37 mm, 40 mm, 88 mm.

291. 12 May 1936, memo on the organization of Greece's war industry, Metaxas Archive.

292. Hill, Vol.II, pp.28-31.

293. Angela Raspin, 'Wirtschaftlische und politische Aspekte der Italienischen Aufrüstung Anfang der dreissiger Jahren bis 1940', in Forstmeier and Volkmann 1975, pp.202-221.

294. Hill, Vol II, pp.28-31.

295. Papagos, pp.172-175.

296. 6 January 1940, Lt. Col. Sir Thomson Moore M.P. to Lord Halifax, PRO, FO 371-24914 R 441/441/19.

297. 5 May 1941, WiRü Amt Vortragsnotiz für den Herrn Reichsmarschall, Geheime Kommandosache, Sicherung deutscher Wirtschaftsinteressen in Griechenland, BA-MA, WI/IC1. 10.

298. Besprechung im Auswärtigen Amt am 7. juni 1941 bei dem Gesandten Clodius über Sicherung von Rohstoffe und wehrwichtigen Unternehmungen in Griechenland, geheim, BA-MA, WI/IC1. 10.

299. Brasida Ch. Sotiropoulos, *Bodosakis*, place and year of publishing not stated, pp.174-176.

300. The Greek Foreign Ministry, 1939/B/3/AG, Oikonomikai schesis, Eghiptos.

301. Institut für Weltwirtschaft an der Universität Kiel, May 1940, BA-MA, RW 19/3329.

302. PRO, Annual Report 1938, FO 371/23777.

303. Die Chemiewirtschaft Griechenlands und wichtige Unternehmen der chemischen Industrie, Vowi 4204, Zentrales Staatsarchiv Potsdam (ZStA Potsdam), 80 IG Farben/IG Farben/A 421.

304. BA Abt. Potsdam, 80 BA1/ Dresdner Bank/2363.

305. 1 June 1940, Orientierungsheft, Griechenland, Der Oberbefehlshaber der Luftwaffe, BA-MA, RLD 13/94.

306. 11 September 1939, IG Farben VoWi 3632 Griechenland, Kurze Übersicht über Wirtschaft und Politik, BA-MA, RW 19 Anhang 1/916.

307. Drista, p.282. Drista relies on documents from the National Bank of Greece.

308. Papagos. p.174.

309. Volkmann 1975, p.85. See also Berlin 1 February 1938, OKW, Wehrwirtschaftsstab, Stand der wirtschaftlichen Lage, BA-MA, RM 11/3.

310. Volkmann 1975, pp.88-92.

311. Fleury, p.49.

312. Grenzebach, p.215.

313. See Part I, Germany.

314. Milward, p.118.

315. Grenzebach, p.120.

316. Wendt 1987, pp.128-129, Volkmann, 'Die NS-Wirtschaft in Vorbereitung des Krieges', in Wilhelm Deist, Manfred Messerschmidt, Hans-Erich Volkmann and Wolfram Wette, eds, *Die Ursachen und Vorraussetzungen des Zweiten Weltkrieges*, Frankfurt am Main 1991 (Originally published under the title *Ursachen und Vorraussetzungen der Deutschen Kriegspolitik*, 1979), p.260.

317. Grenzebach, p.124.

318. Volkmann 1975, p.97. See, also Wendt 1987, pp.130-131.

319. Volkmann 1975, pp.97-98.

320. Wendt 1987, pp.187-191.

321. 22 November 1938, Erstehung, Entwicklung und Arbeit der MWT, Bundesarchiv Koblenz (BAK), R 43/368a.

322. "... Man könnte von einer neuen und modernen Epoche des Kolonial – oder besser Kolonisationsproblems im

Zeitalter der Nationalisierungs- und Industrialisierungstendenzen sprechen..." Bad Kirsingen 15 April 1937, Max Ilgner to Schacht, BAK, R7/3441.

323. "... auf lange Sicht betrachtet – [wird] dasjenige hochentwickelte Land am meisten seinen politischen und wirtschaftlichen Einfluss verankern [...], welches sich als Verbündeter an dem Ausbau der bestehenden Möglichkeiten aktiv beteiligt hat..." Ibid.

324. Wendt 1981, pp.423-424.

325. In January 1927 the International Control Commission withdrew from Germany. On 27 July 1927 the Germans passed a law prohibiting all imports and exports of war equipment. *Akten zur deutschen auswärtigen Politik 1918-1945* (ADAP), C IV 116. See also Karl-Heinz Ludwig, 'Strukturmerkmale national-sozialistischer Aufrüstung bis 1935', in Forstmeier and Volkmann 1975, pp.39-64.

326. Originally the agreement was only valid in relation to the so-called "Russentransporte", i.e. freight of war equipment to the Soviet Union, where, among other things, Germany had a training camp for armoured troops. Ludwig, pp. 43-44. Later the agreement was extended to include all other transportation of war equipment that was of interest to the rearmament. ADAP C IV 116.

327. Rheinmetall-Borsig used Waffen-fabrik Solothurn AG. in Switzerland. ADAP C, I, 357.

328. Berlin 10 July 1933. Note to the Vortragenden Legationsrat Michelsen, ADAP C, I, 357.

329. Kube, pp.166-167.

330. Volkmann 1975, p.93.

331. Manfred Funke, *Sanktionen und Kanonen: Hitler, Mussolini und der internationale Abessinienkonflikt*, Düsseldorf 1971, pp.36-37; 43-45. See also, Esmonde M. Robertson, 'Hitler und die Sanktionen des Völkerbunds – Mussolini und die Besetzung des Rheinlands', *Vierteljahrshefte für Zeitgeschichte* 26 Jahrg. 1978 pp. 237-264; p.237.

332. "...Die Förderung und Erleichterung der deutschen Kriegsgeräteausfuhr und des Waffen- und Munitionshandels nach dem Auslande ist aus wirtschaftlichen und wehrpolitischen Gründen dringend erwünscht. Die Waffenherstellung für die Ausfuhr ist das wertvollste und auch einzige Mittel um unsere Rüstungsfirmen – auf weite Sicht betrachtet – leistungsfähig und finanziell selbständig zu erhalten..." Berlin, 24 June 1935, ADAP C IV 168.

333. 27 June 1935, Neurath to the Ministry of War, ADAP, C, IV, 168 note 5.

334. Ibid.

335. Francis Nicosia, 'Arab Nationalism and National Socialist Germany, 1933-1939: Ideological and strategic incompatibility', *International Journal of Middle East Studies*. 12 (1980), pp.351-372; pp.362-363.

336. ADAP C IV 394 Anmerkung.

337. Funke, pp.67-68.

338. Volkmann, 'Die NS-Wirtschaft' pp.317-323. See also Kube, pp. 163-166, and Robert H. Whealy, *Hitler and Spain: The Nazi Role in the Spanish Civil War 1936-1939*, Kentucky 1989, pp.72-94.

339. Ausfuhr von K.-G. nach Ländern in den Jahren 1936 und 1937, PAAA, Ha.Pol., Geheim, Handel mit Kriegsgerät allgemeines, Bd. 3. Teichert (pp.197-198) and Volkmann 1975 (p.90) consider that the trade with China did not fulfil the expectations of the German authorities.

However, neither mentions the revenues in hard currency from 1937.

340. Kube, pp.170-171.

341. Berlin, 10 February 1937, Reichsgruppe Industrie an den Beauftragten für den Vierjahresplan, PAAA, Ha.Pol., Geheim, Handel mit Kriegsgerät, allgemeines, Bd.2.

342. In 1936 the Little Entente set up a so-called 'commercial centre' in Prague, which later established sub-branches in Belgrade and Bucharest. The purpose was to offer credits to the Yugoslav and Romanian governments, earmarked for the purchase of arms from Czechoslovakia. Berlin 1 June 1937, OKW, Wehrwirtschaftsstab, Stand der wirtschaftlichen Lage, geheime Kommandosache, BA-MA, RM 11/2.

343. The increasing number of orders from the Czechoslovak armament industry led to a considerable enlargement of the labour force at several of the most important plants of the Skoda concern in Pilsen. In September 1937 25,000 men were employed. BA-MA, Berlin 1 November 1937, OKW, Wehrwirtschaftsstab, Stand der wirtschaftlichen Lage, geheime Kommandosache, RM 11/3.

344. AGK, Jahresbericht 1937, PAAA, Ha.Pol, Handel mit Kriegsgerät, allgemeines, Bd.3.

345. Ausfuhr von K.-G. nach Ländern in den Jahren 1936 und 1937, PAAA, Ha.Pol., Handel mit Kriegsgerät, allgemeines, Bd.3.

346. Two recent important works on Göring, apart from Kube, are R.J. Overy, *Goering the 'Iron Man'*, London 1984 and Stefan Martens, *Herman Göring, 'Erster Paladin des Führers' und 'Zweiter Mann im Reich'*, Paderborn 1985.

347. Overy, 1984, pp.32-33.

348. Kube, pp.53-56.

349. Ibid., p.141.

350. Whealy, p.94.

351. Kube, p.166.

352. Whealy, pp.81-82. Veltejns had also been delivering arms to Abyssinia. Funke, pp.36-37; 43-45.

353. Whealy, pp.2-24.

354. Kube, p.166.

355. Whealy, pp.77-79.

356. Overy 1984, pp.56-57.

357. Kube, pp.185-201.

358. "...in engem Einvernehmen zwischen dem Stab des Generaloberst Göring und dem Wehrwirtschaftsstab..." Berlin, 15 December 1936, Der Reichskriegsminister und Oberbefehlshaber der Wehrmacht, geheime Kommandosache, Betr. Ergebnis der Besprechungen bei Generaloberst Göring als Beauftragter für den Vierjahrsplan am 5.12.36, BA-MA, RW 11/2.

359. Kube, pp.186-187.

360. Ibid., pp.175-176. In 1937 Göring approved arms deliveries to the Soviet Union, Germany's potential enemy, thus indicating the extent to which he was willing to go. Ibid., p.182.

361. Ibid., p.186.

362. Ibid., pp.176-180.

363. Ibid., pp.187-188.

364. Ibid., pp.192-197.

365. Ibid., pp.164-169.

366. For this reason, the Japanese Ambassador filed a complaint to Göring. Göring did not attempt to deny that German arms were exported to China; however, he stressed that it was difficult to control the activities of the armament industry due to the economic opportuni-

ties on the Chinese market. Ibid., p.169. In June 1938 trade was conducted through the (German) Ministry of Economy. Ibid., p.170.

367. Ibid., pp.169-170.

368. Jens Petersen, 'Italien und Südosteuropa 1929-1932', in Josef Becker and Klaus Hildebrand, eds, *Internationale Beziehungen in der Weltwirtschaftskrise 1929-1932*, Munich 1980, pp.393-409.

369. *South-Eastern Europe*, pp.24-25.

370. Kube, pp.80-81.

371. Ibid., pp.78-79.

372. Ibid., p.91.

373. Ibid., p.137.

374. Overy 1984, p.32.

375. Ibid., p.29.

376. Kube, p.90.

377. *South-Eastern Europe*, pp.29-30.

378. Kube, pp.82-83.

379. Ibid., p.90.

380. Ibid., pp.82-83.

381. *South-Eastern Europe*, pp.30-32.

382. Funke, pp.36-37.

383. Ibid., pp.45-46.

384. Ibid., pp.42-43.

385. Kube, p.102. In November 1935 Hitler came to the conclusion that Germany should stop the aid to Abyssinia. Hitler was, at that time, pessimistic about Italy's possibilities of winning the war. Funke, pp.137-138.

386. Francesca Schinzinger, 'Kriegsökonomische Aspekte der deutsch-italienischen Wirtschafsbeziehungen 1934-1941', in Friederich Forstmeier and Hans-Erich Volkmann, eds, *Kriegswirtschaft und*

Rüstung 1939-1945, Düsseldorf 1977, pp.167-168.

387. *South-Eastern Europe*, pp.32-34.

388. Funke 1976, pp.833-835.

389. *South-Eastern Europe*, p.34.

390. Funke 1976, pp.837-838.

391. Schinzinger, pp.166-170.

392. The Bank of Greece, Tsouderos Archive, fak.95/16.

393. Statistical Abstracts 1935 No. 502, 1940 No. 570.

394. 11 June 1937, MacVeagh to Metaxas, *Foreign Relations of the United States*, 1937, (FRUS) Vol. II, 611/6831/176.

395. Statistiki epiritis 1939, anadromiki pinakes 28, p.459.

396. 11 June 1937, MacVeagh to Metaxas, FRUS 1937, Vol. II, 611/6831/176.

397. 24 May 1937, Assistant Secretary of State to MacVeagh, FRUS 1937, Vol.II.

398. Athens, 4 October 1937, Shantz, Chargé d'Affairs in Greece, to the Foreign Minister, FRUS 1937, Vol.II, No. 1892.

399. Athens, 18 December 1937, Metaxas to MacVeagh, FRUS 1937, Vol. II, 26458/ gamma/ 7/lambda.

400. *The Week* 28 April 1937, PRO, FO 286/1143/106.

401. 20 August 1936 'Memorandum respecting German penetration in Central Europe , the Balkans and Turkey' Southern (General) Confidential, PRO, FO 286/1136/R 4969/1167/67.

402. See Kolipoulos and Annual Reports.

403. Lawrence R. Pratt, *East of Malta, West of Suez: Britain's Mediterranean Crisis 1936-1939*, Cambridge 1975, p.198. Pratt underlines the fact that British

policy in the Mediterranean, as well as her overall foreign policy, can only be understood in the context he defines as Britain's declining marginal strength, i.e. her lack of resources to fight a war against Italy, Germany or Japan on her own.

404. Ibid., pp. 108-117.

405. Afaf Lutfi al-Sayyid-Marsot, *Egypt's Liberal Experiment 1922-1936*, Berkeley 1977.

406. Koliopoulos, p.27.

407. Pratt pp.108-117.

408. 22 March 1937, Waterlow to Orme G. Sargent, Southern Department, PRO, FO 286/1143/106/1/37.

409. See documents of FO 286-1136; FO 286-1137.

410. 29 March 1937, Waterlow to Eden confidential, PRO, FO 286-1143-106-5-37.

411. 12 July 1939, Waterlow to Eden, PRO, FO 286/1137/106/71/36/37.

412. 22 March 1937, Waterlow to Orme G. Sargent, Southern Department, PRO, FO 286/1143/106/1/37.

413. With the exception of officials at *Auswärtiges Amt* and *Auslandsorganisation der NSDAP*, Göring was the only to have an information service at his disposal. Kube, p.56.

414. Athens, 9 July 1937, Erbach to AA, politischer Bericht, PAAA, POL. IV, POL. 2 Griechenland Bd.1.

415. Annual Report 1938.

416. 18 January 1937, telegram no. 26, Waterlow to FO, PRO, FO 286/1142/R 71/2/37.

417. Annual Report 1937.

418. Alexis Alexandris, 'To istoriko plaisio ton ellinotourkikon scheseon' (Greek-Turkish relation in a historical context), in Alexis Alexandris, Thanis Veremis et alii, eds, *Ellinotourkiki schesis, 1923-1987* (Greek-Turkish relations, 1923-1987) Athens 1988, pp.31-172; p.83.

419. In 1936 Göring tried to bring Yugoslavia and Bulgaria closer together under German leadership. *South-Eastern Europe*, p.41; See also MacVeagh, p.108 and Annual Report 1937.

420. *South-Eastern Europe*, pp.41-42.

421. Alexandris, 'Turkish Policy towards Greece during WW II', *Balkan Studies*, 23, 1, 1982, pp.157-197; pp.166-167.

422. James Barros, *Britain, Greece and the Politics of Sanctions. Ethiopia 1935-1936*, London 1982, pp.1-9.

423. Ibid., p.70; pp.224-226.

424. Athens, 15 July 1936, Mittelmeer-Politik Griechenlands, politischer Bericht, streng vertraulich!, PAAA, Pol. IV. Po.2 Gr. 1. Bd.

425. Athens, 27 July 1936, Kordt to AA, ADAP C, V, 482.

426. Athens, 25 August 1936, Wirtschaftspolitische Unterhaltung mit dem Viezegouverneur der Bank von Griechenland und dem Ministerpräsidenten, PAAA, Ha.Pol.IV., Handel 11 Bd. 1.

427. Ibid.

428. Kitsikis, pp.74-75.

429. Annual Report 1934, PRO, FO 371/19518.

430. Milch had been an officer during the First World War, and saw service in a fighter squadron. In 1935 he was appointed Lieutenant General in the Luftwaffe, in 1939 Inspector General and Colonel-in-Chief and on 19 July 1940 Field Marshal.

431. In 1936 Körner acted as deputy for Göring in terms of the Four Year Plan; later he became President of the General Council to the plan 1939-1942. In 1941-1943 he was leader of *Wirtschaftsführungsstab Ost*, General Secretary in the of Bergund Hüttenwerke Ost GmbH., and General Secretary in the administrative council of Reichswerke "Hermann Göring" für Erzbau und Eisenhütten.

432. Annual Report 1934.

433. Kube, p.87.

434. Athens, 23 May 1934, Waterlow to John Simon, PRO, FO 371/18407.

435. Kube, p.93.

436. Athens, 23 May 1934, Waterlow to John Simon, PRO, FO 371/18407.

437. Athens, 6 June 1934, Waterlow to FO, PRO, FO 371/18407.

438. Annual Report 1935.

439. Kacarkova, pp.54-55.

440. *Manchester Guardian* 31 January 1936.

441. Athens, 8 April 1935, Waterlow to John Simon, PRO, FO, 286/1126/71.

442. Protokoll über die Besprechungen zwischen der deutschen und der griechischen Delegation vom 2-6 April 1935 über den deutsch-griechischen Waren- und Zahlungsverkehr, BA Abt. Potsdam, 0901 Auswärtiges Amt, 68719, Handakten Clodius, Griechenland.

443. 18 September 1935, letter from Philaretos to Alexandros Korizis, Vice President of the National Bank of Greece and chairman to the Committee for Purchase and Administration of Tobacco, the National Bank of Greece, XXIII Proionda A Kapnos fak.6.

444. Mazower 1988, pp.603-619. In 1936 the state's debt to the bank amounted to more than 2.7 billion Dr., the Greek State Archives, 4 May 1937. (Estimating the Greek economy in 1936 by Georgios Pesmazoglou (former Minister of National Economy) for the Superior Economic Council).

445. Among other things the Dresdner Bank controlled the German Aviation Bank, which financed the rearmament through funds from the state. The Dresdner Bank was given responsibility for the financing of various projects, among them was the Four Year Plan. Overy 1984, p.56.

446. 14 April 1935, letter from Philaretos to Ioanis Drosopoulos, President of the National Bank of Greece, the National Bank of Greece's Archive, XXVIII Proionda A Kapnos fak.6.

447. Tsouderos Archive, fak.95/22.

448. 20 May 1935, the Council of Ministers' office to the Central Committee for the Purchase and Administration of Tobacco, the National Bank of Greece's Archive, XXVIII Prioionda Kapna fak.18. The initiative to establish a private clearing seems to originate in 29 September 1934. Hans Pilder, the president of the Dresdner Bank, called a meeting with Philaretos. Pilder was at that time one of Schacht's associate employees and a member of the board of directors in Reemtsma. From this position Pilder had the authority to inform the National Bank of Greece and the Greek Government that Reemtsma was interested in the purchase of the so-called state tobacco, i.e. the stores held by the Committee for the Purchase and Administration of Tobacco. However, a preliminary condition was that the Greek Government placed orders to the German industry. 30 September 1934, letter from Philaretos to Korizis, the National Bank of Greece's Archive, XXVIII Proionda A Kapnos fak.6.

449. 20 May 1935, the Committee for the Purchase and Administration of Tobacco, the National Bank of Greece's Archive, XXVII Proionda Kapna fak. 18.

450. *Athinaika Nea* 1 June 1935, Tsouderos Archive, fak. 138/4.

451. 3 August 1935, Memorandum by Mr. E.J. Tsouderos to the Minister of Finance, Tsouderos Archive, fak. 79/1.

452. *Anexartitos* 2 August 1935, Tsouderos Archive, fak.138/17.

453. 30 September 1934, letter from Philaretos to Korizis, the National Bank of Greece's Archive, Proionda A Kapnos fak.6.

454. Philaretos does not mention the name of the cartel; nevertheless, he notes that it was based in Amsterdam. He must be referring to the Quinine Salt Producers' Organization, as it was the only such cartel in the world. The organization was shared by three German firms, four French, one British, three Dutch and one Swiss. It was linked to the so-called China Bureau, which represented Cinchona bark producers from Java and Dutch quinine salt producers. (Cinchona bark was the basic raw material used in the production of quinine.) The China Bureau set the price for quinine. Ervin Hexner, *International Cartels*, Chapel Hill N. C. 1945, pp.336-339.

455. 29 July 1935, letter from Philaretos to Korizis, the National Bank of Greece's Archive, XXVIII Proionda A Kapnos fak.6.

456. Berlin, 13 November 1935, Clodius to Rizo-Ragavis, PAAA, Abt. IIb Rohstoffe und Waren, Chinin. Bd.1.

457. 18 September 1935, letter from Philaretos to Korizis, the National Bank of Greece's Archive, XXVIII Proionda A Kapnos fak.6.

458. 28 July 1935, letter from Philaretos to Korizis, the National Bank of Greece's Archive, XXVIII Proionda A Kapnos fak.6.

459. 18 September 1935, letter from Philaretos to Korizis, the National Bank of Greece's Archive, XXVIII Proionda A Kapnos fak.6.

460. Athens 25 September 1935, Philaretos to Korizis, the National Bank of Greece's Archive, XXVIII Proionda A Kapnos fak.6.

461. Hellenic and General Trust had been established by Hambros Bank Ltd. and the National Bank of Greece in 1927; Mazower 1988, pp.606-607.

462. Athens, 27 August 1939, short summary about the National Bank of Greece's and Hambros Bank's engagement in SPAP, the National Bank of Greece's Archive, XXV Erga B Sidirodromi fak.30. When control of the company fell into British hands at the end of the 1920s an office was opened in London to conduct British interests in the company and to look after the railway's technical and financial administration. Memo SPAP 20 May 1936, the National Bank of Greece's Archive, XXV Erga B Sidirodromi fak.30.

463. Berlin, 12 December 1934, Siemens-Schuckert to AA, PAAA, Abteilung II, Wirtschaft, Griechenland, Handel 30 Lieferungen, Bd.3.

464. Vertraulicher Sonderbericht, Nr. 19, 18 February 1935, PAAA, Abteilung II, Wirtschaft Griechenland, Handel 30, Lieferungen, Bd. 3.

465. 29 July 1935, letter from Philaretos to Korizis, the National Bank of Greece's Archive, XXVIII Proionda A Kapnos fak.6.

466. Hambros Bank Ltd. London 15 April 1935 to Drosopoulos, chairman of the board of directors in SPAP; the

National Bank of Greece's Archive, XXV Erga B Sidirodromi fak.30.

467. The council coordinated economic and financial problems of national importance. It was headed by the Prime Minister and the other members were: the Minister of Finance, the Minister of National Economy, the Minister of Foreign Affairs, the Governor of the Bank of Greece and the President of the Public Audit Office. Thus the council was made up of some of the most important figures in economic policy.

468. 16 January 1936, secret letter from Philaretos to the Minister of Economy; the National Bank of Greece's Archive, XXVIII Proionda A Kapnos fak.6.

469. Memo SPAP 20 May 1936; the National Bank of Greece's Archive, XXV Erga B Sidirodromi fak.30. In the following years the British sought to wind up their business with the company. In August 1939 Hambro's share was as little as seven per cent, while the General Hellenic Trust had 43.3 per cent and the National Bank of Greece 49.7 per cent of the shares. In 1940 the Peloponnese Railway was taken over by the Greek state.

470. Athens, 14 November 1935, Eisenlohr to AA, PAAA, Handakten Wiehl Griechenland Bd.2.

471. Berlin, 30 November 1935, AA to the Embassy in Athens, PAAA, Handakten Wiehl Bd.2.

472. 16 January 1936, secret letter from Philaretos to Matzavios, the Minister of Economy; the National Bank of Greece's archive, XXVIII Proionda A Kapnos fak.6.

473. Annual Report 1937.

474. Annual Report 1936, PRO, FO 371/21147.

475. D.C.M. Platt, ed., *Business Imperialism 1840-1930: an inquiry based on British experience in Latin America*, Oxford 1977.

476. Annual Report 1935.

477. Joseph Goebbels, *Die Tagebücher* Bd.2. 1931-1936, Munich 1987, p.687.

478. Athens 21 and 23 January 1937, Erbach to AA, PAAA, Ha.Pol.VIa, Handel 10, Förderungen des Aussenhandels, Handelskreditte, Ausfuhrprämien, Subventionen und ähnl. in Griechenland.

479. Athens, 28 January 1937, Memo by Finlayson, 'The Greek Rearmament Programme and the German Clearing Balances', PRO, FO 286/1142/71.

480. Athens, 25 January 1937, department of political affairs to the Embassy in Berlin, Hitler's visit, confidential, the Greek Ministry of Foreign Affairs, 1937 A Pol. A/11/3.

481. Berlin, 7 January 1937, Rizo-Ragavis to the Ministry of Foreign Affairs, confidential, the Greek Ministry of Foreign Affairs, A Pol.A/11/3.

482. "...der Ministerpräsident Metaxas [steht] Deutschland mit ganz besonderen inneren Sympathien gegenüber..." Athens, 10 March 1937, The German Legation to AA, Politischer Bericht, Geheim, Deutsche Kulturpolitik in Griechenland. Ein Bericht des Griechischen Gesandten in London, BAK, R 43 II/1445.

483. Goebbels, Bd.3, p.108.

484. Athens, 28 July 1937, Kordt to AA, PAAA, Pol.IV. Po.5 Gr. 2 Bd. 1.

485. The Gestapo's aim was to make Berlin a so-called, 'centre for the prevention of political crime.' The purpose was mainly propagandist and to show foreign countries that National Socialism had saved Europe from the Bol-

shevik danger. Agreements with the secret police in Italy, Hungary and Finland had already been made and a practical cooperation agreement with Poland and Yugoslavia was instituted. Berlin, 8 October 1936, Note by Heinrich Himmler's Deputy State Secretary, PAAA, Inland IIg, Polizei Abkommen mit Griechenland und Bulgarien.

486. Athens, 27 November 1936, Erbach to AA Telegram No. 143, geheime Reichssache, PAAA, Inland IIg, Polizei Abkommen mit Griechenland und Bulgarien.

487. Athens, 28 July 1937, Erbach to AA, PAAA, Pol.IV Po.5 Gr. Bd.1.

488. PRO, FO 286/1142/71/71/49/37.

489. The source for this was from Mr. Bartlett, agent for the Bristol Aeroplane Company in Europe. He gained the information during a stay in Germany. According to the same source the Greek King found out and consulted Göring. London, 17 March 1938, Southern Department to the Embassy in Berlin, PRO, FO 371/22354/R 2314/18/19.

490. Athens, 23 March 1938, PRO, FO 371/22354.

491. PRO; see British annual reports from 1937-1939.

492. Various frequently-cited scholars have suggested that the regime was a Fascist one; Nikos Psiroukis, *O fasismos ke i 4e augoustou* (Fascism and the 4th of August) Athens 1974, Linardatos, and Heinz Richter, *Griechenland zwischen Revolution und Konterrevolution, 1936-1946*, Frankfurt am Main 1973.

493. PAAA, Pol.IV, Griechenland Bd.1.

494. PRO, See FO 286-1136; FO 286-1137 passim.

495. Annual Report 1936.

496. Athens, 16 October 1937, Erbach to AA, PAAA, Pol.IV Pol.5, Gr Bd.1. The thesis in question is the so-called Fallmerayer's thesis, from *Geschichte der Halbinsel Morea während des Mittelalters*, Stuttgart 1830; concerning the thesis and its significance in Greece, see G. Veloudis, 'Jakob Philipp Fallmerayer und die Entstehung des Neugriechischen Historismus', *Südost-Forschung*, 29, 1970, pp.43-90.

497. Annual Report 1936, 1937.

498. Annual Report 1935.

499. Renate Meissner, 'I ethniko-sosialistiki Germania ke i Ellada kata tin diarkia tis metaxikis diktatorias' (National Socialist Germany and Greece during the Metaxas dictatorship), in Hagen Fleicher and Nikos Svoronos, eds, *Ellada 1936-1940, diktatoria – ka-tochi – antistasi*, Athens 1989, pp. 50-57; p. 56.

500. "...Da dräut der Olymp, dort der Parnass. Es wird einem dabei ganz heiss. Alte Jugenderinnerungen tauchen auf. Ein Traum geht in Erfüllung. Die Sonne geht wunderbar unter. Über dem ewigen Hellas...[...] Athen! O, wie ich glüchlich bin..." Goebbels Bd.2, p.682.

501. "...Gestern: einer der schönsten und tiefsten Morgen meines Lebens. Herauf zu Akropolis. Mit nur wenigen Leuten. Und Stundenlang durch diese edelste Stätte nordischer Kunst gestreift..." Ibid., p.683.

502. "...Meine Seele ist voll von Schönheit. Glückliches Alterum, das noch ohne Christentum in ewiger Heiterkeit lebte und schuf.[...] Spaziergang durch die abendliche Stadt. Dieses heitere, höchste Leben. Dieser Duft von Freude [...] Wie glüchlich würde der Führer sein, bei uns zu sein!..." Ibid., p.684.

503. "...Auf der Akropolis. O, diese erschütternde Schau! Die Wiege der arischen Kultur..." Ibid., Bd.3, p.586.

504. Annual Report 1938, PRO, FO 371/23777.

505. Athens 17 September 1937, Kordt to AA, die innerpolitische Entwicklung in Griechenland, PAAA, Pol.IV. Po.5. Gr. Bd.1.

506. See above.

507. The Greek Ministry of Foreign Affairs, 1937, A8/3.

508. Dritsa, p.195. Dritsa's figures are based on accounts from the Bank of Greece.

509. See below.

510. Figures for 1936-37 are from Deutschlands Kriegsgeräte-Ausfuhr nach den südosteuropäischen Ländern seit 1936, geheim, PAAA, Ha.Pol., Geheim, Handel mit Kriegsgerät allgemeines, Bd.3 1 January 1938 to 31 December 1938.

511. Figures from 1938-1940 are from Abschlüsse der Reichs- und Protektoratfirmen in den Jahren, 1938, 1939 und I/1940 nach Ländern und Länderngruppen geordnet, PAAA, Ha.Pol., Geheim, Handel mit Kriegsgerät, allgemeines, Bd.5.

512. See below.

513. 8 April 1937, Rheinmetall-Borsig to Überwachungsstelle für Eisen und Stahl, W III SE 3414, PAAA, Ha. pol. IVa Handel 11-1 Allgemeine Ein- und Aus- und Durchfuhr, Bd. 2.

514. Athens 31 March 1939, the German Legation to AA, W III 2652/39, PAAA, Ha.Pol.IVa, Handel 24 Nr. 6, Auskünfte über Ruf und Leistungsfähigkeiten von Firmen in Ausland, Griechenland.

515. 5 May 1941, WiRü Amt Vortragsnotiz für den Herrn Reichsmarschall, geheime Kommandosache, Sicherung deutscher Wirtschaftsinteressen in Griechenland, BA-MA, WI/IC1. 10.

516. Berlin, 30 October 1936, Wirtschaftsgruppe Eisenschaffende Industrie to AA, PAAA, Ha.Pol.IV, Industrie 7, Bd. 1.

517. ZEG fell under Internationale Rohstahlgemeinschaft and included the south-eastern European markets in Albania, Yugoslavia, Bulgaria and Romania. Alice Teichova, *Kleinstaaten im Spannungsfeld der Grossmächte*, Munich 1988, pp.169-171.

518. Berlin, 30 October 1936, Wirtschaftsgruppe Eisenschaffende Industrie to AA, PAAA, Ha.Pol.IV, Industrie 7, Bd. 1 Griechenland.

519. Athens, 4 December 1936, Erbach to AA, PAAA, Ha. po. IV, Industrie 7, Bd.1, Griechenland.

520. 12 May 1936 (confidential to the heads of the general staff) memo recording the need for an organization of Greece's war industry. Metaxas Archive, fak. 97.

521. Athens, 7 July 1937, unsere Wirtschaftspolitik gegenüber Griechenland. Eilt, Geheim, PAAA, Ha.Pol.IVa, Handel 11.

522. "...Es kommt hinzu, dass die griechische Wirtschaftspolitik mehr und mehr den bisher beobachteten vernüftigen Grundsatz aufzugeben scheint, wonach einheimische Industrien nur dann aufgebaut werden sollen, wenn sie sich auf einheimische Rohstoffe und einheimische Arbeit stüzten können..." Athens, 7 July 1937, unsere Wirtschaftspolitik gegenüber Griechenland. Eilt, Geheim, PAAA, Ha.Pol.IVa, Handel 11.

523. "...Alle hinweise der Gesandtschaft, dass diese Politik die Aufnahmfähigkeit des griechischen Marktes für bestimm-

ten Deutschland interessierenden Waren vermindern müsste, führten zu nichts. Es bleibt z.B. der deutschen Stickstoffindustrie nur übrig, sich selbst an dem Aufbau des neuen Werkes zu beteiligen, um so wenigsten zu verhüten, dass Griechenland sich an ausländischen Konkurrenten wendet..." Ibid.

524. Ibid.

525. Ibid.

526. Ibid.

527. Athens, 22 July 1937, Kordt to AA, PAAA, Ha.Pol.IVa, Handel 11.

528. Metaxas', tome IV, p.279.

529. Athens, 29 March 1937, confidential, Waterlow to Foreign Office, PRO, FO 286/1143/ 106/5/37.

530. 6th Office of the General Staff, Head of the General Staff to the President, confidential, Athens 11 May 1938, Metaxas Archive, fak.97.

531. Christos Hadziiosif, 'Griechen in der deutschen Kriegsproduktion' in Ulrich Herbert, ed., *Europa und der 'Reichseinsatz': Ausländische Zivilarbeiter, Kriegsgefangene und KZ-Häftlinge in Deutschland 1938-1945*, Essen 1991, pp.210-233.

532. This would leave the mill with Greek scrap metal for production, and, according to German calculations would meet about 25 per cent of Greece's metal demand. However, due to the poor quality of the metal, the products would be difficult to sell. Athens, 10 January 1939, Erbach to AA, PAAA, Ha.Pol.IVa, Industrie 7, Griechenland Bd. 1.

533. Hexner, pp.102-103.

534. Verena Schröter, pp.511-512.

535. In the spirit of the *Neuer Plan*, Germany replaced import of cotton from the USA with import from South America, mainly Brazil, during 1934 and 1935. Germany's trade with South America was settled on clearing accounts. Hans-Jürgen Schröder, 'Die Neue Deustche Südamerika Politik', *Jahrbuch für Geschichte von Staat, Wirtschaft und Gesellschaft Lateinamerikas*, Band 6 1969, pp.337-452.

536. Kindleberger, pp.262-277.

537. Berlin, 13 January 1937, AA to the Legation in Athens, PAAA, Ha.Pol.IVa, Handel 10.

538. This can be explained by the significance olive oil had to the Greek market and to the decrease in the Spanish export: Spain was the leading exporter of olive oil until the outbreak of the Civil War.

539. *Statistiki epiteris*.

540. Athens, 7 July 1937, Unsere Wirtschaftspolitik gegenüber Griechenland, Eilt. Geheim, PAAA, Ha.Pol.IVa, Handel 11.

541. Athens, 22 July 1937, Kordt til AA, PAAA, Ha.Pol.VIa, Handel 11.

542. Berlin, 16 August 1937, Der Reichs- und Preussische Wirtschaftsminister to AA, PAAA, Ha.Pol.IVa, Handel 11 W III SE 6573.

543. The agreement was extended automatically in 1938, while in August 1939 and 1940 it was renegotiated.

544. Abkommen zur Regelung des deutsch-griechischen Warenverkehrs, PAAA, Handakten Wiehl Griechenland Bd. 2.

545. Athens, 9 December 1937, Underredung mit dem Vizeminister des Auswärtigen Amtes und dem Bankgourverneur Varvaresos über die Entwicklung der deutsch-griechischen Wirtschaftsbeziehungen, im Besondere die zukünftige Gestaltung des Rüstungsgeschäfts. Vertraulich, PAAA, Ha.Pol.IVa, Handel 11-1.

546. Ibid.

547. Athens, 19 April 1938, The German Legation to AA, PAAA, Ha.Pol.IVa, Rohstoffe und Waren, Tabak Bd. 1.

548. Kavalla, 12 June 1938, memo from the German Vice Consulate in Kavala to AA, PAAA, Ha.Pol.IVa, Rohstoffe und Waren, Tabak Bd.1.

549. *Mineon Deltion* 1935,1937,1939,1940 Pinax B. Milward has stressed that the growth in Greek exports of bauxite was made possible by extending mining and not by curtailing exports to free currency markets. Milward, pp.390-92.

550. Berlin, 2 December 1940, memo from Morath, PAAA, Handakten Clodius, Griechenland Bd.4.

551. *Bodosakis*, pp.125-129.

552. Ibid.

553. Waldemar Pabst had been an officer in the German Army. He participated in the Spartacus Riot in Berlin 1919 and was the leader of the group that killed Rosa Luxemburg and Karl Liebkneckt on 15 January 1919. He belonged to the close and narrow circle around the extremist right-wing politician Wolfgang Kapp and the officer General Freiherr von Lüttwitz who between them masterminded the so-called Kapp Putsch 13-17 March 1920. MA-BA, Nachlass Pabst N 620/26. See also interview with Pabst, *Der Spiegel* 1962, Heft 16. Subsequently, Pabst went to Austria but was ordered to leave the country because of his activities in the Austrian Home Guard ADAP C, II, 2 289, Note 1. He then held a leading position in Rheinmetall-Borsig's department of arms exports.

554. Berlin, 28 February 1934, Aufzeichnung des Vortragenden Legationsrat Frohwein, ADAP C II, 289.

555. The objection raised was that it was wrong to deliver arms to a member of the Balkan Entente because this was opposed to the interests of revisionist Bulgaria, Germany's ally in the First World War. Ibid.

556. "...M.E. [Meines Erachtens] wäre es falsch nur befreundeten Nationen Waffen zu liefern. Wir würden uns dadurch noch mehr verdächtig machen. Die vorläufige Tarnung verausgesetzt [delivery through Rheinmetall-Borsigs plant in Solothurn in Switzerland], halte ich Lieferungen an frühere Gegner für besonders reizvoll..." Bülow's remark was made on 6 March 1934. ADAP C II, 289, Note 3. During the summer of 1934 it became clear that the intended trade amounted to somewhere between 75 million RM and 100 million RM. The orders were not expected to be placed before the first half of 1935. ADAP C III, 124.

557. Ibid., note 8.

558. 24 October 1934, *Abteilung Süd-Ost im Aussenpolitischen Amt der NSDAP* (APA). Wolfgang Schumann and Ludwig Nestler, eds, *Weltherrschaft im Visier. Dokumente zu den Europa- und Weltherrschaftsplanen des deutschen Imperialismus von der Jahrhundertswende bis Mai 1945*, Berlin 1975, p.238.

559. Jerzy W. Borejsza, 'Greece and the Balkan Policy of Fascist Italy, 1936-1940' *Journal of the Hellenic Diaspora* Vol XIII, Nos 1 & 2 1986, pp.53-70; p.63.

560. Athens, 5 September 1935, Kordt, to AA, ADAP C, IV, 286.

561. See below.

562. "Griechenland benötigt dringend Kriegsmaterial" The Greeks wanted bombers, hydroplanes, wireless receivers, aircraft machine guns, anti-submarine guns, optical and meteorological

instruments, gas protection equipment, vehicles and sanitation equipment.

563. Athens, 30 September 1935, Kordt to AA, ADAP C, IV, 312.

564. Berlin, 21 October 1935, Frohwein to the Legation in Athens, ADAP C IV 369.

565. Berlin, 1 November 1935, Oberbefehlshaber der Kriegsmarine, PAAA, Geheimakten II FK 118, Aus- und Einfuhr von Kriegsgerät nach den Balkanländern. See also ADAP C, IV, 459 note 5.

566. *Vradini* 4 September 1935, PAAA, Ab. II FK 118, Geheimakten.

567. Barros, p.118.

568. Athens, 18 October 1935, personal letter from Theotokis to Canaris, PAAA, Geheimakten II FK 118, Aus- und Einfuhr von Kriegsgerät nach den Balkanländern.

569. Athens, 19 October 1935, Eisenlohr to AA, eilig und geheim, PAAA, Geheimakten II FK 118, Aus- und Einfuhr von Kriegsgerät nach den Balkanländern.

570. "...Gesamte Finanzkraft Landes [Greece] werde in den Dienst Rüstungsgedankens gestellt..." Athens, 24 October 1935, Eisenlohr to AA, M 2417, Geheimakten II FK 118, Aus- und Einfuhr von Kriegsgerät nach den Balkanländern. In the meantime Polish and Czechoslovak arms producers had said that they were ready to deliver bomber aircraft. Furthermore, the Minister of Aviation wanted to obtain British Gloster Gladiators, while Kondilis and Thetokis wanted German Heinkel He 51s.

571. Athens, 20 November 1935, Eisenlohr, geheim, PAAA, Geheimakten II FK 118 Aus- und Einfuhr von Kriegsgerät nach den Balkanländern.

572. Berlin, 1 November 1935, Oberbefehlshaber der Kriegsmarine, PAAA, Geheimakten II FK 118, Aus- und Einfuhr von Kriegsgerät nach den Balkanländern. See also ADAP C, IV, 459 note 5.

573. Berlin, 8 November 1935, Frohwein AA to the Ministry of Economy and War, PAAA, Geheimakten II FK 118, Aus- und Einfuhr von Kriegsgerät nach den Balkanländern.

574. Berlin, 11 November 1935, Reichsgruppe Industrie to AA, II M 2607, PAAA, Geheimakten II FK 118. The consortium's commercial head was Eltze, Managing Director of the Dresdner Bank, assisted by Rambow, also from the Dresdner Bank. Auer, formerly leader of *Heereswaffenamt*, was its technical leader. (ADAP C, IV, 459 note 5) The following persons were also in Athens at the turn of the year 1935/36: Admiral Heusinger von Waldegg, the chairman of the board at the shipyard Deutche Werke in Kiel and Quilitsch, the representative of *Reichsverband der deuschen Luftfahrtindustrie*. Ibid.

575. Kondilis and Theotokis wanted German Heinkel He 70s. The aeroplane was introduced in 1932 and was seen as an innovation: it was a monoplane built of metal with wheels that could be raised and it had a high top speed. The plane was used, among other places, in the Spanish Civil War at the Legion Condor.

576. Delivery of the most modern types, i.e. Gloster Gladiator, Fury II, Bristol Bulldog IV or Gauntlet, was not possible. On the other hand, it was possible to deliver the older Bristol Bulldog II at short notice. London, 14 November, Foreign Office to the Greek Embassy, Metaxas Archive, fak. 80.

577. If the attempt failed the planes would be purchased in Poland or

Czechoslovakia. Athens, 15 November 1935. Note from a meeting between the Prime Minister, Vice Prime Minister, Minister of Aviation and the leaders of the three military services. Metaxas Archive, fak. 80.

578. Athens, 16 November 1935, Theokis to Canaris, geheim, PAAA, Geheimakten FK 118.

579. Athens, 15 November 1935, note from a meeting between the Prime Minister, Deputy Prime Minister, Minister of Aviation and the leaders of the three military services, Metaxas Archive, fak. 80.

580. Athens, 18 November 1935, Waterlow to FO, PRO, FO 286/1125/23.

581. Athens, 19 November 1935, telegram No. 288 to Sir Samuel Hoare, PAAA, FO 286-1125-23.

582. Ibid.

583. Ibid.

584. Koliopoulos, p.25. The King told the German Minister that Greek officers seriously lacked practical skills. Athens, 6 January 1936, Eisenlohr to AA, PAAA, Geheimakten Griechenland Pol.2.

585. Athens, 12 December 1935, Eisenlohr to AA, ADAP, C, IV, 459.

586. Koliopoulos, pp.25-26.

587. Athens, 4 November 1935, Eisenlohr, geheim, PAAA, Geheimakten II FK 118, Aus- und Einfuhr von Kriegsgerät nach den Balkanländern. Germany recieved information that Britain was not capable of delivering arms to Greece. Theotokis told the German Minister, strictly confidentially, yet suprisingly frankly, that Britain was unable to deliver modern bombers.

588. Berlin, 11 December 1935, AA to RKM, RWiM, RLM, geheim, PAAA, Geheimakten II FK 118, Aus- und Einfuhr von Kriegsgerät nach den Balkanländern.

589. "... dass Griechenland ohne den deutschen Kunden nicht leben könne und dass inbesondere eine Einschränkung oder Unterbrechung unserer Tabakkäufe zur Verelendung der mazedonischen Bauern und damit schweren innerpolitischen Störungen in Griechenland führen müsse. Die sorgfältige Pflege dieser Bezieungen [trade relations] sei somit ein wirtschaftlisches wie ein politisches Gebot..." Athens, 12 December 1935, Eisenlohr to Auswärtiges Amt, ADAP, C, IV, 459.

590. "... Deshalb sei es auch naturgegeben, dass Griechenland seinen Bedarf an Kriegsmaterial aus Deutschland beziehen müsse, wo es die Lieferungen grossenteils mit eigener Warenausfuhr bezahlen könne..." Ibid.

591. Ibid.

592. Ibid.

593. Athens, 6 January 1936, Eisenlohr to AA, PAAA, Geheimakten Griechenland Pol. 2.

594. Bericht über die Sachlage und meine Tätigkeit in Athen nach der Abreise des Herrn Eltze von 18.Dezember 1935 bis 10.Januar 1936, streng geheim, PAAA, Geheimakten, II FK 33, Kriegsgerät Allgemeines Geheimsachen.

595. Ibid.

596. "...Nun haben gerade *die* Provinzen an unseren Tabakeinkaüfen ein Lebensinteresse, die am 26. überwiegend Veniselistisch gestimmt haben, d.h. in der Hauptsache Thrazien und Mazedonien. Die Veniselisten müssen aber alles aufbieten, um diese Provinzen bei guter Laune zu erhalten. Es ist nicht zu viel gesagt, wenn man feststellt, dass eine Einstellung unsere Tabakbezüge aus Nordgriechenland in ganz kurzer Zeit zu einer Revolution führen würde.

Der Veniselismus hat also allen Anlass, sich mit uns freundlich zu stellen..." Athens, 28 January 1936, Kordt to AA geheim, PAAA, Ab II, Pol. 7 Gr. Bd.2.

597. Athens, 4 February 1936, Kordt to Counsellor of Legation von Schmieden, vertraulich, ADAP C IV, 539.

598. Ibid.

599. Ibid.

600. AGK die Geschäftsjähre 1935-1936, PAAA, Ha.Pol., geheim, Handel mit Kriegsgerät, allgemeines Bd.1.

601. Kacarkova, p.55.

602. Kitsikis, p.49 note 2, letter from Varvaresos to Tsouderos, 7 September 1937.

603. Athens, 27 February 1936, Kordt to AA, W 1918, PAAA, Handakten Wiehl. Griechenland Bd.2.

604. Memorandum by H.C.Finlayson, 'German Clearing Credit Balances' 20 February 1936, PRO, FO 286-1136 R-71-12-36.

605. The tobacco sector owed the National Bank of Greece 137 million Dr. 20 February 1936, letter from the subbranch of the National Bank of Greece in Salonika to the board of directors, National Bank of Greece archive, XXVIII Proionda A Kapnos fak.20.

606. H.C. Finlayson, who worked as an adviser to the Bank of Greece, had himself been informed by Varvaresos.

607. Athens, 5 March 1936, Waterlow to Eden, PRO, FO 286/1136/71.

608. Ibid.

609. Athens, 13 March 1936, Gesandtschaftsrat Kordt to AA, ADAP C, V, 97. See also ADAP C, V, 110, Berlin, 14 March 1936. Aufzeichnung des Vortragenden Legationsrat von Renthe-Fink.

610. Athens, 18 March 1936, Kordt to AA, politischer Bericht, PAAA, Abt. II, Pol.7, Griechenland, Ministerien Bd 2.

611. 17 March 1936, Reichsgruppe Industrie, Eltze to Demerdzis, AA IIM 1091g, PAAA, Geheimakten Abt.II FK 118 Geheimakten, Aus- und Einfuhr von Kriegsgerät nach dem Balkan Bd.2.

612. 19 March 1936 AA II M 293, PAAA, Geheimakten Abt.II FK 118 Geheimakten, Aus- und Einfuhr von Kriegsgerät nach dem Balkan Bd.2.

613. Berlin, 31 March 1936, von Lupin Reichsgruppe Industrie to von Bülow, Geheimakten Abt.II FK 118, PAAA, Geheimakten, Aus- und Einfuhr von Kriegsgerät nach dem Balkan Bd.2.

614. Athens, 31 March 1936, Kordt to AA, PAAA, Geheimakten Abt.II FK 118 Geheimakten, Aus- und Einfuhr von Kriegsgerät nach dem Balkan Bd.2.

615. Athens, 2 April 1936, Kordt to AA, PAAA, Geheimakten Abt.II FK 118 Geheimakten, Aus- und Einfuhr von Kriegsgerät nach dem Balkan Bd.2.

616. Athens, 8 April 1936, Kordt about a meeting between Metaxas, Eltze and Kordt, AA II M 1161g, PAAA, Geheimakten Abt. II FK 118 Bd.2, Aus- und Einfuhr von Kriegsgerät nach dem Balkan Bd.2

617. Athens, 15 April 1936, Kordt to AA, PAAA, Abt.II, Griechenland Politik 7, Ministerien Bd.2.

618. Athens, 16 July 1936, Anlage 2 geheim, PAAA, Ha.Pol.IVa, wirtschaftliche Beziehungen zu Deutschland (Griechenland) Wirtschaft 6 Bd.1.

619. Salonika, 20 May 1936, report from the German Consul, PAAA, Ha.Pol.IVa, Tabak Bd.1. See also Chapter 1.1.4.

620. The German cigarette company, Brinkmann, had about two million kg.

tobacco stored in Greece and consequently the firm asked AA to react. Berlin, 12 May 1936 to the Legation in Athens, PAAA, II Balk. 995gr., Handakten Wiehl Bd. 2.

621. Koliopoulos, p.42.

622. Athens, 28 May 1936, Walker to Eden, PRO, FO 371/20391.

623. "...Die Fragen der Offiziere waren zum Teil so wenig begründet, dass Herr Metaxas verschiedlich sehr ungnädig wurde. Um nur ein Beispiel zu nennen: Ein Oberst versuchte deutsche Preisüberhöhungen dadurch nachzuweisen, dass er auf ein deutsches Angebot auf Pistolen aus dem Jahre 1930 verwies [...] Der Ministerpräsident liess den unkundigen [...] mit der griechischen hingeworfenen Bemerkung abfallen: ' Halt'den Mund, davon verstehst Du nichts'..." Athens, 14 May 1936, Kordt to AA, geheim, Verhandlungen über deutschen Kriegsmaterial Lieferung, PAAA, Ha.Pol., Geheimakten, Handel mit Kriegsgerät, Balkan Bd.1.

624. Ibid.

625. Athens, 16 July 1936, Anlage 2 Geheim, PAAA, Ha.Pol.IVa, wirtschaftliche Beziehungen zu Deutschland (Griechenland), Wirtschaft 6 Bd.1.

626. Athens, 2 June 1936, Kordt to AA, Telegram, geheim, PAAA, Ha.Pol., Geheimakten, Handel mit Kriegsgerät, Balkan Bd.1.

627. Athens, 14 June 1936, Anlage 2, WIII SE 1093, PAAA, Ha.Pol.IVa, Wirtschaft 6, Bd.1.

628. Ibid.

629. Athens, 15 June 1936, telegram from Pistor to AA, PAAA, Pol.1 464g, Geheimakten. Handel mit Kriegsgerät. Balkan Bd.1.

630. Athens, 20 June 1936, von Lupin to AKG, streng vertraulich, PAAA,

Ha.Pol., Geheimakten, Handel mit Kriegsgerät, Balkan Bd.1.

631. Ibid.

632. Berlin, 29 June 1936, Dieckhoff, Pol.I 652g, PAAA, Ha.Pol., Geheimakten, Handel mit Kriegsgerät, Balkan Bd.1.

633. Athens, 11 July 1936, Pistor to AA, Pol.I 804g, PAAA, Ha.Pol., Geheimakten, Handel mit Kriegsgerät, Balkan Bd.1.

634. Athens, 14 July 1936, Pistor to AA, Pol.I 828g, PAAA, Ha.Pol., Geheimakten, Handel mit Kriegsgerät, Balkan Bd.2.

635. *Financial Times* 15 or 16 July 1936 and *Neue Freie Presse* Vienna 17 July 1936, BA Abt.Potsdam, 80 BA1/Dresdner Bank/725.

636. ADAP C, V, 383, note 8.

637. A Greek condition was, however, that the value of the precious metals delivered to Germany (3 million RM) was to be deducted from the price to be paid in hard currency, Berlin, 22 July, Rizo-Ragavis to von Neurath, Tsouderos archive, fak.95/5.

638. Koliopoulos, p.44.

639. This was a subsidary bank of the German Reichsbank and subsidized exports, Teichert, p.59.

640. See below.

641. Berlin, 15 December 1936, Der Reichskriegsminister und Oberbefehlshaber der Wehrmacht, geheime Kommandosache, Betr. Ergebnis der Bersprechungen bei Generaloberst Göring als Beauftragter für den Vierjahresplan am 5.12.36, BA-MA, RW 11/2.

642. Berlin, 10 February 1937, Reichsgruppe Industrie an den Beauftragten

für den Vierjahresplan, PAAA, Ha.Pol., geheim, Kriegsgerät, allgemeines Bd.2.

643. Jahresbricht der AGK 1935/36, PAAA, Ha.Pol. geheim, Kriegsgerät, allgemeines Bd.1.

644. Berlin, 10 February 1937, Reichsgruppe Industrie an den Beauftragten für den Vierjahresplan, PAAA, Ha.Pol., geheim, Kriegsgerät, allgemeines Bd.2.

645. Berlin, 22 March 1937, Reichsgruppe Industrie to AA, Streng vertraulich, PAAA, Gesandschaft Athen, Geheimakten 1, Bd.50.

646. AGK Berlin, 28 May 1937, Stand über die zur Zeit laufende Geschäfte und Verhandlungen, PAAA, Ha.Pol., geheim, Kriegsgerät, allgemeines Bd.2.

647. Athens, 1 June 1937, Tsouderos to Deutsche Golddiskontobank, PAAA, Ha.Pol.IVa, Handel 10, Bd.1

648. Athens, 9 June 1937, Erbach to AA, PAAA, Ha.Pol.IVa, Handel 10, Bd.1.

649. Athens, 17 October 1937, the German Military Attaché, Colonel Rohde to Reichsluftfahrtsministerium, PAAA, Gesandtschaft Athen Nr. 21, Waffenlieferungen der Griechischen Regierung.

650. *Alverdens Fly i Farver: Krigsfly 1939-1945* (Aircraft of the World: Military Aircarft), Copenhagen 1970, pp.160-161.

651. Athens, 17 October 1937, Colonel Rohde, the German Military Attaché to Reichsluftfahrtsministerium, PAAA, Gesandtschaft Athen Nr. 21, Waffenlieferungen der Griechischen Regierung.

652. Sofia, 9 October 1937, Rheinmetall-Borsig, Aktennotiz concerning the visit to Athens 3-8 October 1937, IWM, Speer Documents, FD 790/46.

653. Athens, 17 October 1937, the German Legation to AA, PAAA, Gesandt-

schaft Athen Nr. 61, Waffenlieferungen der Griechischen Regierung.

654. Berlin, 19 October 1937, the German Ministry of Aviation to the German Legation in Athens, PAAA, Gesandtschaft Athen Nr. 61, Waffenlieferungen der Griechischen Regierung.

655. Berlin, 28 November 1937, Reichsgruppe Industrie, Einschreiben an Griechenlandsgeschäfte interessierte Firmen, streng vertraulich, PAAA, Ha.Pol., Geheim, Kriegsgerät, Griechenland Bd.1.

656. Athens, 9 December 1937, Underredung mit dem Vizeminister des Auswärtigen Amtes und dem Bankgouverneur Varvaresos über die Entwichlung der deutsch-griechischen Wirtschaftsbeziehungen, im Besondere die zukünftige Gestaltung des Rüstungsgeschäfts. Vertraulich!, PAAA, Ha.Pol.IVa, Handel 11-1 Bd.1.

657. Ibid.

658. Mackensen was the German Ambassador in Budapest from 1933 to 1937, State Secretary in AA from April 1937 to March 1938 and Ambassador in Rome from 1938 to 1943.

659. Athens, 10 December 1937, personal letter from Erbach to Mackensen, WIII 8E 10099, PAAA, Ha.Pol.IVa, Handel 11-1 Bd.2.

660. Berlin, December 1937, zu W III SE 9655 Vermerk, PAAA, Ha.Pol.IVa, Handel 11-1 Bd.2.

661. Berlin, 11 January 1938, W III SE 10099 37, PAAA, Ha.Pol.IVa, Handel 11-1 Bd.2.

662. Turkey paid 100 per cent in hard currency and so did Romania (a country, however, capable of delivering oil and wheat). Bulgaria and Hungary paid 25 per cent in hard currency. Outline of trade in war equipment, not dated, AA

W 66 30g (arrived on 25 January 1937), PAAA, Ha.Pol., Geheim, Handel mit Kriegsgerät, allgemeines Bd.2.

663. However, the sales of arms to Greece must not be seen as mere loss of hard currency because Germany had more than her currency expenses covered. According to AGK calculations, the production of one aircraft included only 3 per cent currency demanding raw materials, one piece of artillery 4-5 per cent and one piece of ammunition 7 per cent. AGK, Jahrsbericht 1937, PAAA, Ha.Pol. Geheim, Handel mit Kriegsgerät, allgemeines Bd.3.

664. *Ionomikos Tachidromos* no. 992, 26 April 1973, p.67.

665. Hexner, pp.352-353.

666. Wirtschaftsnachrichten Nr. 32, 12 August 1938. Die Chemiewirtschaft Griechenlands, ZStA, 80IG/IG Farben 512. These are extremely high figures. In 1936 the production value of Greece's most important industry was: textiles 3.3 billion Dr., chemicals 2.1 billion Dr., foodstuffs 1.9 billion Dr.

667. Rheinmetall-Borsig was founded in 1889 and played a significant role as an army contractor during the First World War. As a result of article 168 in the Treaty of Versailles and a regulation from the German Ministry of War dated 4 July 1921, Rheinische Metallwaren und Maschinenfabrik in Düsseldorf (later Rheinmetall-Borsig) was the only German firm allowed to produce guns up to a calibre of 170 mm. The company reorganized a part of its production to manufacture office equipment, agricultural and mining tools and railway equipment, including locomotives. Moreover, the company established an office for construction which, in cooperation with the army and the navy, developed armoured tanks, among other things. When the National Socialists assumed power the company was ready to launch a mass production of various newly-developed types of arms. In connection with the German rearmament several new types of arms were developed. Meanwhile the company started production to meet the demands of the Four Year Plan. (Waffenschmiede der deutschen Wehrmacht, geheime Kommandosache, IWM, Speer Documents, FD 4556/45). In connection with the trial against Krupp held after the Second World War, Major Pabst, Rheinmetall-Borsig's ex-president of Waffen- und Verkaufszentrale, stated, in a personal letter defending Krupp, that Rheinmetall-Borsig had played a significant role in the rearmament of Germany's forces. While Krupp delivered heavy artillery, Rheinmetall-Borsig delivered light artillery. Lucerne, 11 March 1948, Pabst to Krupp's defence attorney, BA-MA, N 620/48, Nachlass Pabst.

668. Annual Report of Rheinmetall-Borsig, 1939, IWM, Speer Documents, FD 783/46.

669. *50 Jahre Rheinmetall-Borsig*, 1889-1939, p.75. VIAG was controlled by the Ministry of Finance and was, until the establishment of Reichswerke Hermann Göring, the biggest state-owned company in Germany.

670. In mid-1937 Roehnert became a member of the National Socialist Party. (Berlin Document Centre). Roehnert was President of Rheinmetall-Borsig AG, Berlin, managing director and entrepreneur at Reichswerke AG Hermann Göring, Busch-Jaeger, Lündenscheider Metallwerke AG and Lüdenscheid, chairman of the board of directors at Junkers Flugzeug- und Motorwerke AG, Kardex AG für Büroartikel Saarbrücken, Kardex System GmbH., Reichswerke AG. für Binnenschiffahrt "Hermann Göring" AG, Berlin, Säch-

sische Metallwarenfabrik August Wellner Söhne AG., Aue/Sachsen, Reichswerke AG. für Waffen- und Maschinenbau "Hermann Göring", and at Torpedo-Werke AG. Frankfurt/Main. The list is much longer, but the abovementioned posts were the most important. Berlin Document Centre.

671. Overy, 'Göring's Multi-National Empire', in Teichova and Cottrell, p.285. Roehnert became leader of Block B 'Waffenblock' in Reichswerke Hermann Göring, controlling armament industries inside and outside Germany. (Ibid.) In 1942 Roehnert and several other armament firms in Reichswerke Hermann Göring left the organization and joined Albert Speer. Idem 1984, p.213.

672. Rheinmetall-Borsig to *Überwachungsstelle für Eisen und Stahl*, W III SE 3414 29 April 1937, PAAA, Ha.Pol.IVa, Handel 11-1 Bd.2, Allgemeine Ein- und Aus- und Durchfuhr.

673. Sophia, 9 October 1937, confidential Aktennotiz, Rheinmetall-Borsig, IWM, Speer Documents, FD 790/46.

674. Letter from Rheinmetall-Borsig to *Überwachungsstelle für Eisen und Stahl*, W III SE 3414 29 April 1937, PAAA, Ha.Pol.IVa, Handel 11-1 Bd.2, Allgemeine Ein- und Aus- und Durchfuhr.

675. Reinmetall-Borsig to *Überwachungsstelle für Eisen und Stahl*, W III SE 3414, 29 April 1937, PAAA, Ha. Pol.IVa, Handel 11-1 Bd.2, Allgemeine Ein- und Aus- und Durchfuhr.

676. Sophia, 9 October 1937, confidential Aktennotiz, Rheinmetall-Borsig, IWM, Speer Documents, FD 790/46.

677. Berlin, 11 March 1938, strictly confidential, from Rheinmetall-Borsig to *Oberkommando der Wehrmacht*, IWM, Speer Documents, FD 790/46.

678. Sophia, 9 October 1937, confidential Aktennotiz, Rheinmetall-Borsig, IWM, Speer Documents, FD 790/46.

679. Rheinmetall-Borsig to *Überwachungsstelle für Eisen und Stahl*, W III SE 3414 29 April 1937, PAAA, Ha.Pol.IVa, Handel 11-1 Bd.2, Allgemeine Ein- und Aus- und Durchfuhr.

680. Established 28 July 1932, *Les conditions* p.255.

681. *Statistiki epetiris* 1939, V Emborion, p.150.

682. See above.

683. *Bodosakis*, p.134.

684. Rheinmetall-Borsig to *Überwachungsstelle für Eisen und Stahl*, W III SE 3414 29 April 1937, PAAA, Ha.Pol.IVa, Handel 11-1 Bd.2, Allgemeine Ein- und Aus- und Durchfuhr.

685. Ibid.

686. Teichova 1974, pp.200ff.

687. Idem, 1988, pp.169ff.

688. Rheinmetall-Borsig to *Überwachungsstelle für Eisen und Stahl*, W III SE 3414 29 April 1937, PAAA, Ha.Pol.IVa, Handel 11-1 Bd. 2, Allgemeine Ein- und Aus- und Durchfuhr.

689. Sophia, 9 October 1937, Rheinmetall-Borsig, confidential Aktennotiz, IWM, Speer Documents, FD 790/46.

690. Ibid.

691. Frank Gervasi, 'Devil Man' *Collier's*, 8 June 1940.

692. *Statistiki epetiris* 1939, V Emborion p.155.

693. Hill, Vol.II, p.31.

694. "...unsere Anlagen und unsere technischen Fortschritte unserem Unternehmen einen Weltruf verschafft und dasselbe zu einem wichtigen Faktor des internationalen Marktes gemacht haben..." The German version of the account appears in IG Farben's archives, Athens 15 June 1938, Bericht des Verwaltungsrat der S.A. de POUDRERIES ET CARTOUCHERIES HELLENIQUES, an die Generalversamlung, BA Abt.Potsdam, 80 IG1/IG Farben/A 3849.

695. MacVeagh, Athens, 17 February 1937. MacVeagh to Franklin D. Roosevelt. pp.107-108.

696. Moses Rosenberg was the son of a former Soviet Ambassador to Madrid. Rosenberg supplied the Republicans (in Spain) with arms on a contractual basis, i.e. he received the orders and purchased the arms afterwards. He had offices throughout the Mediterranean area, with Marseilles and Piraeus as the most important. The Greek Ministry of Foreign Affairs, press cutting, 1937, Pol.A/11/3.

697. Annual Report 1937.

698. Koliopoulos, p.69 note 5.

699. Gervasi.

700. See below.

701. Griechenlands Seeschiffart und Seehäfen, Institut für Weltwirtschaft an der Universität Kiel, May 1940, BA-MA, RW 19/3329.

702. *Bodosakis*, pp.153-156.

703. Ibid.

704. 16 December 1937, Morton, Department of Overseas Trade to Gwatkin. Civil, Economic and Industrial Mobilisation in Greece, PRO, FO 371/22354.

705. Koliopoulos relies on a report from the manager of the aircraft factory in Phaliro, 6 April 1937. (Koliopoulos p.69). – Schacht had already asked the Greek government for permission to export aircraft from Greek soil to Franco in Spain. Koliopoulos refers to a letter dated 26 April 1937 from the manager of the aircraft factory to Waterlow. According to this letter Schacht made his request during a visit to Athens in June 1936. (Koliopoulos, p.69). However, this is unlikely because the Spanish Civil War did not start until 17 July 1936. German initiatives to support Franco with military equipment can be dated as early as 26 July 1936. In the same period Sonderstab W was established by order of Göring, with the purpose of taking a German military unit to Spain in secrecy. (Whealy, p.7) In relation to the flight of German aircraft from Greece and Schacht's role in this, it must be added that Greek government representatives were in Berlin from mid-July 1936. They returned to Berlin the same autumn to negotiate for arms. Moreover, a Greek military commission was in Germany in the second half of 1936. Contact might have been established through one of these channels.

706. MacVeagh, Athens, 17 February 1937, MacVeagh to Roosevelt, p. 108.

707. *Bodosakis*, pp.157-158. Bodosakis mentions that he invested all the money in the Powder and Cartridge Company.

708. Metaxas Archive, fak. 14.

709. Burgos is situated in the part of Spain controlled by the Nationalists at that time.

710. Dr.N. Lorandos was one of Metaxas's close friends and a confirmed anglophile. Koliopoulos, p.107.

711. *Bodosakis*, p.155.

712. See above.

713. Koliopoulos, p.69.

714. The Bank's customers were mainly wealthy refugees from Asia Minor. It was founded by the Ottoman Bank in London after the exodus from Anatolia. The board and management consisted of Greek businessmen who had been born and raised in Constantinople. The bank undertook several transactions for the Ottoman Bank's departments in Yugoslavia, Romania, Syria and Turkey. The Bank had a reputatation for giving loans on unorthodox terms. Hill, Vol.IV, p.18.

715. Athens, 31 March 1939, German Legation to AA, W III 2652/39, PAAA, Ha.Pol.IVa, Handel 24 Nr. 6, Auskünfte über Ruf und Leistungsfähigkeiten von Firmen in Ausland, Griechenland.

716. Berlin, 1 February 1938, OKW, Wehrwirtschftsstab, Stand der wirtschaftlichen Lage, BA-MA, RM 11/3.

717. Whealy, pp.86-87.

718. Ibid., p.94.

719. Berlin, 28 February 1934, Aufzeichnung des Vortragenden Legationsrats Frohwein, ADAP C II, 289.

720. Krupp was also mentioned as a possible supplier *qua* Bofors in Sweden, Berlin 18 July 1935, Der Staatssekretär des Auswärtigen Amts von Bülow an den Reichsminister des Auswärtigen Freiherrn von Neurath, Konzept, ADAP, C,IV, 212.

721. Athens, 2 July 1935, PRO, FO 286/1126/71.

722. Barros, pp.63-64.

723. Kube, p.164.

724. Berlin 11 March 1938, Rheinmetall-Borsig, Vorstand, an das Oberkommando der Wehrmacht, Wehrwirtschaftsstab zu Händen von Herrn Korvettenkapitän Koch, Berlin

15 March 1938, Rheinmetall-Borsig, IWM, Speer Documents FD 790/46.

725. "...Es erscheint undenkbar, dass alle jene Persönlichkeiten, – wären die Gerüchte zutreffend –, heuchlerisch nur einer Waffenschiebung nach Sowjet-Spanien Vorschub geleistet haben sollten – , und dies umsomehr, als insbesondere Seine Majestät der König der Hellenen und Ministerpräsident Metaxas ihre besondere Anerkennung für die Leistungen des Dritten Reiches ausgesprochen und sich offen als Freunde nationalsozialistischen Gedankengutes bekannt haben..." Berlin, 11 March 1938, Rheinmetall-Borsig, Vorstand, an das Oberkommando der Wehrmacht, Wehrwirtschaftsstab zu Händen von Herrn Korvettenkapitän Koch, IWM, Speer Documents, FD 790/46.

726. Berlin, 29 March 1938, Niederschrift über die Besprechungen mit Herrn Oberst Rohde, Deutscher Militär-Attaché in Ankara und Athen, streng vertraulich, IWM, Speer Documents, FD 790/46.

727. Figures from AGK state that in the period 1 January 1936 to 30 June 1938 agreements were made for the delivery of 33 (30) 88 mm Flak, 128 (50) 37 mm guns and 97 (57) 20 mm guns. PAAA, AGK, Griechenland, Gemeldte Abschlüsse 1 January 1936 – 30 June 1938, Ha.Pol., Geheim, Handel mit Kriegsgerät, allgemeines Bd.3. The figures in parentheses have been taken from British Annual Reports for 1937 and 1938. Finally, it is significant that the huge Greek order for German war material was placed before 31 December 1937.

728. Berlin, 29 March 1938, Niederschrift über die Besprechungen mit Herrn Oberst Rohde, Deutscher Militär-Attaché in Ankara und Athen, streng

vertraulich, IWM, Speer Documents, FD 790/46.

729. Athens, 4 November 1936, Kordt to von Schmieden, BA Abt.Potsdam, 0901/68428 Auswärtiges Amt Kriegsgerät Balkan. There is good reason to believe that Sarsentis was one of the middlemen who tried to obstruct Greek-German arms negotiations in 1936. Sarsentis was doing business on a commission basis and would lose the prospect of income as a result of the so-called "government to government" trade.

730. Aktennotiz May 1937, IWM, Speer Documents, FD 790/46.

731. Ibid.

732. Berlin, 19 February 1938, Likourgos Sarsentis to Wessig, IWM, Speer Documents, FD 790/46.

733. Berlin, 25 February 1938, Director Schröder to Managing Director Luther, IWM, Speer Documents FD 790/46.

734. Berlin, 19 February 1938, Likourgos Sarsentis to Wessig, IWM, Speer Documents FD 790/46.

735. Berlin, 25 March and 1 April 1938, Rheinmetall-Borsig, IWM, Speer Documents FD. 790/46.

736. Sophia, 9 October 1937, Aktennotiz, IWM, Speer Documents FD 790/46.

737. Berlin, 12 October 1937, PAAA, Gesandtschaft Athen Nr. 50, Geheimakten Bd.1.

738. It is implicit from the sources that the meeting with Göring took place after Bodosakis had obtained a patent, in October 1937, to manufacture Rheinmetall-Borsig's grenades. Apparently the meeting was held at Göring's castle, Carinhall.

739. *Bodosakis*, pp.161-165. On 6 May 1938 the Minister of Foreign Affairs of Nationalist Spain informed the German Embassy in Burgos that substantial amounts of German war material had fallen into the hands of the Republicans. The information came from a reliable source at the Republican Embassy in Paris. This was Krupp equipment and included the latest anti-aircraft model. The Nationalists presumed that it had been delivered through Holland and Switzerland (Burgos, 6 May 1938, The Spanish Minister of Foreign Political Affairs to the German Embassy in Burgos, Geheim, PAAA, Ha.Pol., Geheim, Handel und Kriegsgerät, Spanien Bd.1) On 20 June 1938 OKW informed AA that Krupp and other German armament companies refuted the accusation. OKW asked AA to tell the Nationalists that their information was incorrect (Berlin, 20 June 1938, OKW to AA, PAAA, Ha.Pol., Geheim, Handel mit Kriegsgerät, Spanien Bd.1) German treatment of the Spanish complaints was, as in other cases, far from exhaustive. A unilateral denial from the German companies was apparently sufficient evidence for OKW to refute the Nationalist accusations.

740. Berlin, 2 May 1938, Besprechung vom 2. Mai 1938 über die weitere Gestaltung der K.G.-Ausfuhr, PAAA, Ha.Pol., Geheim, Handel mit Kriegsgerät, allgemeines, Bd.3.

741. See below.

742. *Bodosakis*, pp.176-178. Originally Bodosakis was to go to China to discuss arms deliveries with Chiang Kai-shek; nevertheless, Metaxas hindered his departure, probably because Bodosakis's presence in Greece was essential at the time.

743. Ibid., pp.169-170.

744. Francis Nicosia, 'Arab Nationalism and National Socialist Germany, 1933-1939: Ideological and Strategic incompatibility', *International Journal of Middle East Studies*, 12, 1980, p.361.

745. Annual Report 1938, PRO, FO 371/23777.

746. Berlin, 31 March 1939, BA Abt. Postdam, 0961/Auswärtiges Amt/68445, Handel mit Kriegsgerät Palästina.

747. Waterlow 12 December 1938, to FO, PRO, FO 371/22371/762 R 9566-726-19.

748. According to Waterlow, Moshe Krivoshein was controlling a secret organization with its headquarters in Athens and the object of smuggling Jews to Palestine and that *Anschluss* helped to initiate Krivoshein's business. Krivoshein was greedy when it came to prices. The fare to Palestine was settled individually and could cost the refugees their total savings. Krivoshein had a good relationship with the Greek Ministry of the Interior and he had several Greek police officers on his payroll. This made it difficult for Britain to persuade the Greek authorities to stop the traffic. However, they seem to have succeeded by the end of 1938, when Krivoshein moved his headquarters to Romania. PRO, Annual Report 1938.

749. 28 September 1938, Colonial Office, PRO, FO 371/21888.

750. Ibid.

751. Waterlow to FO 12 December 1938, PRO, FO 371/22371/762 R 9566-726-19.

752. Cairo, 27 November 1939, British Embassy to FO, PRO, FO 371/23372. Germany started to sell Czechoslovak arms after the march into Prague.

753. Cairo, 24 June 1938, The German Legation to AA geheim, BA Abt.Potsdam, 0961/Auswärtiges Amt/68445, Handel mit Krigsgerät, Ägypten.

754. Nabil Abbas Ibrahim Halim was educated in Germany and participated on the German side on the Belgian, French and Russian fronts during the First World War. He was wounded several times and received the German Iron Cross of the first degree. Later, he served in the Turkish Air Force and was head of the Egyptian workers' union for ten years. In August 1942 he was imprisoned by the British for, among other things, his close relations to the Germans. Joel Beinin and Zachary Lockman, *Workers on the Nile: Nationalism, Communism, Islam, and the Egyptian Working Class, 1882-1954*, Princeton 1988, pp.195-196; p.210.

755. Aziz Ali al-Masri was seen as a veteran within Arab Nationalist circles. He had undertaken his military education in the Ottoman army. He had several military decorations and a good reputation in the Ottoman Empire due to his efforts in Tripolitania during the war with Italy 1911-1912. After the outbreak of the Second World War he was sent on "compulsory sick leave" until being pensioned off in August 1940 and replaced with a more pro-British officer. Richard P. Mitchell, *The Society of the Muslim Brothers*, London 1969, pp.20ff.

756. Israel Gershoni, 'The Muslim Brothers and the Arab Revolt in Palestine, 1936-39' *Middle Eastern Studies*, pp.367-397.

757. According to the late Egyptian President, Anwar al-Sadat, the riot was planned by young rebels in the entourage of the ex-general. However, still according to Sadat, al-Masri, warned them against the use of force. James P. Jankowski, *Egypts Young Rebels: 'Young Egypt' 1933-1952*, Stanford 1975, pp.83-84.

758. Mitchell, p.25.

759. Nicosia, p.364.

760. Heinz Tillmann, *Deutschlands Araberpolitik im Zweiten Weltkrieg*, Berlin 1965, p.31.

761. Nicosia, p.363.

762. Tillmann, p.27.

763. Helmut Mejcher, 'Saudi-Arabiens Beziehungen zu Deutschland in der Regierungszeit von König Abd al-Aziz ibn Saud', in Linda Schatkowski Schiller and Claus Scharf, eds, *Der Nahe Osten in der Zwischenkriegszeit 1919-1939: Der Interdependenz von Politik, Wirtschaft und Ideologie*, Stuttgart 1989, pp.109-127.

764. In this connection it is interesting to note that, according to Nicosia, Canaris met the Grand Mufti of Jerusalem and the leader of the Arab Revolt, al-Hadj Amin al-Husaini, when he stayed in Lebanon incognito. In 1938 *Abwehr* planned to send two secret shipments of arms to Palestine through both Saudi Arabia and Iraq. Moreover, the Germans supplied the Arabs with money. This was only known in the small circle around the leading persons of the party and by Fritz Grobba, the German Ambassador in Baghdad and *Abwehr*. Nicosia, p.364.

765. Tillmann, p.23.

766. Athens, 17 June 1937, Waterlow to Eden, PRO, FO 286-1142-71-28-37.

767. Ibid.

768. Cairo, 17 August 1937, Dresdner Bank, streng vertraulich, to Dresdner Bank, Auslands-Sekretariat VI, Betr., Iraq/ Rheinmetall-Borsig/Otto Wolff. Also Ramleh-San Stefano 21 August 1937, Deutsche Gesandtschaft, BA Abt.Potsdam, 0961/68445, Handel mit KG, Ägypten.

769. "...Der Präsident der Gesellschaft, Herr Bodossaki, sowohl wie seine Direktoren [...] wiesen des öfteren darauf hin, dass sich ihr Werk deshalb ganz beson-ders für den Export nach den Umliege-staaten eigne, weil die Löhne in Griechenland ungefähr nur ein Zehntel ausmachen, die wir in Deutschland bezahlen. Es liegt offenbar bei der Leitung der C.& P. der Wunsch vor, mit uns eines Tages auch ernstlich über eine evtl. gemeinschaftliche Arbeit im Export zu verhandeln..." Sophia, 9 October 1937, Rheinmetall-Borsig, confidential Aktennotiz, IWM, Speer Documents, FD 790/46.

770. Athens, 4 August 1938, Hans Dyckhoff, representative of Auergesellschaft, draft of a letter to the Egyptian Embassy about sales of gas masks, PAAA, Gesandschaft Athen Nr. 21, Heer und Flotte, Lieferungen. Bodosakis had at that time established EKAP and had based the production on a German patent: Stoltenberg.

771. Ramleh, 23 September 1938, the German Legation to AA, WIII 7333/38, PAAA, Gesandtschaft Athen Nr. 21. EKAP's Stoltenberg patent was found to be unsuitable for gas masks.

772. When the Germans occupied Greece they checked EKAP's production facilities. From a report on the subject it is evident that EKAP was producing gas masks according to an Auer patent. 31 May 1941, Bericht über die Tätigkeit der Abteilung Rohstoff-Allgemein, Unterabteilung Immobilien, Übernahme wichtiger Betriebe in Besitz und Eigentum, PAAA, Handakten Clodius, Griechenland Bd.4.

773. MacVeagh, p.132.

774. *Bodosakis*, pp.31-56.

775. In Bodosakis's memoirs the German company is spelled with both Greek and Latin letters. In Greek it is called Philips Hosman; however, there is no doubt that he is speaking of Philipp Holzmann, founded in 1847 and

with its headquarters in Frankfurt am Main.

776. *Bodosakis*, pp.20-21.

777. Gervasi.

778. Ibid.

779. *Bodosakis*, p.68.

780. Alexandris, pp.68-70.

781. The conflict was intensified when the Venizelist Meletios Metaxakis was elected Patriarch in December 1921. The government in Athens disputed the result and refused to recognize the newly elected Patriarch. The result was a rupture between the head of the Ottoman Greeks and the Greek state which undermined Athens' authority over the Ottoman Greeks in Asia Minor. Meletios supported demands for an autonomous Ionian state. In 1922 he visited London, Paris and the United States of America in an inept attempt to gain support. It has been pointed out that these visions of an autonomous Ionia undermined the Greek government's reputation and authority among the Ottoman Greeks and especially in the area around Smyrna, and that this contributed to the political and military collapse in 1922. Whether the catastrophe in 1922 could have been avoided in different circumstances or not remains mere speculation; nevertheless, it is a fact that a considerable number of the Ottoman Greeks who arrived in Greece had strong anti-Venizelist sympathies. Alexandris, pp.71-76.

782. *Bodosakis*, p.80.

783. Ibid., pp.72-74.

784. Heinz Richter, *British Intervention in Greece: from Varkiza to Civil War: February 1945 to August 1946*, London 1986, p.208.

785. Basil Zaharoff was born in Anatolia in 1846 and died in 1936. Like Bodosakis he was an Ottoman Greek. Zaharoff started his career in Constantinople and then moved to Europe, where, on the strength of the Greek financier and diplomat Stefanos Skulodis's recommendation, he became sales agent for T. V. Nordenfelt, a Swedish arms designer, in the Balkans. In 1888 T. V. Nordenfelt and H. S. Maxim, the inventor of the machine-gun, merged to form a new company. Zaharoff was appointed to represent the firm in Eastern Europe and Russia. In 1895 the British arms company, Vickers, took over Maxim-Nordenfelt and Zaharoff's sales area was extended even further under the new company. Zaharoff became a multi-millionaire from the arms trade before, during and after the First World War. Moreover, he had political assignments at the highest level and participated in the negotiations at Versailles. He was a friend of Lloyd George and used this connection to expedite the development that led to the Greek-Turkish War in 1919-1922. He supplied the Greek forces with arms during the war in Asia Minor even when the Allies established an embargo. *Encyclopædia Britannica, Micropædia*, Vol.X, 15th edition, 1975, p. 855. See also, Robert Neumann, *Zaharoff, The Armaments King*, London 1938, pp.216-230.

786. Documents from the National Bank of Greece's branch in Smyrna reveal that Bodosakis had widespread assets in Smyrna, Cappadocia and outside Asia Minor. The bank closed on the 23 August 1922. Thanos Veremis and Kostas Kostis, p.253.

787. *Bodosakis*, pp.69-71; pp.89-91. Bodosakis mentions 300,000 gold francs. pp.97-99.

788. Bodosakis felt that the refugee issue should be considered economically and that the crucial point was to give compensation for lost property to the refugees. According to Bodosakis this could be handled by transferring all abandoned property and land in Turkey to a special non-state organization. Bodosakis believed that this would largely settle the outstanding that the refugees had in Turkey. On this basis the refugees would have the opportunity to contribute actively and enterprisingly to the Greek economy, which would in turn help to make them respected in 'Old Greece'. Furthermore, Bodosakis felt that the refugee loans were not large enough. Article in the Greek newspaper *Embros*, 7 April 1924, reproduced in *Ikonomikos Tachidromos*, 26 April 1973.

789. Bodosakis's hotel, Pera Palace, was on a list compiled by the Greek representative in Constantinople of the largest assets among confiscated property. Alexandris, pp.118-119.

790. The dispute was connected to article four of the Agreement, which reduced total recognition of compensation to those refugees who had a valid passport on the day they left. Ibid., pp.125-126.

791. Bodosakis states that he left property to the value of about 3.5 million Turkish pounds behind, but was only going to receive about 500,000 Turkish pounds in compensation. *Bodosakis*, p.111.

792. Alexandris, pp.126-127.

793. Leading Personalities in Greece, PRO, FO-371/23776/183057.

794. *Bodosakis*, pp.114-115.

795. Ibid, pp.114-118.

796. Alexandris, p.127.

797. Kondilis was born in 1878. He became an officer in the Greek army and committed himself to the realization of the Great Idea. He fought as an irregular behind Greek-Turkish borders in Mace-

donia and on Crete. (Koliopoulos, *Brigands with a Cause: Brigandage and Irredentism in Modern Greece 1821-1912*, Oxford 1987, p. 231. See also Veremis 1983, p. 337). He joined *Ethniki Amina*, deserted after the return of King Constantine, and took up residence in Constantinople at Bodosakis's hotel, Pera Palace.

798. Veremis 1983, p.300.

799. *Bodosakis*, pp.119-120.

800. Ibid., pp.126-127.

801. Ibid., pp.70-71.

802. Approval of the agreement was delayed for several years by the Greek parliament before the final contract was signed in February 1930. Ibid., pp.126-127.

803. Gervasi.

804. *Bodosakis*, p.146. See also below.

805. Ibid., p.145.

806. The Counsulate was contacted by Vasilis Pervana, a leading member of the Greek royalist association *l'Union Hellénique*, Geneva 4 May 1935, PAAA, Pol. Abteil. II, Pol.2.

807. Metaxas had made an electoral pact with dissidents from the Peoples' Party (*to Laiko Koma*), the biggest party in the anti-Venizelist coalition, to win the royalist votes.

808. Mavrogordatos, p.50.

809. Athens, 19 June 1935, PAAA, Pol.Abt. II, Pol.2 Gr.

810. *Bodosakis*, p.147.

811. The Venizelist admiral, Petros Voulgaris, is an example of the success of Bodosakis's long-term investments of this kind. He was employed as a manager in the Powder and Cartridge Company. After the Second World War, Voulgaris became Prime Minister in

Greece for a short period. William Hardy MacNeill, *The Greek Dilemma: War and Aftermath*, London 1947, pp.173-174.

812. The King had informed Waterlow that the best thing to do would be to put Greece under British administration and rule her like a colony. Koliopoulos, p.8.

813. Athens 17 September 1937, Kordt to AA, die innerpolitische Entwicklung in Griechenland, PAAA, Pol.IV. Po.5. Gr. Bd.1. Pol.IV 3168.

814. *Istoria tou ellenikou ethnous*, pp.379ff.

815. Kodzias was a retired athlete, a fencer, who represented Greece at the 1912 Olympics in Stockholm.

816. Report on leading personalities in Greece, PRO, FO 371/23776. An account of ministerial appointments in the Metaxas government can be seen in Katerina Dambassina-Kamara, *Le Regime du '4 Aout 1936' en Grèce: les répercussions politiques et sociales*, Paris 1983. See also the diaries of Goebbels bd. 2, pp. 682ff. Kodzias's visit to Berlin is described in BAK R 43 II/1445.

817. When Drosopoulos died in 1939, Korizis became president of the National Bank of Greece, and when Metaxas died in January 1941, he took over the control of country. He committed suicide as a result of the German occupation of Greece, April 1941. Berlin 31 January 1941, geheim, Abw. Nr. 695/41 g IH OST S, Nachfolger des Ministerpräsidenten Metaxas, BA-MA, W1 IC1. 10.

818. Andricopoulos, p.581.

819. It has been maintained that Diakos's influence on Metaxas was so huge that he was actually ruling Greece. (Athens, 29 December 1936, Kordt to AA, Spannungen in der griechischen Innen-politik, PAAA, Pol. IV Po.5 Bd. 1) After the German occupation of Greece several of the people from the Metaxas regime were accused of abuse of power and public mismanagement of funds. According to Graevenitz, the German Reich commissioner, Diakos and Kodzias were particularly incriminated. (Athens, 4 July 1941, BA-MA, WI/IC1. 10).

820. Marder, p.61.

821. Erbach mentions that Prince Andreas, a member of the royal family, told him in confidence that the King planned to replace Metaxas. Athens, 8 February 1938, Erbach to AA, Innerpolitische Lage in Griechenland. Politischer Bericht, PAAA, Pol. IV Po.Gr. Bd.1.

822. Annual Report, 1938.

823. Ibid.

824. MacVeagh, p.131.

825. Annual Report, 1938.

826. MacVeagh, pp.131-132.

827. Ibid., p.142. 24 October 1938.

828. Metaxas felt that Georgakopoulos had strengthened his position at the royal court and thus weakened his own position. The Minister of Culture and Education had also weakened the position of Metaxas's 'darling', EON. The election of Damaskinos, who was Georgakopoulos's man, would strengthen the minister's position even further. Shortly after the election Metaxas relieved Georgakopoulos, Spiridonos, and Logothetis, the Minister of Justice, of their duties. Metaxas tome IV, pp.312-316.

829. Athens, 7 January 1939, Erbach to AA, innerpolitische Lage. Politischer Bericht, PAAA, Pol. IV Po.5. Gr. Bd 1.

830. Annual Report 1938.

831. MacVeagh. p.153.

832. Ibid., pp.148-149.

833. MacVeagh suggests this explicitly in a letter to the State Department written at the beginning of 1939. The American Ambassador believed that Waterlow, because of his lack of personal and professional skills, created unnecessary problems in relations with the Greek government. This, according to MacVeagh, made it difficult for Waterlow to see matters in the right perspective. He gave the following description to the State Department on 31 January 1939: "to begin with, I may perhaps say that Sir Sidney [Waterlow] is a large, pinkcheeked, walrus-mustachioed, bureaucratic martinet, [...] As might be expected from this, he is also thoroughly flat-footed and tactless in diplomacy, but it is impossible not to have a warm spot in one's heart for him, since among the wily Greeks he often appears like some bewildered old bear, badgered by a lot of naughty boys. He is cordially disliked by his colony and laughed at by many people behind his back, but the natives respect him to his face, as the local blunderbuss of the British Raj.[...]" MacVeagh also refers to an earlier report in which he explained: "... that the British were beginning to sour on the dictatorship, but that Sir Sidney's [Waterlow's] confidence in His Majesty and estimate of his personal influence and ability run far ahead of anything I would care to hazard. Indeed, in the light of the record, his attempt, under instructions [...] to guide the King in his choice of advisers, takes on a decided aspect of the blind leading the blind. As the Department knows from past history, British intervention in Greece's internal affairs has often been astonishingly inept, and it appears to be maintaining its standard in this respect." MacVeagh, pp.151-152, Athens, 31 January 1939, MacVeagh to State Department.

834. Ibid., p.156.

835. Ibid., p.164, note 71.

836. Koliopoulos, pp.107-108.

837. MacVeagh, p.164.

838. *I documenti diplomatici italiani* (DDI) 9,V, 293.

839. Kitsikis, pp.34-40.

840. Kindleberger, pp.262-277.

841. Volkmann 1975, pp.98-100.

842. Wendt 1987, pp.11-22.

843. Ibid., pp.23-24. Wendt bases his findings on the so-called 'Hossbach protocol' which provides the only summary of the meeting. Since the Nuremberg trial in 1946 this has been used as a key document to prove that the German leaders were preparing a war of aggression. Hossbach made his summary a few days after the meeting, basing it on private notes and memory. The protocol is particularly difficult to use for discussion of Hitler's monologue because this is reproduced very briefly. Ibid., pp.11; 23; 191-192.

844. Ibid., p.29.

845. Wendt 1987, p.142.

846. Kube, p.196.

847. Ibid, pp.169-170.

848. Das Kriegsziehl im Falle 'Grün' "werde stets die rasche Besitznahme von Böhmen und Mähren unter gleichzeitiger Lösung der österreichischen Frage im Sinne der Einbeziehung Österreichs in das Deutsche Reich..." Wendt 87, p. 33.

849. Kube, pp. 183-185.

850. Ibid., p. 185.

851. Norbert Schausberger, 'Österreich und die nationalsozialistische Anschluss-Politik', in Manfred Funke, ed., *Hitler, Deutschland und die Mächte:*

Materialen zur Aussenpolitik des Dritten Reiches, Kronberg 1978, pp. 728-756.

852. Ibid., pp. 265-278; Carl-Axel Gemzell, *Raeder, Hitler und Skandinavien. Der Kampf für einen maritimen Operationsplan*, Lund 1965, pp. 72-104.; Wendt 1987, pp. 158-159.

853. Klaus Wittmann, *Schwedens Wirtschaftsbeziehungen zum Dritten Reich 1933-1945*, Munich 1978, passim.

854. Overy 1983, pp. 272-273.

855. Shortly after the establishment of Reichwerke Hermann Göring, Göring began to challenge the monopoly positions of the German industry, to deprive it of its possessions and force his own will through. These efforts were especially fruitful in connection with the Vereinigte Stahlwerke and Vögler-Poensgen-Thyssen group. Accordingly Reichswerke Hermann Göring's position was strengthened in Germany as well. Gerhard Mollin, *Montankonzerne und 'Drittes Reich': der Gegensatz zwischen Monopolindustrie und Befehlswirtschaft in der deutschen Rüstung und Expansion 1936-1944*, Göttingen 1988, pp. 102-129.

856. "...das Deutsche Reich [grenzt] durch den Anschluss nunmehr unmittelbar an den südosteuropäischen Raum, der als Nahrungsmittel- und Rohstofflieferant und als Absatzgebiet für die industriellen Fertigerzeugnisse sein natürliches Hinterland darstellt. Österreich bildet also in Zukunft das im Frieden und Kriege gleich wichtige Tor des Reiches nach dem Südosten..." Berlin, 1 April 1938, OKW, Wehrwirtschaftsstab, Stand der wirtschaftlichen Lage, BA-MA, geheime Kommandosache. RM 11/3.

857. Kube, pp. 253-254

858. Berlin, 1 April 1938, OKW, Wehrwirtschaftsstab, Stand der

wirtschaftlichen Lage, BA-MA, geheime Kommandosache. RM 11/3.

859. AGK, Jahresbericht 1937, PAAA, Ha.Pol., Geheim, Handel mit Kriegsgerät, allgemeines Bd. 3.

860. Berlin, the date is uncertain, either 1 May or 1 June 1938, OKW, Wehrwirtschaftsstab, Stand der wirtschaftlichen Lage, geheime Kommandosache, BA-MA, RM 11/3.

861. Overy 1983, pp.274-277.

862. Teichova 1988, pp.169 ff.

863. Abschlüsse der Reichs- und Protektoratfirmen in den Jahren, 1938, 1939 und I/1940 nach Ländern und Ländergruppen geordnet, PAAA, Ha.Pol., Geheim, Handel mit Kriegsgerät, allgemeines, Bd. 5.

864. *South-Eastern Europe*, pp.126 ff.

865. Volkmann 1975, p.106.

866. Overy 1984, pp.134-135; Waffenschmiede der deutschen Wehrmacht, von Wollen, Werden und Wirken der Rheinmetall-Borsig AG, geheime Kommandosache, IWM, Speer Documents, FD 4556/45.

867. Berlin, 27 February 1939, Herrn Ministerpräsident Generalfeldmarschall Göring mit der Bitte um Kentnisnahme vorgelegt, ADAP, D, V, 306.

868. "...die Industrialisierung Rumäniens soll sich in allgemeinem nur auf die Ergänzung einfacher Verbrauchsgüter einschränken und nur dann angefängt..." Berlin, 26 May, Vermerk über die Förderung der wirtschaftlichen Beziehungen zwischen dem Deutschen Reich und dem Königreich Rumänien von 23. März 1939, Dem Reichsminister zur Kenntnisnahme, BAK, R43 II/1445.

869. Grenzebach, p.166.

870. Kube, p.291.

871. Ibid., p.167.

872. Wendt 1973, pp.108-109.

873. Volkmann 1977, pp.112-119.

874. Marguerat, pp.205-210.

875. See Introduction.

876. Joseph Rothschild, *East Central Europe between the Two World Wars*, Washington 1974, pp.365-366.

877. Bernhard R. Kroener, Rolf Dieter Müller and Hans Umbreit, eds, *Das deutsche Reich und der zweite Weltkrieg: Organisation und Mobilisierung des deutschen Machtbereichs*, Band 5, Stuttgart 1988, p.71.

878. Berchtesgaden 12 August 1939, Verbale del primo colloquio tra il ministro degli esteri, Ciano, e il cancelliere del Reich, Hitler, DDI, 8. ser, XIII, 4.

879. Erwin Oberländer, ed., *Hitler-Stalin-Pact 1939: Das Ende Ostmitteleuropas?*, Frankfurt am Main 1989. Until 1988 the secret protocol was rejected as a western forgery by Soviet authorities. Lothar Gruchmann, *Totaler Krieg: Von Blitzkrieg zur bedingungslosen Kapitulation*, Munich 1991, p.269.

880. Volkmann 1977, pp.98-99.

881. Klaus Olshausen, 'Die deutsche Balkan-Politik 1940-1941', in Funke, pp.709-711.

882. Martin Broszat, 'Deutschland-Ungarn-Rumänien', in Funke, pp.552-553.

883. Gruchmann, pp.91-92.

884. According to Crevel Hitler formed an offensive strategy to dislodge British forces from their positions in the eastern Mediterranean and thus force a British capitulation or conclusion of peace. Thus, according to Crevel, Hitler should have called on Mussolini to attack Greece at a meeting in Brenner on 4 October 1940. Martin van Creveld, *Hitler's Strategy 1940-1941: The Balkan Clue*, Cambridge 1973, pp.33-39.

885. MacGregor Knox, *Mussolini Unleashed 1939-1941: Politics and Strategy in Fascist Italy's Last War*, Cambridge 1982, pp.186-188.

886. Schinzinger, p.171.

887. This aspect of Italian Fascism has been explored thoroughly by A. James Gregor, *Italian Fascism and Developmental Dictatorship*, Princeton 1979.

888. Knox, pp.286-290.

889. John Louis Hondros, *Occupation and Resistance: the Greek Agony 1941-44*, New York 1983, p.36.

890. Gruchmann, p.95.

891. From Mersa Matruth it was possible for Italian bombers to reach the British naval base at Alexandria.

892. DDI 9. ser, V, 728.

893. Frank Mazzari, 'Projects for an Italian-led Balkan Bloc of Neutrals, September-December 1939', *The Historical Journal*, XIII, 4, 1970, pp.767-778.

894. "...I Balcani erano un campo dove la concorenza fra le nazioni europee per la conquista dei mercati era acutissima, ed è quasi superfluo dire che i più accaniti competitori che noi trovavamo sulla nostra strada erano sempre i Tedeschi. Senza la nostra entrata in guerra, noi avremmo potuto conquistare in tutto il Levante..." Emanuele Grazzi, *Il principio della fine: L'Empresa di Grecia*. Rome 1945, pp.89-90.

895. Wolfgang Schumann, ed., *Griff nach Südosteuropa: Neue Dokumente über die Politik des deutschen Imperialismus und Militarismus gegenüber Südosteuropa im zweiten Weltkrieg*, Berlin 1973, p.97.

896. Grazzi, p.90.

897. Knox, p.52, note 43.

898. MacVeagh p.179. Letter from Mac-Veagh to President Roosevelt dated 3 December 1939.

899. Knox, p.203.

900. Gruchmann, p.95.

901. Hondros, p.37.

902. Borejsza, pp.67-68.

903. 5 July 1941, BA-MA, RW 29/96.

904. Mollin, p.197.

905. Dietrich Eizholtz and Wolfgang Schumann, eds, *Anatomie des Krieges: Neue Dokumente über die Rolle des deutschen Monopolkapitals bei der Vorbereitung und Durchführung des zweiten Weltkrieges*, Berlin 1969, pp.332-333.

906. Dusan Lukas, 'Aggression of Italy against Greece and the Consequences of Failure of Italian Expansion', *Balkan Studies*, Vol 23, No. 1, 1982, pp.81-99.

907. Gruchmann, p.93.

908. Koliopoulos, pp.177-178.

909. Gruchmann, p.96.

910. Ehrengard Schramm-von Thadden, *Griechenland und die Grossmächte im zweiten Weltkrieg*, Wiesbaden 1955, pp.138-139.

911. Alexandris 1982, pp.176-179.

912. Gruchmann, p.98.

913. Alexandris 1982, pp.178-179.

914. Gruchmann, pp.98-106.

915. Schramm-von Thadden, p.122.

916. Hondros, p.40.

917. Schramm-von Thadden, p.144.

918. Hondros, pp.42-43.

919. 6 December 1940, Der Chef der Sicherheitspolitzei und des SD to AA, PAAA, Inland IIg.

920. Schramm-von Thadden, pp.150-151.

921. Ibid., p.140.

922. Ibid., p.151.

923. Athens, 20 December 1940, note by Metaxas, the Greek Ministry of Foreign Affairs, 1940/9 A Pol.A/4.

924. Schramm-von Thadden, p.169.

925. Lukas, p.92.

926. Schramm-von Thadden, p.152.

927. Koliopoulos, p.213, note 1.

928. Schramm-von Thadden, p.170.

929. Hondros, p.47.

930. Ibid, pp.50-51.

931. *Les conditions* 1938-1939, p.257.

932. Berlin 30 May 1938, PAAA, Ha.Pol.IVa, Bd.1; Berlin 24 May 1938. Reemtsma used 750,000 RM. for such schemes., ibid.

933. 27 January 1939, PRO, FO 371/23776/R 821.

934. 6 November 1938, Memo from the British Consulate in Salonika, PRO, FO 371/22366/R-1360.

935. MacVeagh p.132, 27 September 1938.

936. Mavrogordatos, pp.253-263.

937. Lars Nørgaard, 'Den Græske arbejderbevægelse før 1918 og Føderationen i Saloniki' (The Greek Workers Union before 1918 and the Federation in Salonika), in Lars Bærentzen, Lars Nørgaard and Ole L Smith, eds, *Mens vi venter: Studier i det moderne Grækenlands historie* (While We Are Waiting: Studies in Modern Greek History) Copenhagen 1980, pp.11-53.

938. Salonika, 2 December 1938, The German Consulate to the Legation in

Athens, PRO, Ha.Pol.IVa, Rohstoffe und Waren, Tabak Bd. 1, W III 9290.

939. Athens, 27 May 1938, The Legation to AA, PAAA, Ha.Pol.IVa, Rohstoffe und Waren, Tabak Bd. 1; Berlin 3 August, AA to the Legation in Athens, Ibid.

940. Kavalla, 29 June 1939, Memo from the German Vice Consulate, PAAA, Ha.Pol.IVa, Rohstoffe und Waren, Tabak Bd.1.

941. Ibid.

942. I have been unable to find material alluding to these negotiations in either Greek or German archives.

943. Anlage 4, Exposé über die Förderung des Baumwollanbaus im Königreich Griechenland, PAAA, Handakten Wiehl Griechenland Bd. 2.

944. György Ranki, *Economy and Foreign Policy: the Struggle of the Great Powers for Hegemony in the Danube Valley 1919-1939*, New York 1983, p.150.

945. Athens, 9 September 1939, Palairet til FO, PRO, FO 371/23776.

946. The German consumption of cigarettes in 1937 made up 37.7 per cent of the total tobacco consumption. 46.3 per cent of this was met by Greek tobacco, and 23.1 per cent of the total German tobacco import came from Greece. (16 March 1939, Memo from Lord Dulverton. Appendix II, Consumption and Disposal of Oriental Tobaccos in Germany, PRO, FO 371/23764/R 3155.) Compared with the German consumption of tobacco in the period 1929-1933, total consumption grew by about 11 per cent in the period 1934-1938 (from 129.5 million kg to 143.8 million kg). This was 9.4 per cent above the average in the period 1924-1928, when the consumption was 131.4 million kg. (*Les grands produits agricoles*, p.221.)

947. 16 March 1939, Memorandum from Lord Dulverton.

948. Pratt, p.147.

949. Ibid., p.148.

950. Ibid., pp.146-149.

951. 21 April 1938, Waterlow to FO, PRO, FO 371/22364/R 3536/368/19.

952. 9 May 1938, Halifax to the Treasury, PRO, FO 371/ 22364/4292/368/19.

953. 14 May 1938, Waley to the Treasury, PRO, FO 371/ 22364/4842.

954. 15 June 1938, Mr. H.W Cole, Miners Department to Foreign Office, PRO, FO 371/ 22364/R 5628.

955. 21 June 1938, Forsyth, Board of Trade, PRO, FO 371/22364/R 5788.

956. 29 June 1938, Sterling, Export Credit Guarantee Department, PRO, FO 371/22364/R 5429.

957. The decrease in British coal exports to the Mediterranean has been linked with her efforts to establish Scandinavian markets. Derek H. Aldcroft, *The British Economy, Vol.1: the Years of Turmoil 1920-1951*, London 1986, p.81 note 23.

958. Pratt, p.148.

959. Memo from the Leith-Ross Committee dated 27 June 1938, PRO, FO 371/22364/R 5871.

960. Pratt, pp.146-147.

961. Memo from The Leith-Ross Committee dated 25 July 1938, PRO, FO 371/22365.

962. Mr Jenkins, Board of Trade, to the Treasury 20 July 1938, PRO, FO 371/22365/R 6495.

963. Athens, 25 October 1938, PRO, FO 371/22368/R 8634/108/19.

964. Minute by Leith-Ross 2 November 1938, PRO, FO 371/22368/ R 8634/108/19.

965. Minute by Ingram 7 November 1938, PRO, FO 371/22368/ R 8634/108/19.

966. Political Review of the Year 1939, PRO, FO 371/24914. The Romanian forgery had a decisive impact on the decisions leading to British guarantees to Poland on 31 March 1939, Davenport-Hines, pp.309 ff.

967. Koliopoulos, p.96.

968. Annual Report 1938.

969. Minute by Orme Sargent 24 March 1939, PRO, FO 371/ 23764/R 1902.

970. Athens, 28 March 1939, PRO, FO 371/23776.

971. 16 March 1939, memo from Lord Dulverton ITC, private and confidential, PRO, FO 371/23764/R 1834.

972. 6 November 1938, memo from the British Consulate in Salonika, PRO, FO 371/22366/1360.

973. Stephen Constantine, *Buy and Build: the Advertising Posters of the Empire Marketing Board*, London 1986.

974. Report from the Board of Trade from 1944 concerned with the cartellization of the British tobacco industry, PRO, BT 64/283.

975. 31 March 1939, PRO, FO 371/23764/R 2204.

976. Minute by Orme Sargent, 13 April 1939, PRO, FO 371/23764/R 2204.

977. Political Review of the Year 1939, PRO, FO 371/24914 R 441/441/19.

978. Kitsikis, pp.80-82.

979. Ibid., See also Mazower 1988, pp.617-619.

980. Koliopoulus, pp.130-131.

981. The Bank of Greece's accounts for 1940. XX, The National Bank of Greece Archive, Trapeza tis Ellados. fak.13.

982. 30 April 1940, The British Legation in Athens to Southern Department, PRO, FO 371/24925.

983. Annual Report from the Bank of Greece, 1940, the National Bank of Greece Archive, XXI trapezes, Trapeza tis Ellados, fak. 13.

984. Political Review of the Year 1939, PRO, FO 371/24914/R 441/441/19.

985. Koliopoulos, 'Unwanted Alley: Greece and the Great Powers 1939-1941' *Balkan Studies*, Vol.23, No.1.

986. See below.

987. Documents that describe the way in which the agreement came into existence can be found in FRUS 1938 Vol.II, pp.516-552.

988. Vertraulicher Sonderbericht Nr. 18, 6 February 1939, PAAA, Ha.Pol.IVa, Handel 11, Bd. 1.

989. Teichova 1974, p.381.

990. Nilson, pp.117-119.

991. See above.

992. The negotiations started in October 1937 during a meeting of the permanent council of the Balkan Entente. In February 1938 the two states declared that they had signed a protocol to the previous agreement. Alexis Alexandris, 'Turkish Policy towards Greece during WW II', *Balkan Studies*, 23,1,1982 pp.166-167.

993. Pratt, pp.135-136.

994. Koliopoulos, p.87.

995. MacVeagh p.134. Athens, 20 May 1938, MacVeagh to Franklin D. Roosevelt.

996. Koliopoulos, pp.89-90.

997. Ibid.

998. Kitsikis, p.76.

999. Metaxas, tome IV, p. 311. "Negotiations with Waterlow. My suggestions [concerning a Greek-British alliance]. I am sure that they will not be accepted. But I am relieved."

1000. Kitsikis, pp.74-77.

1001. Koliopoulos, pp.88-93.

1002. MacVeagh, pp.148-149.

1003. Koliopoulos, pp.102-106. In March 1939 Lord Lloyd tried in vain to persuade Metaxas and the King to introduce certain liberal reforms. Ibid.

1004. Athens, 16 March 1938, Erbach to AA, Athens Academy, GSR T120/1042.

1005. Knox, p.33.

1006. Athens, 8 October 1938, Erbach to AA, vertrauchlich, Politischer Bericht, ADAP, D, V, 233.

1007. Berlin, 6 March 1939, Rizo-Ragavis to Metaxas, Metaxas Archive, fak. 30.

1008. Athens, 6 March 1939, Metaxas to Rizo-Ragavis, Metaxas Archive, fak.30. In the commentary to Metaxas's diary the event has been dated to 9 March 1939, tome IV pp. 335-336. However, as this must be the same event, the discrepancy may have occurred as a result of the publisher printing 6 upside down.

1009. Goebbels, Bd.3, p.587.

1010. Athens, 9 April 1939, Waterlow to Halifax, *Documents on British Foreign Policy 1919-1939* (DBFP) 3, V No. 97.

1011. London, 8 April 1939, Halifax to the Earl of Perth, DBFP 3, V, 95.

1012. London, 9 April 1939, Halifax to the Earl of Perth, DBFP 3, V, 95.

1013. Athens, 10 April 1939, Waterlow to Halifax, DBFP 3, V, 118.

1014. Athens, 12 April 1939, Waterlow to Halifax, DBFP 3, V, 140.

1015. Koliopoulos, pp.111-112.

1016. DBFP 3, V, 119-121.

1017. London, 11 April 1939, Halifax to Knatchbull-Hugessen, Ankara, DBFP 3, V, 128.

1018. Berlin, 12 April 1939, ADAP, D, VI, 186.

1019. Athens, 13 April 1939, ADAP, D, VI, 147.

1020. Athens, 19 April 1939, Erbach to AA, ADAP D, VI, 231.

1021. Berlin, 20 June 1939, Aufzeichnung des Leiters der Politischen Abteilung, ADAP, D, VI, 550.

1022. Political Review of the Year 1939, PRO, FO 371/24914. On 12 July 1939 Greece made a so-called Greek-Anglo Guarantee Agreement, which ensured Greece the financial possibility of arms purchases in Britain to a value of about £2 million.

1023. MacVeagh, p.161.

1024. Rome, 12 September 1939, Mussolini to Grazzi, DDI 9, I, 166.

1025. Knox, pp.49-53.

1026. *Bodosakis*, pp.211-213.

1027. This information is based on documents from the French army which the Germans seized after the fall of France. A selection of these was published in connection with the German assault on Yugoslavia and Greece in, "Zur Konflikte mit Griechenland und Jugoslawien". The aim was to show that the two Balkan states had supported France and Britain. Greece was accused of having opened a flank south of "the German Lebensraum" to France and Britain.

1028. Athens, 31 May 1940, Grazzi to Ciano, DII,9,IV, 676.

1029. Berlin, 25 May 1940, Woermann to the German Legation in Athens, ADAP, D, IX, 318.

1030. Metaxas, tome IV, pp.470-471.

1031. "...In Wirklichkeit aber brenne er [Metaxas] darauf, dass Deutschland unverzüglich in dieser für Griechenland letzten Minute den Schutz der griechischen Grenzen aussprechen möge, und die Deutsche Regierung möge sicher sein, dass dieser Schutz von der Griechischen Regierung und von der Mehrzahl des griechischen Volkes mit grösster Begeisterung aufgenommen würde..." Berlin, 4 June 1940, Aufzeichnung für den Reichsaussenminister, ADAP, D, IX, 384.

1032. Ibid.

1033. ADAP, D, IX, 395, 403.

1034. Athens, 15 July 1940, Head of general staff to Metaxas, confidential, Metaxas Archive, fak.43.

1035. Athens, 23 July 1940, Grazzi to Ciano, DDI, 9, V, 293.

1036. Berlin, 25 July 1940, Rizo-Ragavis to Metaxas, Greek Ministry of Foreign Affairs, 1940/A Pol/A/4.

1037. Athens, 27 July 1940, Metaxas to Rizo-Ragavis, coded, Greek Ministry of Foreign Affairs 1940/A Pol/A/4.

1038. Athens, 12 July 1940, Grazzi to Ciano, DDI, 9, V, 232.

1039. Knox, pp.167-172.

1040. Athens, 13 August; 413, Berlin 14 August, DDI, 9, V, 409.

1041. Borejsza, p.67 note 45.

1042. 'Elli' was sunk by the Italian submarine 'Delfino' from a unit based in the Dodecanese. Official Italian sources attributed the affair to an unknown submarine, even after the war. However, from the memoirs of Cesare Maria de Vecchis, Governor of the Dodecanese, it is clear that it was an Italian submarine that sank the Greek cruiser. Knox, p.174. In addition, one of the topedoes hit a mole and fragments from this show that it was an Italian torpedo.

1043. ADAP, D, X, 353, Berlin 16 August 1940.

1044. Rome, 17 August 1940, Ciano to Alfieri, Italian Ambassador to Germany, DDI, 9, V, 435.

1045. Rome, ... August 1940, Ciano to Politis, DDI, 9, V, 429. The note has not been dated; however, it was probably given to the Greeks after the talks with Ribbentrop. From Ciano's diary it appears that on 15 August Ribbentrop suggested that the Greek-Italian problems were solved by sending a note. On 17 August Mussolini replied that Italy would naturally accept the German point of view, also in respect to Greece.

1046. Metaxas, tome IV, p. 498.

1047. Knox, pp.176-177.

1048. Metaxas, Tome. IV, p.498.

1049. Athens, 21 August, Erbach to AA, ADAP, D, X, 372.

1050. Koliopoulos, p.139.

1051. ADAP, D, X, 386 note 3.

1052. Berlin, 24 August 1940, note by the head of the political department. ADAP, D, X, 387.

1053. Rome, 24 August 1940, Mussolini to Hitler, DDI, 9, V, 484.

1054. Fuschl, 27 August 1940, Aufzeichnung des Legationsrats v. Sonnleithner, Aufzeichnung über dem Empfang des griechischen Gesandten Rizo-Ragabé durch den Aussenministers am 26. 8. 1940 in Fuschl, ADAP D, X, 394.

1055. Metaxas, Tome. IV, pp.501-502.

1056. Hondros, p.36.

1057. In a note from Metaxas's diary dated 24 October 1940, it appears that the Greek dictator heard rumours about an Italian assault the following morning, i.e. 25 October 1940. Metaxas, Tome. IV, p.512.

1058. Athens, 24 October 1940, Erbach to AA, ADAP D, XI, 226.

1059. Athens, 25 October 1940, Grazzi to Ciano, DDI, 9, V, 785.

1060. DDI, 9, V 789.

1061. See, documents in FO 371-23781, 23782.

1062. Athens, 17 October 1939, Erbach to AA, PAAA, Ha.Pol.IVa, Handel 11-1 Bd. 3.

1063. Koliopoulos, p.125.

1064. Athens, 17 October 1939, Erbach to AA, PAAA, Ha.Pol. IVa, 11-1, Bd.3.

1065. Salonika, 15 December 1939, the German Consulate to AA, W IIIa 879/39, PAAA, Ha.Pol.IVa 11a, Auswirkungen der britischen Seekriegsfürung auf dem deutschen Handel mit Griechenland.

1066. Patras, 30 December 1939, Gianoutsos & Co. to Herm. Nagel Hamburg, W IIIa 751/40, PAAA, Ha.Pol.IVa 11a, Auswirkungen der britischen Seekriegsfürung auf dem deutschen Handel mit Griechenland.

1067. Berlin, 24 January 1940 to the German Legation in Athens, W IIIa 344, PAAA, Ha.Pol.IVa 11a, Auswirkungen der britischen Seekriegsfürung auf dem deutschen Handel mit Griechenland.

1068. Athens, 17 October 1939, Erbach to AA, PAAA, Ha.Pol. IVa, Handel 11-1 Bd. 3.

1069. See below.

1070. Berlin, 28 October 1939, Weizäcker to Erbach, ADAP D, VIII, 310.

1071. Athens, 1 November 1939, Erbach to AA, ADAP, VIII, 319.

1072. Koliopoulos, p.130.

1073. Dienststelle Ribbentrop, PAAA, Aufbringen und Versenkung von Handelsschiffen durch Deutschland, Griechenland 1939-1943, Bd. 1.

1074. Berlin, 17 February 1940, the Greek Embassy in Berlin to AA, PAAA, Ha.Pol.IVa 11a, Auswirkungen der britischen Seekriegsfürung auf dem deutschen Handel mit Griechenland.

1075. Berlin, 25 April 1940, Aufzeichnung des Oberkommandos der Kriegsmarine, die Schiffahrt des Balkanraums als Feindversorger, Dokumente zum Konflikt mit Jugoslawien und Griechenland Berlin 1941, Griechenland, 133.

1076. See, documents in FO 371-24914.

1077. Athens, 20 June 1940, Erbach to AA, PAAA, Ha.Pol.IVa, Wirtschaft 1, Griechenland Bd. 1.

1078. Berlin, 14 June 1940, Wiehl to the German Legation in Athens, ADAP D,IX, 435.

1079. Berlin, 21 August 1940, note from Clodius, ADAP, D, X, 37.

1080. Berlin, 27 August 1940, Morath, PAAA, Ha.Pol., Handakten Clodius, Griechenland, Bd. 4.

1081. Koliopoulos, p.131.

1082. Berlin, 2 December 1940, memo by Morath, PAAA, Handakten Clodius, Griechenland Bd.4.

1083. Metaxas notes: "...Much work. – The question about the Greek ships and supplies. I fear that the British goodwill [towards us] will be reduced..." Metaxas, tome IV, p.507.

1084. See above.

1085. See above.

1086. Athens, 30 March 1939, Erbach to AA, PAAA, Ha.Pol., Geheim, Kriegsgerät, Griechenland Bd.1.

1087. Athens, 4 May 1939, Erbach to AA, ADAP D, V 323.

1088. Ibid., note 2.

1089. Undated memo by the Greek Naval Attaché in Berlin, W 2160 40g, PAAA, Ha.Pol., Geheim, Kriegsgerät Griechenland Bd. 2.

1090. Sitzung des Exportgarantie Ausschusses für Regierungs-geschäfte, 14.-17. February 1939, PAAA, Gesandtschaft Athen Nr. 21, Heer und Flotte, Lieferungen.

1091. Berlin, 28 February 1940, Kriegsmaterial für Griechenland geheim, PAAA, Ha.Pol., Geheim, Handel mit Kriegsgerät, Griechenland, Bd.2.

1092. Auergesellschaft had considerable experience within the fields of chemistry and radiation, including the use of X-rays. In 1939 the company was involved in a project for the development of the German nuclear bomb. Mark Walker, *German National Socialism and the Quest for Nuclear Power, 1939-1949*, Cambridge 1989.

1093. Athens, 13 October 1938, Waterlow to Halifax, confidential, PRO, FO 371/22354; *Bodosakis*, pp.185-189.

1094. *Bodosakis*, pp.187-189.

1095. Ibid.

1096. Kube, p.293; 20 July 1939 Reichsgruppe Industrie AGK to Rheinmetall-Borsig, PAAA, Ha.Pol., Geheim, Kriegsgerät Griechenland Bd.1.

1097. Berlin, 7 November 1939, Reichsgruppe Industrie to Rheinmetall-Borsig,

PAAA, Ha.Pol.IV, Handel 12, Kriegsgerät Griechenland Bd.1.

1098. Athens, 18 November 1939, Erbach to AA, PAAA, Handakten Wiehl, Griechenland, Bd.2.

1099. "...dieses Geschäft [ist] nicht nur ein Geschäft zwischen der Rheinmetall-Borsig und der Poudreries & Cartoucheries sondern vielmehr von lebenswichtiger Bedeutung für die griechische Regierung [...], so dass sogar der Herr. Ministerpräsident [Metaxas] persönlich dazu Stellung nimmt und seinen Neffen in besonderer Mission zu uns geschickt hat [...] es [erscheint] auch dem Auswärtigen Amt wünschenswert [...], die mit der griechischen Regierung noch bestehenden guten Verbindungen aufrechtzuerhalten, insbesondere aber, die freundliche Einstellung des Herrn Ministerpräsidenten, Se. Excellenz Metaxas, nicht zu trüben..." Berlin, 1 February 1940, Rheinmetall-Borsig to AA, PAAA, Ha.Pol., Handel 12, Kriegsgerät Griechenland. Bd.2.

1100. 12 February 1940, Reichswirtschaftsministerium, PAAA, Ha.Pol., Handel 12, Kriegsgerät Griechenland. Bd.1.

1101. Athens, 13 February 1940, Air Attaché, Betr. Deutsche Flugzeuglieferungen an Griechenland, PAAA, Ha.Pol., Geheim, Kriegsgerät, Griechenland Bd.2.

1102. Ibid.

1103. Berlin, 28 February 1940, Abt. W to RAM, geheim zu W 1035 g/I, PAAA, Ha.Pol., Geheim, Kriegsgerät, Griechenland Bd.2.

1104. 21 March 1940, OKW, PAAA, Ha.Pol., Handel 12, Kriegsgerät Griechenland. Bd.1.

1105. 22 March 1940, Aufzeichung über Waffenlieferungen an fremde Staaten, geheime Reichssache, PAAA, Ha.Pol.,

Geheim, Handel mit Kriegsgerät, allgemeines Bd.5.

1106. OKW, Wi Rü Amt, Stellungnahme zu der Aufzeichnung des Auswärtigen Amtes v. 26. 3. 40. geheime Reichssache, PAAA, Ha.Pol., Geheim, Handel mit Kriegsgerät, allgemeines Bd.5.

1107. Raspin, pp.212-213.

1108. 5 May 1940, Ribbentrop to Göring, personal , PAAA, Ha.Pol., Geheim, Handel mit Kriegsgerät, allgemeines Bd.5.

1109. This appears in a report from AGK: "...In Juni [1940] trat das rüstungsmässig bisher unabhängige *Italien* mit einem dringenden Bedarf an schweren Flaks an uns heran..." AGK Geschäftsbericht 1939/1940, PAAA, Ha.Pol., Geheim, Handel mit Kriegsgerät, allgemeines Bd.5.

1110. On 27 June 1940 Hitler granted permission for the delivery of arms to Sweden. Wittmann, pp.302-305.

1111. 27 June 1940, Abkommen betreffend die Bezahlung deutscher Kriegsmateriallieferungen an Griechenland, PAAA, Ha.Pol., Handakten Wiehl Griechenland Bd.3.

1112. Kolipoulos, p.70 note 1.

1113. *Bodosakis*, pp.180-183.

1114. Athens, 13 October 1938, Waterlow to Halifax, confidential, PRO, FO 371/22354.

1115. Minute by Leith-Ross, 26 October 1938, PRO, FO 371/22354.

1116. Vickers-Armstrong Ltd., the leading armaments company in Britain. The company produced guns, tanks, aircraft and battle ships.

1117. 19 December 1938, Leith-Ross, PRO, FO 371/22354. R-10190/18/19.

1118. *Aide-memoire*, the Cartoucheries et Poudreries Helléniques. Probably from February 1939, PRO, FO 371/23767.

1119. Vickers tried to compete with Schneider-Creusot in south-eastern Europe and in the Balkans after the First World War. The stronghold of the British company was situated in Romania. However, the venture turned out to be a bad investment. Romania's membership of the French-dominated Little Entente and the fact that the Schneider-Creusot dominated firm Skoda held a leading position within the Romanian armaments industry became a considerable hindrance for Vickers in obtaining orders from the Romanian army. In addition, the British found it hard to accept the Romanian business mentality. In 1937 Vickers sold its interests in Romania. Davenport-Hines, pp.287-319.

1120. Athens, 8 March 1939, PRO, FO 371/21767.

1121. 29 March 1939, Colonel Harding, WO, to FO, PRO, FO 371/23767/R2178/44/19.

1122. 21 November 1939, note, PRO, FO 371/23767/R 10303/44/19.

1123. Foreign Office, 9 January 1940, cypher telegram to Palairet Athens, PRO, FO 371/24922.

1124. Athens, 12 January 1940, telegram from Palairet, PRO, FO 371/24922.

1125. London, 14 January 1940, J.E. Coulson, Ministry of Economic Warfare to H.C. Budden, Ministry of Supply, PRO, FO 371/23767.

1126. London, 16 January 1940, PRO, FO 371/24922.

1127. London, 15 January 1940, E. Ambatielos to N.E. Ambatielos, PRO, FO 371/24924/R 1188/1188/19. The correspondence between E. and N.E. Ambatielos was intercepted by the FO.

1128. London, 10 April 1940, PRO, FO 371/24922.

1129. London, 12 June 1940, Ministry of Supply, secret and by hand to the Southern Department, PRO, FO 371/24922.

1130. London, 1 August 1939, N.G. Drakopoulos to the Secretary to the Minister of War, PRO, FO 371/23767.

1131. These were the same conditions of payment that Bodosakis required from the Republicans in Spain. The demand for dollars was a considerable tightening of the conditions, as the Lend-Lease agreement between the USA and Britain was not made until the following year.

1132. London, 13 July 1940, Turner, Ministry of Supply to the Southern Department, PRO, FO 371/24922.

1133. 16 July 1940, note 1940, PRO, FO 371/24922.

1134. 16 August 1940, Ministry of Supply to Southern Department, PRO, FO 371/24922.

1135. Athens, 17 August 1940, Palairet to Ministry of Supply, PRO, FO 371/24922.

1136. London, 21 August 1940, Ministry of Supply to Southern Department, PRO, FO 371/24922.

1137. 28 August 1940, War Office to FO, PRO, FO 371/24922.

1138. Athens, 8 September 1940, Armaments Supply Situation in Greece, PRO, FO 371/ 24922.

1139. 9 October 1940, FO to Palairet, PRO, FO 371/24922.

1140. Berlin, 10 August 1940, Clodius to the Legation in Athens, ADAP D, X, 324.

1141. Berlin, 21 August 1940, note by Clodius, ADAP D, X, 375.

1142. Athens, 23 August 1940, Erbach to AA, PAAA, Handakten Clodius Bd.3.

1143. Berlin, 27 August 1940, Clodius, zu W 4083g I. Sofort, Schnellbriefe Geheim, BA Abt. Potsdam, 09.01/Auswärtiges Amt/68435/ Handel mit KG Griechenland, Bd.3.

1144. Berlin, 6 September 1940, der Reichsmarchall des Grossdeutschen Reiches und Beauftragter für den Vierjahresplan, Schnellbrief Geheim, Firma Bodosakis, Griechenland, BA Abt. Potsdam, Auswärtiges Amt/68435/ Handel mit KG Griechenland, Bd.3.

1145. Berlin, 28 August 1940, OWK Sonderstab für Handelskrieg und Wirtschaftliche Kampfmassnahmen (HWK), to AA, BA Abt. Potsdam, Auswärtiges Amt/68435/ Handel mit KG Griechenland, Bd.3.

1146. Berlin, 30 August 1940, HWK to AA, geheim, BA Abt. Potsdam, Auswärtiges Amt/68435/ Handel mit KG Griechenland, Bd.3.

1147. Berlin, 7 September 1940, Morath to HKW geheim, BA Abt. Potsdam, Auswärtiges Amt/68435/ Handel mit KG Griechenland, Bd.3.

1148. Berlin, 16 September 1940, HWK to Ritter AA, Wiru, BA Abt. Potsdam, Auswärtiges Amt/68435/ Handel mit KG Griechenland, Bd.3.

1149. Berlin, 17 October 1940, Morath to the Legation in Athens, geheim mit Kurier, BA Abt. Potsdam, Auswärtiges Amt/68435/ Handel mit KG Griechenland, Bd.3.

1150. Athens, 2 November 1940, from the Military Attaché to the War Office. C-in-C Middle East, PRO, FO 371/24922.

BIBLIOGRAPHY

A) Unpublished sources

1)Imperial War Museum, London
Speer Documents, FD 783/46.
Speer Documents, FD 790/46.
Speer Documents, FD 4556/45.

2) Public Record Office, Kew Gardens, Surrey

Foreign Office
FO 286/1125/23.
FO 286/1126/71.
FO 286/1136/71.
FO 286/1137.
FO 286/1143/106.
FO 371/18407.
FO 371/19518.
FO 371/20391.
FO 371/21888.
FO 371/22354.
FO 371/22364.
FO 371/22365.
FO 371/22366.
FO 371/22368.
FO 371/22371.
FO 371/23372.
FO 371/23764.
FO 371/23767.
FO 371/23776.
FO 371/23777.
FO 371/23781.
FO 371/23782.
FO 371/24913.
FO 371/24914.
FO 371/24922.

Board of Trade
BT 64/283.

3) Berlin Document Centre
Hellmuth Roehnert.

4) Bundesarchiv Abteilung Potsdam (BA Abt.Potsdam)
0901/Auswärtiges Amt/68428, Handel mit Kriegsgerät Balkan.
0901/Auswärtiges Amt/68435, Handel mit Kriegsgerät Griechenland, Bd.3.
0901/Auswärtiges Amt/68719, Handakten Clodius, Griechenland.

0961/Auswärtiges Amt/68445, Handel mit Kriegsgerät, Ägypten.
0961/Auswärtiges Amt/68445, Handel mit Kriegsgerät Palästina.
80 BA1/Dredsner Bank/725.
80 BA1/Dresdner Bank/2363.
80 IG1/IG Farben/1617.
80 IG1/IG Farben/A 3849.
80 IG1/IG Farben/B 4006.
80 IG1/IG Farben/B 6549/107.

5) Bundesarchiv Koblenz
R7/3441.
R 43/368a.
R 43 II/1445.

6) Bundesarchiv Militärarchiv Freiburg
N 620/48, Nachlass Papst.
RLD 13/94.
RM 11/2.
RM 11/3.
RW 19/3329.
RW 19 Anhang 1/916.
RW 29/96.
WI/IC1./7B.
WI/IC1.10.

7) Politisches Archiv des Auswärtigen Amtes, Bonn

Abteilung IIb(Ab IIb)
Griechenland, Pol.7 Bd.2.
Griechenland, Pol.7 Ministerien Bd 2.
Griechenland, Pol.11-4. Militär.
Griechenland, Wirtschaft.
Griechenland, Wirtschaft, Handel 30, Lieferungen Bd.3.
Griechenland, Wirtschaft, Rohstoffe und Waren, Chinin.

Dienststelle Ribbentrop
Aufbringen und Versenkung von Handelsschiffen durch Deutschland, Griechenland
1939-1943 Bd.1.

Geheimakten
II FK 33, Kriegsgerät Allgemeines Geheimsachen.
II FK 118, Aus- und Einfuhr von Kriegsgerät nach dem Balkan.
II FK 118, Aus- und Einfuhr von Kriegsgerät nach dem Balkan, Bd.2 Griechenland
Pol.2.

Gesandtschaftsakten
Gesandtschaft Athen Nr.21, Heer und Flotte. Waffenlieferungen der griechischen Regie-
rung.
Gesandtschaft Athen Nr.50, Geheimakten Bd.1.
Gesandtschaft Athen Nr.61, Waffenlieferungen der Griechischen Regierung.

Handelspolitische Abteilung

Geheimakten
Handel mit Kriegsgerät, allgemeines Bd.1.
Handel mit Kriegsgerät, allgemeines Bd.2.
Handel mit Kriegsgerät, allgemeines Bd.3.
Handel mit Kriegsgerät, allgemeines Bd.5.
Handel mit Kriegsgerät, Balkan Bd.1.
Handel mit Kriegsgerät, Griechenland Bd.1.
Handel mit Kriegsgerät, Griechenland Bd.2.
Handel mit Kriegsgerät, Iraq Bd.1-2.
Handel mit Kriegsgerät, Spanien Bd.1.

Handakten
Clodius, Griechenland Bd.3.
Clodius, Griechenland Bd.4.
Wiehl, Griechenland Bd.2.

Abteilung IVa: (Ha.Pol. IVa.)
Handel 10 Förderungen des Aussenhandels, Handelskreditte, Ausfuhrprämien, Subventionen und ähnl. in Griechenland.
Handel 11.
Handel 11-1 Bd.1-3. Ein-, Aus- und Durchfuhr Allgem. und Grundsätzliches.
Handel 11-3 Bd.1. Austauchgeschäfte Griechenland.
Handel 11-10 Bd.1.
Handel 11-11a Auswirkungen der britischen Seekriegsfürung auf dem deutschen Handel mit Griechenland. Bd.1. Handel 12, Griechenland Grossbritanien, WIIIa 551/40. Handel 24 Nr.6.
Handel 30, Lieferungen Bd. 3.
Industrie 7.
Rohstoffe und Waren Tabak Bd.1. Wirtschaft 1,Bd.1.
Wirtschaft 6,Bd.1.

Inland II
Griechenland.
Inland IIg.
Polizeiabkommen mit Griechenland und Bulgarien.

Politische Abteilung II(Pol.Ab.II)
Pol 2. II.

Politische Abteilung IV(Pol Ab. IV)
Po. 2, Politische Beziehungen Griechenlands zu Deutschland Bd. 1.
Pol. IV Po.
Po. 5

8) Zentrales Staatsarchiv Potsdam
80 IG1/IG Farben 421
80 IG1/IG Farben 512

9) Akademia Athinon (The Academy of Athens)
GSR T120/1042.

10) Genika archia tou kratous (The Greek State Archives)
Metaxas Archive fak.14.
fak.33.
fak.37.
fak.42.
fak.43.
fak.77.
fak.77.
fak.80.
fak.82.
fak.86.
fak.96.
fak.97.

11) Istoriko archio tou Ypourgio exoterikon
(The Historical Archive of the Greek Ministry of Foreign Affairs)
1935 Politiki AAK 36.
1935 A/13.
1936 A/13.
1937 A/11/3.
1940 A/4.
1940 A/13.

12) Istoriko archio tis ethnikis trapezas Ellados
(The Historical Archive of the National Bank of Greece)
XXI Trapeza tis Ellados.fak.13.
XXV Erga B Sidirodromi fak. 30.
XXIII ZT Diafores alles eteries.
XXVIII Proionda Kapna fak. 18.
XXVIII Proionda A Kapnos fak. 6.
XXVIII Proionda A Kapnos fak. 7.
XXVIII Proionda A Kapnos fak. 20.

13) Trapeza tis Ellados
Bank of Greece
Tsouderos Archive
fak. 25/5.
fak. 79/1.
fak. 95/5.
fak. 95/16.
fak. 95/22.
fak. 138/4.

B) Published Sources

1) Diplomatic sources
Akten zur deutschen auswärtigen Politik 1918-1945:
Serie C: 1933-1937 Göttingen 1971 ff.

Serie D: 1937-1941 Baden-Baden u. Göttingen 1950 ff.

I documenti diplomatici italiani:
ser. 8 XIII: 1935-1939 Rome 1953 ff.
ser. 9 I-V:1939-1943 Rome 1953 ff.

Documents on British Foreign Policy 1919-1939:
III. Series Vol 5, London 1951 ff.

Dokumente zum Konflikt mit Jugoslawien und Griechenland, Berlin 1941.

Foreign Relations of the United States:
1937 Vol II, Washington 1955.
1938 Vol II, Washington 1955.

2) Greek National Statistics
Georijiki ke ktinotrofiki statistiki tis ellados, 1938 Athens 1939. (Greek Year Book of Statistics on Argiculture and Stock Breeding)

Mineon deltion tou idikou emboriou tis Ellados meta ton xenon epikraton, december: (Monthly Bulletin on Greece's Net Trade with Foreign Nations)
1934 Athens 1934.
1935 – 1935. 1936 – 1936. 1937 – 1937. 1938 – 1938. 1939 – 1939. 1940 – 1940.

Statistiki epetiris tis ellados:
(Year Book of Greek Statistics)
1931 Athens 1932.
1935 – 1936. 1936 – 1937. 1937 – 1938. 1938 – 1939. 1939 – 1940.

3) Other statistics
Les conditions de l'agriculture mondiale en 1938-39, Rome 1940.
Les grands produits agricoles, compendium international de statistique 1924-1938, Rome 1948.
Hill, Henry A, *The Economy of Greece: Prepared for the Coordinating Committee of American Agencies in Greece,* Vol. I-V, New York. (No year or place of publication)
Mousmoutis N.D., *The Estimate of the National Income of Greece: From the Production Side,* Athens 1950.
Statistical Abstract of the United States 1935, Washington 1935.
Statistical Abstract of the United States 1940, Washington 1940.

4) Military Publications
I pros polemon paraskevi tou ellinikou stratou, 1923- 1940, (The Preparation of the Greek Army for War, 1923- 1940) The General Staff, The Directorate for Military History, Athens 1969.

C) Diaries, memoirs and personal papers
Ambassador MacVeagh's Reports: Greece 1933-1947, ed. John O.Iatrides, Princeton 1980.
Bodosakis-Athansiadis, Prodromos, recollections published by Brasida Ch. Sotiropoulos under the title, "Bodosakis" (No year or place of publication)
Goebbels, Joseph, *Die Tagebücher* Bd.2 1931-1936, Munich 1987. Bd.3
Grazzi, Emmanuele, *Il principio della fine: L'Impresa di Grecia,* Rome 1945.

Metaxas, Ioanis, *To prosopiko imerolojio tou*, tome IV, Athens1960, published by Fedon Varnas.

Papagos, Alexandros, *O ellinikos stratos ke i pros polemon proparaskevi tou, 1923-1940*. (The Greek Army and its Preparation for War) Athend 1945.

D) Books and articles

1) contemporary literature

The Balkan States, The Royal Institute of International Affairs, London 1936.

50 Jahre Rheinmetall-Borsig, 1889-1939.

Gervasi, Frank, "Devil Man", *Collier's* 8 June 1940.

Greek Refugee Problem. League of Nations, Geneva 1926.

Gross, Hermann, *Südosteuropa: Bau und Entwicklung der Wirtschaft*, Leipzig 1937.

Hexner, Ervin, *International Cartels*, Chapel Hill N.C. 1945.

International Capital Movements during the Inter-War Period, U.N., Lake Success 1949.

MacNeill, William Hardy, *The Greek Dilemma: War and Aftermath*,London 1947.

Momtchiloff, N., *Ten Years of Controlled Trade in South-Eastern Europe*, Cambridge 1944.

Neumann, Robert, *Zaharoff: the Armaments King*, London 1938.

Politis, Athanse G., *L'Hellénisme et l'Egypte moderne: Histoire de l'Hellénisme égyptien de 1798 à 1927*, Paris 1929-1930.

The Problem of International Investment: The Royal Institute of International Affairs, London 1937.

South-Eastern Europe, A Political and Economic Survey, The Royal Institute of International Affairs, London 1939.

2) New Literature

Aldcroft, Derek H., *The British Economy, Vol 1: The Years of Turmoil 1920-1951*, London 1986.

Alverdens Fly i Farver: Krigsfly 1919-1939 (Aircraft of the World: Military Aircarft), Copenhagen 1972.

Alverdens Fly i Farver: Krigsfly 1939-1945 (Aircraft of the World: Military Aircarft), Copenhagen 1970.

Alexander, Alec P, *Greek Industrialists: An Economic and Social Analysis*, Athens 1964.

Alexandris, Alexis, Thanos Veremis et alii, eds, *I ellinotourkiki schesis, 1923-1987* (Greek-Turkish Relations, 1923-1987), Athens 1988

Alexandris, *The Greek Minority of Istanbul and Greek-Turkish Relations*, Athens, 1983.

Alexandris, 'To istoriko plaisio ton ellinotourkikon scheseon' (The Historical Framework of Greek-Turkish Relations), in Alexandris, Thanos Veremis et alii, pp.31-172.

Alexandris, 'Turkish Policy towards Greece during WW II', *Balkan Studies*, 23, 1, 1982, pp.157-197.

Andersen, Lars Erslev, ed., *Middle East Studies in Denmark*, Odense 1994

Anderson, Irvine H., *Aramco, the United States and Saudi Arabia: A Study of the Dynamics of Foreign Oil Policy, 1933-1950*, Princeton 1981.

Andricopoulos, Yannis, 'The Powerbase of Greek Authoritarianism', in Hagtved and Larsen, pp. 568-584.

Barros, James, *Britain, Greece and the Politics of Sanctions:Ethiopia 1935-1936*, London 1982.

Becker, Josef and Klaus Hildebrand, eds, *Internationale Beziehungen in der Weltwirtschafskrise 1929-1933*, Munich 1980.

Beinin, Joel and Lockman, Zachary, *Workers on the Nile: Nationalism, Communism, Islam, and the Egyptian Working Class, 1882-1954*, Princeton 1988.

Berov, L., 'Le Capital financier occidental et les pays balkaniques dans les années vingt', *Études Balkaniques* 2-3, 1965 Sofia, pp.139-169.

Borejsza, Jerzy W, 'Greece and the Balkan Policy of Fascist Italy, 1936-1940, *Journal of the Hellenic Diaspora* Vol. XIII, Nos 1 & 2 1986, pp.53-70.

Bosworth, R.J.B. *Explaining Auschwitz & Hiroshima: History Writing and the Second World War 1945-1990*, London and New York 1993

Botsas, Eleftherios N., 'Greece and the East, The Trade Connection, 1851-1984', *Journal of Modern Greek Studies*, October 1987, Vol. 5, No.2, pp.207-235.

Broszat, Martin, 'Deutschland-Ungarn-Rumänien, in Funke 1976, pp.524-564.

Bussière, Eric, 'The Interests of the Banque de l'Union parisienne in Czechoslovakia, Hungary and the Balkans', in Teichova and Cottrell, pp. 399-410.

Bærentzen, Lars, Lars Nørgaard and Ole L. Smith, *Mens vi venter: Studier i det moderne Grækenlands historie* (While We Are Waiting: Studies in Modern Greek History), Copenhagen 1980.

Cliadakis, Hary, 'The Political and Diplomatic Background to the Metaxas Dictatorship, 1935-36', *Journal of Contemporary History*, January 1979 Vol. 14, No 1, pp.117-138.

Clogg, Richard, *A Short History of Modern Greece*, Cambridge 1979.

Constantine, Stephen, *Buy and Build: The Advertising Postersof the Empire Marketing Board*, London 1986.

Creveld, Martin van, *Hitler's Strategy 1940-1941: The Balkan Clue*, Cambridge 1973.

Dafnis, Griogrios, *I Ellas metaxi dio polemon* (Greece between the two Wars), Tome II, Athens 1955.

Davenport-Hines, RPT, 'Vickers' Balkan Conscience: Aspects of Anglo-Romanian Armaments 1918-1939', *Business History*,Vol XXV 1983, pp.287-319.

Dambassina-Kamara, Katerina, *Le Regime du 4 Aout 1936, en Grèce: les répercussions politiques et sociales*, Paris 1983.

Davis, Eric, *Challenging Colonialism: Bank Misr and Egyptian Industrialization, 1920-1941*, Princeton 1983.

Deist, Wilhelm, Manfred Messerschmidt, Hans-Erich Volkmann and Wolfram Wette, eds, *Die Ursachen und Vorraussetzungen des Zweiten Weltkrieges*, Frankfurt am Main 1991, (Originally published under the title Ursachen und Vorraussetzungen der Deutschen Kriegspolitik, 1979)

Dritsa, Margarita, *Biomichania ke trapezes stin Ellada tou mesopolemou* (Industry and Banks in Inter-War Greece), Athens 1990.

Due-Nielsen, Carsten, Hans Kierchoff, Carl-Christian Lammers and Torben Nybom, eds, *Konflikt og Samarbejde, Festskrift for Carl-Axel Gemzell* (Conflict and Co-operation, *Festschrift* for Carl-Axel Gemzell), Copenhagen 1993

Eizholtz, Dietrich and Wolfgang Schumann, eds, *Anatomie des Krieges: Neue Dokumente über die Rolle des deutschen Monopolkapitals bei der Vorbereitung und Durchführung des zweiten Weltkrieges*, Berlin 1969.

Elefandis, Angelos G., *I epangelia tis adinatis epanastatis: KKE ke astismos ston mesopolemo* (The Promise of the Impossible Revolution: KKE and the Bourgeoisie in the Inter-War Period), Athens 1976.

Fischer, Fritz, *Griff nach der Weltmacht: Die Kriegszielpolitik des kaiserlichen Deutschland 1914-18*, Düsseldorf 1961.

Fischer, *Krieg der Illusionen: Die deutsche Politik von 1911-1914*, Düsseldorf 1969.

Fleicher, Hagen and Nikos Svoronos, *Ellada 1936-1940, diktatoria-katochi-antistasi* (Greece 1936-1940, Dictatorship, Occupation, Resistance), Athens 1989.

Fleury, Antoine, *La pénétration allemande au Moyen-Orient 1919-1939: Le cas de la Turquie, de l'Iran et de l'Afghanistan*, Leiden 1977.

323

Forstmeier, Friderich and Hans-Erich Volkmann, eds, *Wirtschaft und Rüstung am Vorabend des Zweiten Weltkrieges*, Düsseldorf 1975.

Forstmeier, Friderich and Hans-Erich Volkmann, eds, *Kriegswirtschaft und Rüstung 1939-1945*, Düsseldorf 1977.

Funke, Manfred, 'Die deutsch-italienischen Beziehungen:Antibolschewismus und aussenpolitische Interessenkonkurrenz als Strukturprizip der 'Achse', in Funke, pp. 823-846.

Funke, ed., *Hitler, Deutschland und die Mächte*: *Materialen zur Aussenpolitik des Dritten Reiches*, Düsseldorf 1976.

Funke, *Sanktionen und Kanonen. Hitler: Mussolini und der internationale Abessinienkonflikt*, Düsseldorf 1971.

Geiss, Immanuel and Bernd-Jürgen Wendt, eds, *Deutschland in der Weltpolitik des 19. und 20 Jahrhundert: Fritz Fischer zum 65.Geburtstag*, Düsseldorf 1973

Gemzell, Carl-Axel, *Raeder, Hitler und Skandinavien. Der Kampf für einen maritimen Operationsplan*, Lund 1965.

Gershoni, Israel, 'The Muslim Brothers and the Arab Revolt in Palestine, 1936-39', *Middle Eastern Studies*, pp.365- 397.

Gregor, James A., *Italian Fascism and Developmental Dictatorship*, Princeton 1979.

Grenzebach Jr., William S., *Germany's Informal Empire in East-Central Europe: German Economic Policy toward Yugoslavia and Romania, 1933-1939*, Stuttgart 1988.

Gruchmann, Lothar, *Totaler Krieg: Von Blitzkrieg zur bedingungslosen Kapitulation*, Munich 1991.

Hadziiossif, Christos, 'Griechen in der deutschen Kriegsproduktion', in Herbert, pp.210-233.

Hagtved, Bernt, and Stein Uglevik Larsen, eds, *Who were the Fascists?*, Bergen 1980.

Herbert, Ulrich, ed., *Europa und der 'Reichseinsatz': Ausländische Zivilarbeiter, Kriegsgefangene und KZ- Häftlinge in Deutschland 1938-1945*, Essen 1991

Hirschfeld, Gerhard and Lothar Kettenacker, eds, *'Der Führerstaat' Mythos und Realität: Studien zur Stuktur und Politik des Dritten Reiches*, Stuttgart 1981.

Hondros, John Louis, *Occupation and Resistance: The Greek Agony 1941-44*, New York 1983.

Hoppe, Hans Joachim, *Bulgarien – Hitlers eigenwilliger Verbündeter: Eine Fallstudie zur nationalsozialistischen Südosteuropapolitik*, Stuttgart 1979.

Ioakimidis, P.C., 'Greece: from Military Dictatorship to Socialism', in Allan Williams, ed., *Southern Europe Transformed: Political and Economic Change in Greece, Italy, Portugal and Spain*, London 1984, pp.33-60.

Ikonomikos Tachidromos, no. 992, 26 April 1973.

Istoria tou ellenikou ethnous: neoteros ellinismos apo 1913 os to 1941 (A History of the Greek Nation: Modern Hellenism 1913-1941).

Jankowski, James P., *Egypt's Young Rebels: 'Young Egypt' 1933-1952*, Stanford 1975.

Jecchinis, Christos, *Trade Unionism in Greece*, Chicago 1967.

Joachim, J.G., 'Writing the Biography of John Metaxas' in Macrakis and Diamandouros, pp.136-149.

Kacarkova, Vera, 'Handelsbeziehungen zwischen Deutschland und Griechenland in den 30er Jahren des XX. Jh.', *Études balkaniques* 12, 1976, 3 Sofia, pp. 43-61.

Kaiser, David E., *Economic Diplomacy and the Origins of the Second World War: Germany, Britain and Eastern Europe, 1930-1939*, Princeton 1980.

Kindleberger, Charles P., *The World in Depression 1929-1939*, Los Angeles 1973.

Kitroeff, Alexander, *The Greeks in Egypt, 1919-1937: Ethnicity and Class*, London 1989.

Kitsikis, Dimitris, *I ellas tis 4s augoustou ke i megale dinamis* (Greece of the Fourth of August and the Great Powers), Athens 1974.

Kofas, Jon V., *Authoritarianism in Greece: The Metaxas Regime*, New York 1983.

Koliopoulos, John S., *Brigands with a Cause: Brigandage and Irredentism in Modern Greece 1821-1912*, Oxford 1987.

Koliopoulos, *Greece and the British Connection 1935-1941*,Oxford 1977.

Koliopoulos, 'Unwanted Alley: Greece and the Great Powers 1939- 1941' *Balkan Studies*, Vol.23, No.1.

Knox, MacGregor, *Mussolini Unleashed 1939-1941: Politics and Strategy in Fascist Italy's Last War*, Cambridge 1982.

Kroener, Bernhard R., Rolf Dieter Müller and Hans Umbreit, eds, *Das deutsche Reich und der zweite Weltkrieg: Organisation und Mobilisierung des deutschen Machtbereichs*, Band 5, Stuttgart 1988.

Kube, Alfred, *Pour le mérite und Hakenkreuz: Hermann Göring imDritten Reich*, Munich 1986.

Linardatos, Spiros, *I 4e augustou* (The Fourth of August), Athens 1966.

Loulos, Konstantin, *Die deutsche Griechenlandspolitik von der Jahrhundertwende bis zum Ausbruch des Ersten Weltkrieges*,Frankfurt am Main, Bern, New York 1986.

Lukas, Dusan, 'Aggression of Italy against Greece and the Consequences of Failure of Italian Expansion', *Balkan Studies*, Vol 23, No.1, 1982, pp.81-99.

Ludwig, Karl-Heinz 'Strukturmerkmale nationalsozialistischer Aufrüstung bis 1935', in Forstmeier and Volkmann 1975, pp.39-64.

Lugs, Jaroslav, *Firearms Past and Present*, London 1973.

Macrakis, A. Lily and P. Nikoforos Diamandouros, eds, *New Trends in Modern Greek Historiography*, 1982.

La Marca, Nicola, *Italia e Balcani fra le due guerre: Saggio di una recerca sui tentativi italiani di espansione economica nel Sul Est Europa fra le due guerre*, Rome 1979.

Marder, Everett J, 'The Second Regime of George II: His Rolein Politics.', *Southeastern Europe* II, 1, 1975, pp.53-69.

Marguerat, Philippe, *Le IIIe Reich et le pétrole roumain 1938-1940*, Leiden and Geneva 1977.

Marrus, Michael R., *The Unwanted: European Refugees in the Twentieth Century*, Oxford 1985.

Martens, Stefan, *Herman Göring, 'Erster Paladin des Führes' und 'Zweiter Mann im Reich'*, Paderborn 1985.

Mavrogordatos, George Th., *Stillborn Republic: Social Coalitions and Party Strategies in Greece 1922-1936*, Berkeley 1983.

Mazower, Mark, 'Economic Diplomacy between Great Britain and Greece in the 1930s', *The Journal of European Economic History*, Vol. 17, No. 3, Winter 1988, pp. 603-619.

Mazower, *Greece and the Inter-war Economic Crisis*, Oxford1991.

Mazzari, Frank, 'Projects for an Italian-led Balkan Bloc of Neutrals, September-December 1939', *The Historical Journal*, XIII, 4, 1970, pp.767-778.

Meissner, Renate, 'I ethnikososialistiki Germania ke i Ellada kata tin diarkia tis metaxikis diktatorias' (National Socialist Germany and Greece during the Dictatorship of Metaxas), in Fleicher and Svoronos, pp.50-57.

Mejcher, Helmut, 'Saudi-Arabiens Beziehungen zu Deutschland in der Regierungszeit von König Abd al-Aziz ibn Saud', in Schiller and Scharf, eds, pp.109-127.

Milward, Alan S., 'The Reichsmark Bloc and the International Economy', in Hirschfeld and Kettenacker, pp.377-413.

Mitchell, Richard P., *The Society of the Muslim Brothers*,London 1969.

Mollin, Gerhard, *Montankonzerne und 'Drittes Reich': DerGegensatz zwischen Monopolindustrie und Befehlswirtschaft in der deutschen Rüstung und Expansion 1936-1944*,Göttingen 1988.

Nicosia, Francis, 'Arab Nationalism and National Socialist Germany, 1933-1939: Ideological and Strategic Incompatibility', *International Journal of Middle East Studies*, 12, 1980, pp.351-372.

Nikolianakos, Marios, 'Materialen zur kapitalitischen Entwicklung in Griechenland', *Das Argument* 57, 12. Jg.Mai 1970, Heft 2/3.

Nilson, Bengt, *Handelspolitik under skärpt konkurrens: England och Sverige 1929-39* (Trade Policy during Increased Competition: Britain and Sweden, 1929-1939), Lund 1983.

Nørgaard, Lars, 'Den græske arbejderbevægelse før 1918 og Føderationen i Saloniki' (The Greek Labour Movement prior to 1918 and the Federation in Salonika), in Bærentzen, Nørgaard and Smith, pp.11-53.

Oberländer, Erwin, ed., *Hitler-Stalin-Pakt 1939: Das Ende Ostmitteleuropas?* Frankfurt am Main 1989.

Olshausen, Klaus, 'Die deutsche Balkan-Politik 1940-1941', in Funke, ed, 1976, pp.707-727.

Overy, R.J.,'German multinationals and the Nazi state in occupied Europe', in Teichova, Lévy-Leboyer and Nussbaum, pp.299-325.

Overy, *Goering the 'Iron Man'*, London 1984.

Overy, 'Göring's Multi-national Empire', in Teichova and Cottrell, pp.269-305.

Pelt, Mogens, 'Bodosakis-Athanasiadis, a Greek Businessman from the East: A Case Study of the Interrelationship between State and Business', in Andersen, pp.65-86.

Pelt, 'Germany and the Economic Dimension of the Metaxas Regime' *Journal of the Hellenic Diaspora*, Vol.20.2. 1994

Pelt, 'Greece and Germany's Policy toward Southeastern Europe, 1932-1940', *Epsilon*, No.2 1988.

Pelt, 'Grækenland mellem Centraleuropa og Middelhavet' (Greece between Central Europe and the Mediterranean), in Due-Nielsen, Kierchoff, Lammers and Nybom, pp.89-106.

Petersen, Jens, 'Die Aussenpolitik des faschistischen Italiens als historiographisches Problem', *Viertelsjahrhefte für Zeitgeschichte 22*. Jhg.1974 1.Heft Januar pp. 417-461.

Petersen, 'Italien und Südosteuropa 1929-1932', in Becker and Hildebrand, pp.393-413.

Petropulos, John A., 'The Compulsory Exchange of Populations:Greek-Turkish Peace-making, 1922-1930', *Byzantine andModern Greek Studies*, Vol.2, 1976, pp.135-160.

Platt, D.C.M., ed., *Business Imperialism 1840-1930: An Enquiry Based on British Experience in Latin America*, Oxford 1977.

Pratt, Lawrence R., *East of Malta, West of Suez: Britain's Mediterranean Crisis 1936-1939*, Cambridge 1975.

Psiroukis, Nikos, *O fasismos ke i tetarti augustou* (Fascism and the Fourth of August), Athens 1974.

Ranki, György, *Economy and Foreign Policy: The Struggle of the Great Powers for Hegemony in the Daunube Valley 1919-1939*, New York 1983.

Radandt, Hans, 'Berichte der Volkswirtschaftlichen Abteilung der IG Farbenindustrie AG über Südosteuropa' *Jahrbuch für Wirtschaftsgeschichte*, Berlin 1966 IV, pp.289-314.

Raspin, Angela, 'Wirtschaftliche und politische Aspekte der italienischen Aufrüstung Anfang der dreissiger Jahre bis 1940', in Forstmeier and Volkmann 1975, pp.202-221.

Richter, Heinz, *British Intervention in Greece. From Varkizato Civil War: February 1945 to August 1946*, London 1986.

Richter, *Griechenland zwischen Revolution und Konterrevolution, 1936-1946*, Frankfurt am Main 1973.

Rigos, Alkis, *I B elliniki dimokratia 1924-1935, kinonikesdiastasis tis politikis skinis* (The Second Greek Republic and the Dimensions of the Political Scene), Athens 1988.

Robertson, Esmonde M., 'Hitler und die Sanktionen des Völkerbunds – Mussolini und die Besetzung des Rheinlands', *Vierteljahrshefte für Zeitgeschichte* 26 Jahrg. 1978, pp. 237-264.

Rothschild, Joseph, *East Central Europe between the Two World Wars*, Washington 1974.

al-Sayyid-Marsot, Afaf Lutfi, *Egypt's Liberal Experiment 1922-1936*, Berkeley 1977.

Schausberger, Norbert, 'Österreich und die Nationalsozialistische Anschluss-Politik', in Funke 1976, pp.728-756.

Schiller, Linda Schatkowski and Claus Scharf, eds, *Der Nahe Osten in der Zwischenkriegszeit 1919-1939: Der Interdependenz von Politik, Wirtschaft und Ideologie*, Stuttgart 1989.

Schinzinger, Francesca, 'Kriegsökonomische Aspekte derdeutsch-italiensichen Wirtschaftsbeziehungen 1934-1941', in Forstmeier and Volkmann 1977, pp.164-181.

Schlarp, Karl-Heinz, *Wirtschaft und Besatzung in Serbien 1941-1944*, Stuttgart 1986.

Schramm-von Thadden, Ehrengard, *Griechenland und dieGrossmächte im zweiten Weltkrieg*, Wiesbaden 1955.

Schröder, Hans-Jürgen, 'Deutsche Südosteuropapolitik 1929- 1936: Zur Kontinuität deutscher Aussenpolitik in der Weltwirtschaftskrise', *Geschichte und Gesellschaft* 2.Jg. Heft 1, 1976, pp.5-32.

Schröder, 'Die Neue Deutsche Südamerikapolitik', *Jahrbuch fürWirtschaft und Gesellschaft Latinamerikas*, Band 6, 1969,pp.337-452.

Schröder, 'Südosteuropa als 'Informal Empire' Deutschlands 1933-1939: Das Beispiel Jugoslawien', *Jahrbücher für Geschichte Osteuropas*, Bd.23, 1975, pp.70-96.

Schröter, Harm G., *Aussenpolitik und Wirtschaftsinteresse: Skandinavien im aussenwirtschaftlichen Kalkül Deutschlands und Grossbritanniens 1918-1939*, Frankfurt amMain, Bern, New York 1983.

Schröter, 'Siemens and Central and South-East Europe between the two World Wars', in Teichova and Cottrell pp.173-192.

Schröter, Verena, *Die deutsche Industrie auf dem Weltmarkt 1929-1933. Aussenwirtschaftliche Strategien unter dem Druck der Weltwirtschaftskrise*, Frankfurt am Main 1984.

Schumann, Wolfgang, ed., *Griff nach Südosteuropa: Neue Dokumente über die Politik des deutschen Imperialismus und Militarismus gegenüber Südosteuropa im zweiten Weltkrieg*, Berlin 1973.

Schumann and Ludwig Nestler, eds, *Weltherrschaft im Visier. Dokumente zu den Europa- und Weltherrschaftsplänen des deutschen Imperialismus von der Jahrhundertswende bis Mai 1945*, Berlin 1975.

Smith, Michael Llewellyn, *Ionian Vision: Greece in Asia Minor1919-1922*, London 1973.

Stegmann, Dirk, Bernd-Jürgen Wendt and Peter Christian Witt, eds, *Industrielle Gesellschaft und politisches System: Beiträge zur politischen Sozialgeschichte: Festschrift für Fritz Fischer*, Bonn 1978.

Stegmann, Dirk, 'Mitteleuropa, 1925-1934: Zum Problem der Kontinuität deutscher Aussenhandelspolitik von Stresemann bis Hitler', in Stegmann, Wendt and Witt.

Teichert, Eckart, *Autarkie und Grossraumwirtschaft in Deutschland 1930-1939*, Munich 1984.

Teichova, Alice, 'Besonderheiten im Strukturwandel der mittelost-und südosteuropäischen Industrie in der Zwischenkriegszeit' in Stegmann, Wendt and Witt, pp.31-150.

Teichova, *An Economic Background to Munich: International Business and Czechoslovakia 1918-1938*, Cambridge 1974.

Teichova and P.L.Cottrell, eds, *International Business and Central Europe, 1918-1939*, Leicester 1983.

Teichova, *Kleinstaten im Spannungsfeld der Grossmächte*, Munich 1988.

Teichova, Maurice Lévy-Leboyer and Helga Nussbaum, eds, *Multinational Enterprise in Historical Perspective*, Cambridge 1986.

327

Tignor, Robert, 'The Economic Activities of Foreigners inEgypt, 1920-1950: From Millet to Haute Bourgeoise', *Comparative Studies in Society and History*, Cambridge 1980, pp.416-449.

Tillmann, Heinz, *Deutschlands Araberpolitik im Zweiten Weltkrieg*, Berlin 1965.

Tsoukalas, Konstandinos, *Exartisi ke anaparagoji: O kinonikos rolos ton ekpedeftikon michanismon stin Ellada 1830- 1922* (Dependence and Reproduction: The Social Role of the Mechanisms of Education in Greece 1830-1922), Athens 1981 (Originally published in French, Paris 1975).

Veloudis, G, 'Jakob Philipp Fallmerayer und die Entstehung desNeugriechischen Historismus', *Südost-Forschung*, 29, 1970, pp.43-90.

Veremis, Thanos, *I epemvasis tou stratou stin elliniki politiki, 1916-36* (The Intervention of the Army in Greek Politics 1916-1936), Athens 1983.

Veremis og Kostas Kostis, *I Ethniki Trapeza sti Mikra Asia, 1919-1922* (The National Bank of Greece in Asia Minor, 1919-1922), Athens 1984.

Veremis, *Ikonomia ke diktatoria: I sinkiria 1925-1926* (Economy and Dictatorship: The Case of 1925-1926), Athens 1982.

Veremis, 'The Officer Corps in Greece, 1912-1936', *Byzantine and Modern Greek Studies*, Vol.2 1976, pp.130-132.

Volkmann, Hans-Erich, 'Aussenhandel und Aufrüstung in Deutschland 1933 bis 1939', in Forstmeier and Volkmann 1975, pp.81-131.

Volkmann, 'NS-Aussenhandel im geschlossenen Kriegswirtschaftsraum (1939-1941)', in Forstmeier and Volkmann 1977, pp.92-133.

Volkmann, 'Die NS-Wirtschaft in Vorbereitung des Krieges', in Deist, Messerschmidt, Volkmann and Wette.

Walker, Mark, *German National Socialism and the Quest for Nuclear Power, 1939-1949*, Cambridge 1989.

Wehler, Hans-Ulrich, *Modernisierungsteorie und Geschichte*,Göttingen 1975.

Wendt, Bernd-Jürgen, *Aussenpolitik und Kriegsvorbereitung des Hitler-Regimes*, Munich 1987.

Wendt, 'England und der deutsche 'Drang nach Südosten' Kapitalbeziehungen und Warenverkehr in Südosteuropa zwischen den Weltkriegen', in Geiss and Wendt, pp.483-511.

Wendt, 'Südosteuropa in der nationalsozialistischen Grossraumwirtschaft: Eine Antwort auf Alan S. Milward', in Hirschfeld and Kettenacker, pp.414-427.

Whealy, Robert H., *Hitler and Spain: The Nazi Role in the Spanish Civil War 1936-1939*, Kentucky 1989.

Wittmann, Klaus, *Schwedens Wirtschaftsbeziehungen zum Dritten Reich 1933-1945*, Munich 1978.

Wurm, Clemens A., 'Aussenpolitik und Wirtschaft in den internationalen Beziehungen: Internationale Kartelle, Aussenpolitik und weltwirtschaftliche Beziehungen 1919-1939: Einführung', in Wurm, pp.1-31.

Wurm, ed., *Internationale Kartelle und Aussenpolitik, Stuttgart 1989*.

NOTE ON SOURCES

My research relies to a great extent on files from *Auswärtiges Amt*. These were scattered after the Second World War but those that still exist either as documents or as microfilms are now kept in *Politisches Amt des Auswärtigen Amtes* in Bonn or in *Bundesarchiv Abteilung Potsdam*. (Before Germany's reunification these belonged to the state archives of the former German Democratic Republic).

The files in *Politisches Amt des Auswärtigen Amtes* regarding Greek-German economic relations are incomplete for the period before 1936 and complete in the period from 1936-1941. Regarding Greek-German political relations, the situation is reversed, as the files are almost complete for the period leading up to 1936, while after 1936 they are available only in part.

These files include correspondence between the German Legation in Athens and the *Auswärtiges Amt* in Berlin, as well as communications between *Auswärtiges Amt* and institutions and persons relevant to Greek-German relations. It is significant that the correspondence with the semi-official arms cartel *Ausfuhrgemeinschaft für Kriegsgerät*, which from 1936 onwards was in charge of arms negotiations between Germany and Greece, features in the files from both *Handelspolitische Abteilung* (Department of Commercial Policy) and the so-called *Geheimakten* (Secret Files). These files are, of course, central to the Greek-German arms trade but they also provide valuable evidence of political developments in Greece, as numerous documents are reports from meetings between Greek and German officials. In relation to this it is important to note that the files from *Handelspolitische Abteilung* often provide a valuable insight into the development of Greek-German relations and German attitudes not strictly related to commercial matters. This is true to such an extent that any further study of Greek-German relations would benefit from a consultation of these documents.

The material from *Bundesarchiv Abteilung Potsdam*, offers, often in addition to the above-mentioned files from *Auswärtiges Amt*, a very rich and extensive collection of files of financial provenance, such as reports, memoranda and correspondence from German banks and industries. Of particular importance are the documents from IG Farben, the world's largest chemical firm in the interwar period. These documents include reports of business negotiations, cartel agreements and extensive statistical material. The so-called 'Vowi-Berichte' from IG Farben's *Volkswirtschaftliche Abteilung* (Department of National Economy) are particularly important. The latter are concerned with a broad variety of aspects of the economy of foreign countries, including the analysis of national economies and investigations of specific branches and industries. Among these investigations are 35 reports on Greece and leading Greek industries in the period 1935 to 1942. (In the bibliography a number of these are listed under the signatures 'ZStA-Potsdam' (i.e. *Zentrales Staatarchiv Potsdam*) as used in the former GDR: these were still in use when I was working on this material.

Bundesarchiv Militärarchiv Freiburg, also provide a valuable resource, especially in providing documents from *Oberkommando der Wehrmacht, Abteilung Wehr-*

wirtschaftsstab and the *Wirtschafts- und Rüstungsamt*. These include monthly and daily reports covering the military aspects of the Greek economy, as well as reports and statistics from *Weltwirtschaftsinstitut* in Kiel describing the various sectors of the Greek economy.

The archives of Albert Speer at the Imperial War Museum in London offered an important insight into relations between the Greek and German armaments industries and the German attitude to Greece's trade in arms on the international market, especially her connection with the Republicans during the Civil War in Spain. The Speer archives also include a vast amount of material associated with the staff of Hermann Göring during the 1930s and early 1940s, such as files relating to the Four Year Plan and to the German armaments concern Rheinmetall-Borsig. The latter played a crucial role in the Greek-German armaments trade, as well as providing an informal connection between the political entourage of Metaxas and the German authorities, especially Göring.

While I was conducting research in Greece, it soon became clear to me that the Greek Ministry of Foreign Affairs possesses little material concerning Greek-German relations. The material that exists from the period prior to 1939 is strikingly irrelevant to high-level politics, notably, for example, the correspondence concerning maintenance of German burial places in Greece. One probable explanation for this is that Greek-German contacts were maintained through other and often informal channels. In this relation it is significant that the Greek-German commercial negotiations were led by Emanuil Tsouderos and Kiriakos Varvaresos, respectively the Governor and the Deputy Governor of the Bank of Greece. The archives of the Bank of Greece provide a valuable resource, as they hold much relevant material in the files of Emanuil Tsouderos.

The National Bank of Greece also played a crucial role in Greek-German relations. It was the largest private bank in Greece, with many business interests including the tobacco industry. The archives of the bank hold a quantity of valuable material regarding Greek-German relations and the impact of these on Greek and foreign business interests, particularly during the period 1933 to 1936.

Finally, I have used the files formally belonging to Metaxas, the so-called Metaxas Archive. These are held in the Greek National Archives. The Metaxas Archive contains a tangled collection of documents from the Greek dictator's own hand and from his offices. The correspondence between Metaxas and the armed forces dealing with Greek rearmament is of particular interest in this context.

This material of German and Greek provenance must be supplemented with other material in order to balance what might otherwise result in a one-sided approach. To this effect the files of the British Foreign Office in the Public Record Office provide rich and fruitful material. The British Legation in Athens and the Foreign Office in London followed closely the development of Greek-German relations. This resulted in the production of various assessments of the contemporary situation. Furthermore, the British Minister in Athens and various British officials held a number of meetings with the Greek King and Metaxas, as well as with other Greek government officials, concerning these matters. In addition, the Greeks often turned to the British for advice or, at times assistance and in this way have willingly or unwillingly provided important insights. Last but not least, these files offer a wealth of material regarding the development of the British attitude towards counteracting the German penetration of Greece and they reveal, in particular, the impotence experienced by the British government in 1938 in attempts to mobilize British business and industry to concert their efforts with those of the government and meet the German challenge in Greece.

It is also important to mention published diplomatic files. Of these I consulted *Akten zur deutschen auswärtigen Politik* (ADAP), Foreign Relations of the US (FRUS), Documents of British Foreign Policy (DBFP) and *Documenti Diplomatici Italiani* (DDI). ADAP offers a number of important documents relating to the 1930s and 1940s and provides essential reference material for anyone intending to work on subjects related to Greek-German relations in this period.

DBFP offers only a few documents about Greece during this period. FRUS contains a rich correspondence that covers a variety of interesting issues with special emphasis on commercial relations between the United States and Greece. In this connection it is pertinent to mention John O.Iatrides's edition of the papers of Lincoln MacVeagh, the American Ambassador to Greece. Iatrides's edition consists of the correspondence between MacVeagh and the Department of State as well as with President Roosevelt. This is a very valuable publication for anyone working on Greece in the interwar period, as a result of the editor's excellent commentary and MacVeagh's personal interest in Greece. These documents range from specific issues relating to Greek-American relations to detailed and very keen analyses of internal developments in Greece and of the relations between Greece and the Great Powers.

DDI are especially relevant for the period 1939-1940 and offer extensive and rich material. The main bulk of this concentrates on the period from Italy's entry into the war and her assault on Greece on 28 October 1940.

The memoirs of Emanuel Grazzi, the Italian Ambassador to Greece, also constitute a valuable source, albeit to be approached with caution. Grazzi published his book just after the end of war and it is coloured by a desire on his part to distance himself from the Fascists and, in particular, from the policy of Ciano; this turns the book into a personal apology.

The diaries of Metaxas constitute an important Greek source. These were published in 1960, when Metaxas's daughter gave her father's personal papers to the Greek State Archives. They contain extracts from Metaxas's diary, speeches and interviews, as well as selected documents from Metaxas's files covering his long career. The emphasis is on the period immediately preceding and during the successful war against Italy which in Greece was symbolized by the so-called 'I Magali Ochi' (The Great No), i.e. Metaxas's rejection of Italy's ultimatum to Greece on 28 October 1940. After the Axis Occupation (1941-1944) and the Civil War (1946-1949) this was the only wartime experience to be celebrated nationwide in a country which, during the first post-war decades, was torn apart politically and ideologically by cleavages originating in the period of dictatorship, occupation and civil war. It is conspicuous that Greek-German relations, especially in the commentary to the diaries, have been given so little attention. One reason may be that these issues were mainly economic and therefore undertaken by Kiriakos Varvaresos, Metaxas's economic adviser.

Finally, I have consulted the memoirs of Prodromos Bodosakis-Athanasiadis, the Greek business tycoon and arms dealer, published by Vrasidas Ch. Sotiropoulos, an Athens-based lawyer. From 1934 Bodosakis became an increasingly important figure in Greek commerce and industry and from 1936 a central figure in Greek rearmament, as well as in Greek sales of war material on the international market. In this capacity he was also of significant importance for Metaxas in matters of national economy and in the realm of internal politics as well as in relations with Germany. It has not been possible to establish whether the recollections, which often have an almost anecdotic form, were written by Bodosakis himself, or dictated by him or whether they have been edited. However, to the extent that I have been able to check them against German documents, in particular in matters concerning armaments and trade in arms, they turn out be precise in details of prices, terms of payment, calibres of guns, patents and names of contact persons, as well as chronology, etc.

INDEX

336

Sidi Barrani, 203
Siemens, 56, 89; and central Europe, 33, 34; & Halske 56, 180; Hellenic Electrotechnical Co.Ltd. Athens, 54; Siemens-Schuckert 54, 56, 115; Österreichische Siemens-Schuckert Werke 54, 56
Simmonds, S., 217
Simon, John, 216
Skaramanga, 77
Skilakakis, 185, 187
Skoda, 71, 248 n1119; and south-eastern Europe, 90, 159, 197
Slovakia, 197, 201
Smoot-Hawley Tariff Act, 35
Smyrna, 22, 25, 42, 178
Societé des Matiéres Colorantes, 54
Sollum, 203
Soloturn, 133
Somaliland, 98
Sonderstab für Handelskrieg und wirt-schaftliche Kampfmassnahmen (HWK), 252, 253 Holland 16, 199, 202, 229, 237; delivery of arms through, 170 n739
Sophia, 206
Southern Bokuvina, 203
Southern Department, 105, 250, 251
Southern Rhodesia, 215
Soviet Union, 17, 43, 88, 93, 210, 232, 246, 258; and arrangements with Germany in 1939 and 1940, 202, 203; and German preparations for an attack on, 206-208
Spain, Civil War in, see: Spanish Civil War; Greek exports of war material to, 70, 161-166, 168, 170, 172, 176, 248, 251, 260, 330
Spanish Civil War, 15, 89, 90, 92, 137, 156, 162, 164, 166; Germany's in-volvement in, 90, 93; Italy's involvment in, 100, 101
Spanish gold reserves, 92
Spanish Nationalists, 162, 164, 165, 170 n739
Spanish Republicans, Greek arms deliveries to, 15, 162-166; and cooperation with Germany, 92, 100, 168-170, 177, 260, 330
Sparta, 121
Special Security Department, 62

Speer, Albert, 85, 122, 154, 330
Spitta, 155
St. Jean de Maurienne agreement, 42
STAMAG, Stahl- und Maschinen-gesellschaft mbH., 88
Stavsky, 172
Sté Hellénique des lampes à l'incan-descance, 56
steel industry, 80, 157, 159, 160, 166, 196-200; establishment of Greek, 126, 127, 129; German, 34, 126, 127, 129
Steffen, Major H., 98
Stettin, 88
Stresa Conference, 96, 99
Stresemann, Gustav, 31, 32
Sudan, the, 48, 105
Sudetenland, 197, 201
Superior Council of the National Economic Defence, 116, 143
Supreme Council for the National Defence, 66
Sweden, 45, 245, 246
Syria, 42, 213
technology, as means for control and domination, 15, 34, 76, 78, 118, 134, 212, 256
Theophanidis, 163, 165, 173
Theotokis, Ioanis, 134-138, 140, 142, 149
Third Reich, 12, 168
Thomas, George, 93, 94
Tirana treaty, 42
tobacco workers 29, 30, 63
tourist trade, 49
Thrace, 24, 25, 27, 29, 30, 60, 142
Transjordan, 41
Transsylvania, 203
Treasury, the, 215, 218, 259
Tripartite Pact, 206, 207
Tsaldaris, Panages, 24, 59, 60, 62, 110, 181
Tsouderos, Emanuil, 112, 113, 147-149, 153, 165, 190, 330
Turkey, 14, 24-28, 38, 43, 45, 46, 67, 99, 152, 156, 161, 165, 205, 235, 252, 262; the Barbarossa Plan and the friend-ship pact with Germany dated June 1941, 207-208; in Britain's policy after *Anschluss*, 213-215; co-operation with